COUNTRY LIVING
MAGAZINE

GUIDE TO RURAL ENGLAND

THE SOUTH EAST OF ENGLAND

D1369175

By Peter Long

© Travel Publishing Ltd.

Published by:
Travel Publishing Ltd
7a Apollo House, Calleva Park
Aldermaston, Berks, RG7 8TN
ISBN 1-904-43414-2
© Travel Publishing Ltd

Country Living is a registered trademark of The National
Magazine Company Limited.

First Published: 2001 *Second Edition:* 2004

COUNTRY LIVING GUIDES:

East Anglia	Scotland
Heart of England	The South of England
Ireland	The South East of England
The North East of England	The West Country
The North West of England	Wales

PLEASE NOTE:

All advertisements in this publication have been accepted in good faith by Travel
Publishing and they have not necessarily been endorsed by *Country Living*
Magazine.

All information is included by the publishers in good faith and is believed to be
correct at the time of going to press. No responsibility can be accepted for errors.

Editor: Peter Long

Printing by: Scotprint, Haddington

Location Maps:© Maps in Minutes ™ (2004)   © Crown Copyright, Ordnance Survey 2004

Walks: Walks have been reproduced with kind permission of the internet
                   walking site www.walkingworld.com

Walk Maps: Reproduced from Ordnance Survey mapping on behalf of the
                   Controller of Her Majesty's Stationery Office, © Crown Copyright.
                   Licence Number MC 100035812

Cover Design: Lines & Words, Aldermaston

Cover Photo: Oast Houses, Headcorn, Kent   © www.britainonview.com

Text Photos: Text photos have been kindly supplied by the Britain on View photo library
                   © www.britainonview.com

Foreword

From a bracing walk across the hills and tarns of The Lake District to a relaxing weekend spent discovering the unspoilt hamlets of East Anglia, nothing quite matches getting off the beaten track and exploring Britain's areas of outstanding beauty.

Each month, *Country Living Magazine* celebrates the richness and diversity of our countryside with features on rural Britain and the traditions that have their roots there. So it is with great pleasure that I introduce you to the *Country Living Magazine Guide to Rural England* series. Packed with information about unusual and unique aspects of our countryside, the guides will point both fair-weather and intrepid travellers in the right direction.

Each chapter provides a fascinating tour of the South East area, with insights into local heritage and history and easy-to-read facts on a wealth of places to visit, stay, eat, drink and shop.

I hope that this guide will help make your visit a rewarding and stimulating experience and that you will return inspired, refreshed and ready to head off on your next countryside adventure.

Susy Smith

Susy Smith
Editor, Country Living magazine

PS To subscribe to *Country Living Magazine* each month, call 01858 438844

Introduction

This is the second edition of the *Country Living Guide to Rural England - The South East* and it is full of information on the traditional English countryside in Surrey, Sussex and Kent. It is over 2 years since publication of the very popular first edition and we hope that you enjoy this thoroughly updated version just as much.

Peter Long, the editor, is an experienced travel writer who spent many years as an inspector and writer with Egon Ronay's Hotels & Restaurants Guides before joining the Travel Publishing editorial team. Peter has ensured that this edition is packed with vivid descriptions, historical stories, amusing anecdotes and interesting facts on hundreds of places in the South East.

The coloured advertising panels within each chapter provide further information on places to see, stay, eat, drink, shop and even exercise! We have also selected a number of walks from walkingworld.com (full details of this website may be found to the rear of this guide) which we highly recommend if you wish to appreciate fully the beauty and charm of the varied rural landscapes and coastlines of Surrey, East Sussex, West Sussex and Kent.

The guide however is not simply an "armchair tour". Its prime aim is to encourage the reader to visit the places described and discover much more about the wonderful towns, villages and countryside of the South East. In this respect we would like to thank all the Tourist Information Centres who helped us to provide you with up-to-date information. Whether you decide to explore this region by wheeled transport or on foot we are sure you will find it a very uplifting experience.

We are always interested in receiving comments on places covered (or not covered) in our guides so please do not hesitate to use the reader reaction form provided at the rear of this guide to give us your considered comments. This will help us refine and improve the content of the next edition. We also welcome any general comments which will help improve the overall presentation of the guides themselves.

Finally, for more information on the full range of travel guides published by Travel Publishing please refer to the details and order form at the rear of this guide or log on to our website at www.travelpublishing.co.uk

Travel Publishing

Locator Map

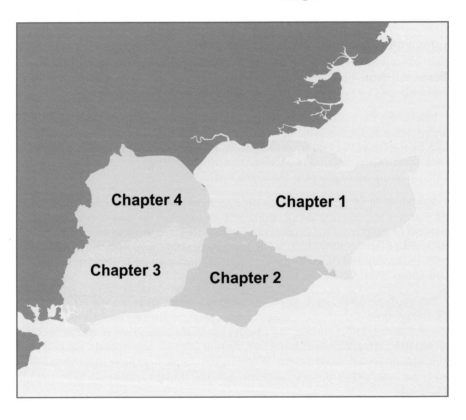

Contents

LOCATOR MAP

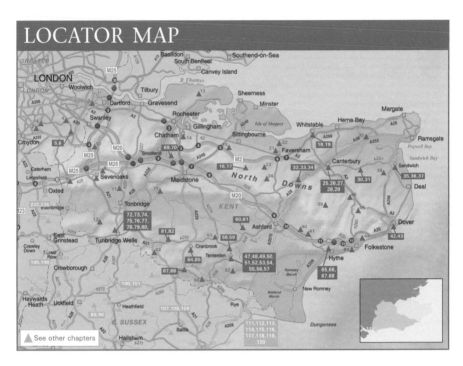

ADVERTISERS AND PLACES OF INTEREST

KENT 1

Kent is a land of gardens and orchards, of historic castles and churches, of pretty villages and fine market towns, but above all it is a land that is inescapably linked to the sea. Its proximity to Europe across the narrow channel means that invaders through the centuries have chosen the Kent coast as a gateway to Britain. The Romans landed here over 2,000 years ago, the Vikings followed almost

Canterbury Cathedral

1,000 years later and the land was widely settled by the Normans following the defeat of Harold in 1066. All these peoples and the prehistoric tribes that preceded them have left their mark on the landscape and the language. Many place names, such as Rochester and Whitstable, are derived from Roman, Saxon or Norman origins. Norman churches and castles in various states of ruin or preservation still stand in the tranquil rural countryside that belies the bloodshed of centuries of successive invasions.

Cricket at the Vine Ground, Sevenoaks

On the south coast, the Cinque Ports were set up in the 11th century as a commercial alliance of significant ports, although silting up of channels over the centuries has left many of them several miles from the sea. Henry VIII established a dockyard at Chatham, which was a major factor in Britain's dominance of the seas in the centuries that followed. The whole length of the Kent coast has been the historic haven of smugglers, and every rocky cove and sheltered bay has seen daring and ruthless smugglers pursued by brave and determined but generally ineffective excise men. In villages across Kent, ancient tales of smuggling are still told and houses, churches and caves are remembered as places where the smugglers' booty was hidden away. However Kent's maritime tradition did not depend entirely on lawlessness and many villages plied a legitimate trade in fishing. Ancient fishing villages like Deal retain their quaint alleyways and traditional fishermen's cottages around the harbour areas. Whitstable has been famed for centuries for oyster fishing and Whitstable oysters are still regarded as gourmet fare. In the 19th century as the fashion grew for taking holidays by the sea, seaside towns and resorts grew up in former fishing ports like Herne Bay. Margate with its glorious sands was one of the first resorts to attract visitors. Even before the railways, pleasure boats brought Londoners to Margate in search of sun, sea and sand.

Churchill, Darwin and Charles Dickens all had homes in Kent. Geoffrey Chaucer and Christopher Marlowe, Somerset Maugham and Mary Tourtel, the creator of Rupert Bear, all lived part of their lives at Canterbury. The abbey and cathedral here, along with St Martin's Church, form a fascinating World Heritage Site, the place where St Augustine brought Christianity to England in the 6th century.

Although Kent lies very close to the spreading suburban sprawl of Greater London, much of it has managed to retain a tranquil rural feel, despite commuter developments. Rolling wooded countryside is dotted with windmills and attractive villages, surrounded by orchards, market gardens, hop fields and countless gardens.

WEST KENT

Although the western region of Kent lies so close to the spreading suburban areas of Greater London, it has still managed to maintain an identity that is all its own, illustrated by the offbeat pronunciations of some of its towns and villages. Water dominates much of the history of Kent, reflected in the strong maritime heritage along the banks of the River Thames. The glorious countryside attracts many visitors yet it still manages to retain a tranquil rural feel. The short crossing to Europe via Dover and the Thames estuary has always made this one of the first targets for invaders.

Prehistoric remains have been found here along with evidence of Roman occupation at Lullingstone near Eynsford and Croft Roman Villa at Orpington. Danes and Vikings also invaded and the now picturesque village of Aylesford has, over the centuries, been witness to more than its fair share of bloodshed.

More peaceful times saw the creation of grand manor houses and the conversion of castles into more comfortable homes: this area abounds with interesting and historic places such as Cobham Hall, Knole House, Old Soar Manor, Ightham Mote, Penshurst Place and the magnificent Hever Castle.

Two of these places stand out as being of particular interest. Chartwell, the home of Sir Winston and Lady Churchill from the 1920s until the great statesman's death in 1965, has been left just as it was when the couple were alive and it remains a lasting tribute to this extraordinary man. At Downe, just south of Farnborough, lies Down House, the home of Charles Darwin and the place where he formulated his theories of evolution and wrote his most famous work *The Origin of Species by Means of Natural Selection*.

DARTFORD

This urban settlement is best known today as the home of the **Dartford Tunnel,** which runs for roughly one mile beneath the River Thames, re-emerging on the Essex bank near West Thurrock. Dartford is a place of some historical significance: it stands on the old London to Dover road, at the crossing of the River Darent, and this is the reason for its name, which actually means 'Darent Ford'.

Local legend has it that Wat Tyler, leader of the Peasant's Revolt, was from Dartford. The revolt was supposedly sparked off when Tyler's daughter was indecently assaulted by a tax assessor. Deptford, Colchester and Maidstone also lay claims to Wat Tyler. However the historical sources are unreliable and the legend is perpetuated in Dartford, which even has a Wat Tyler Inn.

In the 20th century Dartford has changed from Victorian market town to sprawling commuter land with 80,000 residents. Most of the town's older buildings have disappeared down the centuries, victims of war, modern transport systems or the dead hand of urban planning. Holy Trinity church, mainly 18th and 19th century with a Norman tower, a few cottages nearby and a couple of 18th century buildings on the High Street including the galleried Royal Victoria and Bull Hotel are among the few survivors of old Dartford. The church has a memorial to the railway pioneer Richard Trevithick, who died in poverty at the Royal Victoria and Bull (then just the Bull) in 1833. He had been working nearby on new inventions, and his colleagues clubbed together to provide him with a decent funeral.

AROUND DARTFORD

CRAYFORD
2 miles NW of Dartford on the A206

This is the point at which the Roman road Watling Street crosses the River Cray. The parish church St Paulinus dates back to the 12th century but additions have been made over the centuries. A settlement was discovered just to the west of St Paulinus where Iron Age pottery was unearthed.

On the banks of the River Cray, the **World of Silk** provides visitors with an insight into the historic and traditional craft of silk making and the origins of silk are explained. Believed to have been discovered in around 1640 BC by the Empress of China, Hsi-Ling-Shi, silk found its way to Europe along the arduous silk route and, from the humble silk worm through to the beautiful printed fabrics, the whole of the story of this luxury material is explained.

BEXLEYHEATH
3 miles W of Dartford on the A207

Despite being located between Dartford and Woolwich, Bexleyheath is somewhat surprising in that, although there was a great deal of development here in the 19th and early 20th centuries, expanses of parkland still remain. As the town's name might suggest, this area was once heathland and, following enclosure in 1814, some of this land has managed to escape the hands of the developers. In the heart of Bexleyheath lies one of these areas, **Danson Park**, covering more than 180 acres. Originally a private estate, the garden was landscaped by Capability Brown. The **Danson Mansion** within the park, a Grade I Listed Building, completed in 1762 and designed by Sir Robert Taylor, architect of the Bank of

BECKENHAM UPHOLSTERY & SOFT FURNISHINGS

1-2 The Mews, rear of 32 High Street,
Beckenham, Kent BR3 1AY
Tel: 020 8650 3340
website: www.southlondonguide.co.uk/beckenham

In a mews just behind Beckenham High Street, **Beckenham Upholstery and Soft Furnishings** has been in business since 1987, but the experience of its founding partners Frank Geoghegan and Antony Mee goes back some 40 years. They specialise in upholstery and re-upholstery, loose covers, curtains and blinds, and French polishing. They also restore antique furniture. As well as restoration and repair work they will design pieces from scratch to meet customers' individual requirements.

All the work is carried out on the premises, and the partners' ability to turn furniture that has seen better days into treasured heirlooms of the future has earned them a reputation for quality and reliability that goes far beyond the southern suburbs of London. They provide free estimates and free local delivery. Antony and Frank are members of the Association of Master Upholsterers. Opening hours of Beckenham Upholsterers and Soft Furnishings are 9am to 5.30pm Monday to Friday and 12 noon to 4pm on Saturday.

L'ARAGOSTA

8 Eden Park Avenue, Elmers End,
nr Beckenham, Kent BR3 3HN
Tel: 020 8650 3959

Italian cooking using the finest ingredients is what Peppe offers at **L'Aragosta**, which he has made into one of the most popular restaurants in this part of town. The dining room is bright and modern, but with a delightfully traditional feel, and one wall is covered with a lovely, evocative mural of an Italian coastal scene. At the

front, but well protected by plants and bushes, is an outside eating area.

Aragosta means lobster, and the long and varied menu offers lobster in several guises: with prawns and crab on a bed of rocket and radicchio; with spaghetti, garlic, basil and cherry tomatoes; as a main course *a piacere* (to the customer's choice); and *medaglione* - a tower of beef filled with lobster meat and served on a bed of spinach and polenta with a rich lobster sauce. There's plenty more to choose from among the starters, pasta dishes, meat and fish main courses and tempting desserts, and the extensive wine list has bottles from Italy and all over the globe.

England, is sometimes open to the public. At the centre of the park, a great oak tree, which is over 200 years old, is now designated one of the 'Great Trees of London'.

To the southeast lies **Hall Place** (see [anel on page 8), a charming country house that was built in 1540 for Sir John Champneis, a Lord Mayor of London and substantially added to around 100 years later. As well as the fine splendid great hall, the house is particularly noted for its beautiful award-winning formal gardens on the banks of the River Cray.

One of Bexleyheath's most famous former residents lived at **The Red House**, in Red House Lane. Designed by Philip Webb, it was built in 1860 for the newly married William Morris. The interior was decorated by Webb, Morris, Burne-Jones, Madox Brown and Dante Gabriel Rossetti. William Morris described the house as "a joyful nook of heaven in an unheavenly world", while for Rossetti it was "...more a poem than a house - but an admirable place to live in too". The house is one of the most recent acquisitions of the National Trust.

The ruins of **Lesness Abbey** are in the area between Belvedere and Abbey Wood. The Augustinians occupied the abbey from 1178 until the 16th century when it was razed to the ground. The foundations excavated in the 20th century give a good idea of the layout of a monastic community.

HEXTABLE

3 miles S of Dartford on the B258

Surrounded by market gardens and orchards, this village is home to **Hextable Gardens**. This heritage centre lies in the former Botany Laboratory of Swanley Horticultural College, believed to be the first horticultural college in the world. The Botany Lab is not listed but

HALL PLACE

Bourne Road, Bexley, Kent DA5 1PQ
Tel: 01322 526574 Fax: 01322 52292
website: www.hallplaceandgardens.com

Surrounded by its award-winning gardens, **Hall Place** is an attractive mansion house that dates from the 16th century that was substantially added to around 100 years later.

Originally the home of Sir John Champneis, a Lord Mayor of London, the house, over the centuries, has served many purposes and it has been a school on three separate occasions and, during World War II, it was an American Army communications centre.

However, today, parts of the house are open to the public and visitors here can not only see the magnificent Great Hall, the Tudor Parlour and the recently redecorated Drawing Room and Long Gallery but Hall Place contains Bexley Museum and there are also exhibitions galleries. The gardens, through which the River Cray flows, are impressive and perhaps most eye-catching of all is the outstanding topiary with its chess pieces and Queen's beasts. Meanwhile, there are rose gardens laid out in the Tudor style, herb, rock and heather gardens and a nursery with a display of designs for the smaller garden. Guided tours can be booked of both the house and the gardens. Hall Place is open throughout the year whilst the summer opening Visitors Centre, that doubles as a Tourist Information Centre, hosts exhibitions on local history and arts and crafts.

JESSICA JONES

2 Donna Alexandra Mews, 5 Royal Parade, Chislehurst,
Kent BR7 6NR
Tel: 020 8467 2868

Jessica Jones is a lovely little shop in a quaint Victorian mews, with every inch of space filled with delightful items to keep, to give or to receive. Everything is lovingly chosen and displayed by the shop's three owners, Candice, Jan and Debbie. They worked together elsewhere in Chislehurst and became the best of friends, so when Pennington Jewellers closed they decided to open this lovely shop.

They have put their flair, expertise and eye for design to good

use in choosing and displaying their stock, which includes fun things for children, candles, lamps, bags, cushions and soft furnishings, silver and costume jewellery, homewares, photo frames and albums, cards and wrapping paper. Most of the items are unique, and since the stock is constantly changing, every visit to this pretty little place will result in something new to buy and treasure or to delight a friend with a special gift.

Shop hours are 9.30am to 5pm Tuesday to Saturday.

is an attractive 1930s white-painted brick building with metal-framed windows, now sensitively restored. Also in the village is **Hextable Park**, a charming place that has been specifically designed to attract a wide variety of wildlife and butterflies. Pictorial information plaques aid visitors in identifying the many species found here.

CHISLEHURST
5 miles SW of Dartford on the A208

Following the arrival of the railways, Chislehurst developed as one of London's more select and fashionable suburbs as businessmen moved here lured by the fresh air and the downland scenery that lies on the doorstep. The town has managed to remain relatively unspoilt by further development thanks, in large part, to **Chislehurst Common**, an oasis of greenery criss-crossed by a number of small roads.

The suburb is also home to **Chislehurst Caves**, one of Britain's most interesting networks of underground caverns. There are over 20 miles of caverns and passageways, dug over a period of 8,000 years. The vast labyrinth of caves is a maze of ancient flint and chalk mines dug by hand over the centuries. It comprises three sections that each relate to a specific era and the oldest section, known as the Druids, dates back approximately 4,000 years. The largest section is Roman while the smallest, and youngest, was excavated some 1,400 years ago by the Saxons. Royalists took refuge here during the Civil War and the pit that was built to trap their Parliamentarian pursuers can still be seen. At the height of the Blitz during World War II, the caves became the world's largest air raid shelter when some 15,000 people hid here from the German bombing raids. Visitors can take a lamp lit guided tour of the various sections including the air raid shelters, the Druid Altar and the Haunted Pool.

A quiet and pleasant residential area today, Chislehurst has two famous sons: William Willet Junior, the enthusiastic advocate of the Daylight Saving Scheme, who unfortunately died a year before British Summer Time (BST) was introduced in 1916, and Sir Malcolm Campbell, the racing driver and pioneering land and water speed record holder of the 1930s. A memorial to Willet is in nearby Petts Wood.

ORPINGTON
6 miles SW of Dartford on the A224

Once a country village, Orpington changed dramatically in the 1920s and 1930s into the commuter town that it is

BROMLEY MUSEUM

The Priory, Church Hill, Orpington, Kent BR6 0HH
Tel: 01689 873826

Housed in a museum piece itself, an interesting medieval building dating from 1290, and surrounded by attractive gardens **Bromley Museum** has numerous exhibits and displays that cover the history of the area around Bromley. From prehistoric Stone Age tools, Roman lamps and Saxon jewellery to a recreated 1930s dining room and memorabilia from World War II there are many interesting items that will fire the imagination. The museum is also home an archaeological collection that was put together by Victorian 'Renaissance man' Sir John Lubbock of nearby Hall Place.

RUTH BRUSHETT

94 High Street, Orpington, Kent BR6 0JY
Tel: 01689 823035
website: www.ruthbrushett.com

Designer jeweller **Ruth Brushett** offers a range of beautiful jewellery that has few equals, and a visit to her shop and showroom in Orpington's High Street is always a delight. The selection attempts to give the customer a feel for what is available in the UK but also draws on tastes and influences from other European countries. Many of the items tend to the more 'unusual' in terms of jewellery and gift

ideas and offer a platform for customers' own ideas through working with Ruth. She is not competing with mainstream high street jewellers, but offers a totally personal experience.

Some of the jewellery on display is imported from Italy, Germany and Switzerland, providing an interesting contrast in styles, and the shop is also a showcase for young and emerging British talent. Ruth will undertake one-off commissions and also offers a repair and alteration service.

today. However, thanks to William Cook, a 19th century local poultry farmer, the town has not lost its rural connections as Cook introduced a breed of poultry - the Black Orpington - that was to become famous throughout the farming world in Britain, Europe and beyond.

In the heart of the town, next to the library, stands **Bromley Museum** (see panel on page 9), which is an ideal starting point for an exploration of this area. Housed in what is a museum piece itself, an interesting medieval building dating from 1290, and surrounded by attractive gardens, Bromley Museum has numerous exhibits and displays that cover the history of the area around Bromley. From prehistoric Stone Age tools, Roman lamps and Saxon jewellery to a recreated 1930s dining room and

memorabilia from World War II there are many interesting items that will fire the imagination. The museum also houses an archaeological collection, put together by Sir John Lubbock of nearby Hall Place.

Adjacent to the railway station, and protected from the elements by a modern cover building, is **Crofton Roman Villa**, built in around AD 140 and inhabited for over 250 years. Presumed to have been at the centre of a farming estate, the villa, which was altered several times during its occupation, probably extended to some 20 rooms although the remains of only 10 have been uncovered. Evidence of the underfloor heating arrangements, or hypocaust, can still be seen as can some of the tiled floors, and there is a display of the artefacts that were also uncovered during the excavations here.

GRAVESEND

The Thames is half a mile wide at Gravesend. This is where ships take on board a river pilot for the journey upstream. It is a busy maritime community, with cutters and tugs helping to maintain a steady flow of river traffic. Gravesend is where the bodies of those who had died on board were unloaded before the ships entered London; but the name Gravesend is not a reference to its being the last resting place of these poor unfortunates but is derived from 'Grove's End' from the Old English 'graf' meaning grove and 'ende' meaning end or boundary.

Much of the town was destroyed by fire in 1727. One of the many buildings that did not survive the fire was the parish **Church of St George**, and the building seen today was rebuilt in Georgian style after the disaster. However the graveyard is more interesting than the church as this is thought to be the final resting place of the famous Red Indian princess, Pocahontas. Pocahontas was the daughter of a native American chieftain, who reputedly saved the life of the English settler, John Smith, in Virginia. She died on board ship (either from smallpox, fever or tuberculosis) in 1617 while she was on her way back to America with her husband, John Rolfe. A life-sized statue marks Pocahontas's supposed burial place in the churchyard.

A building of interest in the town, that did survive the 18th century fire, is the 14th century **Milton Chantry**. A chantry is a place set aside for saying prayers for the dead. This small building was the chantry of the de Valence and Monechais families. It later became an inn and, in 1780, part of a fort. Milton Chantry is now a heritage centre with fascinating displays detailing the history and varied uses of the building.

AROUND GRAVESEND

COBHAM
4 miles SE of Gravesend off the A2

This picturesque village is home to one of the largest and finest houses in Kent - **Cobham Hall** - an outstanding redbrick mansion that dates from 1584. Set in 150 acres of parkland and demonstrating architectural styles from Elizabethan, Jacobean, Carolean eras and the 18th century, the house has much to offer those interested in art, history and architecture. The Elizabethan wings date from the late 16th century. The central section of the house is later and here can be found the magnificent Gilt Hall that was decorated by Inigo Jones's famous pupil, John Webb, in 1654. Elsewhere in the house there are several superb marble fireplaces. The beautiful **Gardens** were landscaped by Humphry Repton for the 4th Earl of Darnley. Over the centuries many notable people have stayed here, including English monarchs from Elizabeth I to Edward VIII, and Charles Dickens used to walk through the grounds from his home at Higham to Cobham's village pub. However, perhaps Cobham Hall's most famous claim to fame dates back to 1883 when Ivo Blight, who later became the 8th Earl of Darnley, led the English cricket team to victory against Australia and brought the Ashes home to Cobham. Today, the hall is a private girls' boarding school and is occasionally open to visitors.

Back in the village more evidence can be found of past members of the Cobham family and, in the 13th century parish church of **St Mary Magdalene**, a series of superb commemorative floor brasses can be seen that date back to the late Middle Ages. Behind the church are some **Almshouses** that incorporate a 14th century kitchen and hall that were once part of the Old College that was founded by the 3rd Lord Cobham. He endowed them as living quarters for five priests who were to pray for the repose of his soul. After 1537, when the college was suppressed, the buildings became almhouses for 20 poor men and women from local parishes.

In the heart of the village stands the half-timbered **Leather Bottle Inn**, made famous by Charles Dickens when he featured his favourite inn in the novel *The Pickwick Papers*. It was at the Leather Bottle Inn that Tracey Tupman was discovered by Mr Pickwick after being jilted by Rachel Wardle.

Close by, just to the north of the village, lies **Owletts**, a lovely redbrick house that was built in the late 17th century by a Cobham farmer. Still retaining a charming sense of rural comfort, the house has an imposing staircase, a notable 17th century plaster ceiling and a beautiful garden.

Swanscombe

2½ miles W of Gravesend on the A226

This former agricultural village, which has long since been swamped by the growth of industry along the banks of the River Thames, was the site of an important archaeological find in 1935. Excavations in a gravel pit unearthed fragments of a human skull and analysis of the bones revealed that the remains (those of a woman) were around 200,000 years old, making them some of the oldest human remains found in Europe. This riverside settlement also has remnants from more recent historical periods and, while the parish church of Saints Peter and Paul dates mainly from the 12th century, its structure incorporates bricks from Roman times and parts of its tower predate the Norman invasion. Although the church was substantially restored in the Victorian era, making it difficult to detect the original features, it does provide tangible evidence of the many layers of human settlement here along the Thames.

SEVENOAKS

With its easy road and rail links with London and its leafy and relaxed atmosphere, Sevenoaks has come to epitomise the essence of the commuter belt. While this perception is not far from the truth, the town retains a rural feel from the once wooded countryside that surrounded the ancient settlement that stood here some nine centuries ago.

Sevenoaks began as a market town in Saxon times, although an older settlement is believed to have been sited here previously, and it grew up around the meeting point of the roads from London and the Dartford river crossing as they headed south towards the coast.

The first recorded mention of the town came in 1114, when it was called 'Seovenaca' and local tradition has it that the name refers to the clump of seven oaks that once stood here; those trees disappeared long ago but were replaced in 1955 with seven trees from Knole Park. These replacement trees made headline news in the autumn of 1987 when several were blown down in the Great Storm that hit the southeast of England in October.

Rural Sevenoaks changed little over the centuries until the arrival of the railway in 1864, when the town became a popular residential area for those working in London. Despite the development, which was again accelerated when the railway line was electrified in the 1930s, Sevenoaks has managed to maintain its individuality and there are still various traditional Kentish tile-hung cottages to be found here. In the **Sevenoaks Library Gallery** an imaginative programme of contemporary exhibitions of modern art, by both local and international artists, shows that the town does not dwell in the past. The exhibits range from photography and textiles to fine art, and Andy Warhol and John Piper are among the famous names to be featured here over the years.

Not far from the centre of Sevenoaks is another reminder of the town's heritage in the form of the **Vine Cricket Ground** that lies on a rise to the south. It was given to the town in 1773 but the first recorded match held here - between Kent and Sussex - was in 1782, when the Duke of Dorset (one of the Sackville family of Knole) and his estate workers defeated a team representing All England. This remarkable victory was particularly sweet as the Duke's team also won a bet of 1,000 guineas! The weatherboard pavilion at the club is 19th century. The Cricket Club pay Sevenoaks Town Council a peppercorn rent, literally two peppercorns per year - one for the ground and one for the pavilion. The council may be required to pay Lord Sackville one cricket ball each year, but only if he asks.

The pride of Sevenoaks is **Knole House**, one of the largest private homes in England that lies to the southeast of the town and is surrounded by an extensive and majestic deer park. The huge manor house, with its 365 rooms, stands on the site of a much smaller house that was bought by the Archbishop of Canterbury in 1456 and

HORNSHAW HOUSE

47 Mount Harry Road, Sevenoaks,
Kent TN13 3JN
Tel: 01732 465262
e-mail: embates@hornshaw47.freeserve.co.uk
website: www.hornshaw-house.co.uk

Hornshaw House, the home of Jeremy and Elizabeth Bates and their family, is furnished with traditional and antique furniture, with family pictures on the walls. The two rooms that they let on a bed & breakfast basis (Tourist Board 4

Diamonds) provide excellent accommodation for two couples, with large, comfortable beds, central heating and en suite bathrooms with both bath and shower.

One room has extra-long twin beds that can be zipped together to make a super-kingsize bed. The day starts with a Continental or full English breakfast. The house is surrounded by gardens and trees and is well protected from traffic noise. Sevenoaks station is a five-minute walk away, and the house is only two miles from Junction 5 of the M25. There's ample off-road parking at Hornshaw House, which is a totally non-smoking establishment.

Deer in Knole Park, Sevenoaks

used as an ecclesiastical palace until 1532 when it was taken over by Henry VIII. In 1603, Elizabeth I granted the house to the Sackville family and, although it is now in the ownership of the National Trust, the family still live here. A superb example of late medieval architecture, with Jacobean embellishments that include superb carvings and plasterwork, visitors to Knole can also see the internationally renowned collection of Royal Stuart furnishings, 17th-century textiles, important English silver and works by Van Dyck, Gainsborough, Lely, Kneller and Reynolds. Little altered since the 18th century, it was here that Vita Sackville-West was born in 1892 and, as well as being the setting for Virginia Wolf's novel *Orlando*, it is believed that Hitler intended to use Knole as his English headquarters.

The trees in the 1,000-acre deer park were smashed by the great storm of 1987, and it fell to Lionel Sackville-West and a team of volunteers to plant more than 250,000 trees, mostly beech but with some oak and chestnut. He tended the trees personally until shortly before his

death in March 2004, and had the distinction of beating the Queen into third place in a forestry competition for replantings after the storm. Lord Egremont won first prize, but as Lord Sackville commented, "he had professional foresters". In the late 1960s Lord Sackville restored the chapel at Knole, since when it has been used regularly by his family and by Sevenoaks School. Knole has 365 rooms, a handful of which are open to the public for visits.

AROUND SEVENOAKS

FARNBOROUGH
8 miles N of Sevenoaks on the A21

Just to the south of the village lies **High Elms Country Park**, a delightful park of woodlands, formal gardens and meadows, that was once part of the High Elms Estate.

FRENCH STREET
6 miles W of Sevenoaks off the B2042

A tiny hamlet, tucked away in the folds of narrow, wooded hills, French Street appears to be one of the most hidden away places in Kent, but a particular reason brings visitors here in droves. In 1924, Winston Churchill purchased **Chartwell** as a family home and, with its magnificent views looking out over the Kentish Weald, it is easy to see why the great statesman said of Chartwell, "I love the place - a day away from Chartwell is a day wasted." From the 1920s until his death in 1965, Churchill lived here with his wife and the rooms have been left exactly as they were when the couple were alive: daily newspapers lie on the table, fresh flowers from the garden decorate the rooms and a box of his famous cigars lie ready. The museum and

TIMOTHY CONSTABLE

Workshop 6, Chart Farm, Seal Chart,
nr Sevenoaks, Kent TN15 0ES
Tel: 01732 763263

In a workshop filled with an impressive array of tools and materials, cabinet maker, furniture maker and designer **Timothy Constable** produces top-quality pieces that range from elegant jewellery boxes to chairs, tables and bedroom furniture. He served his apprenticeship with the internationally renowned musical instrument makers Arnold Dolmetsch Ltd at Haslemere in Surrey.

After 20 years spent making early keyboard instruments, Timothy took up the challenge of designing and making contemporary furniture, which he has been doing since the mid-1980s. Among many accolades, he was awarded a coveted Guild Mark Award by the Worshipful Company of Furniture Makers for a superb music stand. The Dolmetsch Workshops were run very much in the Arts & Crafts tradition (Arnold Dolmetsch was a friend of William Morris) and that influence is still evident in the way Timothy approaches his work. Working mainly to commission enables him to control closely the standard of craftsmanship that goes into pieces that are pleasing to both the eye and the touch. His workshop is located close to the A25 a mile east of Sevenoaks.

Chartwell House in Springtime

exhibition rooms contain numerous mementoes from his life and political career, while the garden studio contains many of his paintings along with his easel and paintbox.

The gardens have also been kept just as they were during his lifetime, so visitors can see not only the golden rose walk that the couple's children planted on the occasion of Sir Winston and Lady Churchill's 50th wedding anniversary but also the brick wall that Churchill built with his own hands. The house is now in the care of the National Trust.

WESTERHAM

4 miles W of Sevenoaks on the A25

A pleasant, small town close to the Surrey border, the building of the M25 close by has eased the town's traffic congestion and it is now a quieter and calmer place that is more in keeping with its former days as a coaching station. Along the town's main street and around the tiny green are a number of old buildings, including two venerable coaching inns, while, in the town centre, by the green, are two statues of British heroes who had connections with Westerham. The first dates from 1969 and it is a tribute to Sir Winston Churchill, who made his home close by at Chartwell, and the other statue is that of General James Wolfe, who defeated the French at Quebec in 1759. Wolfe was born in Westerham and his childhood home, renamed **Quebec House**, can be found to the east of the town centre. Dating from the 17th century, this gabled redbrick building, now in the care of the National Trust, contains portraits, prints and other memorabilia relating to the family, the general and his famous victory over the French.

There has been a house on the site that is now occupied by **Squerryes Court** (see panel below) since 1216 and, in 1658, when the diarist John Evelyn visited the medieval mansion he wrote the following description: "A pretty, finely wooded, well watered seate, the stables good, the house old but

convenient." However, this building was not to last much longer, as in 1681 the then owner, Sir Nicholas Crisp, pulled it down and built in its place the glorious redbrick house seen today. Bought by the Warde family in 1731, it remains in their hands today and is perhaps best known for the important collection of 18th century English and 17th century Dutch paintings, many of them commissioned by the family. The sumptuously appointed rooms also contain some splendid furniture, porcelain and tapestries, as well as some Wolfe memorabilia. A friend of the family, James Wolfe received his first commission here at the tender age of 14. Outside lie superb gardens, restored to their original formal state after the Great Storm of 1987 using a garden plan of 1719.

In Westerham's churchyard is the grave of Sir Peter Nissen, who designed the hut that was widely used in the Second World War.

OTFORD

3 miles N of Sevenoaks off the A225

Found in a pleasant location beside the River Darent, this village has a history

SQUERRYES COURT

Westerham, Kent TN16 1SJ
Tel: 01959 562345/563118 Fax: 01959 565949

There has been a house on the site that is now occupied by **Squerryes Court** since 1216 and, in 1658, when the diarist John Evelyn visited the medieval mansion he wrote the following description: "A pretty, finely wooded, well watered seate, the stables good, the house old but convenient." However, this building was not to last much longer as, in 1681, the then owner, Sir Nicholas Crisp, pulled it down and built in its place the glorious red brick house seen today. Bought by the Warde family in 1731, it remains in their hands today and Squerryes Court is perhaps best known for the important collection of 18th century English and 17th century Dutch paintings housed here - many of which were commissioned by the family. Meanwhile, there are also sumptuously decorated rooms that are home to some splendid furniture, porcelain and tapestries. Outside lie the superb gardens that, following the Great Storm of 1987, have been restored to their original formal state using a garden plan of 1719 as a guide. Beyond lie the less formal landscaped grounds and parkland that was laid out in the mid-18th century.

that stretches back to Roman times and beyond - as does much of the Darent Valley. Lying at an important crossroads for many centuries, it was here in AD 775 that King Offa of Mercia won the battle that brought Kent into his kingdom; several centuries later, Henry VIII stopped at Otford on his way to the historic encounter with François I of France at the Field of the Cloth of Gold. The King is believed to have stayed the night at one of the many palaces belonging to the Archbishop of Canterbury. The palace at Otford, of which little remains, stood adjacent to the Church of St Bartholomew and opposite the village's duck pond.

The **Pond**, which lies at the heart of Otford, is itself something of an historic curiosity as it was documented as early as the 11th century and is thought to be the only stretch of water in England to be classified as a listed building. The **Otford Heritage Centre** is just the place to find out more about this interesting village and here can be seen displays on the village's natural history, geology and archaeology, including artefacts from nearby Roman sites and the medieval Archbishop's Palace.

Connections with the Archbishops of Canterbury continue at **Becket's Well**, which once supplied water to the palace and is thought to have miraculous origins. Local folklore suggests that when he was visiting Otford, Archbishop Thomas à Becket was so displeased with the quality of the local water that, to remedy the situation, he struck the ground with his crozier and two springs of clear water bubbled up from the spot.

SHOREHAM

4 miles N of Sevenoaks off the A255

Shoreham is situated beside the River Darent, which features prominently in

THE HOP SHOP

Castle Farm, Shoreham, nr Sevenoaks, Kent TN14 7UB
Tel: 01959 523219 Fax: 01959 524220
e-mail: sales@hopshop.co.uk
web: www.hopshop.co.uk

Hops are just part of the life of The Hop Shop, a small independent business run by William and Caroline Alexander and based on a family farm in the beautiful Darenth Valley, only 20 miles from central London. An intriguing and tempting range of crops is produced - a rare variety of eating apple that makes superb juice, aromatic lavender, succulent beef grazed on the water meadows, hop bines for interior decoration, and a selection of dried flowers that earned them an international reputation and won five consecutive Gold Medals at the Chelsea Flower Show.

In June and July, the air is filled with the scent of lavender grown for its essential oil, and tours can be booked of the flower fields. In August the harvesting of the hop bines begins and in September the orchards open for P-Y-O apples.

The Hop Shop sells a distinctive and eclectic mixture of flowers, farm foods, honey, local produce (asparagus, strawberries, cherries etc), unusual gifts and seasonal decorations. It is directly accessible from the A225, halfway between Shoreham and Eynsford. The flowers and hops are available by mail order. **Open daily all year from 10am to 5pm.**

Hosey Common

Distance:	5.7 miles (9.1 kilometres)
Typical time:	200 mins
Height gain:	140 metres
Map:	Explorer 147
Walk:	www.walkingworld.com ID:552
Contributor:	Nina Thornhill

Access Information:

The walk starts from Hosey Common car park. From the A25 at Westerham follow the signs to Chartwell, which takes you into Hosey Common Road. The car park is on the left, just after the turn for French Street. The walk can also be started from Westerham itself; this may be useful if you arrive by bus, or if you would rather avoid the climb up Hosey Hill on the return to Hosey Common car park. A car park is signposted from the main road (A25).

Additional Information:

The height gain of 140 metres is a bit deceptive, as a total of four hills have to be climbed (making it more like 140 x 4). Westerham has a good choice of pubs, restaurants and tea rooms. There are three historic houses open to the public, the National Trust-owned Chartwell and Quebec House and Squerryes Court. A good place to stop for a picnic is the viewing point at the top of Toys Hill.

Description:

The walk starts just south of Westerham through the wooded Hosey Common, then follows the secluded hamlet of French Street, offering a host of treasures including an oast house and fine views. In 1927, the Westerham Gold was found by workers digging for gravel. This consisted of 14 Iron Age gold staters which were hidden by the Celts. The Greensand Way is

followed from here to the National Trust-owned Toys Hill; at just over 800 feet it is Kent's highest point. On a clear day, Ashdown Forest and the South Downs are visible.

From here we start to head west, towards the National Trust-owned Chartwell, home of Sir Winston Churchill for more than 40 years. Although the grounds of the estate are not entered, it is still possible to see some interesting outlying buildings and more views.

Another stretch of National Trust countryside is next at Mariners Hill, before climbing up Crockham Hill. This is the woodland section of the walk and continues all the way to Squerryes Park. Here the countryside opens out again to fine views of The High Chart to the west and The Chart to the east. Further on, views of the North Downs and Westerham can be seen. The historic town of Westerham is reached towards the end of the walk.

Features:

Hills or Fells, Lake/Loch, Pub, Toilets, National Trust/NTS, Wildlife, Birds, Great Views

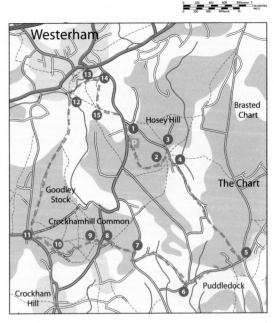

Walk Directions:

1 From the car park at Hosey Common, look for a footpath in the right hand corner, marked by a yellow-arrowed post (there are two paths which go from here but they both join up a little further on). Keep to this path, until you reach a fork in about a ¼ mile. At the fork bear left and continue to follow the yellow marker-posts, until another fork is reached close by.

2 Bear left at this fork. Almost immediately you are faced with a choice of three paths. You need to take the middle one, which is surrounded by little ridges either side. Be careful to stay on this main path, as several paths lead off from this one. At a small fork, bear left downhill in about 20 yards; you should arrive at a hollow on the left. Keep left alongside the hollow and after ¼ mile, look out for a post and path on the right. Turn right here. When a crossroads is reached, keep ahead. Further on, ignore two paths on the left; you should soon arrive at a country lane.

3 Turn right and walk along the lane, which passes through the hamlet of French Street. At a fork in the road, keep ahead downhill (ignoring the right turn). Some old cottages are passed before reaching another fork. At this fork, keep left to join the Greensand Way which we follow all the way to Toys Hill. Just after climbing uphill, a fork is reached.

4 Bear right at the fork to take the bridlepath to Toys hill. Follow the Greensand Way arrows through Toys Hill, ignoring a series of paths going off to the left, until you reach a crossroads. Keep ahead at this crossroads and follow the blue arrows (this is where you part from the Greensand Way). A few paces ahead at a fork, bear right. This path goes downhill to Puddledock Lane.

5 When Puddledock Lane is reached, turn right and enjoy some breathtaking views. Follow the lane downhill and after passing a small lane on the right at Windswept Cottage, look out for a stile on the right.

6 Turn right onto this path, which leads to the grounds of Chartwell. When you reach a lane, keep left and head towards an oast house. Keeping the oast house to your right you join a lane. Keep ahead on this lane until you reach a road (Mapleton Road) and turn right into it. Look out for a bridleway on the left, near some houses.

7 Turn left onto this bridleway to climb Mariners Hill. Stay on the bridleway ignoring all paths on the right, until the gate of Windmill Bank is reached.

8 At Windmill Bank take the path ahead through the woods, to rejoin the Greensand Way. Keep ahead to reach Hosey Common Road and go straight over to take the path by April Cottage. Soon after you come to a fork.

9 At this fork, turn left and continue ahead to follow the Greensand Way until you reach a crossroads of paths. At the crossroads, keep ahead to climb up Crockham Hill. Do the same at another crossroads of paths further on. When The Warren house is reached continue to follow yellow arrows. Continue until this track meets a road. You should see a bench on the right.

10 Turn right here and be sure to follow the yellow Greensand Way markers ahead. Follow this path until a T-junction is reached.

11 Turn right at this T-junction. The yellow Greensand Way markers are now followed all the way to Westerham (this is no longer the actual Greensand Way, but a route that links Westerham to it). Continue ahead for more than a mile, going over a series of four stiles.

12 At this, the fifth stile (immediately before the pond), turn left. Another pond is passed on the left. Take the footpath on the right, which goes through a field. Keep to the path along the left-hand side of field and in the next field look out for a gate on the left.

13 Go through this gate. This path leads you along Water Lane to Westerham. When you reach the main road turn right until you reach Mill Street. Turn right down here and re-cross the stream. Keep to the path along the right-hand side and look for a gap in the trees.

14 Go through the gap and you should see a marker-post just ahead. Turn left here to walk up Hosey Hill. Keep to the left of the field. Go over two stiles and as soon as you pass Glebe House look out for a path on the left.

15 Turn left and go down this path, which comes out by Hosey Common Road. Turn right at the road and head back to the car park.

the village. As well as the footpaths that run along its banks it is also crossed by a handsome hump-backed bridge. Close to this bridge lies the **Water House** that was the home of Samuel Palmer, the great Romantic painter, for some years. Here Palmer entertained his friend, the poet and visionary William Blake.

On the hillside across the valley can be seen a large cross, carved into the chalk that commemorates those who fell in the two World Wars. **Shoreham Aircraft Museum** is dedicated to the Battle of Britain and the air war over southern England. Among the numerous exhibits are aviation relics and homefront memorabilia from the 1940s.

EYNSFORD

6½ miles N of Sevenoaks off the A225

The centre of this pretty and picturesque village manages to preserve a sense of history and, crossing the River Darent, there is a small hump-backed bridge and an ancient ford along with a number of old timbered cottages and a church with a tall shingle spire. The ford that gives the village its name has a depth chart that shows that the depth of the ford can reach six feet when the river is swollen with floodwater.

Leslie Hore-Belisha made his home here for a time. It was while Minister of Transport in the 1930s that he gave his name to the Belisha beacon street crossings; he also inaugurated the driving test for motorists.

Tucked away down a lane just a short distance from the village is **Eagle Heights**, Kent's bird of prey centre. Concentrating on explaining the importance of conservation and the birds' environment, the centre hosts free flying shows where visitors can see eagles soaring high above the Darent Valley and watch the condor, the world's largest bird of prey, in flight.

Further down the lane lies **Lullingstone Roman Villa**, only uncovered in 1949 although its existence had been known since the 18th century, when farm labourers uncovered fragments of mosaics that had been pierced as the men drove fence posts into the ground. Although not the largest find in the country, Lullingstone is recognised to be the most exciting of its kind made in the 20th century. The villa, which was first occupied in AD 80, has splendid mosaic floors and one of the earliest private Christian chapels.

Close by, in a quiet spot beside the River Darent, lies **Lullingstone Castle**, a superb manor house whose 15th century gatehouse is one of the first ever to be built from bricks. The house remains in the hands of the descendants of John Peche, who built it. John Peche was a city alderman and a keen jouster; he laid out a jousting ground in front of the gatehouse and entertained the young Henry VIII. The house has some fine state rooms, as might be expected of a place with royal connections, as well as family portraits and armour on display. John Peche's jousting helmet is on display in the dining room. The castle is surrounded by beautiful grounds, that also house the tiny Norman church of St Botolph. A little further south again lies **Lullingstone Park and Visitor Centre** that incorporates both parkland, with ancient pollard oaks, and chalk grassland. A full programme of guided walks, special events and children's activities take place from the visitor centre, where there is a countryside interpretation exhibition.

FARNINGHAM

8 miles N of Sevenoaks off the A225

This attractive village, in the Darent valley, was once on the main London road and much of the Georgian architecture found in the village centre reflects the prosperity that Farningham once enjoyed. A handsome 18th century brick bridge stands by lawns that slope down to the river's edge, alongside which runs the **Darent Valley Path**, following the course of the river as far as Dartford. Despite its rural appeal, Farningham is close to the M25 and M20 motorway intersection, but **Farningham Woods Nature Reserve** provides a delightful area of natural countryside that supports a wide variety of rare plants and birdlife.

MEOPHAM

10 miles NE of Sevenoaks on the A227

This pretty village, whose name is pronounced 'Meppam', still acts as a trading centre for the surrounding smaller villages and hamlets. In addition to the well maintained cricket green, the village is home to **Meopham Windmill**, a fully restored black smock mill dating from 1821 that is unusual in that it has six sides. The village was the birthplace of the great 17th century naturalist and gardener John Tradescant, who introduced many non-native species of flowers and vegetables into England.

TROTTISCLIFFE

9½ miles NE of Sevenoaks off the A20

As its name, pronounced 'Trossley', implies, this village occupies a hillside position. A pretty, neat village with views over the North Downs, it was the beauty of this quiet place that lured the artist Graham Sutherland to make Trottiscliffe his home (he is buried with his wife in the churchyard).

Just to the north of the village, on high ground that offers commanding views eastwards over the Medway Valley, stands **Coldrum Long Barrow**, some 24 columns of stone that once marked the perimeter of a circular long barrow that

was originally 50 feet in diameter. Only four of the huge stones are still standing and, although the huge burial mound inside the circle has long since disappeared, this ancient site remains an evocative and mysterious place.

WROTHAM

6 miles NE of Sevenoaks off the A227

This ancient village was once a staging post on one of the important routes southeastwards from London. It was here, in 1536, that Henry VIII received news of the execution of his second wife, Anne Boleyn.

PLATT

6 miles E of Sevenoaks off the A25

This village lies close to **Great Comp Garden**, one of finest gardens in the country and one with a truly unique atmosphere. Around the ruins of the house that once stood here, there are terraces and a sweeping lawn along with a breathtaking collection of trees, shrubs and perennials and tranquil woodland walks. The whole amazing garden was designed and created by Eric Cameron and his wife after they retired in 1957.

IGHTHAM

4½ miles E of Sevenoaks on the A227

This delightful village is a charming place of half-timbered houses and crooked lanes. Inside **Ightham Church** is a mural dedicated to Dame Dorothy Selby, who, according to legend, was instrumental in uncovering the Gunpowder Plot. The story goes that James I showed Dame Dorothy an anonymous letter he had received that hinted at 'a terrible blow' that would soon befall Parliament and, while the king dismissed the letter as the work of a crank, Dame Dorothy, reading between the lines, urged him to take the warning with the utmost seriousness.

IVY HATCH

3½ miles E of Sevenoaks off the A227

Just to the south of this small village lies **Ightham Mote**, one of England's finest medieval manor houses, owned by the National Trust. Covering some 650 years of history, this beautiful moated house, set in a narrow, wooded valley, dates back to the 14th century. It is constructed around a central courtyard that retains the meeting place purpose that is referred to in its name - 'mote' probably comes from the Old English word meaning 'meeting place'. There is plenty to see here, from the medieval Great Hall and Tudor chapel to the Victorian housekeeper's room and the billiard room. The manor house had a crypt where unlucky prisoners could be simply dispatched by the opening of a sluice gate from the moat. There was also a trap in the floor of a room in the tower from where unsuspecting victims could be dropped into a small dark hole.

An exhibition details the traditional skills that were used during the major conservation programme, which took place here in 1998. The delightful garden and grounds, with their lakes and woodland, provide numerous opportunities for pleasant country walks.

PLAXTOL

4½ miles E of Sevenoaks off the A227

This hilltop village, on a prominent ridge near Ightham Mote, has a charming row of traditional Kentish weatherboard cottages that surround the parish church. Just to the east of the village, and reached via a circuitous succession of narrow lanes, is **Old Soar Manor**, another fine National Trust owned manor house, dating from the late 13th century. The solar end of the old house survives on a tunnel vaulted undercroft, along with the chapel. An 18th century redbrick house stands where the original hall was located. While the house itself is charming it is the idyllic setting of Old Soar Manor, with its surrounding orchards and copses, that makes this such a delightful place to visit. The woods grow more dense as they climb the ridge and rise up from the orchards and, at the top, is one of southern England's largest forests, **Mereworth Woods**. Wild boar once roamed through this forest of oak and beech trees and, though today the wildlife is of a tamer variety, the woods are still enchanting.

MEREWORTH

8 miles E of Sevenoaks on the A228

Found on the southern boundary of Mereworth Woods, the village is something of a curiosity. Early in the 18th century, John Fane, a local landowner, built himself a large Palladian mansion here. He soon found that the village obscured some of his views of the surrounding

Medieval Manor House, Ightham Mote

THE OLD STABLES

Great Oaks House, Puttenden Road, Shipbourne,
nr Tonbridge, Kent TN11 9RX
Tel: 01732 810739 Fax: 01732 810738
e-mail: kent-lets@virgin.net
website: www.kent-lets.co.uk

Top-quality self-catering accommodation is offered at
The Old Stables, which is set in a beautiful part of the
country surrounded by green fields, woods and
farmland. Newly renovated to a very high standard,
the 19th century stables in the grounds of Great Oaks
House comprise a ground-floor double bedroom; an attic room up an open-tread stairway with two
single beds; a large, light, open-plan living room with French doors opening on to a courtyard garden;
and a fully equipped kitchen. Facilities include a TV with video, radio and tape, fridge-freezer, microwave

oven, dishwasher, washer-dryer, central heating,
picnic table and barbecue, books and games and off-
road parking - everything to provide a worry-free break
with all the home comforts.

The Old Stables is very close to many places of
historic interest, including Knole House and Ightham
Mote, as well as gardens and nurseries. Tonbridge is
four miles away, Sevenoaks seven miles. A network of
footpaths runs through woods and fields from the
property itself; there's a golf course nearby, and several
pubs serving meals are within walking distance.

countryside and so he had the village
demolished and moved to a site that
could not be seen from his new home.
The new village had houses for all the
original inhabitants and Fane even built
a new church. The architecture of the
church owes a lot to the style of Sir
Christopher Wren and the result is a
faithful copy of St Martin in the Fields,
London.

BIGGIN HILL

7½ miles NW of Sevenoaks on the A233

This village is best known for its
association with the RAF and, in
particular, with the role that the local
station played in the Battle of Britain. A
Spitfire and a Hurricane flank the
entrance to **Biggin Hill RAF Station**. A
chapel at the station commemorates the
453 pilots from Biggin Hill who lost their
lives during the conflict.

The location of Biggin Hill - high on a
plateau on the North Downs - made it an
obvious choice for an airfield and the
views from here, over the Darent Valley,
are outstanding.

The village itself, which sprawls along
this plateau, has a particularly
interesting church. Saint Mark's was built
between 1957 and 1959, using material
from the derelict All Saints' Church at
Peckham. The windows were engraved by
the vicar - Rev V. Symons.

DOWNE

7 miles NW of Sevenoaks off the A233

Found high up on the North Downs and
commanding spectacular views,
especially northwards towards London,
Downe has managed to retain a real
country atmosphere. Its central core of
traditional flint cottages has not been
engulfed by the growing tide of modern

suburban housing spreading from the capital. Seemingly at a crossroads between Greater London and the countryside, Downe's natural setting, still evident in the outskirts of the village, also marks something of a boundary as it is poised between the open uplands of the Downs themselves and the more wooded areas of Kent, such as the Weald, further south.

It was in this village, at **Down House**, that one of the world's greatest and best known scientists, Charles Darwin, lived for over 40 years until his death in 1882. Following his five year voyage on *HMS Beagle*, Darwin came back to this house where he worked on formalising his theory of evolution and it was here that he wrote his famous work *The Origin of Species by Means of Natural Selection* that was published in 1859. The house is now a museum dedicated to the life and work of this famous scientist and visitors can find out more about his revolutionary theory and gain an understanding of the man himself. The study, where he did much of his writing, still contains many personal belongings and the family rooms have been painstakingly restored to provide a real insight into Charles Darwin, the scientist, husband and father.

TONBRIDGE

This pretty old town stands at the highest navigable point on the River Medway and, as well as having a Victorian cast-iron bridge across the river, the substantial remains of Tonbridge's Norman **Castle** can be found on a rise in the town centre. The walls of the castle date from the 12th century while the shell of the keep, along with the massive gatehouse and drum towers, were built in the early 14th century.

Within the castle walls is a mound that is believed to have been the site of an earlier Saxon fort that provides further evidence of the importance of the river crossing. The castle was all but destroyed during the Civil War and, today, the ruins are surrounded by attractive landscaped gardens.

While the castle is certainly one of the town's oldest buildings, its most famous institution is **Tonbridge School**, founded in 1553 by Sir Andrew Judd, Master of the Skinners' Company and a former Lord Mayor of London. The school received a charter from Elizabeth I, and on Judd's death the administration was left in trust to the Skinners' Company, the Governors to this day.

AROUND TONBRIDGE

TUDELEY
2 miles E of Tonbridge on the B2017

The most striking feature of **All Saints Church** is a stained-glass window commissioned from Marc Chagall by Sir Henry and Lady d'Avidgor Goldsmith in memory of their daughter Sarah, who drowned in a sailing accident off Rye in 1963. The work was so well received on its installation in 1967 that more were commissioned, the last being installed in 1985, the year of Chagall's death. The glass was made and fitted by Charles Marq of Rheims.

PENSHURST
4½ miles SW of Tonbridge on the B2176

With its hilly, wooded setting and Tudor architecture, Penshurst is renowned as being one of Kent's prettiest villages. The houses at its core are all old, dating as far back as the 16th century, and each has its own sense of charm and identity.

At the heart of the village, the Church of St John the Baptist appears completely 19th century from the outside, but inside are architectural details from the 13th century onwards. Particularly noteworthy is the carving on a medieval tomb of a supplicant woman. The entrance to the church is by an ancient lychgate. Close by is one of the village's equally ancient houses, a two-storey Tudor dwelling that is particularly quaint with its bulging walls and crooked beams.

Just to the north of the village lies **Penshurst Place**. Set in the peaceful landscape of the Weald of Kent, it is recognised as being one of the best examples of 14th century architecture in the country. The house was built of local sandstone in 1341 by Sir John de Pulteney, four times Lord Mayor of London. In 1552, Edward VI granted Penshurst Place to his steward and tutor, Sir William Sidney, grandfather of the famous Elizabethan poet, soldier and courtier, Sir Philip Sidney. Additions to the original house over the centuries have seen it become an imposing fortified manor house and it remains in the Sidney family today. Visitors to Penshurst Place have the opportunity to

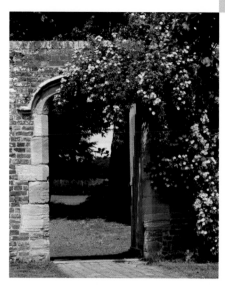

Garden Gate at Penshurst Place

see the magnificent Barons Hall and the impressive staterooms, and a marvellous collection of paintings, furniture, tapestries, porcelain and armour.

The Gardens surrounding the house are equally impressive and are a rare example of Elizabethan design. The records here go back to 1346, making this one of the oldest gardens in private ownership, and over a mile of yew

PENSHURST VINEYARDS

Grove Road, Penshurst, Tonbridge, Kent TN11 8DU
Tel: 01892 870255 Fax: 01892 870255
website www.penshurst.co.uk

Penshurst Vineyards welcomes visitors to a vineyard with a difference. Not only are you offered an insight into the production of high quality wines, but you can also enjoy a unique collection of wildlife - a delightful combination that attracts thousands of visitors each year. The picturesque location just outside the village of Penshurst, close to the Eden Valley, makes this an ideal family day out.

The wildlife collection includes a mob of wallabies which, with the black swans and flock of rare breed sheep, are a great attraction. The wallabies, which are bred here, feature strongly in the history of Penshurst Vineyards, with a picture of one being incorporated into the wine label. The estate has also become a breeding centre for more than 30 species of exotic wildfowl.

hedging separates the walled garden into a series of individually styled 'rooms'. Designed as a garden for all seasons, it provides a riot of colour from early springtime right through to the autumn.

Penshurst Place is also home to a Toy Museum, where the world of the nursery is brought to life through an interesting collection of dolls, tin soldiers and many other toys that originally belonged to several generations of Sidney family children.

Also close by is one of the most modern vineyards in England, **Penshurst Vineyards** (see panel on page 25), where adults can enjoy the lovely walks and the wine tastings, and children can watch the unusual range of animals, including wallabies, rare breeds of sheep and birds.

CHIDDINGSTONE

6 miles W of Tonbridge off the B2027

This pretty village, set in pleasant open woodland, is one of the most picturesque in Kent and is owned by the National Trust. Along a footpath behind the main street, which is lined with houses from the 16th and 17th centuries that were built during the village's prosperous period, lies a block of sandstone known as the **Chiding Stone**. Legend has it that in the past miscreant, vagrants and assorted petty criminals were taken here for public humiliation

Also found in this village is one of Kent's best kept secrets, **Chiddingstone Castle**, a traditional country squire's house that has the appearance of a grand castle. In 1805 Henry Streatfield rebuilt his

family home in grand Gothic style.

In 1955 the house was bought by Denys Eyre Bower, a self-made man with a passion for collecting. Today, the castle houses Bower's vast and varied collection, covering themes that range from relics from ancient Egypt and artefacts from Japan to pictures and mementoes from the Royal Stuart dynasty.

BOUGH BEECH

6½ miles W of Tonbridge on the B2027

To the north of this village lies **Bough Beech Reservoir**, whose surrounding nature reserve provides excellent opportunities for bird watching. The reservoir's visitor centre has a series of exhibitions and displays on the local wildlife, the area's hop growing industry and the history of this reservoir.

HEVER

7½ miles W of Tonbridge off the B2027

This tiny village, set in a delightfully unspoilt countryside of orchards and woodlands, is home to one of Kent's star attractions - **Hever Castle**. The

Castle and Grounds, Hever

original castle, which consisted of the gatehouse, outer walls and inner moat, was built in the 1270s by Sir Stephen de Penchester, who received permission from Edward I to fortify his home. Some two centuries later, the Bullen (or Boleyn) family purchased the property and added the comfortable Tudor manor house that stands within the castle walls. Hever Castle was the childhood home of Anne Boleyn and the ill-fated mother of Elizabeth I was courted here by Henry VIII. Many of Anne's personal items, including two books of hours (prayer books) signed by Anne, along with other Tudor mementoes, can be seen here.

In 1903, the castle was bought by the American millionaire, William Waldorf Astor, who put his great wealth to use in restoring the original buildings and the grounds - work that included laying out and planting over 30 acres of formal gardens. Visitors are particularly drawn to these award-winning gardens but the castle also houses fine collections of paintings, furniture, tapestries and objets d'art.

EDENBRIDGE

9 miles W of Tonbridge on the B2026

This small town, found near the upper reaches of the River Eden, a tributary of the Medway, has been a settlement since Roman times and, although the present bridge spanning the river dates from the 1830s, there has been a bridge here since that early occupation. Its High Street is a straight line through the town and across the river. It was originally the Roman road and an important route through the forest of the Kentish Weald. Along its route can still be found some ancient coaching inns, some dating from as long ago as the 1370s, that catered to the needs of travellers.

The Crown Inn became notorious in the 17th century as a haunt of the Romney gang of smugglers.

IDE HILL

7½ miles NW of Tonbridge off the B2042

Situated in the upper Darent Valley, this remote little village is the highest spot in Kent at 800 feet above sea level. In bygone days the hill was used as a beacon to signal danger to Shooters Hill on the outskirts of London. From its elevated position, it commands glorious, panoramic views stretching out over the Weald. During the 16th century its hunting grounds became a secret meeting place for Henry VIII and his future queen, Anne Boleyn of Hever.

Just outside the village, and set on a hillside of mature beech trees, is **Emmetts Garden**, an informal National Trust maintained garden that boasts the highest tree top in Kent - a 100-foot Wellingtonia planted on Kent's highest point. Noted for its rare trees and shrubs, as well as its rose and rock gardens, Emmetts also offers wonderful views across the Kentish Weald.

NORTH KENT COAST

From Margate, on the northeastern tip of Kent, to Rochester, on the River Medway, the history of the north Kent coastal area has been dominated by the sea. It was invaded over 2,000 years ago by the Romans and, ever since, the land, villages and towns have endured occupation by successive invaders. Many of the place names, such as Rochester and Whitstable, are derived from Roman, Saxon or Norman origins.

The cathedral at Rochester was built on a Saxon site by William the

Conqueror's architect Bishop Gundulph, and it was also he who designed the massive fortress of Rochester Castle. While this ancient city, with numerous connections with Charles Dickens, is one of the best known places along the Medway, it is Chatham that really captures the imagination. Henry VIII, looking to increase his sea power, established a dockyard at this originally Saxon settlement. This was the beginning of the Royal Navy that was to be instrumental in the building and maintenance of the British Empire. The Naval Dockyards at Chatham, where Nelson's ship *HMS Victory* was built, and the Napoleonic fortress, Fort Amherst, are two of the best monuments to the great seafaring traditions of England. In conjunction with the naval loyalties of Chatham, Gillingham is the home of the Royal Engineers, and their museum highlights the valuable work that the Corps has done over the centuries in many areas, including civil engineering and surveying.

Further east lie the seaside towns and resorts of Whitstable, Herne Bay and Margate. Certainly the most popular is Margate, the natural destination for many people of southeast London looking for a day beside the sea. While offering all the delights of the seaside, such as amusements, a funfair, candyfloss and fish and chips, Margate is older than it seems. It probably comes as no surprise to learn that the bathing machine was invented in the town. Whitstable, which remains famous for its oysters, presents a calmer and less brash appearance to those looking for a seaside break. With a history that goes back to Roman times, this fishing village, once the haunt of smugglers, has managed to retain an individuality that inspired writers such as Somerset Maugham and Charles Dickens.

ROCHESTER

First impressions of this riverside city are misleading as the pedestrianised main shopping area and steady flow of traffic hide a history that goes back over 2,000 years. Rochester was first settled by the Romans, whose Watling Street crossed the River Medway at this point. To protect this strategic crossing point, they fortified their camp here and, in so doing, created a walled city of some 23 acres. Some five centuries later the Saxons arrived. Still an important strategic town and port, it was at Rochester that King Alfred, determined to thwart Viking sea power, built a fleet of ships and thereby created the first English navy.

Following the Norman invasion in 1066, William the Conqueror,

Rochester Castle

also aware of the importance of the town and its port, decreed that a castle be maintained here permanently and set his architect, Bishop Gundulph, the task of designing a suitable fortification. Still dominating the city today, **Rochester Castle** is recognised as one of the finest surviving examples of Norman architecture in England. Over 100 feet tall and with walls that are around 12 feet thick, this massive construction comprised four floors from which there were many lookout points. Despite the solidity of the fortress, it has had a very chequered history and over the centuries was subjected to three sieges. In 1215 the rebellious barons were held here by King John for seven weeks. The barons held out despite being bombarded by missiles thrown from huge siege engines, and it was only when the props of a siege tunnel were burnt away and the tunnel collapsed that the barons surrendered. The collapsing of the tunnel also caused the massive tower above to collapse. This was later reconstructed in a round form rather than the original square shape, giving the castle its odd appearance. Rochester Castle was again severely damaged during the Civil War and much of the building seen today is the result of restoration work undertaken in the 19th century.

As well as ordering the construction of the massive fortification, William the Conqueror put his architect to the task of building **Rochester Cathedral** on the site of a Saxon church that was founded in AD 604. Today's building still contains the remains of the 12th century chapter house and priory, along with other Norman features including the fine

Rochester Cathedral

west doorway. Like the castle, the cathedral was badly damaged during the Civil War and restoration work was undertaken by the Victorians. The remains of former monastic buildings surround the cathedral and there are three ancient gates: Prior's Gate, Deanery Gate and Chertsey's Gate, all leading on to the High Street.

Not far from Rochester Bridge is the **Guildhall Museum** that covers the history of this city from prehistoric times through to the present day. The Guildhall was built 1687 and features in Dickens's novel *Great Expectations* as the place where Pip goes as an apprentice. The reconstruction of a Medway prison hulk ship, from the turn of the 19th century covers three floors. It is undoubtedly the most haunting exhibit in the museum depicting the inhuman conditions on board. There are domestic reconstructions of Victorian and Edwardian vintage, and many exhibits relating to Rochester's maritime history. There are scale models of local sailing barges and a diorama of the Dutch raid of the Medway in 1667.

Although the castle, cathedral and river dominate Rochester, the city is perhaps most famous for its connections with the great Victorian novelist, Charles Dickens.

There are many other buildings in the city with a Dickens' connection that are well worth seeking out. **The Royal Victoria and Bull Hotel** featured as The Bull in *The Pickwick Papers* and again in *Great Expectations* as The Blue Boar. The addition of the 'Royal Victoria' to the hotel's name came in the 1830s following a visit by the as yet uncrowned Queen Victoria, who was prevented from continuing to London by a violent storm in 1836.

The busy port here and the routes to and from London that pass through Rochester have always ensured that the city has a steady stream of visitors. After 11 years in exile, Charles II found himself staying overnight at Rochester while making his triumphal march from Dover to London in 1660. On a less happy note, it was at Abdication House (now a bank on the High Street) that James II, fleeing from William of Orange in 1689, spent his last night in England.

AROUND ROCHESTER

BORSTAL

1½ miles S of Rochester off the B2097

Found on the eastern side of the elegant **Medway Bridge**, which carries the M2 over the River Medway, this village gave its name to young offenders institutions when the first prison of this type was opened here in 1908. The original Borstal buildings can still be seen.

STROOD

1 mile W of Rochester off the A228

Situated on the opposite bank of the River Medway from Rochester, it was here that, during the Roman invasion of Britain masterminded by Claudius from Richborough, the Roman legions were halted by a force of Britons led by Caractacus. After two days, the Romans won the battle but only after Claudius had ordered some of his men to swim the river while others crossed higher up and surprised the Britons from behind.

However, it is as the home of **Temple Manor** that Strood is better known. Built in the 13th century by the Knights Templar, this was originally a hostel where the knights could find shelter, food and fresh horses while going to and from the Crusades. A building of simple design, this is all that survives from an earlier complex that would also have contained stables, kitchens and barns. Later, it became a nunnery that was dissolved under Henry VIII and eventually a farmhouse before falling into disrepair. Sympathetically restored after World War II, the original 13th century hall, with its vaulted undercroft, and the 17th century brick extensions have all survived.

A local legend tells that during the bitter feuding between Henry II and Archbishop Thomas à Becket the men of Strood, who were loyal to the king, cut off the tail of Becket's horse while he was riding through the town. Becket suggested that the descendants of those involved in the incident would be born with tails and so, apparently, they were!

As with other Medway towns, Strood has its connections with the sea and, moored at **Damhead Creek** is *The Medway Queen*, an old paddle steamer that was one of the many thousands of unlikely craft that took part in the evacuation of Dunkirk in 1941.

UPNOR

2 miles NE of Rochester off the A228

With a river frontage along the Medway and a backdrop of wooded hills, Upnor became something of a resort for the people of the Medway towns. However, while this is indeed an ideal place to spend some leisure time, the village has not always been so peaceful. In the 16th century, Elizabeth I ordered the construction of several fortifications along the Medway estuary to protect her dockyard at Chatham from invasion and, in 1559, **Upnor Castle** was constructed. Fronted by a water bastion jutting out

into the River Medway, this castle saw action in 1667 when the Dutch sailed up the river with the intention of destroying the English naval fleet. The gun batteries at Upnor were the primary defence against this attack but they proved to be ineffective as the Dutch captured, and made off with, the British flagship the *Royal Charles*.

After this failure, the castle became a magazine and, at one time, more gunpowder was stored here than at the Tower of London. One of the guns that failed to stop the Dutch has been salvaged from the river and now stands guard outside the entrance to the fort and visitors here can tour the gatehouse and main body of the castle.

STABLE COTTAGES

Fenn Croft, Newlands Farm Road,
St Mary's Hoo, nr Rochester, Kent ME3 8QS
Tel: 01634 272439 Fax: 01634 272205
e-mail: stablecottages@btinternet.com
website: www.stable-cottages.com

Set in 20 acres of farmland, with lovely views over open countryside to the River Thames, **Stable Cottages** provides a perfect getaway from the hustle and bustle of city life. Each of the modern oak-beamed cottages has two bedrooms, one with a double bed, the other including bunk beds (single or double). The fully tiled bathrooms have bath and shower, the lounge-diner has a three-piece suite and a dining table with room for 6 guests, and the kitchen is fully equipped, with oven, hob, microwave, kettle, toaster and coffee-maker.

There is a shared utility room with a washing machine, tumble dryer, iron, ironing board and

sewing kit. In the garden is a barbecue, furniture and some garden toys for the children. This is great walking and cycling country, and owner Debbie Symonds, who lives with her family on site, has a selection of Wellington boots for guests venturing out for a walk in wet weather. Local attractions include an RSPB reserve and the largest heronry in Europe, and the city of Rochester is only 15 minutes away.

Lower Upnor

Distance:	3.5 miles (5.6 kilometres)
Typical time:	90 mins
Height gain:	37 metres
Map:	Explorer 163
Walk:	www.walkingworld.com ID:873
Contributor:	Ian Elmes

Access Information:

From the A228 turn towards Lower Upnor on Upchat Road. Shortly thereafter turn left on Upnor Road, at the end of which is the car park.

Additional Information:

There are toilets at the car park in Lower Upnor (starting point).

Description:

A fantastic short walk for those wishing just to get out and about for a little while, especially good after a stressful day in the office. The walk takes you along past the Saxon Shore Way by the River Medway at Lower Upnor, returning along field paths back to Lower Upnor. The village of Lower Upnor is ideally suited to relaxed evenings; it boasts two pubs, toilets and great views across to the old dockyard at Chatham. It is also a good place to sit and watch the yachts going up and down the river. Just up the road from Lower Upnor is the aptly-named Upper Upnor, which also boasts two pubs and the castle (English Heritage).

Features:

River, Pub, Toilets, Castle, Great Views, Food Shop

Walk Directions:

1 From the car park at Lower Upnor, turn left along the road towards the Medway Yacht Club. Once at the gate to the yacht club, bear right onto the footpath; be careful here as it can be quite a steep drop into the river if you're not careful. Follow the path past the clubhouse on your left. At the end of the path drop down onto the beach and follow the line of the woods. Continue along the beach past the old Boat House and the old war gun placement towards the Wilsonian Sailing Club, where there is a raised concrete footpath. Continuing on your journey along the beach, you will pass the ruins of an old fortress.

2 Follow the line of the river; it can be muddy and slippery at this point after high tide. Shortly you will reach a relatively new raised footpath. Continue along this path.

3 Follow the well-defined footpath past the remains of a wooden ship in the riverbed and past a rather large houseboat named "Anserava" on your right. Continue to the end of the path, past the numerous house barges and through the Hoo Ness Yacht Club.

4 Once through the gate follow the track straight ahead, bearing right onto another track just before the white gate. Follow this path past the Saxon Shore Walk marker-post. Continue along the path until it opens out into a car parking area, with mobile homes on the left. Follow the high metal fence and then along the tarmac road past the Riverside Diner.

5 Continue straight ahead. Should you be hungry or thirsty, there is a supermarket-type shop along the road to the left. Head along the gravel track and through a footpath at the end. Once out in the open, by the garages on the right, bear right at the house in front of you, following the Saxon Shore marker-post. Follow the path past the yachts and out onto the road. At the end of the path, by the fence, turn right to cross the road and walk along the path between the bus depot and steelworks. Cross the road to take the slightly overgrown footpath to the left of Whitton Marine.

6 Follow the path and come out at an opening. At the red-windowed factory straight in front of you, turn left along the road. Take the footpath directly in front of you, heading towards three large houses in the distance.

7 Before the houses, bear left onto another path towards the main road and church. At the main road, turn left and then right onto the farm track by Church Farm Lodge.

8 Follow this track up the hill, past the vicarage and a few other houses, all the way to the gate at the top.

9 Go straight ahead at the gate, past the farmhouse on the left and keep straight ahead at the crossroads, taking the track to the right of the chicken-houses. Continue up along the track, ignoring the footpath on the right, past the large house behind the walled railings. Go straight ahead through an enclosed footpath taking you past the gardens of the houses of Elm Avenue.

10 At the road, turn left and follow the road up the hill.

11 At the top of the hill (the highest point at 135ft) follow the footpath marker down through the enclosed footpath straight ahead. Instead of following the path to the right, carry straight on to a bench offering fantastic views across the River Medway. Continue along the footpath down towards the river. Bear left at the yellow marker-post. At the bottom, follow the road with the Arethusa Venture Centre on the left and continue along the road, past the toilets and into the car park.

HIGHAM

3 miles NW of Rochester off the A226

This scattered village, with its ancient and charming marshland church, is famous for being the home of Charles Dickens - the great novelist lived with his family at **Gad's Hill Place** from 1857, when he bought it for £1,770, until his death in 1870. Dickens made various alterations to the 18th century house to accommodate his family and, in particular, he added a conservatory that has been restored to its former glory. While living at Gad's Hill, Dickens wrote several of his novels. Although the house is now a school, some of the rooms and the grounds that Dickens so loved are open to the public at various times throughout the year. Visitors can see the study where Dickens worked on his novels and the restored conservatory, and stroll around the grounds.

COOLING

4½ miles N of Rochester off the A228

This isolated village lies on the Hoo peninsula, an area of bleak marshland lying between the Medway and the Thames. In 1381, John de Cobham of Cooling applied to Richard II to be granted the right to fortify his manor house as, at that time, the sea came right up to his house and he feared a seaborne attack. His fears were well founded, as a couple of years earlier the French had sailed up the river and set fire to several villages in the area. So the king was happy to allow the construction to go ahead. The result of de Cobham's work, which became known as **Cooling Castle**, can still be seen clearly from the road (although it is not open to the public) but the sea has receded over the years and no longer laps the castle's massive outer walls. In the 15th century, Cooling Castle became the home of Sir John Oldcastle, Lord of Cooling, who was executed in 1417 for the part he played in a plot against Henry V. Shakespeare is said to have modelled his character Falstaff on Sir John.

Close by the substantial castle remains stands **St James' Church** (redundant but open for visits) where, in the graveyard, can be seen the 13 lozenge-shaped stones that mark the graves of various Comport children who all died of malaria in the 18th century. Not one of the children lived to be older than 17 months and these were, supposedly, the graves of Pip's brothers in Dickens's novel *Great Expectations*.

ALLHALLOWS
8 miles NE of Rochester off the A228

This remote village, which takes its name from its small 11th century church of All Saints, overlooks the River Thames estuary and, beyond, the busy Essex resort of Southend. Nearby is an **Iron Beacon** that was erected in Elizabethan times and it is one of many such beacons that were set up along the coast to warn

of imminent invasion. In the 1930s there were plans to develop the coastal strip to the north of the village as a holiday area and, although the resort never quite came to fruition, the Art Deco style railway station still remains and has been put to other uses.

CHATHAM
1 mile E of Rochester on the A2

Although there has been a settlement here since Saxon times, it was not until Henry VIII established a dockyard that Chatham began to grow from being a sleepy, riverside backwater into a busy town. The dockyard flourished and was expanded by Elizabeth I during the time of the Armada. Sir Francis Drake, who took part in the defeat of the Spanish fleet in 1588, moved here with his family at the age of six and, while his father was chaplain to the fleet based here, the young Francis learned his sailing skills on the reaches around Chatham and Gillingham. Of the many famous ships that were built at the naval dockyard, perhaps the most famous is Nelson's *HMS Victory*, which was launched in 1765.

The naval connection continued to boost the growth of the town and its present commercial centre originally saw to the needs of navy personnel. Among these was John Dickens, who was employed by the Navy Pay Office. His son, Charles, spent some of his boyhood years at Chatham. The family moved to **2 Ordnance Terrace** (now number 11) when Charles was five years old and it was his father who was to provide the inspiration for the character Mr Micawber in *David Copperfield*.

Clock Tower Building at No. 2 Dock, Chatham

Just to the north of the town centre on the banks of the River Medway is **The Historic Dockyard** (see panel below), founded by Henry VIII, which became the premier shipbuilding yard for the Royal Navy. With its 450 years of history, visitors can appreciate the scale of the 20th century submarine and battleship dry docked here and the architecture of the most complete Georgian dockyard in the world. Samuel Pepys, the famous diarist, first made reference to the dockyard in his diaries in 1661 and he was here to witness the audacious Dutch raid six years later when de Ruyter managed to capture the English flagship, *Royal Charles*. The Ropery at the Historic Dockyard is a building a quarter of a mile long. Rope can be seen being made in the traditional way here, using machines dating back to 1811. The 175-year history of the lifeboats is told at the National Collection of the RNLI. The dockyard has been the setting for a number of films over the years, including *The Mummy* and *Tomorrow Never Dies*.

The Chatham dockyards were an obvious target for Hitler's bombers during World War II and, at **Fort Amherst Heritage Park and Caverns**, which lie close by, the secret underground telephone exchange that coordinated the air raid warnings can be seen. The country's premier Napoleonic fortress, Fort Amherst was built in 1756 to defend the naval dockyard from attack by land, and it continued to serve this purpose up until the end of World War II. Today, the fort offers visitors an insight into the daily lives of the soldiers who were stationed here, and their families, through a series of displays and through re-enactments in period costumes. The fort's most outstanding feature, and the most interesting, is

WORLD NAVAL BASE

The Historic Dockyard, Chatham, Kent ME4 4TZ
Tel: 01634 823800 Fax: 01634 823801
e-mail: info@worldnavalbase.org.uk
website: www.worldnavalbase.org.uk

On the banks of the River Medway, lies the **World Naval Base** - Chatham's historic dockyard - that saw the foundation of the Royal Navy under Henry VIII and, down the centuries, it was the naval power generated here that helped build the British Empire. The Naval Base covers some 400 years of history and visitors touring the site will see the most complete Georgian dockyard in the world along with displays and exhibits that explain the part the dockyard has played in the country's and the world's history. Samuel Pepys, the famous diarist, first made reference to the dockyard in his diaries in 1661 and he was here to witness the audacious Dutch raid six years later when de Ruyter managed to capture the English flag ship, Royal Charles.

Whilst the dockyard exhibitions certainly dwell on past glories, there is plenty more to see here, including the modern spy submarine Ocelot, HMS Cavalier that saw active service during World War II and HMS Gannet the last surviving sloop of the Victorian navy. In a building that is a quarter of a mile long rope can be seen being made in the traditional way whilst the 175-year history of the lifeboats is told at the National Collection of the RNLI. The newly opened Museum of the Dockyard brings together the 400 year history of the World Naval Base and, with so much to see, the steam railway with its audio tour is an excellent way to begin a tour of this impressive site.

undoubtedly the underground maze of tunnels and caverns that were used as storage, magazines, barracks and guardrooms, and the guided tour around the underground workings highlights the skills of the military engineers.

The extensive outer fortification, which covers seven acres and includes battlements and earthworks, has been turned into a country park style area where visitors can enjoy a picnic or explore the various nature trails.

Like the dockyard, Fort Amherst has been used as a location by both film and television companies and it was here that Robert de Niro shot the prison cell scenes for *The Mission*, Val Kilmer worked on the remake of the 1960s series *The Saint* and the BBC filmed *The Phoenix and the Carpet*.

In the main part of the town can be found the **Almshouses** that were built by one of the two charities that were established by the Elizabethan seafarer, Admiral Sir John Hawkins. As well as helping to defeat the Spanish Armada along with Sir Francis Drake, Hawkins was also an inventor and philanthropist and it was he who introduced 'copper bottoms' to help prevent the deterioration of ship's hulls below the waterline. These almshouses were originally designed as a hospital for retired seamen and their widows.

GILLINGHAM

2 miles E of Rochester on the A2

Although there is evidence of both prehistoric and Roman occupation of this area, a village did not really become established here until the 11th century. The oldest part of this, the largest of the Medway towns, is **The Green**, where can be found the Norman parish church of St Mary. It was the establishment of the dockyard at neighbouring Chatham in

the 16th century that saw Gillingham begin to expand as it became a centre for servicing the naval dockyard and depot. As with many towns along the Medway, Gillingham has many links with the sea and it was the story of the Gillingham sailor, Will Adams, that inspired the novel *Shogun* by James Clavell. In 1600, Adams sailed to Japan and there he befriended Ieyasu, the Shogun, learnt Japanese and was honoured as a Samurai warrior. Beside the A2 is the **Will Adams Monument**, a fitting tribute to the man who went on to become the Shogun's teacher and adviser.

All things maritime have influenced Gillingham greatly over the centuries, but the town is also the home of one of the most fascinating military attractions - **The Royal Engineers Museum**. This museum reflects the diverse range of skills that the Corps has brought to bear both in times of both peace and war. They were the creators of the Ordnance Survey, the designers of the Royal Albert Hall and the founders of the Royal Flying Corps in 1912. The Royal Engineers continue the dangerous work of bomb disposal and throughout the world they build roads and bridges, lay water pipes and assist in relief work after natural disasters. The courtyard display illustrates the wide variety of activities the Corps has undertaken since the 1940s, while inside are a dignified medal gallery, a reconstruction of a World War I trench and numerous artefacts from around the world acquired by members of the Corps. Both the nearby dockyards and Fort Amherst at Chatham were built by the Royal Engineers. Visitors can see the original battlefield map prepared by the Corps and used by the Duke of Wellington to defeat Napoleon at the Battle of Waterloo in 1815. It was a Royal Engineer, Lieutenant John Chard VC, who played a key role in the defence of Rorkes Drift when the mission, with just 130 men, was attacked by thousands of Zulu warriors. The World War I General, Lord Kitchener, of the famous recruitment poster campaign, was also a Royal Engineer.

MILTON REGIS
10 miles E of Rochester off the A2

Once a royal borough, Milton Regis has been all but incorporated into the outskirts of Sittingbourne. However, in the still well-defined village centre can be found the **Court Hall Museum** housed, as its name might suggest, in a 15th century timbered building that was originally Milton Regis's courthouse, school and town gaol. The museum has displays, photographs and documents that relate to the village and surrounding area.

At **Milton Creek** lies **Dolphin Yard Sailing Barge Museum**, housed in a traditional sailing barge yard where commercial work is still undertaken. Along with aiming to preserve the barges and other craft that have been used on the local estuaries for hundreds of years, the museum is dedicated in particular to the sailing barge. While the creek provided a means of transport, its waters were also used to power paper mills and paper manufacturing remains in evidence in this area today.

SITTINGBOURNE
10½ miles E of Rochester on the A2

Lying close to the Roman road, Watling Street, Sittingbourne was, during the Middle Ages, a stopping place for pilgrims on their way to Canterbury. As a result of this the town developed a thriving market

OAD STREET CENTRE

Oad Street, Borden, Kent ME9 8LB
Tel: 01795 843130 Fax: 01795 842266
website: www.arthousegallery.net

In the heart of the Kent countryside, **Oad Street Centre** offers a pleasant day out with plenty of interesting things to see and do. The latest addition to the attractions is the Arthouse Gallery, which houses a range of exciting collections gathered from all over the UK, Europe and the USA. The Gallery is also home to the Artists Quarter, a regularly changing showcase for both new and

established artists to exhibit their work, including paintings, mosaics, sculpture and ceramics.

In the Artists Workshops, visitors can see practising artists at work; among them are Andrew Bull (porcelain), Nigel Wheeler (furniture restoration) and K Frames - a bespoke picture framing and mounting service. The Gift Shop sells an excellent range of unusual gifts, including glassware, ceramics, jewellery and flowers, and the Tea Room prides itself on its home-cooked food. Open all day, it serves a wide selection of cakes, scones and biscuits as well as sandwiches, light snacks, salads and main meals.

DODDINGTON PLACE GARDENS

Doddington, Near Sittingbourne, Kent, ME9 0BB
Tel: 01795 886101 Fax: 01795 886155

Doddington Place was built in 1860 for Sir John Croft of the port and sherry family. It is now the home of the Oldfield family. Surrounded by wooded countryside, orchards and farmland, it is in an officially designated Area of Outstanding Natural Beauty. The lovely landscaped ten- acre gardens are recognised by English Heritage as being of special historical interest. The gardens include a notable

woodland garden established in the 1960's which is spectacular in May and June. It includes many different kinds of rhododendron and azalea, camellias, acers and eucryphia. A large rock garden laid out c.1910 retains a strong Edwardian atmosphere, where the plants include sedum, sempervivens, Helianthemum, dianthus, naturalised cyclamen and irises. A formal sunk garden with borders - at their best in late summer and a spring garden with fruit trees under planted with bulbs.

There is also a fine avenue of Wellingtonia dating from the mid 19th century and a recently completed two storey brick and flint gothic folly. Extensive lawns are framed by impressive clipped yew hedges and many fine specimen trees. The avenues provide several fine walks including Woodland Garden, Pond and Folly Walks.

S W DOUGHTY FAMILY BUTCHER

The Street, Doddington, Kent ME9 0BH
Tel: 01795 886255

S W Doughty of Doddington offers a unique rural shopping experience. Run by the Doughty family for 85 years, it is one of the few remaining butchers with its own slaughterhouse, and the majority of its meat is sourced from Hole Street Farm, less than a mile away.

In recent years the business has won several awards for its sausages, winning accolades for

both traditional pork and speciality varieties such as pork and leek. They supply several pubs in the region in addition to the many regular customers for whom only the best will do. S W Doughty provides bespoke butchering at its best and also offers a full range of meat for the freezer or for barbecues. Other specialities include home-reared free-range geese for Christmas; strawberries in June; cherries in July; free-range Kent chickens; local organic apple juice and a selection of top-quality cheeses and seasonal vegetables.

Shop hours are 8am to 5.30pm Tuesday to Friday and 8am to 2pm on Saturday.

that has continued to this day; the town was also a centre for barge making and for paper manufacturing.

It is from here that the **Sittingbourne and Kemsley Light Railway** runs steam hauled passenger trains along two miles of preserved track. The railway was originally designed to transport paper and other bulk materials but now the journey is taken for pleasure by those fascinated by steam trains and those wishing to view this area of the Kentish countryside at close quarters.

Garden at Doddington Place

DODDINGTON

5 miles SE of Sittingbourne off the A2

The landscaped gardens of **Doddington Place**, in a traditional rural village, are truly magnificent and comprise lawns, avenues and clipped yew hedges. The 10-acre garden was created by the renowned 19th century gardener William Nesfield. The display of rhododendrons and azaleas in the spring is brilliant, and among other attractions are large rock gardens and a formal sunken garden.

THE ISLE OF SHEPPEY

MINSTER

This seaside town on the northern coast of the Isle of Sheppey is an unlikely place to find one of the oldest sites of Christianity in England. However, it was here, on the highest point of the island, that Sexburga, the widow of a Saxon king of Kent, founded a nunnery in the late 7th century. Sacked by the Danes in 855, **Minster Abbey** was rebuilt in around 1130 when it was also re-established as a priory for Benedictine nuns. Sometime later, in the 13th century, the parish church of Minster was built, adjoining the monastic church, and so, from the Middle Ages until the Dissolution of the Monasteries, the building served as a 'double church' with the nuns worshipping in the northern half of the building and the parishioners in the other. To the west of this unusual church lies the 15th century abbey gatehouse, home today to the **Minster Abbey Gatehouse Museum**. Here, the history of Sheppey is told through exhibits of fossils, tools and photographs.

In his *Ingoldsby Legends*, RH Barham retells the story of the fiery Sir Roger de Shurland, Lord of Sheppey, who in 1300 killed a monk who had disobeyed him. Dodging the county sheriff, Sir Roger swam out on horseback to Edward I's passing ship and received the king's pardon for his wicked act. On returning to shore, Sir Roger met a mysterious old hag who foretold that, having saved his life, Sir Roger's horse would also cause his death. On hearing this, the tempestuous knight drew his sword and beheaded his horse. Some time later, while walking on the beach, Sir Roger came across the head of his horse that had been washed ashore. In an angry rage, he kicked the head but one of the horse's teeth penetrated his boot and Sir Roger died later from the infection that developed in the wound. Sir Roger's tomb lies in the abbey church; close to the right foot of his stone effigy can be seen the head of a horse.

AROUND MINSTER

EASTCHURCH
2½ miles SE of Minster off the B2231

This village was once the home of the early pioneers of aviation and a young Sir Winston Churchill flew from the old Eastchurch aerodrome. Another early pilot, Lord Brabazon of Tara, was the holder of the first official pilot's licence. Close to the church is a stone memorial to the early pilots, while close by are the ruins of 16th century Shurland Hall, where Henry VIII and Anne Boleyn stayed on their honeymoon.

A little way outside the village lies **Norwood Manor**, a charming old house

that dates from the 17th century although the Northwoode family have lived on this site since Norman times. On display in the house are numerous artefacts that relate to this long established Kentish family.

LEYSDOWN
5 miles SE of Minster on the B2231

A popular seaside place with visitors for many years - Henry VIII loved the Isle of Sheppey so much that he spent one of his honeymoons here - Leysdown is renowned for its sandy beaches, and there are picnic areas and nature trails close by.

A little to the south, on the southeastern tip of the Isle of Sheppey, **The Swale National Nature Reserve** is home to numerous wildfowl.

ELMLEY ISLAND
3 miles S of Minster off the A249

Situated on southern coastline of the Isle of Sheppey and overlooking The Swale and the north Kent coast, **Elmley Marshes Nature Reserve** is an area of salt marsh that is home to wetland birds, marsh frogs, numerous insects and many species of aquatic plants.

QUEENBOROUGH
3 miles W of Minster off the A249

A historic town that began as a Saxon settlement, Queenborough became an important wool port and a wealthy borough that was graced by a royal **Castle** built by Edward III. The town's reliance on the sea for its prosperity also saw its courthouse captured by the Dutch during their invasion of the Medway in 1667. During the 18th century, the town's prosperity

Kingsferry Swingbridge, Isle of Sheppey

continued, based on the increased naval presence after the Dutch invasion. Many fine buildings were built, which still survive. However the first part of 19th century saw Queenborough decline as enterprising neighbours like Sheerness grew. During World War II, Queenborough became the home of hundreds of mine-sweeping vessels. **The Guildhall Museum**, housed in the building that replaced the earlier courthouse, tells the fascinating story of this town, from Saxon times, through its rise at the hands of Victorian industrialists, to the important role it played during World War II. Queenborough is still a very busy boating centre, with numerous boat builders and chandlers.

Sheerness

2½ miles NW of Minster on the A249

Overlooking the point where the River Medway meets the River Thames, Sheerness was once the site of a naval dockyard and was the first to be surveyed by Samuel Pepys, who held the position of Secretary of the Admiralty during the reign of Charles II. It was at Sheerness that in 1805 *HMS Victory* docked when it brought Nelson's body back to England after the Battle of Trafalgar. In more recent times, Sheerness has developed into a busy container and car ferry port and most of the Isle of Sheppey's wealth is centred on the town.

The Sheerness Heritage Centre is housed in a weatherboarded cottage that was built in the early 19th century as a dwelling for a dockyard worker. Despite being constructed of seemingly temporary building materials, the house and its two neighbours have lasted well. Over the years, the cottage has been a baker's shop and a fish & chip shop. The rooms have now been restored to reflect authentic 19th century life and are furnished with genuine pieces from that period. The heritage centre also has an exhibition describing the development of The Royal Dockyard, which closed here in the 1960s.

WHITSTABLE

Anyone wandering around Whitstable will soon realise that this is no seaside resort but very much a working town that is centred around the busy commercial harbour that was originally the port for Canterbury. The old-fashioned streets of the town are lined with fisherman's cottages and the winding lanes are linked by narrow alleyways with eccentric names - such as **Squeeze Gut Alley** - that recall the town's rich maritime past. Sometimes referred to as the 'Pearl of Kent', Whitstable is as famous today for its oysters as it was in Roman times and it is probable that Caesar himself enjoyed Whitstable oysters.

After the Roman occupiers left Britain, the Saxons came to the area and gave the town its name - then Witanstaple, meaning 'an assembly of wise men in the market'. This later became Whitstable. Later, the Normans built the parish church of All Saints, which provided medieval sailors with a key navigation aid. The ownership of the manor of Whitstable in the Middle Ages proved to be something of a poisoned chalice. John de Stragboli was executed for murder, Bartholomew de Badlesmere was hanged for his part in the rebellion against Edward II and Robert de Vere was convicted for treason. Even in the 16th century, the owner of the manor fared no better and Sir John Gates was executed for his support of Lady Jane Grey over the Catholic Mary Tudor.

Along with oysters and a fishing industry that has lasted over 700 years, the discovery of iron pyrites deposits around Whitstable led to the development of the manufacture of copper to be used for dyeing and making ink and some early medicines. However, it was the sea and the associated boat building and repair yards that were to continue to support many of those living in the town. Now many of the yards have gone, but as recently as World War II ships' lifeboats and other small craft were being built and launched at Whitstable. Going hand in hand with the town's maritime connections was the unofficial trade of smuggling, and during the 18th century there were numerous battles between the gangs and the revenue men in and around the town.

While the authorities clamped down hard on this illegal trading, there was one positive spin-off as the smugglers had such an intimate knowledge of the French coastline that Nelson consulted them while planning his naval campaigns.

For a broad picture of the town, past and present, **Whitstable Museum and Gallery** explores the traditions and life of this ancient seafaring community. There are also references and information on the many 'firsts' to which the town lays claim: the first scheduled passenger train ran between Whitstable and Canterbury; the first steamship to sail to Australia from Britain left here in 1837; the diving helmet was invented in the town; and the country's first council houses were built at Whitstable.

Whitstable also has associations with writers and broadcasters. After his

LYRE STUDIO

20 High Street, Whitstable, Kent CT5 1BQ
Tel/Fax: 01227 280998

Famous since Roman times for its oysters, Whitstable is sometimes known as 'The Pearl of Kent'. Since 2001 the town's residents and its many visitors have been able to treat themselves to gems of another kind at **Lyre Studio** in the High Street. Owner Petra Cable was continuing and developing a lifelong interest in jewellery and stones when she opened this remarkable little shop, which is filled with literally thousands of items of jewellery, rocks, precious and semi-precious stones, crystals and fossils, as well as related gifts, cards and books. Many of the ranges are exclusive to Lyre Studio, and every piece is personally selected by Petra, some bought for stock, others designed in house.

The venture has been a great success, and for anyone looking for something just a little bit different for a gift or a treat, this is definitely a place to visit. And if that something is not in stock, Petra will do her very best to obtain it – personal service is part of the charm of the place.

Shell Fishing, Whitstable

novels, *Of Human Bondage* and *Cakes and Ale*. Charles Dickens visited here and wrote about the town, and Robert Hitchens, the novelist and journalist, lived nearby at Tankerton. One of the town's more notorious residents was William Joyce, who worked in one of the town's radio shops before

parents died, Somerset Maugham came to live with his uncle at Whitstable and the town features strongly in two of his

travelling to Germany to broadcast Nazi propaganda back to England as Lord Haw Haw.

CAROLE RIDLEY

32 Harbour Street, Whitstable, Kent CT5 1AJ
Tel: 01227 275713   web: www.caroleridley.com

Carole Ridley owns two high-class ladies fashion shops that bear her name. This one is close to the front in Whitstable, the other in Sandwich. Carole brings a lifetime's experience in fashion retailing to assemble an excellent range of dresses, trousers, blouses, jumpers and shoes, aimed mainly at the over 25s who are looking for a relaxed style of clothing but one which inspires confidence to the wearer. All the fabrics are natural and represent some of the top names in ladies fashion, including Sarah Pacini, Sonja Marohn, Oska and Ischiko.

To complement the clothing, there is a selection of beautiful and unusual accessories, inlcuding jewellery, bags and belts. Many of the accessories feature leather and the wonderful Sherlings – a type of suede. Carole runs a number of fashion shows each year for charity in the local area and is a regular attender at *Country Living* fairs. The staff are knowledgable and helpful, offering a personal service to their customers.

AROUND WHITSTABLE

HERNE BAY

4½ miles NE of Whitstable on the B2205

Now one of the main resorts on the north Kent coast, Herne Bay was originally, a fishing village that became notorious as a haunt for smugglers. Much of the town seen today was laid out in the mid-19th century as it was developed as a resort to attract Victorian middle classes looking for clean air and safe beaches. It still retains a quiet gentility that is reminiscent of that lost era, and at the **Herne Bay Museum Centre** visitors can discover the history of the town and the story of its famous pier through entertaining displays. The museum also contains relics from prehistoric times such as fossils and stone tools. Also in the town is a superb landmark, the **Clock Tower**, that stands on the promenade and was given to Herne Bay by a wealthy London lady, Mrs Thwaytes, to commemorate Queen Victoria's coronation in 1836.

Just inland, at the ancient Saxon village of **Herne**, stands **Herne Mill**, a Kentish smock mill that has recently undergone extensive repair work. Dating from 1789, this particularly mill is the latest in a long line that have occupied this site.

RECULVER

7½ miles NE of Whitstable off the A299

Reculver is the site of the Roman Regulbium, one of the forts built in the 3rd century to defend the shores of Kent from Saxon invasion. Sometime later the site was taken over as a place of Christian worship and this early fort provided the building materials for the 7th century Saxon church that was later extended by the Normans. It was also around this time that the Normans built the two huge towers within the remains of the Roman fort that provided mariners with a landmark to guide them into the Thames estuary. Today, **Reculver Towers and Roman Fort** is under the management of English Heritage, and although there are only few remains of the fort the towers still stand overlooking the rocky beach and can be seen from several miles along the coast. **Reculver Country Park** offers visitors a lovely walk to these remains, church and towers, and the park's visitors' centre has some fascinating information on the history and natural history of this stretch of coastline.

As a major historic site, Reculver has seen much archaeological activity over the years and in the 1960s excavation unearthed several tiny skeletons that were buried not far from the towers. It is generally believed that these babies were buried alive as human sacrifices and it is said that on stormy nights the babies can be heard crying out. During World War II, the Barnes Wallace 'bouncing bomb' was tested off the coast of Reculver. Several of these were found on the shore in 1997. Fortunately they were found to contain no explosives.

BIRCHINGTON

12 miles E of Whitstable on the A28

This quiet resort, with cliffs and bays, still retains its individuality despite the spread of the Margate conurbation from the east, and it is a particular favourite for families with young children. At **All Saints' Church** there is a monument to one of the most famous British artists of the 19th century, Dante Gabriel Rossetti, the poet and artist who was instrumental in the formation of the Pre-Raphaelite Brotherhood. He lies buried in the doorway and a memorial stone, carved by his mentor, Ford Madox Brown, marks his grave.

About half a mile to the southeast of the village lies **Quex House**, a Regency gentleman's country house that was later expanded into the Victorian mansion seen today. It remains the home of the Powell-Cotton family and visitors looking around the rooms will find that the house still retains the atmosphere of a family home, complete with freshly cut flowers from the garden. A fine collection of period and oriental furniture, family portraits, porcelain and silver can be seen by those wandering through the rooms. One particular member of the family, Major PHG (Percy) Powell-Cotton, was a great explorer and while he was lured to exotic lands by big game, the Major was a true Victorian who also took an interest in the customs and beliefs of the people and tribes that he met on his travels. As a result he put together a vast collection, and the **Museum** here displays that collection in polished mahogany cases. From dioramas of animals and tribal art, costumes and weapons to European and Chinese porcelains and local archaeological finds, there is a vast range of exhibits from right around the world. He once had an uncomfortable brush with a lion, and both the lion and his

The Harbour, Margate

torn jacket are on display. As well as offering visitors a great deal to see inside the house, Quex is surrounded by some superb Gardens, parkland and woodlands that provide the perfect backdrop to this fascinating house. The gardens have wide lawns with mature trees and a walled kitchen garden. John Cotton-Powell's collection of cannons is also displayed in the grounds, and another feature is the Waterloo Tower folly built to house his ring of 12 bells.

MARGATE
15 miles E of Whitstable on the A28

With its long stretch of golden sand, promenades, amusement arcades and candy floss, Margate is very much everyone's idea of a boisterous English seaside resort. This is a well-deserved reputation that has grown up for over 200 years. Before the railway brought holidaymakers in droves from London from the 1840s onwards, those looking for a day by the sea came in sailing boats known as Margate hoys. Many Londoners return here time and time again to wander round the old town and take the bracing sea air. With this background as a seaside resort, it is not surprising to find that the bathing machine was reputedly invented here, in 1752, by a Quaker glover and a Margate resident called Benjamin Beale.

However, there is more to Margate than sun, sea, sand and fish & chips. In King Street stands **Tudor House**, which dates back to the early 16th century and the reign of Henry VIII. It is the oldest house in Margate and it holds a collection of seaside memorabilia. Viewing is by appointment only by prior arrangement with Margate Museum.

Just inland lies medieval **Salmestone Grange**, which originally belonged to St Augustine's Abbey at Canterbury. In what is arguably one of the best preserved examples of a monastic grange in England, the chapel, crypt and kitchen can all still be seen.

Another building that has withstood the test of time is **Drapers Mill**, an old smock corn mill that was constructed in 1845 by John Holman. It continued to be powered by the wind until a gas engine was installed in 1916 and, after being made redundant in the 1930s, the mill was restored to working order in the 1970s.

SARRE

9 miles SE of Whitstable on the A28

This sunken village on the edge of marshland was once an important harbour and ferry point when the Isle of

Thanet was indeed an island. Today, it is home to one of the country's few remaining commercially working mills, **Sarre Mill** (see panel below), a typical Kentish smock windmill built in 1820 by the Canterbury millwright John Holman. The addition of first steam and then gas power ensured that Sarre Mill remained in use well into the 20th century but in the 1940s milling ceased here. Fortunately, in the 1980s, the windmill was restored to working order, and today, Sarre Mill is producing high quality stoneground flour and offering tours of the five floors of the mill. There are small farmyard animals that are sure to delight children, and a rare portable steam engine dating from the 1860s that was used to crush apples for cider making. Numerous other items of rural interest, such as old agricultural machinery, farming implements and domestic pieces, are on display in the exhibition of bygones.

SARRE MILL

Canterbury Road, Sarre, near Birchington, Kent CT7 0JU
Tel: 01843 847573

Found on high ground just to the northeast of the village is one of the country's few remaining commercially working mills, **Sarre Mill**, a typical Kentish smock windmill. Built in 1820 by the Canterbury millwright John Holman, a steam engine was installed here in 1861 to add further power although it was not until the 1920s that the sails were taken down and the mill wheels were completely powered by the gas engine that was installed in 1907. Milling finally ceased at Sarre in the 1940s and, after being left derelict for decades, the building was purchased in 1985 by the Hobbs family and restoration work was begun.

Today, Sarre Mill is back to working order, producing high quality stoneground flour and, as well as touring the five floors of the mill, there is plenty more for the whole family to see. There are small farmyard animals, including Victoria, a Tamworth pig, that are sure to delight children and a rare portable steam engine dating from the 1860s that was used to crush apples for cider making. Numerous other items of rural interest, such as old agricultural machinery, farming implements and domestic pieces, are on display here in the exhibition of bygones. A tea room provides visitors with the ideal opportunity to enjoy some home made bread or cake, all made using Sarre Mill flour, whilst, at the mill shop, not only can the flour be purchased but also a wide range of other country goods.

HERNE COMMON

4 miles SE of Whitstable off the A291

Close to the village and found deep in a leafy forest is **Wildwood**, Kent's unique woodland discovery park that is also the home of the only breeding pack of endangered European wolves in Britain. Although wolves have not been living in the wild in this country for many years, tales of the savage packs that once roamed the countryside live on, and at Wildwood stories of the medieval hunters who killed them for bounty and of the fear of travellers alone on dark nights bring back those days. The Saxons called January 'Wulf monat' as this was when the hungry packs were at their most dangerous. However, Wildwood is not entirely devoted to wolves and here in the forest is a reconstruction of a Saxon village, Regia Anglorum, where history is brought to life as village members, in authentic costume, go about their daily lives and practise the skills and crafts from centuries ago.

Other wildlife also abounds at Wildwood, and along with the badger colony there are rabbits, polecats, shrews and hedgehogs all living in underground burrows. Living in a near natural environment is the park's herd of deer. While this is an interesting, enjoyable and educational place to visit for all the family, much of the work of the park goes on behind the scenes, in the area of conservation, and two species in particular, water voles and hazel dormice, are bred here for re-introduction into the wild.

HERNHILL

5 miles SW of Whitstable off the A299

A secluded and tranquil village that is surrounded by orchards, Hernhill is also home to **Mount Ephraim Gardens**. This family estate also includes a house, woodland and fruit farm. There are magnificent views of both the Swale and Thames estuaries from the gardens. The gardens are essentially Edwardian offering a good balance between the formal and the informal through such delights as herbaceous borders, topiary, rose terraces, a Japanese garden, a rock garden, a vineyard and orchard trails.

FAVERSHAM

As with many places in this area of Kent, Faversham was first settled by the Romans, who gave the town its name (it comes from 'faber' meaning blacksmith), and it was later inhabited by both the Jutes and the Saxons. Despite this period of turmoil, the town continued to grow, so much so that in 811 King Kenulf granted Faversham a charter and the market still plays an important part in the life of the town today. The Market Place, which is also the junction of three of the town's oldest streets, is dominated by the **Guildhall**, which was built in the 16th century. Its open ground floor pillared arcade provided cover for the market. Unusually it has a tower at one end. After the upper floor and tower were damaged by fire in the early 19th century, it was rebuilt in keeping with the original and extended. The clock in the tower was made in 1814 by a clock maker called Francis Crow, whose workshop was in the Market Place opposite the tower.

Over the centuries, Faversham market has dealt in a wide range of goods, and the town was for almost 400 years the centre of the country's explosives industry and **Chart Gunpowder Mills** is a lasting monument to the industry that thrived here between 1560 and 1934. Dating from the 18th century, and now restored, these mills are the oldest of their kind in the world. Chart Mills is an 'incorporating' mill. Incorporating was

FAVERSHAM INTERIORS

7 Court Street, Faversham, Kent ME13 7AN
Tel: 01795 591471

An attractive 450-year-old white painted building on Court Street is home
to **Faversham Interiors**. Behind the eye-catching window display is Ralph
Lane's ever-changing collection of antique French decorative furniture
which, along with the chandeliers and other smaller pieces, chinaware
and glassware, is displayed to best effect in the lovely room. Ralph has been in the antiques business
for almost 20 years, in Faversham since 1996 and here in Court Street since 1999. As a result he has
many long-term clients. Also part of Faversham Interiors are the Periwinkle Press who specialise in
picture framing, antique prints and books.

UPLEES LODGE

Uplees Road, Oare, nr Faversham, Kent ME13 0QR
Tel: 01795 535014   e-mail: upleeslodge@aol.com

Uplees Lodge, an Edwardian country house set among lawns, gardens
and woodland close to the Swale Estuary, provides a quiet, civilised
setting for a Bed & Breakfast break. There's a certain French feel in the
two comfortable bedrooms, one en suite, the other with a private
bathroom, both with tea/coffee-making facilities, TV, radio and hairdryer. Uplees Lodge is an ideal
base for walking, sailing and birdwatching, or for discovering the many places of interest in the region.
Ralph Lane, who runs the lodge with Gary Carlton, also owns Faversham Interiors, a design and antique
shop in Faversham.

THE EASTLING CENTRE

Churchfields Farm, Eastling, Faversham, Kent ME13 0BG
Tel: 01795 890746
e-mail: info@holidayhorse.com
website: www.holidayhorse.com

Located on the North Downs between Faversham and Lenham, the **Eastling
Centre** is set in nine acres of historic cherry orchard with livery yard. The
Centre provides self-catering accommodation in high-quality apartments
having fully fitted kitchens, lounge with TV/video and en suite facilities.
Each apartment has a private patio area with barbecue. Well-behaved horse
friendly dogs are always welcome.

Short breaks and longer stays are offered by the Centre. Each apartment
can accommodate three adults or two adults and two children under 10
years of age. Stabling is available at the Centre for guests who wish to
bring their horse on holiday. An enclosed ride and floodlit sandschool in
the grounds of the Centre is augmented by access to many local
bridleways in this lovely hacking part of Kent. In a quiet rural
setting the village of Eastling provides quintessential English
countryside. A Saxon church, 16th century inn and Manor House
sit at the heart of the village. A five-mile journey allows visits to
the medieval market towns of Faversham and Lenham whilst
numerous pretty villages are scattered across the North Downs
to the sea. Bed & Breakfast and self-catering accommodation is
provided all year round, whilst holidays with horses operate
March to December.

the process by which the ingredients of gunpowder are incorporated together to become explosive.

Faversham has over 400 listed buildings and one that is well worth seeking out is the 15th century former inn that is now home to the **Fleur de Lis Heritage Centre**. Here, displays review the last 1,000 years and tell the story of the town's growth and prosperity. Of the numerous artefacts and exhibitions to be seen here one of the more impressive is Abbey Street, a 16th century thoroughfare that is complete and well-preserved. Also featured are an Edwardian barber shop, a Victorian fireside, a typical village post office, working manual telephone exchange and costume displays.

Close by lies **Faversham Creek**, a tidal inlet of the River Swale that is inextricably linked with the main town's prosperity as the Creek acted as Faversham's port. A limb of the Cinque

Port of Dover and with a shipbuilding tradition that is so rooted in history that the title of 'The King's Port' is retained as an acknowledgment of the royal gratitude for the provision of navy vessels, Faversham Creek is well worth a visit. Between here and Seasalter, to the east, lies the **South Swale Nature Reserve**, which concentrates on the legacy of natural history of this area. A wide range of wildfowl, including Brent geese, make their home along this stretch of coast. There is a pleasant coastal walk here between Seasalter and Faversham.

AROUND FAVERSHAM

THROWLEY

3 miles S of Faversham off the A251

Tucked away amid the orchards of Kent and close to the village lies **Belmont** (see panel below), a beautiful Georgian mansion house and estate.

BELMONT

Belmont Park, Throwley, Faversham, Kent ME13 0HH
Tel: 01795 890202
e-mail: belmontadmin@btconnect.com
website: www.belmont-house.org

Commanding stunning views across the rolling Kent countryside, **Belmont** is a marvellous example of Georgian architecture that has remained completely unspoilt. Until Edward Wilks, the store-keeper of the Royal Powder Mills at Faversham bought this land in 1769 there was no house or estate of Belmont. The house that he had built still survives as a wing of the present building and that in turn was constructed to the designs of Samuel Wyatt between 1789 and 1793 for the new owner, Colonel John Montresor of the Royal Engineers. It was the Colonel who is responsible for creating much of the estate seen today but, unfortunately, his career ended prematurely when he was accused of embezzlement and, in 1801, the estate was purchased, at auction, by General George Harris, with money earned during his successful military career in India.

Created a lord in 1815 following his victory at Seringapatam, he and successive Lords Harris have continued to live at Belmont and also play a distinguished role in the expansion of the British Empire. It is the magnificent clock collection put together by the 5th Lord Harris that takes pride of place and it is the most extensive to be found in private hands.

Meanwhile, the surrounding gardens are equally impressive and here there is not only a walled garden and a pinetum, with a Victorian Shell Grotto, but also an Orangery, designed as an extension to the house, that is planted with orange trees, palms and other tropical trees.

SHELDWICH

3 miles S of Faversham on the A251

Standing at the point where the landscape blends gently from scattered woodlands to open meadows and then farms and orchards, Sheldwich has, at its centre, a Norman parish church with a distinctive squat steeple that is visible from miles around.

Just to the north, at **Brogdale**, can be found the **National Fruit Collection**. Here is the largest collection of fruit trees and plants in the world, with over 2,300 varieties of apples, 550 pears, and numerous plums, cherries and bush fruits along with smaller collections of nuts and vines that are all grown in the beautiful orchards.

BOUGHTON

3 miles E of Faversham off the A2

It is well worth pausing en route to the coast to explore **Farming World at Nash Court**. Almost every aspect of farming is featured here and, with beautiful surrounding countryside and marked trails for walking, there is plenty here to keep the whole family amused for hours.

Farming World's extensive breeding programme ensures that there are usually lots of young animals to see, such as lambs, kids, calves and chicks, but it is also home to a variety of rarer breeds like miniature Shetland ponies, llamas and Britain's smallest breed of cattle.

Along with the animals, the birds of prey and the heavy horses, Farming World has a museum with a fascinating collection of agricultural implements. Throughout the year there are demonstrations on the ancient and traditional skills of farming and other crafts, while specialist talks cover a wide range of subjects, including beekeeping, animal husbandry and falconry.

OSPRINGE

1 mile SW of Faversham off the A2

This hamlet was a thriving Roman settlement and numerous coins, medallions and household items have been unearthed that suggest that the community was quite sizeable. Various excavated artefacts can be found, along with Saxon pottery, glass and jewellery and relics from medieval Ospringe, at **Maison Dieu**. The French Maison Dieu, meaning God's House, was in common usage in medieval times when a mix of French and English was spoken in England. It meant a house that provided hospitality of various kinds. Such houses would provide a haven for the sick as well as a resting place for travellers on Watling Street.

The exact name of this property was the Hospital of the Blessed Mary of Ospringe. Originally founded by Henry III in around 1230, the building served as a combination hospital and hostel for pilgrims on their way to and from Canterbury. As well as having some features still remaining from the 13th century, the house also displays beamed ceilings from the Tudor era. Along with the relics unearthed in the local area, the museum also includes information on the fascinating history of Maison Dieu itself.

TEYNHAM

3 miles W of Faversham off the A2

In 1533, Henry VIII's fruiterer, Richard Harris, planted England's first cherry tree in the village, along with pippins and golden russet apple trees, and thus established Teynham as the birthplace of English orchards. William Lamparde, in his 16th century *Perambulation of Kent*, wrote of Teynham as "the cherry garden and apple orchard of Kent". This would appear still to be true, as fruit trees can be seen in every direction.

CANTERBURY TO SANDWICH BAY

This ancient land, between the city of Canterbury and the east coast of Kent, has seen invaders come and go, religious houses founded and dissolved under Henry VIII and the building of great fortresses. Certainly one of the best places to begin any tour of the area is Canterbury itself, the home of the Mother Church of the Anglican Communion, Canterbury Cathedral. The cathedral was founded by St Augustine in the late 6th century, along with an abbey, and both can still be seen today although the cathedral, which still dominates the city's skyline, is actually a Norman structure. The abbey and the cathedral, along with St Martin's Church, the oldest parish church in England still in constant use, form a fascinating World Heritage Site.

However, it is not just ancient buildings that draw visitors to this very special city. There is much else to see here including the places that were known to the city's several famous literary connections: Geoffrey Chaucer, the Elizabethan playwright and spy Christopher Marlowe, Somerset Maugham and Mary Tourtel, the creator of Rupert Bear.

The land between Canterbury and the coast is characterised by pretty villages, while to the south around Barfreston, was the area of the East Kent coalfield. To the north, around Stourmouth, is an area of very fertile land, which is the home of market gardens and orchards. Centuries ago, the Wantsum Channel separated the Isle of Thanet from the rest of Kent. The channel silted up over the centuries becoming marshland. The land seen today is the result of the drainage of the marshland in the 16th and 17th centuries.

This eastern stretch of Kentish coastline supported numerous fishing villages but, with the constant threat of invasion, they became fortified, particularly in 16th century under Henry VIII. Deal Castle remains one of the best surviving examples of Tudor military architecture while its contemporary, Walmer Castle, has been turned into an elegant stately house that is the home of the Lord Warden of the Cinque Ports. Set up in the 11th century, the Cinque Ports were a commercial alliance of south coast ports but today the title is chiefly ceremonial.

CANTERBURY

England's most famous cathedral city, and also one of the loveliest, Canterbury lies in one of the most attractive areas of rural Kent. It was here, in AD 597, that St Augustine founded an abbey, soon after his arrival from Rome, and it proved to be the roots of Christianity in England. Lying just outside the city walls, **St Augustine's Abbey** is now in ruins but there is an excellent museum and information centre here with exhibits on display that have been excavated from the site. Founded in 598, it is one of the oldest monastic sites in Britain. Destroyed at the dissolution of the monasteries in the 16th century, visitors can see the ruins of the original Saxon and Norman churches as well as the remains of Tudor brickwork from a Royal Palace built by Henry VIII. Before St Augustine had finished the monastery, he worshipped at **St Martin's Church**, England's oldest parish church, which was named after the Bishop of Tours, France. The building is believed to date back to Roman times and it is still in constant use.

However, both these fine buildings are overshadowed by the Mother Church of

CANTERBURY CATHEDRAL

Dean and Chapter of Canterbury, The Precincts, Canterbury, Kent CT1 2EH
Tel: 01227 762862 Fax: 01227 865222/865250
e-mail: enquiries@canterbury-cathedral.org website: www.canterbury-cathedral.org

Continuing to dominate the skyline of the city today, Canterbury Cathedral has a tradition of welcoming visitors that goes back to the days of the medieval pilgrimage. It was founded in AD 597 by St Augustine who was sent to England by Pope Gregory the Great and, as the first archbishop, he made Canterbury his seat (or 'Cathedra'). The earliest part of the present building is the crypt that dates back to around 1100 and that is also the largest of its kind in the country. On top of this was

built the quire that had to be replaced in the 12th century after the original construction was destroyed by fire. Gradually, the building was added to and extended over the centuries and, of the more interesting parts, there is the 14th century nave, with its tall columns rising up like trees to meet the delicate vaulted arches, and the late 15th century 'Bell Harry' tower.

The windows in the cathedral are magnificent and all the more so as they have not only survived the ravages of Henry VIII's Dissolution of the Monasteries but also Hitler's bombs that flatted much of the surrounding city. However, the cathedral's library was not so lucky as this was damaged by a German air raid in 1942. Fortunately, the beautiful and historic stained glass at the cathedral had been removed earlier and only the plain, replacement windows were blown out with the force of the blast.

Naturally, there is much to see here, from the medieval tombs of kings and numerous archbishops to splendid architecture, and the guided tours provide not only information about the building but also of those people who have been associated with it through the centuries. However, it is as the scene of the murder of Archbishop Thomas à Becket that the building is best known. Becket was killed on a December evening in the northwest transept by the knights of Henry II who misunderstood the king's request to be rid of his archbishop. A penitent Henry, full of remorse for the death of his former

friend, later came here on a pilgrimage. Unfortunately, Becket's tomb, that is said to have been covered in gold and jewels, was destroyed in 1538 by the agents of Henry VIII. However, from the time of his death, in 1170, Canterbury Cathedral has been one of the most famous places of pilgrimage in Europe and it continues to be so today. Standing in spacious precincts surrounded by the remains of a monastery, the cathedral, along with St Martin's Church and St Augustine's Abbey, form a World Heritage Site.

the Anglican Communion, **Canterbury Cathedral** (see panel opposite), which still dominates the city skyline. Canterbury Cathedral has a tradition of welcoming visitors that goes back to the days of the medieval pilgrimage. St Augustine was sent to England by Pope Gregory the Great and, as the first archbishop, he made Canterbury his seat (or 'Cathedra'). The earliest part of the present building is the crypt, dating back to around 1100 and the largest of its kind in the country. On top of this was built the quire that had to be replaced in the 12th century after the original construction was destroyed by fire. Gradually, the building was added to and altered over the centuries. The nave, with its tall columns rising up like trees to meet the delicate vaulted arches, is 14th century, and the 'Bell Harry' tower 15th century.

The windows in the cathedral are magnificent. Fortunately they survived the ravages of Henry VIII's Dissolution of the Monasteries and the wartime bombs that flattened much of the surrounding city. However, the cathedral's library was not so lucky as this was damaged by a German air raid in 1942. The beautiful and historic stained glass at the cathedral had been removed earlier and only the plain, replacement windows were blown out with the force of the blast. Eight of the original 12 12th century stained glass windows remain intact with amazing jewel bright colours.

There is a vast amount to see here, from the medieval tombs of kings and archbishops (Lanfranc and St Anselm) to splendid architecture, and the guided tours provide not only information about the building but also of those people who have been associated with it through the centuries. However, it is as the scene of the murder of Archbishop Thomas à Becket that the building is best known. Becket was killed on a December evening in the northwest transept by the knights of Henry II, who supposedly misunderstood the king's request to be rid of this troublesome priest. A penitent Henry, full of remorse for the death of his former friend, later came here on a pilgrimage. Unfortunately, Becket's original tomb, said to have been covered in gold and jewels, was destroyed in 1538 by the agents of Henry VIII. However, from the time of his death, in 1170, Canterbury Cathedral has been one of the most famous places of pilgrimage in Europe and it continues to be so today. One of the best examples of ecclesiastical architecture in the country, the whole precincts of the cathedral, along with St Martin's Church and St Augustine's

ANIMAL ARTS

20 Orange Street, Canterbury, Kent CT1 2JA
Tel: 01227 451145
e-mail: info@animalarts.co.uk
website: www.animalarts.co.uk

Animal Arts is an independent publishing business specialising in wildlife pencil art. All the images are printed in house on their state-of-the-art Giclée system,

and the frames are all made in their own workshops. The show-room in Orange Street displays a constantly changing selection of original drawings and limited edition prints by some of the most talented artists in their field. Featuring prominently are Sue Miles, who has achieved international recognition with her 4B pencil drawings of animals, particularly horses; Martin Sayer, who specialises mainly in drawings of wildlife based on his own photographs; the Russian artist Marianna Cojocar-Drake; and the distinguished illustrator Michael J Woods, who also produces colour images.

The 2004 catalogue also includes prints taken from encaustic art originals by Cornwall-based Judith Treweek; colour prints of big cats by Clare O'Bray; a series of crazy but cute 'Bonkers Beast' by computer graphics ace Roger Harris; and amusing animal studies by Martin Cheek, who is, among other talents, an acclaimed mosaic artist. Business hours of Animal Arts are 10 to 5.30 Monday to Saturday.

UNIQUES PINE EMPORIUM

Parham Road (off Sturry Road), Canterbury,
Kent CT1 1DD
Tel: 01227 479007

'If you want to talk furniture talk to Uniques' is the motto of Uniques Pine Emporium. They have for sale an amazing range of top-quality pine furniture at affordable factory prices. The range on display in the large showroom includes bedroom, kitchen and dining room suites, cupboards, dressers and wardrobes as well as smaller items and one-off imported lines including wine racks, lamps and

lighting, clocks, candleholders, ironware and glassware. Among the most popular lines are the Driftwood Range (marketed solely in Canterbury by Uniques) and the Country Craft range developed specially for Uniques combining traditional styles with a contemporary touch. All the pine items are crafted using traditional techniques and turned to the highest standards, and Uniques can create items to individual customer specifications.

Opening hours are 10am to 5pm Monday to Saturday, 10am to 4pm Sunday. There's ample parking space, and a free delivery service is available within the area.

Abbey, form a World Heritage Site. The Archbishop of Canterbury is the Primate of All England, attends royal functions and sits in the House of Lords.

By the time that Geoffrey Chaucer was writing his *Canterbury Tales*, some two centuries after the death of Thomas à Becket in 1170, Canterbury had become one of the most popular places of pilgrimage after Rome and Jerusalem. Many of the pilgrims set out, on foot or by horse, from London, as did Chaucer himself and, in many cases, the journey seems to have been more of a social event than an act of penance. As well as making the journey at least once himself, as the king's messenger, Chaucer also passed through Canterbury on numerous occasions on his way to the Continent. At the **Canterbury Tales Visitor Attraction** visitors are taken back to the 14th century and invited to embark on the same journey of pilgrimage that was undertaken by the characters in Chaucer's great poem. As they were making the journey, the Knight, the Miller, the Pardoner and the Wife of Bath, along with the other travellers, told tales to keep themselves amused. From the animated farmyard tale of a cock, a hen and a wily old fox to stories of love, chivalry, rivalry and ribaldry, the colourful tales are brought very much to life at this popular attraction. The medieval streets, houses and markets of the pilgrims are faithfully reconstructed, as is Becket's shrine, their destination. In the High Street stands the **Eastbridge Hospital of St Thomas the Martyr**, established for pilgrims to Becket's shrine. It survived destruction during the Reformation, finding a new role as an almshouse for 10 poor townspeople.

Westgate Gardens, Canterbury

While Canterbury is certainly dominated by its great cathedral there is much more to the city than first appearances might suggest. The capital of the Iron Age kingdom, Cantii (a name that lives on in the city and in the county name of Kent), the Romans also settled here for a time and, at the **Roman Museum**, there is a fine display of unearthed remains from Durovernum Cantiacorum (the Roman name for Canterbury). This underground museum centres on the remains of a Roman town house and, along with the fine mosaic floors, there are also reconstructions of other Roman buildings, a gallery of household objects that were excavated in and around this ancient site and some reproduction artefacts that visitors can handle.

Another aspect of life in Kent can be discovered at **The Kent Masonic Library and Museum** where the history of freemasonry over the last 300 years is explored. The vast collections found here cover many aspects of masonic life,

NOTHING BUT THE CAT

1 Iron Bar Lane, Canterbury, Kent CT1 2HN
Tel: 01227 787227
website: www.nothingbutthecat.co.uk

Every cat lover's dream – and every cat's dream. That's **Nothing But The Cat**, a shop where owner Sarah Hunt stocks practically everything that anyone has ever thought of producing to pamper cats and to make their owners purr with delight. For the cats there are cat mats and feeding bowls, catnip sprays and bubbles, collars, novelty beds and all manor of cat toys. For besotted owners there are key rings and clocks, books and playing cards, umbrellas and tote bags, tea cosies and T shirts, ornaments, doormats and mouse mats – all inspired by Britain's favourite pet.

and visitors can see numerous pieces of Masonic regalia and a huge library of books covering all aspects of freemasonry. There are also fine paintings, glassware and porcelain and the Cornwallis collection of documents and presentation items. The museum has limited opening times.

Housed in the former Poor Priests Hospital, which has some fine medieval interiors, is the **Museum of Canterbury** that presents a full history of the city over the last 2,000 years. From prehistoric times through to Canterbury in World War II, this museum has a great wealth of treasures and award winning displays. In the same building is a children's museum, featuring celebrities connected with Canterbury such as Rupert Bear, Bagpuss and the Clangers. Canterbury has had many literary connections down the ages, including Mary Tourtel (creator of Rupert Bear), Chaucer, Somerset Maugham (who went to King's School in the city in the 1890s) and the Elizabethan dramatist Christopher Marlowe (at the same school centuries earlier). A contemporary of Shakespeare's and the author of *Dr Faustus* and *Edward II*, Marlowe, the son of a shoemaker, was born in 1564 in George Street, Canterbury and later went on to Benet (now Corpus Christi) College, Cambridge. As a friend of Sir

Francis Walsingham, Elizabeth I's Secretary of State, Marlowe supplemented his literary career by taking an active role as a spy. At only 29 years of age, he was stabbed to death in Deptford following what is officially referred to as a tavern brawl but may well have been a deliberately planned assassination. He is buried at the church of St Nicholas and the church records simply state: "Christopher Marlowe, slain by ffrancis Archer 1 June 1593." Canterbury's main theatrical venue, the **Marlowe Theatre**, is named after this famous son and, along with the **Gulbenkian Theatre** at the University of Kent, it plays host to the annual **Canterbury Festival** that presents a varied programme of performing arts.

AROUND CANTERBURY

FORDWICH
2½ miles NE of Canterbury off the A28

This village was once a busy port for Canterbury on the River Stour, which was tidal to this point. As the river silted up and commercial vessels became larger, Fordwich was robbed of its major economic activity and the once prosperous town became a quiet and peaceful backwater. However, remnants of the bustling trade remain in what is the smallest town in Britain. Its town council meets in one of the smallest **Town Halls** in the county. Built in Tudor times and sited on the quay, it is timber framed, with the upper storey overhanging on all sides. On the upper floor was the courtroom and on the ground floor, the jail and the jailer's quarters. There is a fascinating collection of items here including the ancient chest with three locks in which all the town's important documents were kept.

PRESTON

7 miles NE of Canterbury off the A28

Listed in the Domesday Book as Prestetune, which means 'priest's farmstead or manor', the village church of St Mildred had, up until the early 18th century, suffered a period of decline and records show that animals were allowed to graze in the graveyard and that the church services were conducted improperly if they were conducted at all. However, some sort of order was returned to the parish when, in 1711, a house was left to the local church for use as a vicarage on condition that two services were held at the church each Sunday. The church itself is quaint in appearance, 14th century with a 19th century pyramidal cap on the tower and slightly odd triangular windows. There are also some beautiful 14th century stained glass windows.

STOURMOUTH

7½ miles NE of Canterbury off the A28

As the village is several miles from the sea, its name seems to make little sense but, centuries ago, this is where the River Stour fed into the **Wantsum Channel**, the stretch of water that separates the Isle of Thanet from the rest of Kent. In fact, such was the depth of the channel

that, in AD 885, it was the site of a sea battle between King Alfred and Danish raiders, who became trapped in the channel while attempting to attack and capture the City of Rochester.

The Wantsum Channel gradually silted up over the years and, in the 16th and 17th centuries, the resultant marshes were drained by Flemish refugees. Still criss-crossed by a network of drainage ditches today, this land remains very fertile and is now home to market gardens, fruit farms and hop fields.

WINGHAM

6 miles E of Canterbury on the A257

On either side of the long tree-lined High Street that runs through this large village, there are some fine and historic buildings, some of which date back to the reign of Henry VIII. There is an interesting story surrounding the wooden arcade of the **Norman parish church**. By the 16th century the building had fallen into a state of acute disrepair and George Ffoggarde, a local brewer, obtained a licence to raise funds for the church's repair. However, Ffoggarde embezzled all the £244 that he had collected and so the intended stone arcade, which should have been a feature of the repairs, was replaced with a wooden one that was considerably cheaper. The village became renowned for rebellion as the villagers were not only active in the Peasants' Revolt of 1381 and other popular protests but they also took part in the Swing Riots of 1830, for which several inhabitants were transported to Australia.

Just to the northeast of the village lies **Wingham Wildlife Park**, which aims to provide safe and secure habitats for many species of bird that are threatened in the wild. Among the many birds here visitors can see waterfowl, parrots, owls and emu

TONY BENHAM CERAMIC WATERFALLS

The Studio, Twitham Court Farm, Staple Road, Wingham,
nr Canterbury, Kent CT13 1LP
Tel: 01227 711324 Fax: 01227 722177
e-mail: tony.benham@amserve.net

Tony Benham has a lifetime's experience in pottery, glazing and reduction kiln firing. In his studio at **Tony Benham Ceramic Waterfalls** he produces a wide range of water features and sculptures using organic elements fired with glass and wood ash glazes in natural flame kilns. The pieces, each one a unique masterpiece, range from Buddha wall plaques to spectacular rockface wall panels with plant containers running down each side of the flowing water area.

THE RAILWAY STATION FARM SHOP

Littlebourne Road, Wingham, Kent CT3 1NH
Telephone 01227 721177 (Opening hours: 9.30am-5.30pm Monday-Saturday and 10am-4pm Sunday)

• **LOCAL PRODUCE • FLORIST • COFFEE SHOP • DELI AND BAKERY**

The Railway Station Farm Shop is located on the site of one of the old railway stations at Wingham. There used to be three...! It now supplies its customers with quality, farm fresh products. Wherever possible they

try to use local farmers and are proud to be members of *Produced In Kent*. They stock a range of deli products, such as salmon, olives, meats [including organic], over 30 cheeses and many other fine foods. John Yonge and his team are always interested in sourcing new, local goods... so, if they don't have what you're after, please let them know.

Why not enjoy a cream tea in the coffee shop or browse the growing number of nursery plants and products for your garden. Whether you're local or just passing pop in and see what's new. Make them your first stop...

Bright Ideas – the Flower Shop. Whether it's a special dinner party or wedding day flowers, Bright Ideas can create beautiful displays that are everything you dreamed of - and more. A graduate of London's prestigious Jane Packer Flower School, Julia Woodcock has launched Bright Ideas to create original arrangements that will express your personality to perfection.

while, in the Orchard Aviary, numerous smaller birds live alongside a range of furry mammals. Children will love the Pet Village, where they can mingle with the animals, and the Landscaped Lake, where they can feed the ducks. A tropical house is home to exotic butterflies and plants.

BEKESBOURNE

3 miles SE of Canterbury off the A2

Just to the north of the village and set within 70 acres of beautiful and ancient parkland, lies **Howletts Wild Animal Park**, which was created by John Aspinall and is dedicated to the preservation of rare and endangered animals. Here, visitors can see the largest family groups of gorillas and breeding herds of Asian and African elephants. Other families of rare monkeys can be seen at the park along with both Indian and Siberian tigers, other large cats and many more endangered animals.

BRIDGE
3 miles SE of Canterbury on the A2

The village stands at a river crossing, where the old Dover Road from London crosses a tributary of the River Stour, and this is, obviously, the source of the village's name. Now by-passed by the main A2 dual carriageway, this village was, for many years, subjected to a constant stream of heavy traffic and the villagers, in the 1970s, caused such a bottleneck while protesting to have the road through the village re-routed that the government relented and the by-pass was opened in 1976.

Close to the bridge lies **Higham Park** a mansion, restored and now open to the public, that was altered for Count Louis Zabrowski, who built and raced the original *Chitty Chitty Bang Bang*.

PATRIXBOURNE
3 miles SE of Canterbury off the A2

This handsome village, with a range of houses dating largely from the 17th and 18th centuries, also has newer dwellings, built in the 19th century. Carefully constructed in the Tudor style, they blend harmoniously with the existing buildings. The village church dates back to Norman times and has some wonderful carvings including the priest's door with a disfigured saint's head above. Bifrons, now demolished, was the seat of the Marquess of Conyngham, the great favourite of George IV.

AYLESHAM
6½ miles SE of Canterbury off the B2046

Following World War I, the eminent town planner, Professor Abercrombie, set out an ambitious scheme for a new town here that was to provide 2,000 houses. When development began in the 1920s, the plans

were scaled down and the village provided 500 dwellings for miners and their families who worked in the East Kent coalfield and, in particular, nearby Snowdown Colliery, which closed in 1987.

GOODNESTONE
7 miles SE of Canterbury off the B2046

Close to the village lies Goodnestone Park, an estate that was originally owned by Brook Bridges, who held an important post in the Treasury during the reign of Charles II. In the 18th century, Jane Austen was a frequent visitor to the house as her brother married Bridges' daughter and, during World War II, the house and park were requisitioned by the army and used as a tank repair depot. The estate is now in the ownership of Lord and Lady FitzWalter, and **Goodnestone Park Gardens** are considered some of the best in the southeast of England. The formal gardens around the house contain several old specimen trees along with a walled garden that still has some of the original 17th century walls. New planting continues here all the time and beyond the formal garden areas lie mature woodlands and a 1920s rockery and pond.

NONINGTON
7 miles SE of Canterbury off the B2046

For many years there were several private estates, with grand and imposing houses, situated close to this village and one, **Fredville Park**, remains to the south of Nonington. Although the superb Georgian house that lay at the centre of this estate was burned to the ground in 1939, the park is still renowned for its collection of fine oak trees and, in particular, the **Fredville Oak** that is several hundred years old and has a circumference of 36 feet.

CHILLENDEN

8 miles SE of Canterbury off the B2046

Found in a prominent position, just outside this village, is **Chillenden Windmill**, one of the last 'open trestle' post windmills to be built in England and one of the last surviving such mills in Kent. It was built in 1868 for Brigadier Speed, who lived at Knowlton Court, although this exposed site has supported windmills for over 500 years. Now restored and with a complete outward appearance, the mill contains some of the old machinery and is open to the public on occasional days throughout the year.

KNOWLTON

8½ miles SE of Canterbury off the A256

The main street through this tiny hamlet leads to **Knowlton Court**, an Elizabethan house remodelled by Sir Reginald Blomfield in 1904. The Lodge was designed by Sir Edwin Lutyens in 1912. Down the years, Knowlton Court has been the home of several military and naval men: the Royalist commander Sir Thomas Peyton lived here at the time of the Civil War while, later, it was the home of Admiral Sir John Narborough. In 1707, Sir John's two sons were drowned off the Isles of Scilly following a naval disaster when navigational error caused the English fleet to be wrecked at night. A tomb in **Knowlton Church**, designed by Grinling Gibbons, illustrates the scene.

BARFRESTON

8½ miles SE of Canterbury off the A2

Barfreston's small **Norman church**, which dates from the 11th and 12th centuries, is remarkable for its detailed stone carvings the best examples of which can be seen around the east door. They represent an array of creatures, scenes from medieval life and religious symbols, an explanatory booklet on these delightful images can be obtained from the nearby public house. There is another curious feature to this church - the church bell can be found attached to a yew tree in the churchyard.

SHEPHERDSWELL

9 miles SE of Canterbury off the A2

This old village, which is sometimes referred to as Sibertswold, grew rapidly after 1861 when the London to Dover railway opened and, again, when housing was built here for the miners working at the nearby Tilmanstone Colliery. In 1911, a junction was established for the East Kent Light Railway to serve the colliery and, while the last passenger service ran in 1948, the railway continued its commercial operations until the colliery closed in 1987. Today, the **East Kent Railway** is open once again and carries passengers from the village's charming station to the nearby village of Eythorne. Those visiting the railway will also find a museum of railway memorabilia, a buffet, a gift shop and a miniature railway to add to their enjoyment.

COLDRED

10 miles SE of Canterbury off the A2

The tidy little village of Coldred is one of the highest settlements in East Kent at nearly 400 feet above sea level. Its name may be from Ceoldred, King of Mercia, who supposedly helped the Kentish men against the Saxons, or perhaps from the Old English word for charcoal burning, which was a local industry. Next to the parish church of St Pancras lies a farm that was originally a manor house owned by Bishop Odo of Bayeux, half-brother to William the Conqueror. In fact, both the church and the farm stand on a site that was a fortified Saxon camp of the 8th century - of which a few remains can still be seen. Archaeological excavations in this ancient village have revealed not only finds from Saxon times but also evidence of earlier, Roman, occupation. In later times the village pond was used for witch trials and, in the 1640s, it was recorded that Nell Garlige, an old woman of the parish, was tied up and thrown into the pond where, presumably, she drowned.

Chilham Castle

CHILHAM

5 miles SW of Canterbury on the A252

This well-preserved village is one of Kent's showpieces and is often used as a location for filming, particularly the area round the square. The houses here are primarily Tudor and Jacobean and are a delightfully haphazard mix of gabled, half-timbered houses, shops and ancient inns. A stopping place for pilgrims on their way to the shrine of Thomas à Becket in Canterbury Cathedral, Chilham today plays host to other visitors, many of whom walk the nearby **North Downs Way**.

THE OLD ALMA INN

Canterbury Road, Chilham, Kent CT4 8DX
Tel/Fax: 01227 731913
e-mail: oldalma@aol.com

Built in 1854 and named after the first battle of the Crimean War, the **Old Alma Inn** offers warm, comfortable Bed & Breakfast accommodation in the heart of Kent. It is owned and run by the Niven family, who have created a very friendly, relaxed atmosphere. The white-painted exterior, adorned with flower tubs and hanging baskets, is a very cheerful sight on the main A28, and the guest lounge has a blazing fire in the winter providing a warm homely welcome.

The bedrooms, including family rooms, all have en suite facilities, TV and hospitality trays, and an excellent English or Continental breakfast is served in the pretty little dining room.

Easy to reach by road or rail (there are regular services from Chilham station to London, Canterbury and Ashford International Terminal), the Old Alma is a perfect centre for exploring Canterbury and the historic towns and scenic attractions of one of England's most beautiful counties. Chilham itself, once a stopping place for pilgrims on their way to the shrine of Thomas à Becket, is one of Kent's showpiece villages and today plays host to walkers on the Pilgrims Way and the North Downs Way.

CHILHAM SHOP
FARM SHOP & PLANT CENTRE

Canterbury Road, Chilham, Kent CT4 8DX
Tel: 01227 730348 Fax: 01227 752657

Located in one of the loveliest villages in the whole of Kent, the family-run **Chilham Shop** attracts customers from near and far with its rich and varied range of produce. Thought to be one of the first 'farm shops' in the county, it has been run by George and Peter Higgs for 21 years and is popular with the local farming community for both buying and selling. Much of the fresh fruit and vegetables on display are locally grown, and other local produce includes eggs, preserves and home baking. Freshly made sandwiches and home made pies and pasties are ideal to take away for a snack or a picnic, and a recently introduced delicatessen range includes olives, cheeses and cooked meats.

Situated on the A28, the main road between Canterbury and Ashford, with ample parking on the forecourt, Chilham Shop is a very convenient place for buying general groceries as well as the local produce, and throughout the wide variety of goods on sale, freshness and quality are always paramount. In summer they sell perennials, shrubs and bedding plants, many grown in their own nurseries, and all year round they stock garden requisites and ceramic and terracotta pots. Cut flowers, pot plants, hand made goods and exotic sweets make excellent last-minute gifts at this outstanding shop, which has few rivals in terms of variety, quality, convenience and friendliness.

BADGERS HILL FARM

Chilham, nr Canterbury, Kent CT4 8BW
Tel: 01227 730573 Fax: 01227 738383
website: www.badgershillfarm.co.uk

Badgers Hill Farm is a family-owned and run company that started up in the early 1990s specialising in the making and selling of wooden barrel products. The best known items in the range are the hugely popular water features, made from traditional wooden barrels strengthened with galvanised steel bands, protected inside with a wax coating and fitted with Victorian-style handpumps converted to electric power to guarantee a constant flow of water. The barrels are also the basis of several other products, including garden furniture, but the company has expanded to deal in many other products for the garden, including pots and planters, terracotta figures, bird houses and much more.

Visitors to this working farm have a barrel of fun in all sorts of ways. A wide range of country food, including pickles and preserves, confectionery and home made cider, is on sale in the barn, along with plants and shrubs, and the farm is also home to chickens, turkeys, goats, donkeys, wallabies and rheas. Open to the public every day from March to Christmas, the farm provides a great day out for all the family, and children can let off surplus energy in a play area with swings and - what else? - a barrel playhouse!

The village is also the home of **Chilham Castle**, a Jacobean Mansion built on to a Norman Keep built on Roman foundations. The house was built for Sir Dudley Digges, an official of James I, and the spacious grounds around the castle were first laid out by Charles I's gardener, John Tradescant. They were reworked in the 18th century by Capability Brown. The lodge gates in the village square were added in the 20th century. It was close to Chilham that the Romans fought their last great battle in Britain; the site is known as Julieberrie Downs in honour of Julius Laberius who was killed there in 54 BC.

HARBLEDOWN
1 mile NW of Canterbury off the A2

This village was for many pilgrims the last stopping place before Canterbury and, so legend has it, the village well was called Black Prince's Well as the prince believed the waters to have healing properties. Despite drinking a flask of the water each day, the prince died in 1376, probably of syphilis contracted in Spain. The Church of St Nicholas, still known locally as the Leper Church, was built by Archbishop Lanfranc around 1084 as the Chapel for the Leper Hospital, which he founded here. The chapel was extended in the 14th century, and there are four delightful 14th century stained glass windows in the chancel. The leper hospital was demolished as leprosy disappeared in England; the almshouses next to the church are Victorian.

Near Harbledon is **Bigbury Hill Fort**, where Caesar fought the local inhabitants in 54BC. The outline of the fort is still clearly visible on the skyline, and the defensive ditches can still be seen. Excavations at the site have unearthed Belgic pottery and iron work, including a slave chain.

BLEAN
2½ miles NW of Canterbury on the A290

Close to the village lies **Druidstone Park and Arts Park**, where visitors can see a wide variety of animals and birds in a peaceful country setting, as well as a collection of indoor and outdoor sculptures.. Along with native species such as otters and owls, the park is also home to more exotic creatures including rhea, mara, wallabies and parrots. Younger children can make friends with the farmyard animals, and there are walks through woodland where the park's herd of deer can be observed. Many of the animals and birds living here have been rescued, and others play an important part in captive breeding programmes. The plant growth in the park provides interest throughout the year, from spring flowers to autumn fungi and winter buds.

RAMSGATE

For centuries, Ramsgate was a small fishing village until, in 1749, a harbour was built and the town began to grow. After George IV landed here in 1822 (the **Obelisk** on the East Pier commemorates this historic event), the town adopted the title of 'Royal Harbour'. By the end of the 19th century, its fishing fleet had grown to make it the largest port on the south coast of England. However, at the beginning of World War I, the fishing industry began to decline and, with a seemingly uncertain future, Ramsgate enjoyed a brief moment of national glory when, in 1940, over 40,000 British troops, evacuated from the Dunkirk beaches by an armada of small boats and vessels, landed here.

The parish church of St George commemorates this important episode in Ramsgate's and England's history with a special stained glass window. The Catholic Church of St Augustine was designed by Augustus Pugin, best known as the designer of the interior of the Houses of Parliament. He is buried in the church in a tomb chest designed by his son.

Still dominated by its harbour and shipping, the town is also home to the **Ramsgate Motor Museum**, where visitors are offered a trip down memory lane and a journey back to the days of stylish motoring. Founded in 1982 and dedicated to the golden ages of motoring, the many cars, motorcycles and bicycles on display here are set out in scenes that depict the past, and cards record the world history of the year each vehicle was made.

Just to the south of Ramsgate lies **Pegwell Bay**, traditionally the landing place of Hengist and Horsa, who led the successful Jutish invasion of Kent in AD449. The badge of Kent today has on it a prancing white horse, the image under which these Jutish warriors fought.

AROUND RAMSGATE

BROADSTAIRS
2 miles N of Ramsgate on the A255

This family seaside resort grew as an amalgamation of St Peter's inland and Broadstairs and Reading on the coast. It still retains its village atmosphere and is widely known for its associations with Charles Dickens. Those coming in search of **Bleak House** will find it in Church Road high up on the cliffs at the northern end of the town, overlooking the popular beach at Viking Bay. Charles Dickens spent his summers here for 20 years. He wrote *David Copperfield* here, at a desk at the window with a splendid view over the English Channel and the Goodwin Sands from his 'airy nest'. The

cellars of Bleak House (originally called Fort House) have various displays on smuggling in Broadstairs. The Dickens House Museum, the 'home' of Betsey Trotwood, is also filled with Dickens memorabilia, including letters, costumes, pictures and a collection of prints by Dickens' illustrator Phiz (HK Browne). The town reinforces its links with the great Victorian novelist by holding an annual Charles Dickens Festival.

Other notables associated with the town include the politician Sir Edward Heath, who was born here in 1916, and another famous sailor, Sir Alec Rose, who lived in Broadstairs for many years. Writers, too, seem to have found inspiration along this stretch of coast as both Frank Richards, creator of Billy Bunter, and John Buchan, author of *The Thirty-Nine Steps* spy thriller, lived here. Buchan wrote the story at a house called St Cuby, on Cliff Promenade and the staircase that gave him the idea for the title stands opposite the house. It comprises 78 steps, but the number was halved by Buchan to provide a catchier title.

SANDWICH
5½ miles SW of Ramsgate off the A256

Sandwich has its origins in Saxon times, when a settlement was established at the mouth of the River Stour. Since those days, the river has silted up and the town now stands a couple of miles from the coast, but its maritime history still lives on. It was one of the original Cinque Ports, hard though it might be to believe today. After the harbour ceased to be navigable, the town turned to cloth manufacturing as its economic mainstay and, with the help of Flemish refugees, once again prospered. This industry has all but ceased and Sandwich has become simply a pleasant and peaceful place, best known for its championship golf

The Old Customs House, Sandwich

though much altered in the 20th century, the Guildhall itself can be toured and there are some fascinating historic items including the Moot Horn that was used as far back as the 12th century to summon the people of the town to hear important announcements. The Horn is still used today to announce the death of the monarch and the accession of the successor. Another fascinating item is the Hog Mace, which was used to round up straying animals after the Goose Bell had been rung; all such animals not repossessed by their owners on payment of a fine were passed on to the Brothers and Sisters of

course, Royal St George's.

The **Sandwich Guildhall Museum** tells the story of the town from early medieval times onwards, with the help of numerous artefacts dating from as far back as the 13th century. Built in 1576,

---

CAROLE RIDLEY

11 High Street, Sandwich, Kent CT13 9EB
Tel: 01304 621620
website: www.caroleridley.com

Carole Ridley owns two high-class ladies fashion shops that bear her name. This one is in a beautiful and quiet part of Sandwich close to the river, the other in Whitstable. Carole has been involved in ladies fashion retailing for most of her working life and uses her experience to select a range of relaxed, confidence-inspiring clothes and accessories aimed mainly at the over 25s. All the fabrics – linen, silk, cotton, cashmere - are natural and represent the leading names in fashion, among them Sarah Pacini, Sonja Marohn, Oska and Ischiko. The unique styles are available in a variety of colours - vibrant, earth hues, pastels and of course, classic black.

Leather and the wonderful Sherlings (a type of suede) are prominent among the accessories which include jewellery, belts and bags for every occassion. Carole runs fashion shows for charity locally and regularly attends *Country Living* fairs around the country. The knowledgable and helpful staff will be pleased to assist you with any prospective purchase and you will be sure to find something a little out of the ordinary.

JAY'S COOKSHOP

2 Market Street, Sandwich, Kent CT1 3DA
Tel: 01304 620233

Shoppers will find an impressive range of goods for the kitchen and the table at **Jay's Cookshop**, an absolute gem of a place run by Pauline and Tracy. All the famous names are represented - Sabatier knives, Salter scales, Le Creuset cast-iron ovenware, Bridgewater and Henry Watson china, tea towels by Ulster Weavers – and Jay's, one of the friendliest shops in town, also stocks a select range of foodstuffs, including Dart Valley chutneys and preserves, and a host of gift ideas that are both practical and attractive.

St John's Hospital. Sandwich Town Council still meets in the Council Chamber twice a month as it has done for over 400 years. The Mayor's chair dates from 1561.

Elsewhere in Sandwich, visitors can see the **Barbican Gate**, a turreted 16th century gatehouse that guards the northern entrance into the town, and **St**

Bartholomew's Hospital, which was founded in the 12th century and consists of a quadrangle of almshouses grouped around an old chapel.

A mile northwest of the town is **Richborough Roman Fort**, believed to date from AD 43. These impressive ruins of a fort and supporting township include the massive foundations of a

CALICO

14 King Street, Sandwich, Kent CT13 9BT
Tel: 01304 620068

If the ladies of Sandwich and the surrounding area are looking particularly smart these days, it could well be that they've being paying visits to **Calico**. Sue Cook's beautifully appointed shop in the heart of town is stocked with fine clothes to suit all ages and for all occasions, from smart casual to society weddings. Quality comes first, and everything on display is personally selected by an owner with a natural feel for clothes. Calico also stocks shoes, scarves, bags and other accessories, as well as lovely jewellery by makers such as Noa and Travis Leigh.

LITTLE SELSON COTTAGE

Little Selson Farmhouse, Selson, Eastry, nr Sandwich, Kent CT13 0EF
Tel: 01304 611482

Not far away from Sandwich, in the tiny rural hamlet of Selson, the Cook family offer excellent self-catering accommodation in a delightful two-bedroom cottage converted from an old milking parlour and stables. **Little Selson Cottage** has a fully fitted kitchen and a comfortable lounge/dining room. A galleried area enjoys views of the countryside, and French doors lead out on to a secluded patio area and garden.

triumphal arch that stood some 80 feet high. The extensive fortifications, which still dominate the surrounding flat land, were designed to repel Saxon invaders and at one time this was the most important Roman military base in Britain. The museum here gives a real insight into life during the heyday of this busy Roman town.

WORTH

6 miles SW of Ramsgate off the A258

The pond in the centre of this pretty village was once part of a navigable creek that lead out to the sea but, over the centuries, as with much of this coastal strip, the waters have silted up. There are several buildings in Worth with distinctive Dutch architectural features; these were constructed in the 17th century by Flemish and Huguenot refugees who fled from the Continent to escape persecution.

WOODNESBOROUGH

7 miles SW of Ramsgate off the A256

The hill at the centre of the village is Woden-hill derived from the Saxon God Woden, from which the village took its name. In the early 8th century the Battle of Wodnesbeorh took place here between the Saxons and the West Mercians. Legend has it that Woden-hill is actually the burial heap of those who died in the battle. Death certainly seems to have been a feature of Woodnesborough as this is also believed to be the burial place of Vortimer, King of the Saxons, who died in AD 457. Near the hill is the Parish Church of St Mary, notable for the wooden tower which replaced its spire in 1745.

MANSTON

2 miles W of Ramsgate on the B2050

This quiet village, surrounded by rich farmland supports intensive market gardening, was, during World War II

home to one of the country's major airfields. Featuring heavily in the Battle of Britain, RAF Manston was the closest airfield to the enemy coast and, as a consequence, it bore the brunt of the early Luftwaffe air attacks. The **Spitfire and Hurricane Memorial Building**, where the main attractions are the two aircraft themselves, provides visitors with an opportunity to gain an understanding of just what life was like for the pilots and other staff stationed at the airfield in the 1940s. Photographs and other memorabilia are on sale here while there is a cafeteria with fine views out across the airfield.

MINSTER

4½ miles W of Ramsgate off the A299

It is likely that there were settlements in the area around this village overlooking Minster Marshes well before the invasion of the Romans, and it is generally accepted that the Isle of Thanet was the first landing place for invading Saxons. Among the many old buildings in the village, some of which date back to the Middle Ages, are the **Old House**, built in 1350, and the **Oak House** that is almost as old. One of the country's first nunneries was established at Minster in the 7th century, on land granted to Princess Ermenburga, who is usually better known by her religious name - Domneva. King Egbert, her uncle, gave the land to Ermenburga as compensation when her two brothers were murdered by one of his men, the thane, Thunor. Legend has it that Thunor secured the throne of Kent for Egbert by murdering the two princes, Ethelbert and Ethelred, and he buried their bodies, secretly, in the grounds of the royal palace. The graves were soon found, revealed, so it is said, by mysterious columns of light, and a penitent King Egbert let loose a deer to run free, declaring that all the land that

it encircled would be given to
Ermenburga. As Thunor watched
he became alarmed at the distance
that the deer was covering and set
out to try halt it but he fell, with
his horse, into a ditch and was
drowned.

In the end, Ermenburga
received over 1,000 acres and the
story of its acquisition is
illustrated in the windows of the
parish church of St Mary.
Ermenburga founded **Minster
Abbey** in 670 and, although the
nunnery was later sacked by the
Danes, it became part of the estate of St
Augustine's Abbey, Canterbury. The
monks set about rebuilding the abbey,
adding a grange, and much of the
Norman work can still be seen in the
cloisters and other parts of the ruins. In
the grounds of Minster Abbey is
**Minster's Agricultural and Rural Life
Museum** centred on the Old Tithe Barn,
parts of which date back to the 8th
century. Agricultural machinery and
implements depict farming methods and
daily life in a rural community from the
early 19th century.

The Beach at Deal

DEAL

This delightful fishing town has changed
little in character since the 18th century,
thanks in part to its shingle rather than
sandy beach, which meant that Deal
escaped Victorian development into a
full-blown seaside resort. The fishing
industry has always played a major role
along this stretch of coastline and the
roots of that trade are still very much in
evidence. Deal's seafront is one of the
most picturesque along the southeast
coast and, with its quaint alleyways,
traditional fishermen's cottages and old
houses, the town is well worth exploring.

Not surprisingly, given its history, Deal
was also the haunt of smugglers and these
illegal activities were centred around
Middle Street. It was in a house along
this street that, in 1801, Nelson's great
friend, Captain Edward Parker, died from
wounds that he received following a raid
on Boulogne. Nelson was a frequent
visitor to the town, and he outraged local
society by staying at the Royal Hotel with
his mistress, Lady Emma Hamilton.

The **Maritime and Local History
Museum** is an excellent place to begin as
the displays here cover many aspects of
the life of the town and its people.
Housed in stables that were once used to
shelter army mules, the museum has a
large collection of real and model boats,
figureheads, compasses and other
navigational aids, pilots' relics and
memorabilia that relate to Deal's
seafaring and fishing past. On the site of
the old Naval yard stands the distinctive
Timeball Tower that was built in 1795
and was used to give time signals to ships
in the English Channel. The four-storey
building had a curious device whereby a
black copper ball was dropped down its
central shaft at exactly one o'clock to
warn ships just off the coast to be ready
to set their chronometers. Although this
original system has long since been

replaced by a modern radio time signal, a replica ball still drops down the shaft each day. The tower is also home to a museum devoted to time and telegraphy.

Not far from the Timeball Tower stands the menacing fortress of **Deal Castle**, which was built by Henry VIII in the early 1540s as one of a number of forts designed to protect the south coast from invasion by the French and Spanish, angered over Henry's divorce of his Catholic wife, Catherine of Aragon. The castle was designed to resemble a Tudor rose and the distinctive 'lily-pad' shape can only really be appreciated from the air or by looking at plans of the site. A huge bastion, Deal Castle had 119 guns trained out across the sea and it must have been a very formidable sight to anyone thinking of making an attack. Despite all these precautions, Deal Castle never actually came under attack from foreign invaders and it was not until the Civil War that the fortress saw action. In 1648, it came under fire from the Parliamentarians and, although it was extensively damaged, it was not attacked again until it was hit by a bomb during World War II. At the northern end of the town lies another of Henry VIII's great fortresses, **Sandown Castle**, but unfortunately time has not been so kind to Sandown and all that remains are some ruined buttresses.

The quiet waters just off the coast of Deal, known as **The Downs**, create a safe anchorage for ships that might otherwise run aground on the treacherous **Goodwin Sands**. Down the centuries these sands proved to be a graveyard for unwary vessels and wrecked ships, with their masts poking above the water, can still be seen at low tide. The sands were mentioned by Shakespeare, in the *Merchant of Venice*, as a place where the merchant lost one of his ships. As many as 50,000 men may have perished on these sands, which have given rise to numerous tales of 'ghost ships'.

AROUND DEAL

WALMER
1½ miles S of Deal on the A258

This residential seaside town merges almost imperceptibly with its neighbour, Deal, to the north, but Walmer does have its very own, distinct, history. It is firmly believed that it was here, in 55 BC, that Julius Caesar and his legions landed in England. However, the town is now best known for its sister castle to Deal. **Walmer Castle**, built as one of Henry VIII's line of coastal defences in the 1540s, has become, over the years, an elegant stately home. Today it is the official residence of the Lord Warden of the Cinque Ports, a title that has been

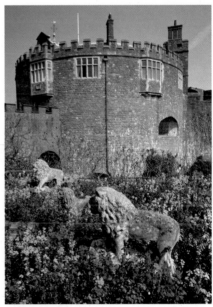
Walmer Castle

South Foreland

Distance: 5.6 miles (9.0 kilometres)

Typical time: 180 mins

Height gain: 107 metres

Map: Explorer 138

Walk: www.walkingworld.com
ID:970

Contributor: Ian Elmes

Access Information:

Take the A2 towards Dover, turn left heading for Deal, then turn right following the signs to St Margaret's Bay. Plenty of parking space is available.

Description:

A moderate circular walk from St Margaret's Bay, taking in the fantastic views of the English Channel along the clifftops and on past the South Foreland Lighthouse (NT) and up to the viewpoint at Fox Hill Down, overlooking the busy ferry terminal at Dover.

Features:

Sea, Toilets, Museum, Play Area, National Trust/NTS, Birds, Great Views, Butterflies, Food Shop, Tea Shop

Walk Directions:

1 This walk starts at St Margaret's Bay car park. There is a charge for parking here at the weekends. From the car park, walk back along the road you drove down to the postbox, then take the road straight ahead (looks like an old disused road).

2 Turn left here along Beach Road, following the sign for the Saxon Shoreway.

3 Take the left fork at this junction, following the sign to the Saxon Shoreway. Follow the path up the hill, it is very clearly defined. At the top of the hill, bear right to follow the footpath to the top of the cliff. At the top of the hill cross the track to the gate.

4 Go through the gate and follow the path to the right, going uphill. Beware that the cliffs are dangerous. To the left of you, on a clear day you may well see France. Ahead of you is the South Foreland Lighthouse (National Trust). This was used by Marconi for his first radio transmission. Follow the pathway to the gate at the top, through the gate and turn left, back onto the track you crossed earlier. Continue along the track to the entrance of the lighthouse.

5 The Lighthouse is National Trust-owned and is open between March and October. Turn left here, following the sign to the Coastal Path and Langdon Cliff. Follow the footpath; there is a diversion as the cliff has eroded as far as the path. Views from here are fantastic, the Port of Dover ahead, together with the cruise terminal.

6 Follow the track from this point, up and over the undulations of the contours, following the line of the cliff.

7 Langdon Hole (National Trust). Go over the stile and follow the path straight in front of you. Keep heading toward the three radio masts straight ahead.

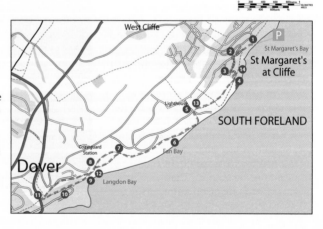

8 Take the steps up the hill towards the coastguard station.

9 Pass through the kissing-gate and follow the footpath all the way along - great views to the left of the ferry terminal at Dover.

10 At this point, take the footpath to the left. The pathway opens out and there is a car park to the right. Here you will see many people just sitting watching the ferries - many of the people have scanners so they can listen to the conversations between ship and shore.

11 At the newly formed footpath, turn right to go back up the hill. At the top of the hill, follow the road into the car park of the National Trust. Follow the roadway, through the car park and gate towards the cafe. Follow the path through the triangular bollards and take the left footpath, signposted Saxon Shoreway.

12 At the kissing gate to Langdon Hole go through and follow the footpath on the right down by the fence. At the end of the fence, follow the footpath straight in front of you, back down the steps and back to the stile at the other end. Just after the stile at the far end, take the right footpath to retrace your steps back to the lighthouse.

13 At the lighthouse entrance, turn right and keep on the track, past Lighthouse Down, through the gate at the cattle grid and follow it down.

14 Go through the gate here and follow the track to the left. At the bottom turn right towards the gift shop and garden etc. The tea shop is a nice place to stop for a bite to eat after this wonderful walk. Carry straight on down the road past the postbox and back to the car park at St Margaret's Bay.

held by William Pitt the Younger, the Duke of Wellington and Sir Winston Churchill as well as Queen Elizabeth the Queen Mother. Visitors to this charming place can see the Duke of Wellington's rooms, and even his famous boots, as well as enjoying a stroll around the Gardens. In honour of the Queen Mother's 95th birthday in August 1995 a special garden was planted. One-time owners of the castle, the Beauchamp family, were the inspiration for the Flyte family in Evelyn Waugh's novel *Brideshead Revisited*.

RINGWOULD
3 miles S of Deal on the A258

Centuries ago, this village stood on the edge of a vast forest that extended westwards almost to the city of Canterbury. The oldest building in the village is undoubtedly the 12th century **Church of St Nicholas**, whose curious onion dome was added to the 17th century tower to act as a navigation aid for ships in the English Channel. The village's old forge also had maritime connections: iron carriage wheels and

chains were made to be used at the naval dockyard in the nearby town of Deal.

ST MARGARET'S AT CLIFFE
5½ miles S of Deal off the A258

This small town stands on cliffs overlooking **St Margaret's Bay**. It was, before World War II, a secluded seaside resort with a number of hotels along the beach. It was the home of playwright Noel Coward, and Ian Fleming, the author of the James Bond spy thrillers, later bought Coward's house. As this is the nearest point to the French coast, which lies some 21 miles away, St Margaret's has long been the traditional starting place for cross-channel swimmers and, also because of its position, a gun emplacement was built here during World War II to protect the Channel and ward off any German invasion. St Margaret's possesses an ancient parish church, the 12th century **Church of St Margaret of Antioch**, which features some interesting rounded arches and an intricately carved doorway.

Just to the south of the town lies **The

Pines, a six-acre park renowned for its trees, plants, shrubs and ornamental lake. The brainchild of a wealthy local builder and philanthropist Fred Cleary, the gardens' imaginative layout includes a Romany caravan, a statue of Sir Winston Churchill and a waterfall. It is a delightfully tranquil setting in which to enjoy the glorious views over the White Cliffs. Opposite The Pines, and opened in 1989, is **St Margaret's Museum** containing collections of artefacts put together by Fred Cleary relating to local or maritime themes and others of world-wide interest.

A little further south again lies **South Foreland Lighthouse**, the highlight of the White Cliffs and a distinctive landmark overlooking the Straits of Dover. Erected in 1843, the lighthouse was used by the radio pioneer Marconi for his early experiments and it was from here that he made the world's first ship-to-shore radio transmission. A guided tour takes visitors around the lighthouse, where its history can be learned and from where there are magnificent long-ranging views.

GREAT MONGEHAM
2 miles SW of Deal off the A258

Hanging from a pole high on the wall of the chancel of the local parish church of St Martin is a helmet said to have been worn at the Battle of Hastings in 1066. More credible is a brass plaque on a pillar that bears a Greek verse written by the poet, Robert Bridges, in memory of his nurse who lies buried in the church.

WEST LANGDON
5 miles SW of Deal off the A256

Close to this small village can be seen the scant remains of **Langdon Abbey**, founded in 1189 by Premonstratensian Canons. After the dissolution, much of the masonry of the abbey was carted to the

coast and used in the construction of Henry VIII's coastal defences;, a farmhouse was later built on the abbey site.

NORTHBOURNE
3 miles W of Deal off the A256

In the church of this small country village can be found a monument to Sir Edwin Sandys, who was responsible for the drawing up of the constitution of Virginia, in America, and who was born in the village at Northbourne Court. Edwin's son also made a name for himself as he became a prominent and notoriously cruel commander in the Civil War on the Parliamentarian side. Although the house that these two gentlemen knew was demolished in the 18th century, the **Ornamental Gardens** survive and are occasionally open to the public.

EASTRY
4½ miles NW of Deal off the A256

Situated along the Roman road that linked Richborough with Dover, this ancient village has a couple of interesting historic connections. It was here in 1164 that Thomas à Becket hid while waiting to travel to Flanders after his quarrel with Henry II. Lord Nelson also visited the village and one of his officers, Captain John Harvey, lies buried in the local churchyard.

NORTH DOWNS TO DOVER

Following the North Downs eastwards to the coast, this area ends, or begins, at Dover, the traditional 'Gateway to England'. As Britain's major cross-Channel port, this is where many start their holiday in England (or leave to go abroad) but the town is well used to 'invaders' and, during the Roman occupation, it was here that they stationed their navy. It is still dominated by its castle, set high above the famous White Cliffs; this originally Norman fortress has, over the centuries, been an impressive repellent to foreign foes. While the huge structure of the castle makes this is wonderful place to wander around, it is the Secret Wartime Tunnels that attract much of the attention. This is a labyrinthine maze of tunnels cut into the cliffs where, during World War II, the evacuation of Dunkirk was masterminded by Winston Churchill and Admiral Ramsey.

Although defence of the country from sea attack is a key aspect of this stretch of coast, it was overhead that one of the great battles of World War II took place and close to the coast are both the Battle of Britain Memorial and the Kent Battle of Britain Museum. They each play tribute, in separate ways, to the courage of the young pilots who fought to win air supremacy over the skies of England and so prevent a German invasion.

It may seem that this area is given over to war, but the idyllic nature of many of the rural villages of this region portray a picture that is both peaceful and tranquil. Inland lie the National Fruit Collection, where literally hundreds of varieties of apples, pears, plums and numerous other fruit trees are grown, and the famous Wye College, the agricultural institution that is now part of the University of London. There are also ancient country houses that open their glorious gardens to the public such as Beech Court Gardens and Belmont.

At the heart of the rural idyll lies Ashford, which, like many places in Kent, has a history that goes back to Roman times. The central location of the town has made it a natural meeting place and, today, with the opening of the Channel Tunnel and its International Station it is beginning to rival Dover for the title 'Gateway to Britain'.

ASHFORD

In the heart of the Garden of England, Ashford boasts some fine Georgian houses and is surrounded by countryside, which has inspired such famous writers as HE Bates, Jane Austen and HG Wells. The town itself is dominated by the great central tower of St Mary's, its splendid 15th century parish church rising high above the other town buildings, each of its four pinnacles crowned by a golden arrow-shaped weathervane.

Ashford's central location makes it an ideal base from which to visit many of the county's attractions but it is well worth spending time here and, at the **Ashford Borough Museum**, where visitors can find out more about this interesting and historic place. Housed in Dr Wilks' Hall, which was formerly the Old Grammar School, the museum has a varied collection that ranges from Victorian patchwork to equipment used by the town's fire brigade.

Ashford is home of the first volunteer Fire Service in the country, formed in 1826 and which purchased its first manual fire engine some 10 years later. In 1925, the first Leyland motor fire engine went into service at Ashford and the funds required to buy the appliance were raised by public subscription.

The town's central location saw a Roman settlement established here in the 1st century and, for several centuries before the Norman Conquest, records show that a town called Esseteford was found here. Growing into a flourishing market town that served the surrounding area, Ashford developed further with the building of turnpike roads and the arrival of the railway. In 1846 the Board of Directors of the South Eastern Railway bought 185 acres of good Kentish countryside on which to lay the foundations of a 'locomotive establishment'. 72 labourers' cottages were built in 1847 and construction of the railway works began. When the old railway companies were grouped in 1923, Ashford became one of the three main works of the Southern Railway dealing with the construction, repair and maintenance of locomotives, carriages and wagons (the others were Eastleigh and Lancing). The railway still influences the town and, with the completion of the Channel Tunnel, a range of Continental European destinations can be reached in just a few hours from Ashford's **International Station**.

Two miles north of Ashford stands **Godington Park**, a Jacobean house built round a 14th century core. Among the main features are an imposing Great Hall and the Great Chamber with a frieze depicting soldiers doing Dutch pike drill. Here, too, are Chippendale furniture, a Dresden tea service, Worcester and Chelsea china and a Reynolds portrait of David Garrick.

AROUND ASHFORD

Boughton Lees
2½ miles N of Ashford on the A251

This delightful village, along with its neighbour Boughton Aluph, lies on the southern fringes of the North Downs, where the wooded hills give way to hedgerows, meadows, field and a network of narrow, twisting lanes. The long distance footpath, the **North Downs Way**, makes the descent from the higher ground at this point and passes right alongside the parish church of Boughton Aluph. A similar network of footpaths and narrow lanes leads southwards to Boughton Lees.

Challock
4½ miles N of Ashford off the A251

This pretty village high up on the Downs, centred around its wide and spacious green, is set in the dense woodlands known as **Challock Forest**. Like so many villages with its roots in the Middle Ages, Challock was built around its church in a forest clearing. However, when the Black Plague struck, the villagers moved to a new site, a mile or so from the church. Dedicated to Saints Cosmus and Damian, the church was the victim of a direct bomb hit during World War II and, now restored, it is worth visiting, not just for its location but also for the fine wall paintings added in the 1950s as part of the restoration.

Set around a medieval farmhouse, **Beech Court Gardens** provides something of interest for everyone right through the year. A riot of colour in the spring when the azaleas, vibernums and rhododendrons are in bloom, the garden has brilliant summer borders and roses while, in the autumn, there are the rich tones of the acers. Well known for its relaxing atmosphere, the garden has more than 90 named trees, woody areas and extensive lawns.

Just to the south of the village lies **Eastwell Park**, which has a public footpath running through its 3,000 acres. On the northern edge of the vast Eastwell Lake is a ruined church that reputedly houses the bones of Richard Plantagenet, son of Richard III.

Stelling Minnis
8 miles NE of Ashford off the B2068

Minnis means 'common', and on the edge of what remains of the once great Lyminge Forest, this village has an attractive rural atmosphere. On the outskirts of Stelling Minnis stands **Davison's Mill**, a smock mill built in

GREAT FIELD FARM

Misling Lane, Stelling Minnis, nr Canterbury,
Kent, CT4 6DE
Tel/Fax: 01227 709223
e-mail: greatfieldfarm@aol.com
website: www.great-field-farm.co.uk

Situated along a quiet country lane in an Area of
Outstanding Natural Beauty, **Great Field Farm** provides
the perfect base for a break from the hustle and bustle
of town life. The farmhouse is set in about 40 acres that
include pleasant south-facing gardens and paddocks
with friendly ponies. Resident owners Lewana and Malcolm Castle provide comfortable, centrally
heated Bed & Breakfast accommodation in a spacious double bedroom with en suite bathroom, with
air bath, and a private twin room in a detatched cottage next to the farmhouse with its own bathroom

and sitting room. They also offer the option of
B&B or self-catering in an annex flat with an en
suite double bedroom, sitting room and kitchen.
Hearty breakfasts include home-grown soft fruits
and eggs from the owners' own chickens.

The location is ideal for exploring some of
Kent's prettiest villages, and Canterbury and
Folkestone are both a short drive away. The
Channel Tunnel is just 10 minutes away, so the
farm is also a good stopover point on a journey
to or from the Continent

1866 that continued to grind corn
commercially until 1970. The mill
wheels were rotated by either wind or
the mill's 1912 Ruston and Hornsby oil
engine, and the museum here has
displays of some of the original mill
maintenance tools along with other
milling implements. It is unlikely that it
will ever be able to run wind-powered
again but it is still in working order.

WYE

3 miles NE of Ashford off the A28

This attractive old market town on the
North Downs has some fine Georgian
houses as well as some half-timbered
buildings in the area surrounding its 15th
century collegiate church. However, it is
not these buildings that have made the
town famous but its agricultural college -
Wye College, now affiliated to the
University of London. Occupying the
buildings of a priests' college built in 1447

by John Kempe, Archbishop of
Canterbury, the college combines
teaching with internationally respected
research into all areas of agriculture
including plants and pests, soils, animals
and agricultural economics.

BROOK

3 miles E of Ashford off the A28

A scattered village - once by the sea - in
the wooded farmland that lies beneath
the North Downs, Brook is home to an
Agricultural Museum that occupies old
farm buildings that stand on a site that
dates back to Saxon times. Beginning as a
small collection of farm implements and
tools that were in the hands of nearby
Wye College, the collection has grown
and now includes such items as ploughs,
man traps, shepherd's crooks and
domestic artefacts like butter pats and flat
irons. However, it is not just the
collection that is of interest here as two of

RICHARDSON & OTTEWILL

Evegate, Station Road, Smeeth, nr Ashford, Kent TN25 6SX
Tel: 01303 814484 Fax: 01303 814730
e-mail: enquiries@r-o.co.uk
website: www.r-o.co.uk

Justin Richardson and Steven Ottewill met at design school, and since 1993 the partnership of **Richardson & Ottewill** has built up a fine reputation in the design and manufacture of gold and silverware. In their purpose-built studio in the heart of the Kent countryside they produce award-winning designs and finished pieces, and their experience and expertise

encompass a wide variety of hollowware, flatware and jewellery. Working to the highest standards of contemporary craftsmanship, they aim to design and manufacture functional, tactile yet innovative pieces, drawing inspiration from all areas of design, using natural, flowing forms to enhance silver's reflective qualities.

They work closely with clients to produce memorable celebration and commemorative pieces, and their workshop and studio have a flexibility and range that can accommodate anything from unique one-off pieces to large-batch products in both silverware and jewellery, from a simple teaspoon to a grand centrepiece. The studio also operates as a retail outlet, and visitors can see the craftsmen at work and look at the display of the finished articles. In addition to all this, the partners undertake commissions to restore and repair antique pieces and jewellery.

THE BARN INTERIORS

Otterpool Manor, Otterpool Lane, Sellindge,
Kent TN25 6DB
Tel/Fax: 01303 813999
website: www.thebarninteriors.com

The Barn is a family business whose owners have spent years acquiring knowledge in the UK and overseas, particularly in France. The business is located in a superbly converted 18th century barn in a courtyard at the back of a farm. The barn, part redbrick, part clapboard, with a marvellous, steeply raked tiled roof, is

an atmospheric setting for showing the collection of furniture and other items that truly make a house a home.

The range runs from antique French furniture including beds, wardrobes, marble-topped wash stands, refectory tables and dressers, a lovely reclaimed pine range, rustic oak range, mirrors, lighting, ornaments, baskets and hampers - and hop bines available later in the year. Also an extensive range of wood-burning stoves, cast iron fireplaces with pine, marble or limestone surrounds with granite or tiled hearths and log baskets, firebacks many different traditional designs to choose from. There is also the courtyard with their garden section offering traditional hazel hurdles in various sizes, garden furniture, trellis, plant climbers, hanging baskets pots and tubs, barbeques, cast iron chimeneas and Braziers.

the buildings in which the displays can be seen are worthy of special note. The barn was constructed in the 1370s and its oak framework is particularly interesting, revealing the skills of the craftsmen involved in its construction. It is about 120 feet long and about 30 feet wide, with a Kent peg tile roof. The oast house, dating from 1815, is an early example of one with a round kiln - thought to give the hops more even drying - and it is possibly unique in having four fireplaces rather that just one.

Brook's **Church of St Mary** has a Norman tower with a winding staircase leading to a first-floor chapel with an altar and wall paintings.

WILLESBOROUGH
1½ miles SE of Ashford off the A20

Now almost swallowed up by the expansion of Ashford, this once rural village is home to **Willesborough Windmill**, a smock mill that dates back to 1869 and which was restored in 1991. Visitors can take a guided tour around the mill and see just what life was like for a miller at the beginning of the 20th century; the mill is also home to a collection of artefacts that relate to Ashford's industrial heritage.

SMEETH
4½ miles SE of Ashford on the A20

A charming and traditional Kentish village, where authentic country games are still played. Smeeth's name means 'a smooth clearing in the woods' and though, today, most of the woods have long since gone remains of ancient forests, such as Lyminge to the north, can still be found.

CHARING
5 miles NW of Ashford on the A20

There has been a settlement here for centuries and the earliest archaeological evidence is of Iron Age flint workings. Archaeologists suggest that there could well have been a Roman villa close by and the village's name is said to be derived from that of a local Jutish chief. In the late 8th century, Charing was given to Canterbury Cathedral by Egbert II, King of Kent. The manor remained the property of the archbishops until 1545, when Henry VIII confiscated it from Archbishop Cranmer. The little that remains of this archbishop's palace today dates from the early 14th century and many of the buildings have been incorporated into a private farm. However, when visiting the parish church of St Peter and St Paul in the village, the archbishop still robes in this ancient palace.

The village lies one day's journey from Canterbury and Charing became one of the many stopping places, in the Middle Ages, where pilgrims would seek rest, shelter and food on their pilgrimage. Just outside the gates of the manor house was a flourishing market which, due to its antiquity, never required a charter. At the top of the street there are some fine red brick houses dating mainly to the 17th and 18th century although Pierce House is 16th century with an even older building beside it, believed to be 13th century.

PLUCKLEY
5½ miles NW of Ashford off the A20

This charming little village clusters around a tidy little square and the surrounding cottages all have a curious feature - 'Dering' windows. Sir Edward Cholmeley Dering, a 19th century landowner, added these distinctive arched windows to all the houses of his estate because he thought them lucky. One of his ancestors had supposedly escaped from the Roundheads through such a window during the Civil War. He also put them into his own mansion but this appears to be where his luck ended as the great house burnt down. Pluckley featured in the successful TV series *The Darling Buds of May* and according to The Guinness Book of Records is the most haunted village in England.

DOVER

Dover Castle

This ancient town, which is often referred to as the 'Gateway to England', is Britain's major cross-Channel port. Many pass through but few stay for long, but with its long history going back to Roman times, it is well worth taking time to explore. It was the Romans who first developed Dover, basing their navy here, and right up to the present day, the town has relied on shipping and seafaring for its prosperity. It was a founder member of Edward I's Confederation of Cinque Ports, and as the old harbour silted up a new one was constructed in the 19th century. Much of the older part of Dover was destroyed by enemy bombs during the World Wars but, among the jumble of modern streets, some of the surviving ancient buildings can still be found.

Situated high on a hill above the cliff tops, and dominating the town from almost every angle, stands **Dover Castle**, dating back to 1180. Although the castle was begun by William the Conqueror, it was under Henry II that the great keep was constructed and the fortress was completed by another surrounding wall which was studded with square towers and two barbicans. Throughout its long life the castle has had an interesting

DOVER ROMAN PAINTED HOUSE

New Street, Dover, Kent CT17 9AJ
Tel: 01304 203279
e-mail: kentarchaeology@aol.com

The Roman Painted House, often dubbed Britain's buried Pompeii, dates from AD 200 and, although it was demolished in 270 by the army to make way for a fortress, it has been remarkably well-preserved. Now covered by a modern building, this excavated site reveals in excellent detail the layout of the house as well as its underfloor heating system. Originally the walls of the house were decorated with wall paintings and these have, miraculously, survived whilst the displays surrounding the excavation site not only explain the discovery of this painted house but also the development of Roman Dover.

history and one event, in particular, occurred towards the end of the reign of King John. By 1216, the barons had become increasingly frustrated with their king and they invited the heir to the French throne, Prince Louis, to invade and take over. He landed with his army at Dover and laid siege to the castle, which was at that time held by Hubert de Burgh, a baron loyal to King John. Powerful though the castle's walls were, the French managed to gain access to the outer barbican and began to undermine the gate to the inner enclosure. At this point, King John died and the barons declared their allegiance to his successor, Henry III, and Prince Louis went home empty handed.

Today, the castle has much to offer the visitor. It is home to the **Princess of Wales' Royal Regiment Museum**, and there are also the remains of a Roman lighthouse and a small Saxon church within the grounds. However, one of the most spectacular sights and, one of World War II's best kept secrets, are the **Secret Wartime Tunnels** that were cut into Dover's famous white cliffs. Now open to the public and reconstructed to provide the most realistic wartime experience possible, it was from this labyrinth of tunnels that Winston Churchill and Admiral Ramsey masterminded the evacuation of nearly 350,000 troops from the beaches of Dunkirk. Also in this maze of caves were an operating theatre and underground hospital and, as the lights dim and bombs drop overhead, the atmosphere of wartime Britain is brought back to life.

Back in the heart of Dover, in New Street, can be found another of Dover's popular attractions - the **Roman Painted House** (see panel on page 78), often dubbed Britain's buried Pompeii.

HIBAU LTD

Enterprise House, Poulton Close,
Coombe Valley Road, Dover, Kent CT17 0HL
Tel: 01304 204203 Fax: 01304 214056
e-mail: hibau@btconnect.com
website: www.hibau.co.uk

Hibau Ltd was founded in 1996 by the current owner, based on 25 years of experience in senior management within the building and associated industries. Based in modern premises in Dover, the company activities encompass panel joinery production, display equipment manufacture, shopfitting, plastic fabrication and furniture development. Quality of service, professionalism and reliability have always been the hallmarks of Hibau, regardless of the size, type or value of the project.

The methodical approach, aided by modern computer technology, enables Hibau to process enquiries and requirements efficiently, with the minimum of fuss and in the shortest time possible. All the company's employees are committed to maintaining the highest standards of workmanship and service. The factory showroom, which is available for viewing by appointment, has three separate room settings and a host of other products on show; these include the very latest products, available at special prices, some of them ready to take away.

The Shakespeare Cliff, Dover

from the time that Dover was a Roman port and fortress, along with finds from one of the most important archaeological sites in Britain, the nearby Buckland Saxon cemetery. The story of Dover as a Cinque Port, the town through both World Wars and numerous Victorian objects all add to the interesting picture of the town that the museum portrays. However, one of the newest exhibits is one of the museum's oldest. After seven years conservation, a 3,500 year old Bronze Age Boat, is now on display.

Just away from the town centre, lies **The Western Heights**, a vast area that stands on what was one of the largest and strongest fortresses in the country. There are some five miles of dry ditches and numerous gun batteries and defences. Some parts date from the late 18th and early 19th centuries, a time when England was expecting to have to defend its shores from French invasion. Other parts date only to World War II. The huge complex has been preserved to include, along with many of the defensive structures, much of the wildlife and the plants that have since colonised the site. The first buildings were erected here in the summer of 1779 and, when Napoleon posed a threat from France, further work was undertaken to strengthen and fortify the area further. The Drop Redoubt is a sunken fortress of the early 19th century that could fire guns in all directions, and St Martin's Battery saw service during World War II. The Grand Shaft is a triple spiral staircase built to allow the

An exceptionally well-preserved town house, thought to date from around AD 200, the building was used as a hotel for official travellers and the excavated remains have revealed extensive wall paintings and an elaborate under-floor heating system. Only discovered in 1970, the house, which has a Roman fort wall built through it, is covered by a modern structure that also houses a major display on Roman Dover.

The Victorian Town Hall incorporates the magnificent **Maison Dieu**, a hostel for Canterbury pilgrims that was founded in the early 13th century as well as typically grand Victorian Council Chambers and function rooms.

In the Market Square can be found the area's largest and newest museum, **Dover Museum**, which has an amazing range of items that illustrate the history of the town from prehistoric times onwards. There are artefacts

THE BATTLE OF BRITAIN MEMORIAL

Capel le Ferne, Folkestone, Kent
Tel: 01304 253286

On a spectacular clifftop position can be found the Battle of Britain Memorial that was built to commemorate those who fought and lost their lives in the summer of 1940. Taking the form of an immense three bladed propeller cut into the chalk hillside with, at its centre, the statue of a lone seated airman, this is a fitting tribute to those young men who so bravely and unselfishly served their country. The memorial was unveiled by HM Queen Elizabeth the Queen Mother in 1993 and an annual memorial day is held here on the Sunday that lies closest to 10th July, the start of the air battle.

The siting of the memorial here is particularly poignant as it was in the skies above, in the summer of 1940, that the RAF struggled to gain air supremacy over the Luftwaffe and so prevent the otherwise inevitable German invasion. The battle, that cost so many their lives, lasted until the end of October and, as well as being the last major conflict over British soil, the victory marked the turning point of World War II.

Close to the memorial, by the flagpole that originally stood at RAF Biggin Hill, is a memorial wall on which Winston Churchill's immortal words, "Never in the field of human conflict was so much owed by so many to so few", are carved. At the adjacent visitors' centre visitors can purchase a range of souvenirs and it should be remembered that this memorial and the site on which it stands relies on public donation for its maintenance. Open daily from 1st April to 30th Spetember, 11am - 5pm.

soldiers to descend quickly from the Heights to the harbour.

One final place of interest, particularly to those who remember World War II, is the **Women's Land Army Museum**, which pays tribute to the women who served their country by working on the land. Among the numerous exhibits on display are personal letters, uniforms and a wealth of factual information.

AROUND DOVER

CAPEL LE FERNE

5 miles SW of Dover off the B2011

This village, close to the cliffs between Folkestone and Dover, is home to the **Battle of Britain Memorial** (see panel opposite) that commemorates the fierce 1940 air battle that took place in the skies overhead.

HAWKINGE

6 miles SW of Dover on the A260

Close to the village, at Hawkinge Airfield, can be found the **Kent Battle of Britain Museum** that is the home of the country's largest collection of 1940 related artefacts on display to the public. Along with the full size replicas of the planes that played such a part in the battle - a Hurricane, Spitfire and Messerschmitt have been painstakingly rebuilt from as many original parts as possible - the museum houses an important collection of both British and German flying equipment of that era. Many of the items on display have been recovered from aircraft that were shot down, and there are also weapons, vehicles and exhibits relating to the home front.

ALKHAM

4 miles W of Dover off the A20

Plans to turn this charming village in the steep Alkham Valley into a large residential area for miners working in the expanding East Kent coalfield never came to fruition, and the village remains much as it has done for centuries. A good place from which to begin a walk in the pleasant countryside around this coastal chalk downland, Alkham is also a pleasant place to stroll around as it has retained its Norman church, 18th century redbrick rectory, ancient houses and, perhaps most importantly, its old coaching inn.

SWINGFIELD

6½ miles W of Dover on the A260

At **MacFarlanes Butterfly and Garden Centre** visitors can walk around the tropical green houses, which not only contain exotic plants but also many varieties of colourful butterflies from all over the world that are allowed to fly freely. The life cycle of the butterfly, from the courtship displays, through the egg and caterpillar stages, to the chrysalis and finally the butterfly, are explained and can be observed at close quarters. Exotic plants on which the butterflies live - such as bougainvillaea, banana and oleander - can also be studied.

ELHAM

9 miles W of Dover off the A260

This relatively unspoilt village, whose name is pronounced 'Eelham', is the starting point for a number of footpaths that lead through the Elham Valley.

During World War II, the now disused railway line through the village carried an 18-inch 'Boche Buster' gun, actually of World War I vintage, that fired shells seven feet long.

RIVER

1 mile NW of Dover on the A2

Almost a suburb of Dover, this village stands on the banks of a river that has, over the centuries, powered several mills as it meanders its way out to sea. Of those fine old mills **Crabble Corn Mill** survives and this beautiful Georgian mill still works on a regular basis. Visitors can join the guided tour of the windmill and see the unique set of automatic 19th century flour mills. Just to the southwest of the village of River lie the ruins of **St Radigunds Abbey** founded by French monks in the 12th century.

WHITFIELD

2 miles NW of Dover on the A2

For centuries this village has stood at an important crossroads where the routes to Canterbury, Dover and Sandwich met and it was also the site of several manor houses. One of the ancient lords of the manor had a particularly unusual service in that it was his duty to hold the king's head whenever he made a Channel crossing and support him through any seasickness to which he might succumb. This village, practically a suburb of Dover, is home to the **Dover Transport Museum**, where a whole range of vehicles, from bicycles to buses, can be seen along with model railways and tramways. Offering a history of the local transport, the museum also includes exhibits on the East Kent coalfield and the area's maritime heritage.

TEMPLE EWELL
2½ miles NW of Dover off the A2

This ancient village, in the valley of the River Dour, was mentioned in a charter as long ago as 772 and for centuries it came under the control of successive religious orders: first the Knights Templar and then the Knights of the Order of St John of Jerusalem. As with the village of River, further down the River Dour, there were two mills in the valley here that were driven by the Dour's waters.

WOOTTON
6½ miles NW of Dover off the A260

This village was the home of Thomas Digges, the inventor of the early telescope who, during the reign of Elizabeth I, was the builder of the original harbour complex at Dover, now incorporated into the Western Docks. Unfortunately, nothing remains of the manor house, demolished in 1952, that was Digges's home.

DENTON
7 miles NW of Dover on the A260

This charming village has a green surrounded by pretty half-timbered cottages. Next to the small 13th century church of St Mary Magdalene, nestling among ancient trees, can be found **Denton Court**, where the poet Thomas Gray was a frequent visitor. Close by are two other interesting, historic houses.

BABYLON TERRACOTTA & BABYLON HORTICULTURE

Shoats Barn, Shelvin Farm, Shelvin,
Canterbury, Kent CT4 6RL
Tel: 01303 844008 Fax: 01303 844001
e-mail: babylon@ukeuro.com

Babylon Terracotta operates from a beautiful family-run farm situated in a lovely Kent valley with easy access from the A2 or A260. The stock includes a vast range of terracotta pots and bowls in all shapes and sizes, colours and finishes, brought together from sources all around the world and displayed in a fine old

granary carefully converted to retain a good deal of period appeal.

In this really delightful part of the world Rupert James and Joe also offer a service for landscape design and construction, covering anything from small gardens to large estates. Their expertise covers traditional English, Japanese and many other styles. Babylon is open on weekdays, also on weekends by prior arrangement. In season, Babylon runs two pick your own strawberry sites locally.

Broome Park, dating from 1635 and designed by Inigo Jones, was at one time the home of Field Marshal Lord Kitchener, the World War I military leader. The other house, **Tappington Hall**, was built by Thomas Marsh in about 1628. Richard Barham wrote many of his *Ingoldsby Legends* here, featuring the Ingoldsby family of Tappington-Everard. The hall is associated with several ghost stories. One suggests that it is haunted by a Royalist killed during the Civil War by his brother, who was fighting for the Parliamentarian cause.

BARHAM

8½ miles NW of Dover off the A2

The village is set in a delightful river valley near the point where the woodlands of the North Downs give way to the flatter agricultural lands. This area was first mentioned in the Arthurian legends as being the site of a great battle and the land around the village was used as a military camp in the early 19th century when an invasion by Napoleon was feared.

WOODLANDS AND MARSHES

This southernmost area of Kent is characterised by two diverse landscapes, the woodland, or once wooded, area around Tenterden and the marshlands of Romney and Welland. Often dubbed the 'Jewel in the Weald', Tenterden lies on the eastern border of the Weald and this place, like other villages and towns close by, has the suffix '-den' that indicates a former setting in a woodland clearing. Developed on the wealth of the woollen trade in the Middle Ages and then becoming a key market place for the area, Tenterden has a pleasing mix of old buildings and is an excellent place to begin a tour of southern Kent. Around it

ELMSTONE

Out Elmstead Lane, Barham, nr Canterbury, Kent CT4 6PH
Tel: 01227 832091 Fax: 01227 832403
e-mail: info@elmstonecourt.com
website: www.elmstonecourt.com

Madeleine and Philip Edwards provide the very best in accommodation at their handsome country house set in the beautiful Elham Valley. At **Elmstone**, tucked away down a country lane, they offer the perfect country retreat, an ideal spot for a relaxing break, combining the delights of a quiet rural setting with easy access to the main A2 and the historic city of Canterbury. The elegantly appointed guest bedrooms range from the muted cream colour scheme of the Minimalist Room to the rich, spicy warmth of the Indian Room.

Each has its own very distinctive appeal, but all are equally comfortable and well-appointed, with en suite shower room, TV, tea/coffee making facilities and connection points for computers. Madeleine is an accomplished cook, and her meals make excellent use of Kent's abundant produce – fruit and vegetables from the 'Garden of England' and the riches of the sea landed at Whitstable. Country pursuits, including golf, riding, fishing, hot-air ballooning, guided walks and painting, can all be arranged locally, and Elmstone Court is available to host meetings and small private occasions for up to 50 guests.

are numerous charming villages including the delightful Biddenden, where lived and died the Biddenden Maids, 12th century Siamese twins. Bethersden has become best known for its marble - a fossil encrusted stone - that has been used in the building work of Kent's two cathedrals and numerous parish churches. At the southern edge of the marshland lies Folkestone, which developed after the arrival of the railways from a little known fishing village into an important ferry port and fashionable seaside resort. To the south are the delightful former ports of Hythe, Dymchurch and New Romney that were linked in the 1920s by the charming Romney, Hythe and Dymchurch light railway. Finally, there are the remote and isolated marshes, once the haunt of smugglers, today an area of rich farmland and home of the hardy Romney sheep.

TENTERDEN

Often referred to as the 'Jewel of the Weald', despite being situated right on the border between the dense woodlands of the Weald and the flatter farmland that leads eastwards to Romney Marsh, Tenterden is a charming town of considerable age. Today's well-earned nickname is, however, a far cry from its earliest days when it was known as 'Tenet-ware-den' or 'pig pasture of Thanet'. Although pigs certainly did flourish here and in the surrounding area, sheep became more profitable. The town developed quickly as the wool trade grew. In 1331, the far-sighted Edward III prohibited the export of unwashed wool and encouraged weavers from Flanders to settle here and bring their dyeing and weaving techniques to England. The town prospered and became one of the most important

MONYX

15/17 Sayers Lane, Tenterden, Kent TN30 6BW
Tel: 01580 763024

Monyx is a beautifully appointed ladies' clothes shop in a smart shopping precinct in the heart of Tenterden. Owner Lyn Qizilbash has worked really hard to build up her little group of shops in Kent, and everything sold in the shops is personally chosen by her. The stock includes clothes for all ages and all occasions, from beach to ballroom. Clothes for special occasions such as weddings and Royal Ascot, shoes, bags and all the accessories along with hats and fascinators that can be hired. Shoes are eye-catchingly displayed on artistically sculpted iron trees.

Other outlets are at:

Monyx, Foremans Walk, High Street, Headcorn, Kent TN27 9NE, Tel: 01622 892444

The Shoe Tree, 15 High Street, Headcorn, Kent, TN27 9NH, Tel: 01622 891065

Evegate, Station Road, Smeeth, nr Ashford, Kent TN25 6SX, Tel: 01303 814907

THE WHISTLE STOP RESTAURANT

2 Coombe Lane, Tenterden,
Kent TN30 6HD
Tel: 01580 765450

Exploring the sights of Tenterden can be guaranteed to work up an appetite, and the **Whistle Stop Restaurant** is just the place to satisfy a visitor's hunger. It's long been a favourite with the local residents, and owner Annie Oliver Wanstall, a gifted chef with 30 years experience and an abundance of enthusiasm, makes a point of using only the very best ingredients in her dishes.

Her prettily appointed licensed restaurant, with neatly laid tables, flowers, pictures, prints and decorative plates, is open from 10am to 5pm every day except Sunday (also open by arrangement on some evenings), and most of what's on the menu is available all day. Baguettes with generous and interesting fillings make tasty, satisfying snacks; the daily roast and daily specials such as salmon and prawn mornay are always in demand; lunchtime offers a two-course set meal as well as à la carte; the superb selection of home made desserts is definitely not to be missed. And experts in the field of cream teas will tell you that Annie's cream teas are the best in Kent!

The Whistle Stop also sells a selection of cards, cushions, jugs, mugs, cards and photos and little gifts as well as delicious home made chutneys and biscuits. Booking is recommended, particularly in high season, and when the weather is fine the tables set out at the front are always in demand.

Some people visit Tenterden, sometimes called 'The Jewel of the Weald', to admire the view of countryside and coast from the tower of the Church of St Mildred; some to learn about life in the old days at the Museum; others to take a nostalgic ride on the Kent and East Sussex Railway. But for those who know good food when they taste it, the Whistle Stop is an essential stop on a visit to this charming place.

Kent and East Sussex Railway

began to decline. There are still buildings in the town built with the profits of the wool trade, along with elegant 18th century houses constructed during Tenterden's days as an agricultural market place serving the surrounding towns and villages.

The **Church of St Mildred**, in the heart of Tenterden, dates from 1180 and its most interesting feature is its unusual twin doors at the western end. From the top of its 15th century tower - some 125 feet above the town - there are panoramic views out across the Weald and to the Channel coast. Another place of prayer, a Unitarian chapel, built in 1695, is particularly interesting as this

centres for the manufacture of broadcloth during the Middle Ages. However, in the 16th century, the fortunes of the clothiers were altered by an act of Parliament and the wool trade

TRUFFLES @. COCO

128 High Street, Tenterden, Kent TN30 6HT
Tel: 01580 763501

Window shopping along Tenterden's charming old High Street is a delightful experience that definitely should not to be rushed. There's something out of the ordinary all the way along, but

perhaps the shop that's most difficult to walk past is **Truffles @. Coco**. Kevin Bryant, Artisan Chocolatier and master of his craft, set up in this lovely old weather-boarded shop in 2002, after a long spell supplying truffles and other chocolates to private clients in the restaurant and pub worlds. He makes his truffles from only the very best and purest of ingredients, with no preservatives or chemicals, and his clientele now reaches across the world.

There's plenty to tempt besides the truffles, including sugared almonds, chocolate coffee beans and crystallised stem ginger. Self-indulgence is the very best reason for a purchase, and any lingering feelings of guilt disappear with the first bite into one of Kevin's creations. His masterpieces are also available to order, and it's hard to imagine a gift more special and more certain to delight than a beautifully wrapped selection of his truffles.

TUSSIE MUSSIES

The Old Stables, 2b East Cross, High Street,
Tenterden, Kent TN30 6AD
Tel: 01580 766224
e-mail: tussiemussies@btinternet.com

Owner Christina Exall offers a warm and friendly welcome at **Tussie Mussies**, a delightful little shop situated down a quiet alley just off Tenterden's High Street. A lot is packed into a little at this Aladdin's Cave, including dried and silk flowers, glass and pottery, local crafts, candles, militaria, antiques and brocante collectables, painted furniture and aromatherapy toiletries. Among the many gift ideas are the exclusive, limited edition hand made collectors' bears from Hyefolk.

The hand made silk Tussie Mussies revive the Victorian tradition of sending messages through posies. Each flower has a meaning and your sentiment is expressed on the attatched card. The complete Wedding Service includes bouquets and corsages which are made to individual requirements and an extensive range of tiaras, handmade jewellery, favours and accessories. To have your wedding party or event dressed in style for the occasion by Christina, choose the hire service for candelabras, table arrangements, wedding arch, cake decorations, flower garlands for tables, walls and staircases.

SANDPIPERS

3 and 6 Sayers Lane, Tenterden,
Kent TN30 6BW
Tel: 01580 763413
e-mail: sandpipers@btconnect.com

Two shops in Tenterden's smart modern shopping precinct provide the very best in ladies' wear and quality gifts. **Sandpipers** at No.3 is stocked with clothes for the discerning lady, including luscious linens by Oska; casual wear from Oui; In Town and Sandwich; hats

to buy or hire; wedding outfits by Libra; and beautiful jewellery by Manouk.

At No.6 there are more clothes, as well as practical items for the house and lots of gift ideas: leather goods, pens, ties, key rings, hip flasks, small silver items, christening gifts, an exquisite range of pottery and glass, artificial flowers, Crabtree & Evelyn, photo frames, candle holders, games to amuse and entertain. Tenterden is well-endowed with interesting, well-run shops, but few provide better browsing opportunities than Maureen Pemble's brace of Sandpipers – perfect places for buying something special in ladies wear or for choosing a special gift for any occasion.

is where, in 1783, Dr Benjamin Franklin, the American statesman, philosopher and scientist, worshipped. As an apprentice typesetter in his brother's newspaper, Franklin came to England to work in a British printing office for 18 months before returning home to set up his own newspaper. Later, and then acting as an agent for several American provinces, he moved back to England for 18 years when also, as a result of his experiments with electricity and his invention of the lightning conductor, he was elected a Fellow of the Royal Society.

For a real insight into the history of the town and the local area a visit to the **Tenterden and District Museum** is well worth while. The displays here cover over 1,000 years of history and they relate to hop-picking, farming, the area of the Weald, the Cinque Ports and

EATON & JONES

120 High Street, Tenterden, Kent TN30 6HT
Tel/Fax: 01580 763357
e-mail: eatonjones@firenet.uk.net

In their 250-year-old weatherboarded premises at the leafy 'West End' of town, Karen and John Eaton work together as consultant designers and goldsmiths. As **Eaton & Jones** they make precious and semi-precious pieces of individual and beautiful designs, many inspired by the Art Nouveau Movement. Curved and linear creations house popular and less known gems, creating a very handsome range of

sumptuous jewellery.

Each pane of the shop's Georgian-style bow window displays its own array of treasures. The display room inside is informal and friendly, with no counter creating a barrier between customer and jeweller. Karen and John offer the usual services, including commissions to customers individual requirements, renovation, re-designing, repairs and restringing. In a beautiful town often referred to as 'The Jewel in the Weald', Eaton & Jones is an undoubted gem.

TOWER HOUSE BED & BREAKFAST

Ashford Road, Tenterden, Kent TN30 6LL
Tel: 01580 761920
e-mail: pippa@towerhouse.biz website: www.towerhouse.biz

Mike and Pippa Carter offer guests a warm welcome at their pretty Georgian town house with a distinctive landmark tower, just a minute's walk from the amenities and sights of Tenterden. The romantic, tastefully decorated double bedrooms have en suite or private shower, TV and tea/coffee facilities, and the day starts with a delicious Aga-cooked breakfast served in the sunny Georgian dining room. The house has a delightful walled garden with mulberry, walnut and peach trees and an old greenhouse with a vine.

TENTERDEN HOUSE INTERIORS

4 WEST CROSS, TENTERDEN, KENT TN30 6JL
Tel: 01580 764481 Fax: 01580 765531

- In Tenterden since 1984, but the original family business of cabinet making was established in Bedfordshire in 1826.

- Specialising in hand made fine quality Traditional English Oak and Cherry furniture, with over 200 items available from stock.

- A custom made service is readily available in a variety of qualities, hardwoods and prices.

- A wide range of sofas and chairs, mirrors, tapestries, table lamps, Smithbrook lighting and many decorative furnishings and fabrics.

- Large selection of gifts including occasional furniture, bronzes, prints and oil paintings, Royal Copenhagen, Limoges and Mangani porcelain, Isle of Wight glass, Italian majolica and William Yeoward glass, together with a very large range of pewter based on classical European designs.

- Situated in a three-storey building at the far west end of High Street. Open 9am–5.30pm except Wednesdays and Sundays.

- Free and immediate delivery to the UK mainland

CELLINI & CELLINI KIDZ

Sayers Square, Tenterden, Kent TN30 6BW
Cellini Tel: 01580 763036 Cellini Kidz Tel: 01580 766823

2004 sees the 21st birthday of **Cellini**, an elegant shop specialising in ladies' shoes. The shop is located in a smart shopping square in the heart of town, and owners Giuseppina Moore and Maria Dyer personally source and select the stock. Most of the shoes are made in factories in Florence, Venice and elsewhere in Italy, and style and quality are paramount. The range covers everything from smart casual to formal, and in addition to the shoes Cellini stocks a full range of matching accessories, including gloves, belts and bags – even umbrellas and brief cases.

At the nearby younger sibling establishment **Cellini Kidz** the

speciality is clothes and shoes for children from birth to ten years. Shoes by Startrite and continental manufacturers cover a wide range of style and colours, and there are expert fitters on hand to ensure the right size is selected. Absorba, Babar, Alphabet, Mayoral and Girandola are among the famous names represented among the stock, and besides the stock for everyday wear Cellini Kidz has a range of christening gowns and clothes for exceptionally tiny babies. Here, too, are lots of toys, both traditional and modern, rag dolls, cuddly animals, books, games and puzzles.

MIA HOME

No. 13 Sayers Square, Sayers Lane,
Tenterden, Kent TN30 6BW
Tel: 01580 766769   Fax: 01303 813900

Jenny Clifton-Holt has put her honours degree in Design Craft
to excellent use in **Mia Home**, a shop stocked with a selection
of beautiful, unusual items for the home and garden. In a square
of exclusive and interesting shops, Mia Home is neat, bright and
attractive, with soft pastels and heavenly smells assisting the
calm, relaxed ambience. Among the wide variety of products sold are items for the table, the kitchen,
the bathroom and the garden, glassware, aprons, napkins, candles, cards and notebooks.

FORREST

5 Sayers Square, Tenterden, Kent TN30 6BW
Tel/Fax: 01580 762536

Interior designer Philippa Forrest keeps a carefully chosen stock of
contemporary womenswear and accessories in the shop that carries
her name. The designers featured at **Forrest** include familiar names
and also some smaller English and Irish designers. Among those
whose clothes are displayed are Farhi, Marilyn Moore, Anonymous,
Orla Kiely, John Smedley, Birkenstock, Lora Rose, Miss Budd and
Anya Hindmarch. The stock changes constantly, and customers can be sure of a warm welcome and
helpful, personal service.

Victorian domestic life. Lying close to
the town's steam railway, the museum is
housed in an interesting 19th century
weatherboarded building that was
originally a coach house and stables.
Comprising six rooms, on two floors, the
museum's collections are extensive and
diverse, including exhibits ranging from
a 1500BC flint axe head to a recreation
of a typical Victorian kitchen.

Tenterden is also the home of the

Kent and East Sussex Railway that
runs between the town and Northiam
just over the county border in East
Sussex. When the railway opened in
1900 it was the first full size light
railway in the world. Passengers today
can journey in beautifully restored
carriages dating from Victorian times
up until the 1960s, pulled by one of
the railway's dozen steam locomotives,
travelling through glorious, unspoilt

SILCOCKS FARM SHOP

Grange Road, St Michaels, nr Tenterden, Kent TN30 6TL
Tel: 01580 763351
e-mail: orders@honournaturalfoods.com
web: www.honournaturalfoods.co.uk

On a 600-acre farm just off the A28 north of Tenterden, **Silcocks
Farm Shop** is known for the quality of its home-raised organic
meat and dairy products. Traditional Hereford cattle, Dorset and
Romney lamb, and Gloucester Old Spot pigs are grazed on pastures with no artificial fertilisers, pesticides
or herbicides, and the meat can be supplied fresh in vacuum packs or frozen. Also on sale in the shop
is their organic milk, cream, and the superb soft, creamy Boresisle cheese. The shop is open Thursday
to Saturday mornings or by appointment.

LONDON BEACH COUNTRY HOTEL & GOLF CLUB

Ashford Road, St Michaels, nr Tenterden,
Kent TN30 6SP
Tel: 01580 766279 Fax: 01580 763884
e-mail: enquiries@londonbeach.com
website: www.londonbeach.net

London Beach Country Hotel & Golf Club
is situated in the Kent countryside just two
minutes' drive from Tenterden, 20 minutes
from Ashford International Station and 40
minutes from the Channel ports. The hotel
was designed for both business and pleasure,
combining state of the art features with
elegance and comfort; its amenities are
among the best in the area, and apart from
being an ideal base for tourists or business people, it's a popular venue for parties, special occasions,
functions or meetings for up to 200 people.

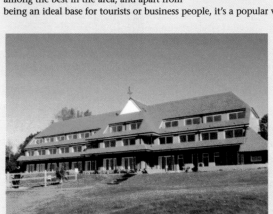

The 24 en suite bedrooms are notable for their space, comfort and facilities, which include telephones with internet access, TV, trouser press, hairdryer and tea/coffee trays. Several of the rooms are large enough for families, and the bridal suite has a romantic four-poster bed; all the rooms have balconies with stunning views over the parkland golf course that is one of the hotel's chief assets. The greens meet US PGA standards, and the facility also includes a driving range and a golf shop.

The elegantly appointed London Beach Brasserie offers a wide variety of dishes to suit all tastes and appetites, and the delicious food is enhanced by fine wines and friendly, professional service. For a more informal meal, Spikes Bar is open from 7am to 9pm and also offers a wide range of food, from a full English breakfast to snacks and full meals. The terrace is a perfect place to relax with a drink or a meal and is also a delightful setting for outside entertainment, buffets and barbecues.

The largest of the hotel's conference rooms is the Long Room, with a capacity of 200; versatility is the keynote, as the room can be subdivided into three smaller rooms – the Botham, Gower and Willis rooms, each with large French doors opening on to a balcony overlooking the golf course. The hotel is licensed to conduct civil weddings, and can provide everything needed to ensure a memorable day. Fishing is available locally, and there is a trout farm within walking distance.

countryside, that will be familiar to anyone who saw the television series *The Darling Buds of May*. Adjacent to the station at Tenterden is the **Colonel Stephens' Railway Museum** where the fascinating story of the Colonel, who built and ran this railway along with several other independent lines, is told.

AROUND TENTERDEN

SMARDEN

5½ miles N of Tenterden off the A262

This ancient Wealden market town's name comes from a Saxon word meaning 'butter valley and pasture' and this charming place has managed to keep its original character along with some beautiful old half-timbered cottages and houses set along the single main street. A centre for the cloth industry in the Middle Ages, the village's 14th century church has become known as the 'Barn of Kent' because of its huge roof.

BETHERSDEN

5 miles NE of Tenterden on the A28

This small village has long been associated with its 'marble' that was quarried in medieval times and used in many of Kent's churches and its two cathedrals. Calling the stone 'marble' is a little misleading as it is actually a type of fossil encrusted stone. Although the village is situated on the main Tenterden to Ashford road and had an abundance of local building materials, Bethersden was considered, in the 18th century, to have some of the worst roads in the County.

POTTERS FARM

Bethersden, nr Ashford, Kent TN26 3JX
Tel: 01233 820341 Fax: 01233 820469
e-mail: pottersfarms@aol.com

Peace and quiet are in plentiful supply at **Potters Farm**, where two twin-bedded rooms in a modern annexe by the main residence provide warm, well-appointed Bed & Breakfast accommodation. The farm is close to many of the prime tourist attractions in Kent as well as the main transport links (the A28 is just a couple of minutes away), the sea ports and the Channel Tunnel. Potters Farm covers 65 acres, all of which is pasture or woodland. Owner Lynne Anderson keeps sheep, horses, ducks, geese and chickens, and stables and paddocks are available for guests who want to bring their own horses.

THE OLD SAWMILLS FURNITURE COMPANY LTD

Colt Works, Units 4 & 5, The Old Sawmills, Pluckley Road, Bethersden, nr Ashford, Kent TN26 3DD
Tel: 01233 822417 e-mail: mick@oldsawmills.com
website: www.oldsawmills.com

Kevin Clark and Michael O'Brien are partners in **The Old Sawmills Furniture Company Ltd**, which specialises in the production of first-class pieces of traditionally styled, custom-made furniture. In their workshop and showroom in the heart of Kent they pass on their expertise direct to the public through an impressive range of top-quality items, from chairs, tables, wardrobes, bookcases, chests and filing cabinets right down to TV cabinets and racks for CDs.

WOODCHURCH

4 miles E of Tenterden off the B2067

In the heart of this large village lies the green around which are grouped several charming typically Kentish houses - including one dating back to Tudor times and others from the Georgian period. It was on this green, in 1826, that a battle took place between a smuggling gang and the Dragoons. The gang members were caught, tried, sentenced and then transported to Australia.

One of the fine buildings to be found here is **Woodchurch Windmill**, an impressive white smock mill that was constructed in 1820. Fully renovated and with its original machinery restored to full working order, the mill also houses a display of photographs that tell of its history and illustrate the restoration work. From the mill there are spectacular views over the marshes to the Channel coast. It is open to the public on a limited basis.

Also found at Woodchurch is the **South of England Rare Breeds Centre** that, as its name might suggest, is home to a large collection of rare British farm breeds, such as the Lincoln Longwool sheep that date back to Roman times and the Bagot goat that was brought to Britain by the Crusaders. Young visitors can meet many of the centre's animals in the Children's Barn and there are trailer rides and woodland walks to enjoy.

SMALL HYTHE

2 miles S of Tenterden on the B2082

Hard though it might be to imagine today, this little hamlet was once a flourishing port and shipbuilding centre. In the Middle Ages, the River Rother flowed past Small Hythe and it was wide enough and deep enough to accommodate the ships of those days. One of Henry VIII's warships was built

here. Today, there is little trace of this village's past life or, indeed, of the river as, even in the wettest weather, it is little more than a tiny stream. One clue, however, to those long ago days lies in the name of the Small Hythe bus stop, called The Ferry.

Close to the village lies **Smallhythe Place**, a charming 16th century half-timbered house, best known for being the home of the famous Shakespearean actress Ellen Terry, between 1899 and 1928. The house, now in the ownership of the National Trust, contains many of her personal items, including some of her stage costumes and numerous artefacts relating to other great thespians. The house retains many of its original features and, outside, there is a delightful cottage garden and an Elizabethan barn that was adapted into a theatre in the late 1920s.

Small Hythe is also the home of **Tenterden Vineyard** (see panel opposite) where visitors can walk around the growing vines, tour the herb garden and take in the rural museum.

APPLEDORE

6 miles SE of Tenterden on the B2080

Appledore was originally a port on the estuary of the River Rother. A violent storm in the 13th century changed the course of the river and the resultant silting has left Appledore some eight miles from the sea. However, this did not prevent French raiders, in 1380, arriving here and setting fire to the village's 13th century church. The **Royal Military Canal**, built in 1806 as a defence against Napoleon, passes through the village. Encircling Romney Marsh, the canal's sweeping bends meant that the whole length of the waterway could be protected by cannon fire and it was designed as a means of quickly flooding the marshland in the event of

TENTERDEN VINEYARD

Small Hythe, Tenterden, Kent TN30 7NG
Tel: 01580 763033 Fax: 01580 765333
e-mail: tourism@englishwinesgroup.com
website: www.englishwinesgroup.com

Tenterden Vineyard, the home of English Wines Group plc, is a great place to taste, enjoy and learn about superb English wines. English Wines Group produces quality red, rosé, and white wines under the 'Curious Grape' brand and fantastic sparkling wines made in the traditional method under the 'Chapel Down' brand which are made by Owen Elias (UK Winemaker of the Year 2002 and 2003) and his winemaking team. The grapes grown at the vineyard include varieties such as Bacchus, Schönburger and Pinot Noir.

Visitors to the vineyard during the summer months can join a guided tour. On the tour visitors are escorted around the vineyards and winery where the company has invested in equipment enabling

them to employ 'Old World' and 'New World' techniques to get the best from the more unusual grape varieties we grow in England. All tours include a wine tasting.

In the Wine and Food Shop all the wines produced at the Vineyard are available for tasting plus wine accessories and gifts, and a selection of fine local foods. The Grapevine Bistro serves great food prepared from the finest local ingredients served inside, or out on the sun terrace. Children can play in the Adventure Play Area or the whole family can walk the vineyard trails around the 25 acres of vines.

the expected invasion. However, by the time that the canal had been completed, in 1807, the threat of invasion had ended but, during World War II, when it seemed likely that Hitler would try to land his forces on English soil, pillboxes were built along the length of the canal. Now there is a public footpath along the full length of the canal with interpretation panels detailing its history. The canal also provides a wonderful habitat for a variety of wildlife including dragonflies and marsh frogs.

WITTERSHAM
4 miles S of Tenterden on the B2082

Situated high above the Rother Levels, some 200 feet above sea level, and right in the middle of the Isle of Oxney, Wittersham has been given the affectionate title of the 'Capital of the Isle' despite being not significantly

larger, or more important, than many of the area's other villages. The skeleton of a prehistoric iguanadon was uncovered here and, more recently, Wittersham was a mooring site for airships during World War I. Nearby lies **Stocks Mill**, the tallest post mill in Kent, erected on this site in 1781 and restored by the County Council in 1980.

BIDDENDEN
4 miles NW of Tenterden on the A262

Well recognised as one of the finest villages in the Weald of Kent, Biddenden has an attractive main street, lined with charming half-timbered houses. Ranging from medieval times through to the 17th century, there are many fine examples of period architecture and also some interesting old weaver's houses - situated on the south side of the street to make the most of the available light - that date back to the time when this was a centre of the cloth trade. Now converted into shops, above the door of one of these old houses is a carved wooden head that is said to have come from a Spanish ship, wrecked during the Armada.

At the western end of the main street stands **All Saints' Church**, founded by the Saxons but the oldest parts remaining, such as the nave, chancel and south aisle, date from the 13th century. The tower, which was funded by the thriving cloth trade, was erected in 1400 and it is made from Bethersden marble.

All Saints Church, Biddenden

Although this is undoubtedly a delightful place to visit with some fine buildings to see it is the **Biddenden Maids** that arouse most visitors' curiosity. Said to have been born in Biddenden in 1100, Eliza and Mary Chulkhurst were Siamese twins

HENDEN HALL

Biddenden, nr Ashford, Kent TN27 8BB
Tel: 01580 291955 Fax: 01580 291426

Staying in a lovely home in a lovely village is always a delightful experience, and guests at **Henden Hall** are certain to leave with happy memories. The oldest parts of Georgina Scott's handsome redbrick house date back to the 17th century, and the tall chimneys at each end are a very distinctive feature. The large entrance hallway sets the tone for the interior, where original oak beams are a feature in many of the

rooms. A splendid log fire keeps things cosy in the oak-panelled sitting room/breakfast room, and the traditionally appointed bedrooms offer peace, comfort and views over the garden.

The grounds of the hall are one of its many attractions, and when the sun shines it's extremely pleasant to sit by the pond, which is surrounded by trees and plants of all shapes and sizes and myriad shades of green. Biddenden itself is one of the finest villages in the Weald of Kent, with some charming half-timbered houses and a church founded by the Saxons.

who, despite being joined at both the hip and shoulders, lived to be 34. Local legend has it that when one of the sisters died the other refused to be separated from her twin, saying, "As we came together we will also go together", and she died some six hours later. The twins bequeathed some land for the poor and needy of Biddenden that is still generating money today. Cakes bearing the womens' images are given to strangers in the village each Easter and a quantity of loaves and cheese, known as **Biddenden Dole** are distributed to the poor of the parish.

HEADCORN

7½ miles NW of Tenterden on the A274

This is another of the charming and ancient Wealden villages, scattered over this area of the county and, as with many of its neighbours, Headcorn was a thriving centre of cloth manufacturing. Evidence of this wealth remains in the many fine buildings to be seen here, including **Shakespeare House** and **The Chequers**, both excellent examples of Elizabethan timbered buildings. Beyond the large 14th century church, constructed of local Bethersden marble, lies **Headcorn Manor**, a magnificent Wealden house that has changed little since it was erected some 500 years ago. Despite all this antiquity, Headcorn is also a modern village and it provides shopping facilities for the smaller surrounding communities.

Just to the south of the village, at **Lashenden**, is the **Lashenden Air Warfare Museum** that commemorates the role played by this area of Kent during World War II and the Battle of Britain in particular. On display are numerous wartime exhibits, from both Britain and Germany, including a V1 flying bomb, ration books and many photographs.

FOLKESTONE

A port and small fishing village since Saxon times, it was the arrival of the South Eastern railway in 1842 that transformed Folkestone into the elegant resort that it is today. Within a year of the first passenger train service running, passenger ships had started to ferry passengers across the English Channel to Boulogne; the journey time from London to Paris was just 12 hours. Much of the town dates from the Victorian age, while the wide avenues and formal gardens remain a legacy of the elegant Edwardian era. What is most unusual about this particular seaside resort, however, is that it does not have a recognisable seafront but, instead, it has **The Leas**, a wide and sweeping promenade with a series of delightful cliff top lawns and flower gardens, with a distinctly Mediterranean feel. The name comes from a Kent dialect word meaning an open space. The **Leas Cliff Lift**, the oldest water-balanced lift in the country, carries people from the clifftops to the beach below.

Throughout all this development in the late 19th and early 20th century Folkestone has managed to retain its original ancient fishing village, concentrated in an area known as **The Lanterns**. One of the oldest buildings in the town is the **Church of St Mary and St Eanswythe** that dates back to the 13th century. St Eanswythe was a Kent princess who founded a nunnery in what is now Folkestone in the 7th century and her bones are buried here. The church also remembers the town's most famous son, William Harvey, in its west window. Born in 1578 in Church Street, a part of the town that was home to traders of cloth and silk, Harvey was a physician to both James I and Charles I but he is best remembered for his discovery of the

DAVID M LANCEFIELD

53 Sandgate High Street, Sandgate, Folkstone, Kent, CT20 3AH
Tel/Fax: 01303 850149
e-mail: David@antiquedirect.freeserve.co.uk
website: www.davidmlancefield.co.uk

David Lancefield specialises in genuine antiques and interior design. With a constantly changing stock there is every reason to become a regular visitor. David has been supplying the American and continental European trade for a quarter century. His dedicated team of suppliers and decorators are based in this Kentish seaside town renowned for its choice selection of antique and fine art establishments. The shop's traditional, bow windowed frontage looks small from the outside, but it opens into a series of interconnected rooms spreading over two floors. The place is full of furniture, silver and metalware, ceramics, bronzes, ivory, clocks, watches, jewellery, paintings, prints and all manner of objets d'art.

On any visit you might discover a handsome rosewood table, perhaps with a set of balloon back chairs, a mahogany Georgian chest of drawers or a Victorian desk and display cabinet. The tables are set with an exquisite collection of dinner services, cutlery, glasses and decanters - to re-create an historic dining room. There is also a fine selection of skilfully made classic reproductions. Regency

inspired sabre leg chairs are available in a range of colour combinations in either carver style or as side chairs. They can be covered with a choice of fabrics or with that supplied by the client. The warmth and luxury of the Roman Baths of ancient Pompeii can be recaptured with a series of hand-painted wall panels. Available in portrait or landscape they can be designed to individual requirements. To accompany them there are Roman inspired, hand-carved and decorated seats complete with imitation animal skin fabrics.

circulation of blood in the human body. Unfortunately, it would seem that all of Harvey's medical skills counted for nothing when it came to his own fate for he is reputed to have committed suicide in 1657 after discovering that he was going blind.

The story of the town, from its Saxon roots right through to the present day, is told at the **Folkestone Museum** and the numerous displays and exhibits here range from the early traders, the growth of the medieval port and the town as a smugglers' haven to its development into a fashionable resort. At **Martello Tower No 3**, one of numerous such towers built as a defence against the possible invasion of the country by Napoleon, there is an exhibition that illustrates the measures taken to defend the south coast.

As long ago as the early 19th century, when a French engineer presented

Napoleon with plans for a tunnel linking France and England, the idea of such a thoroughfare, then designed for horse-drawn carriages, has captured the imagination. So much so, in fact, that, in 1877, a tunnel was started, from both sides, but work on this ceased, almost before it had begun, because of the public outcry in England. However, in 1986, work on the present Channel Tunnel began. The **Channel Tunnel Terminal** in England is at Folkestone, where both passenger cars and freight lorries join the trains that take them under the Channel to continental Europe.

A far cry from the bustle associated with the tunnel terminal, **The Folkestone Warren** is a peaceful country park that provides a habitat for numerous birds, insects and small mammals. The clifftop grasslands that were once grazed by sheep and cattle have now been colonised by, in some cases, rare wild flowers while there are also beautiful plants, such as Wild Cabbage and Rock Samphire, growing on the chalk cliffs.

AROUND FOLKESTONE

SANDGATE
1 mile SW of Folkestone on the A259

Now more a suburb of Folkestone that a village in its own right, Sandgate is a haven for collectors as its main street is littered with interesting antique shops. This is a peaceful place now but, during the threat of an invasion by Napoleon, no fewer than six Martello Towers were built in the area; these impressive granite structures still overlook the village.

In 1898, the author HG Wells moved to Sandgate, and in 1900, on the proceeds of his successful novels, he moved into **Spade House**, specially

designed for him by CF Voysey. It was here at the foot of Sandgate Hill that he entertained his literary friends and continued to write articles and papers advocating social and political change as well as many of his successful novels.

HYTHE
4 miles W of Folkestone on the A259

The recorded history of Hythe goes back to AD 732 when Ethelred, King of the Saxons, first granted it a charter and its name, which means 'landing place', refers to the time when there was a busy harbour here and Hythe played an important role as one of the Cinque Ports.

However, decline set in as the harbour began to silt up and today this historic town lies half a mile from the sea; no sign of its harbour remains. The skyline is dominated by the Norman tower of **St Leonard's Church**, built in 1080 but much extended in the 13th century. Interesting features include the choir

PIXIE OF HYTHE LTD

36 High Street, Hythe,
Kent CT21 5AT
Tel: 01303 267690

Pixie of Hythe Ltd specialises in ladies clothing and has been run by the same family for over 30 years. It is well known for its classic and elegant styles and is a stockist of many well known names including Gina Bacconi, Belmonde, Grazia, C and D, Lewinger, Slimma, Finn

Karelia, Tanya, Poppy, Alice Collins, Double Two and Cornelia James.

Whether it is a mother of the bride outfit, evening or cruisewear, or smart or casual day wear Pixie has a wide selection from which to choose. There is a vast array of slacks, skirts, T-shirts, blouses, jackets, jumpers, and cardigans and scarves. Stocking sizes from 10 to 24 there is also an alteration service. Customers will appreciate the kind and courteous attention of the staff.

CHURCH MOUSE STUDIO LTD

112A High Street, Hythe, Kent CT21 5LE
Tel/Fax: 01303 237554
e-mail: info@churchmousestudio.co.uk
website: www.churchmousestudio.co.uk

Church Mouse Studio is situated in the centre of Hythe High Street and set in a Grade II listed Victorian shop, with its original double-fronted display windows. The gallery specialises in the work of local artists from around the town and also from nearby Romney Marsh and includes original paintings, prints, cards and craftwork.

It is the ideal place to browse through the paintings on view and the range of gifts, prints and cards on offer. The selection includes glassware, ceramics, sculpture, woodturning and games, as well as specialised designer stationery, calligraphy equipment, designer cards and frames. You are welcome to view these at your own leisure, or ask for advice or help from the staff.

The resident artist, Hilary Scoble, has been painting and exhibiting in the South East professionally for over 20 years and is seen regularly painting in the gallery. She will be happy to discuss the current work in progress, give advice or arrange for a commission.

ACORN CRAFTS

139b High Street, Hythe, Kent CT21 5JW
Tel: 01303 265401 Fax: 01303 257210
web: www.acorn-crafts.demon.co.uk

Based on the main street of the charming Cinque Port town of Hythe, **Acorn Crafts** was established to provide high-quality dolls house miniatures and services to miniaturists from all walks of life. Britain's finest miniature builders merchants provide anything from roof tiles to door knobs, carpets, mouldings, lights, stairs, furniture, clothes, porcelain and glassware.....everything needed to add the finishing touches to a dolls house. They have over 25 houses on

display, including Tudor, Georgian, Victorian, Cottages and various styles of shop.

The models are either superbly ready-constructed (the shells are mainly made from medium density fibreboard or birch plywood) or in easy to assemble DIY form. They stock some dolls houses and toys for the younger enthusiast. They also display the wares of several talented miniaturists from the region, as well as standard items stocked by other retail outlets. Customers who cannot visit in person can avail themselves of the mail order service - phone for a catalogue.

stalls restored by Pearson, and the Victorian pulpit by Street, with mosaics by the Italian Salviati. The crypt houses one of two surviving ossuaries in England (the other is at Rothwell in Northamptonshire). Ossuaries were used to store and honour the bones of the dead when the graveyard became too crowded, and at Hythe over 2,000 skulls and various other assorted human bones, dating back to before the Norman invasion, are on display. For more information on the history of Hythe, the **Hythe Local History Room** is the ideal place to visit. This fascinating museum has numerous artefacts on display and a model of the town dated 1907.

Fishing Boats on the Beach at Hythe

Today, this charming place is best known as one of the terminals for the Romney Hythe and Dymchurch Railway, offering passengers a 14-mile journey by steam train across the edge of Romney Marsh to Dungeness (see under New Romney).

A mile to the north of Hythe lies **Saltwood Castle**. It is not open to the public but can be seen from a nearby bridleway. It was once the residence of the Archbishop of Canterbury and it was here that Becket's murderers stayed while journeying from France to commit their evil act. More recently, Lord Clark, the famous art historian and presenter of the pioneering TV series *Civilisation*, made this his home when he purchased the estate from Bill Deedes, the veteran journalist. After his death his son, Alan Clark, a Conservative member of Parliament, lived here and undertook considerable restoration work. He died in 1999.

LYMPNE

2½ miles W of Folkestone off the B2067

Pronounced 'Limm', Lympne was established by the Romans as a port,

THE CANDLE SHOP

25 High Street, Hythe, Kent CT21 5AO
Tel: 01303 262588

The ancient Cinque Port town of Hythe has plenty to interest the visitor, but few of its shops are as delightful and intriguing as **The Candle Shop** in the High Street. Owned and run by Margaret Wells and her son Bruce, its speciality is naturally candles, which come in all shapes and sizes and scents. The Yankee Samplers candles have

particularly lovely scents, and some of the candles are made from pure vegetable wax or beeswax. Also to be found here are jewellery and gems, tarot cards and plaster of Paris figures of dragons and goblins; many of them unique pieces made locally.

known as Portus Lemanis, and, in the 3rd century, they built a fort here. Now standing on the site of this ancient fort is **Lympne Castle**, a fortified manor house with Norman towers that has been extensively remodelled since it was first built in the 12th century. In 1905 Sir Robert Lorimer restored the now almost derelict castle, managing to preserve many original features in the rebuilding. The castle now operates as a hotel for business functions and weddings. From here, there are glorious panoramic views out across Romney Marsh, along the line of the Royal Military Canal and down the coast to Dungeness.

Just beyond the castle lies **Port Lympne Wild Animal Park** that was created by John Aspinall and shares the same aim, of the preserving of rare and endangered species, as its sister park Howletts. The large wild animal wilderness is home to many animals, including Indian elephants, tigers, lions, gorillas and monkeys, and also the largest captive group of black rhino in the world. After taking a safari trailer ride around the park, visitors have the opportunity to discover the delights of the park's historic mansion house, built by Sir Philip Sassoon MP in 1915. A millionaire at 23 and an aide to Lloyd George, he entertained many notables, including Charlie Chaplin, George Bernard Shaw, TE Lawrence, Edward VIII and Winston Churchill. The house contains the Spencer Roberts Animal Mural Room, where the walls are covered with colourful paintings of the exotic animals. Across the hall is the Tent Room decorated in 1934 by Rex Whistler; outside, there are beautiful landscaped gardens.

COURT-AT-STREET
4 miles W of Folkestone on the B2067

The ruined chapel here is connected with

the tragic tale of the Holy Maid of Kent, Elizabeth Arton, who in 1525 claimed that she had direct communication with the Mother of God. Her pronouncements made her famous and she was persuaded to enter a convent at Canterbury by clergy seeking to capitalise financially on the increasing public interest in her powers. However, in 1533 Elizabeth made the mistake of suggesting that Henry VIII would die if he divorced his first wife, Queen Catherine, and married Anne Boleyn and she (along with those clerics who had faith in her) was hanged at Tyburn in 1534.

MERSHAM
10 miles NW of Folkestone off the A20

To the southwest of this village lies **Swanton Mill**, a charming old rural watermill powered by the River East Stour that is surrounded by a beautiful garden. The restoration work undertaken on the mill has won awards and, today, the mill is still working and produces wholemeal flour.

NEW ROMNEY

Known as the 'Capital of the Marsh', New Romney is an attractive old town with some fine Georgian houses, that was, at one time, the most important of the Cinque Ports. However, in 1287 a great storm choked the River Rother, on which the town stood, with shingle and caused the river's course to be diverted to Rye. The town lost its harbour and its status. Although the Cinque Port documents are still housed at the Guildhall, New Romney now lies a mile from the sea. The sole survivor of the four churches in the town that were recorded in the Domesday Book, **St Nicholas' Church** still dominates the town's skyline with its lofty west tower.

Floodmarks that can be seen on the pillars inside the church indicate just how high the floodwaters rose in late 13th century.

The town is best known as being home to the main station of the **Romney Hythe and Dymchurch Railway**, a charming one third scale railway that was built in the 1920s for the millionaire racing driver, Captain Howey. Opened in 1927 as the 'World's Smallest Public Railway', and running between Hythe and Dungeness, it was not uncommon for train loads of holidaymakers to find that their carriages were being pulled by a locomotive driven by a famous friend of the Captain. During World War II, the railway was run by the army who used it move both troops and supplies along this stretch of the south coast. Although revived in the post war boom years, the railway struggled to attract visitors in the 1960s but it was, fortunately, saved by a group of enthusiastic businessmen. The railway is still a delightful way to explore this coastline and makes a fascinating day out for all the family. At the New Romney station can be found the **Romney Toy and Model Museum** housing a wonderful collection of old and not so old toys, dolls, models, posters and photographs. There are also two magnificent working model railways that are sure to captivate children of all ages.

AROUND NEW ROMNEY

St Mary in the Marsh
2 miles N of New Romney off the A259

Set on the lonely and remote flats of Romney Marsh, this village's church steeple is crowned by an interesting ball and weather vane. The ball was obviously used by the villagers for target practice and, during restoration work, honey from the bees who had made their hive in the ball was seen oozing from the bullet holes. In the churchyard lies the simple grave of E Nesbit, the author of many children's books whose most famous work is *The Railway Children*.

Dymchurch
3½ miles NE of New Romney on the A259

This small town's name is derived from 'Deme' the medieval English word meaning judge or arbiter and the town was the home of the governors of Romney Marsh. Known as the Lords of the Level, it was these men who saw that swift justice was carried out on anyone endangering the well being of marshes and they still meet today. Visitors can find out more about the history of Romney Marsh at the **Lords of the Level**, a small museum housed in the town's old courtroom.

At one time a quiet and secluded village, Dymchurch has become a busy seaside resort with a five-mile stretch of sandy beach and all the usual amusements arcades, gift shops and cafés. However, what does make it rather different from other such resorts is the **Dymchurch Wall**, that prevents water from flooding both the town and marsh as Dymchurch lies about seven-and-a-half feet below the level of the high tide. A barrier of some kind has existed here since Roman times.

Visitors can go from one formidable defence to another at Dymchurch as the **Martello Tower** here is, arguably, the best example of its kind in the country. Now fully restored and with its original 24 pounder gun, complete with traversing carriage, still on the roof, this is one of the 74 such towers that were built along the coast as protection against invasion by Napoleon. Their name is derived from their 'pepper-pot' shape as they are similar in style to a tower that stood at Cape Mortella in Corsica. This was an ironic choice of model as Napoleon himself was born on that Mediterranean island.

From the 1890s onwards the children's author, Edith Nesbit (but always E Nesbit for her novels) came to Dymchurch and other places around Romney Marsh to work on her novels. As well as writing, she would explore the marshland churches, riding first on a bicycle and later in a dog cart.

BURMARSH
5 miles NE of New Romney off the A259

At the northern end of Romney Marsh, this village is home to one of the area's marshland churches, All Saints' Church, which boasts an impressive Norman doorway that is crowned by a grotesque man's face. Two of the original late 14th century bells are still rung today while another, dedicated to Magdalene, has been preserved. At nearby **Lathe Barn**, children get the opportunity to meet and befriend a whole range of farm animals including ducks, chicks, barn owls, rabbits, donkeys, calves and sheep.

DUNGENESS
5 miles S of New Romney off the B2075

This southern most corner of Kent, with its shingle beach, has been a treacherous headland, feared by sailors for centuries. Originally simple fires were lit on the beach to warn shipping of the dangers around this headland and, in 1615, the first proper lighthouse was erected. As the sea has retreated a succession of lighthouses has been built and today there are now two at Dungeness. The **Old Lighthouse** dates from 1901 and its modern and current successor, Lighthouse number five was opened in

1961. The Old lighthouse is open to the public and at the top of its 169 steps, there are glorious views out to sea and, inland, over the marshes. As well as the makeshift fishermen's shacks, and the lighthouses, the other key building on the headland is **Dungeness Power Station** where, at the **Visitor Centre**, there is an exhibition on electricity and the generation of nuclear energy. The headland is also home to the **Dungeness Nature Reserve** whose unique shingle flat lands have been described as 'the last natural undisturbed area in the South East and larger than any similar stretch of land in Europe'. This RSPB reserve is noted for the many rare and migrating birds that come here to rest and feed in spring and autumn and a breeding colony of gulls and terns which nest in summer.

LYDD
3 miles SE of New Romney on the B2076

Like Old Romney, Lydd was once a busy port, linked to the Cinque Port of New Romney, but the changing of the course of the River Rother and the steady build up of land along the marsh put paid to this. Despite the loss of the port trade and now lying some three miles from the sea, Lydd is an attractive place that has retained many mementoes of its more prosperous past. Along with some fine merchants' houses and the handsome guildhall, the town is home to one of the tallest and longest parish churches in Kent, the 13th century **All Saints' Church**, often referred to as the 'Cathedral of the Marsh'. While the church was being restored following bomb damage it sustained in 1940, a stone altar that had been thrown out by Reformers was rediscovered; it now stands in the north chancel. Before his meteoric rise to fame, Cardinal Wolsey was the rector of Lydd in 1503.

Housed in the old fire station, **Lydd Town Museum** has a fascinating collection of memorabilia on the history of the town and local area along with a Merryweather fire engine and an early 20th century horsebus. At Lydd Library, the **Romney Marsh Craft Gallery** has a permanent display of crafts from both Romney Marsh and further afield that can be purchased.

OLD ROMNEY

2 miles W of New Romney on the A259

With its setting in the remote Romney Marsh, this tiny village has a forlorn feel and it is hard to imagine that this place was once a prosperous port. However, the Domesday Book records that Old Romney had three fisheries, a mill and a wharf, thereby indicating that it had a waterfront. As the marsh gained more land from the sea, Romney's position - which had been as a busy island - became landlocked and trading became seriously hampered. So Old Romney lost out to New Romney, which ironically also found itself victim of the gradually accretion of land in the marsh.

Just its name, **Romney Marsh**, is enough to conjure up images of smugglers lugging their contraband across the misty marshland and, for centuries, this whole area profited from the illegal trade that was known locally as 'owling' because of the coded calls the smugglers used in order to avoid the excise men. While Rudyard Kipling has painted a charming and romantic picture of the marsh in his poetry, another writer, Russell Thorndyke, told of a rougher side in his children's novel, *Dr Syn*, published in 1915. As well as being the vicar of Dymchurch, Dr Syn was the leader of a gang of smugglers in the 18th century who killed excise men, fought battles with the militia and stored their contraband in the marshland churches.

BROOKLAND

4½ miles W of New Romney on the A259

Brookland certainly has a name that describes its setting - on the southern fringes of Romney Marsh where the landscape is one of flooded meadows, small ditches and dykes. Despite its location, the village is home to an impressive church, that of St Augustine, said to be built from the timber of local shipwrecks. Inside, the church has some fine features, such as the medieval wall painting of the murder of Thomas à Becket and a cylindrical lead Norman font that is unique in Britain, but the most interesting feature is the church's 13th century shingled octagonal bell tower. Built in three vertical wooden stages, it stands quite apart from the rest of the church in much the same way as the campanile of an Italian church or cathedral. Architectural historians suspect that the medieval builders feared that the church, built on such damp foundations, would not support the extra weight of a belfry if it was added to the original building.

In the nearby hamlet of **Fairfield** stands the timber-framed Church of St Thomas à Becket. Isolated on the marshes, with the surrounding land frequently flooded, it was at one time accessed mainly by boat. Features include a complete set of box pews and a three-decker pulpit.

BRENZETT

4 miles NW of New Romney off the A259

This small settlement, lying on the probably Roman **Rhee Wall** sea embankment, is home to one of the smallest of the marshland churches, St Eanswith's Church. Thought to have been founded in the 7th century, although no traces of this building survive, there is an interesting tomb to local landowner John Fagge and his son to be seen here. The **Brenzett Aeronautical Museum** houses a unique collection of wartime aircraft memorabilia including equipment and articles recovered from crash sites.

SNARGATE

5 miles NW of New Romney off the B2080

In the heart of the Romney Marsh, this village's remote location conjures up the days when smugglers plied their illicit trade under the cover of darkness and hid their ill-gotten gains in reed lined streams or in disused and isolated farm buildings. The 600-year-old parish **Church of St Dunstan**, built in an exposed position, seems, on first impressions, to be disproportionately large for the size of this village. However, this extra space was a boon for smugglers as they used it to store their contraband. An excise raid in 1743 uncovered a cask of gin in the vestry and tobacco in the belfry. In the early 19th century the vicar here was the Rev Richard Barham; during his time at Snargate he wrote his humorous tales, the *Ingoldsby Legends*, some of which relate to the people of the Marsh. As he lived at some distance from the village Barham was unaware of the nightly activity in and around his church.

STONE-IN-OXNEY

8 miles NW of New Romney off the B2080

Strikingly situated on the eastern flank of the inland island known as the Isle of Oxney, the stone that gives the village its name is Roman and can be found, preserved, in the parish Church of St Mary. Other archaeological remains within the church suggest that this site once served as a temple to Mithras, a Persian deity beloved of Roman soldiers.

THE WEALD OF KENT

The Weald of Kent is a name to be reckoned with and one that conjures up, quite rightly, images of rolling wooded countryside, orchards and hop fields. Cranbrook, often dubbed the 'Capital of the Kentish Weald', is typical of many of the towns and villages of this area. It is a charming place that prospered in the Middle Ages with the growth of the woollen trade and that, when this industry declined, reverted to being a market town serving the surrounding communities.

Further north lies Maidstone, on the River Medway that forms the border between the Kentish Men and the Men of Kent. In bygone days Kent was divided into two parts, East (Men of Kent), administered from Canterbury, and West (Kentish Men), from Maidstone. In 1814 the two came together and Maidstone became the county town. Of the places to visit here, some of the most interesting, such as Allington Castle and the Museum of Kent Life, can be found beside this main waterway just north of the town. However, Maidstone is home to a 14th century Archbishop's Palace that was a resting place for the clergy travelling between London and Canterbury and that stands on the site of a building mentioned in the Domesday Book.

Close to the county border with East Sussex lies Royal Tunbridge Wells, a particularly charming town that, unlike many places in the Kent, was no more than a forest clearing until the early 17th century when health-restoring waters were discovered here. Developed to provide accommodation and entertainment, with the help of Beau Nash, to those coming here to take the waters, the town also received royal patronage that led to the addition of the prefix granted by Edward VII.

In between these key towns, the countryside is dotted with attractive villages and small towns, surrounded by the orchards and hop fields that typify the Weald. This area is also home to two of the most popular attractions in the county, if not England. Situated on two islands and surrounded by glorious gardens, the former royal palace of Leeds Castle, that was so beloved by Henry VIII, is a wonderful example of Norman defensive architecture that was thankfully restored by Lady Baillie from 1926 onwards. The other is Sissinghurst Castle, the ruin bought by Vita Sackville-West and her husband, Harold Nicholson in 1930, where they lovingly restored the gardens in the Elizabethan style. There are also other, less famous gardens that are sure to enchant visitors such as Scotney Castle, Groombridge Place and Owl House.

MAIDSTONE

Maidstone grew up on the site of an important meeting place and this is reflected in the town's name that means 'the people's stone'. The River Medway, on which it stands, is the ancient boundary that separated East and West Kent with the Kentish Men living in the west and, to the east of the river, the Men of Kent. This important distinction is still used proudly by many of the county's inhabitants today. Despite being extensively developed in the 20th century, Maidstone has retained many handsome Elizabethan and Georgian buildings. **Chillington Manor** is a beautiful Elizabethan residence, now home to the **Maidstone Museum and Bentlif Art Gallery**, founded by generous Maidstone Victorian gentlemen and

holding one of the finest collections in the south east. The many exhibits here cover a wide range of interests including oriental art, ethnography, archaeology and social history. The museum also has The Lambeth Bible Volume Two, a particularly outstanding example of 12th century illumination, and a real Egyptian mummy. The equally impressive art gallery includes works by both English and continental old masters among its permanent displays.

At the **Maidstone Carriage Museum** visitors can see a marvellous range of horse drawn carriages that were enthusiastically collected by Sir Garrard Tyrwhitt-Drake, a former mayor of the town, who wanted to preserve this method of transport as it was being replaced by motorcars. The first collection of its kind in Britain, the museum opened in 1946 and it is housed, appropriately enough, in stables that once belonged to the archbishops of Canterbury. Opposite these stables is the **Archbishop's Palace** that dates from the 14th century which was used by the archbishops as they travelled between London and Canterbury. It is now used for weddings as the Kent Rehistry Office. Close by are the **Dungeons**, a 14th century building from which, it is alleged, Wat Tyler, leader of the Peasants' Revolt in 1381, released John Ball, the 'mad priest of Kent'.

Other interesting buildings in the town include the **College of Priests**, that was founded in 1395 and the early 15th century **Corpus Christi Fraternity Hall**, where business was carried out in medieval times and which housed the Grammar School for over 300 years until the Education Act of 1870. Both of these buildings are now in private hands.

Just north of the town centre, at **Sandling**, on the banks of the River

Medway, stands **Allington Castle**, the earliest parts of which are 13th century. However a fire around 1600 destroyed a large part of it and it was not until the early 20th century that it was restored. It was once the home of Sir Thomas Wyatt, one of the 'silver poets' of the 16th century and author of *They flee from me that sometime did me seek*. He shares, with the Earl of Surrey, the credit for introducing into English poetry the sonnet form, popularised by the Italian poet, Petrarch, and later perfected by Shakespeare. It was also at this castle that Henry VIII is said to have first met Anne Boleyn and, now housed in Maidstone Museum, is a chair from the castle that bears the following inscription: "... of this (chay)re iss entytled too one salute from everie ladie thott settes downe in itt - Castell Alynton 1530 - Hen. 8 Rex". The castle is now in private ownership.

Lying on the opposite bank of the Medway from the castle is the **Museum of Kent Life**. Reflecting the unique character of this area of Britain and set in some 50 acres of land at the foot of the North Downs, the open-air museum covers many aspects of the county, inclduing three preserved hoppers' huts remembering the days when families came down from London to spend a working holiday picking

hops.Maidstone Millenium Park is a new 10 km park running alongside the River Medway, connecting the town centre to the tranquil countryside nearby. Boat trips are available between the Archbishops Palace and the Museum of Kent Life.

AROUND MAIDSTONE

AYLESFORD
2 miles NW of Maidstone off the A20

This charming village on the banks of the Medway is not only one of Kent's oldest villages but has, over the centuries, seen more than its fair share of fighting. Having travelled many miles from Pegwell Bay, the Jutish leaders Hengist and Horsa defeated the ancient Britons here in a great battle in AD 455. Though Horsa died in the battle, Hengist along with his son Aesc established a kingdom here (Cantware - or 'Men of Kent') and, for the next 300 years, the land was ruled by the descendants of Aesc, the dynasty of the Eskings. Later, in 893, the Danes were seen off by King Alfred while, soon afterwards, in 918, Edmund Ironside defeated Canute and the Vikings at Aylesford.

Aylesford has been an important river

AYLESFORD POTTERY

The Friars, Aylesford, Kent ME20 7BX
Tel: 01622 790796
e-mail: info@aylesfordpottery.co.uk
website: www.aylesfordpottery.co.uk

On the site of the ancient Carmelite Aylesford Priory, The Friars is a tranquil, peaceful retreat with a variety of attractions for the visitor. One of the longer established of these is **Aylesford Pottery**, where many years ago David Leach, the pottery's first manager, set the style for the traditional pieces produced here. Head potters Alan and Bill make a wide range of pottery of distinction, including domestic stoneware, terracotta garden pots, raku pottery, floor tiles, glazed earthenware, water features and much

more. They will also design and produce unique items to meet individual customer requirements, and all the outdoor items are guaranteed 100% frostproof for 10 years.

Visitors can watch the potters at work and browse among the items on display in the showroom. Aylesford Pottery runs one-day courses for budding potters.

crossing for centuries and records recall that there was a bridge spanning the river here as long ago as 1287. However, the beautiful five-arched **Bridge** seen today dates from the 14th century and from it there is an excellent view of Aylesford's delightful half-timbered, steeply gabled cottages.

In 1242, when the first Carmelites arrived here from the Holy Land, they founded **Aylesford Priory**. After the Dissolution in the 16th century, the priory became a private house and was rebuilt in 1675 only to be destroyed by a fire in the 1930s. After World War II, in 1949, the Carmelites took over the house and, having restored it to its former glory, they have re-established the priory - now calling it **The Friars** to use its traditional name. Today, it is a peaceful and tranquil retreat set in acres of well tended grounds in which visitors are

invited to picnic. The restored 17th century barn acts as a tea rooms, as well as a gift and bookshop, while the chapels contain some outstanding modern works of religious art. Still a popular place for pilgrimage, there is also a guesthouse here that offers peace and quiet to individuals, groups and families and extensive conference facilities. Just north of the village lies further evidence of the long history of settlement in and around Aylesford in the form of **Kit's Coty House**. Situated on Blue Bell Hill, this is a Neolithic burial chamber (with a capstone lying across three huge upright stones) that is reputed to be the tomb of a British chieftain who was killed by Horsa. Whether this is true or just local legend matters little as the views from the monument, out across the valley to the Medway Gap, make a walk to this site very worth while.

DETLING

1 miles E of Maidstone off the A249

Sheltered by the North Downs and by-passed by the main road, this village has remained relatively unspoilt and, today, it is visited by many walking the nearby **Pilgrims Way** footpath. In earlier times, this was an important coaching stop on several major routes that linked Maidstone with Sittingbourne, Faversham and other towns to the north. The High Street, that had been the main thoroughfare for the stagecoaches, is now more tranquil and along here, and elsewhere in the village, there are quaint old cottages to be found. On top of nearby Delting Hill lies the **Kent County Agricultural Show Ground**, the venue for the county's major annual agricultural, and social events, and where also some World War II buildings still remain from the days when this site was used as an airfield.

BOXLEY

2 miles N of Maidstone off the A249

Very much a hidden village, lying tucked away below the North Downs surrounded by major roads and motorways, Boxley is a small and traditional village of weatherboarded and red brick cottages. Just outside the village, to the west, lie the remains of **Boxley Abbey**, now part of a private house and not open to the public although the abbey's late-13th century ragstone barn can be seen from the road.

Back in the village stands the 13th century **All Saints' Church**, which still retains some features from the original Norman building; inside, visitors can see a monument that recalls the gratitude of one of the village's residents for a cat. In 1483, Sir Henry Wyatt was imprisoned in the Tower of London for denying Richard III's claim to the throne of England. Sir Henry was left to starve to death in one of the tower's cold, damp cells but a cat, by sleeping on his chest at night and bringing him pigeons to eat during the day, saved his life.

OTHAM

3 miles SE of Maidstone off the A274

Despite being only a short distance from Maidstone, this elevated village is a haven of tranquillity with its restored 14th century church, solid yeomen's houses and surrounding orchards. William Stevens, the eccentric writer who called himself 'Nobody' and founded the society of 'Nobody's Friends' lies buried in the churchyard. **Stoneacre**, a National Trust property, is a small and charming 15th century half-timbered yeoman's house, complete with a great hall with a crownpost roof. It was sensitively restored from a state of near dereliction in the early 20th century using windows, fireplaces and wood from other ruined period buildings. The delightful gardens here have been restored to their original cottage style.

HOLLINGBOURNE

4 miles E of Maidstone off the A20

Along with the adjoining hamlet, **Eythorne Street**, Hollingbourne forms a linear village stretching out below the rising North Downs. Of the two, Eythorne Street is the older and here a number of timber-framed and traditional, weatherboarded houses can be found. The 14th century All Saints Church lies by the village pond. In Upper Hollingbourne is the Grade 1 listed Elizabethan manor house, Hollingbourne Manor, once home to a prominent Kentish family, the Culpepers. This tall Tudor manor house was acquired by Francis Culpeper in 1590.

LEEDS

4½ miles SE of Maidstone on the B2163

While most people come to the village on their way to see the 'most beautiful castle in the World', it would be a mistake not to spend some time looking around Leeds itself. The village stands on the grounds of a former abbey, that flourished until the Dissolution in the 16th century, and many of the older buildings in Leeds, such as its oast houses, Norman Church of St Nicholas, and surrounding farms, were part of the abbey complex.

Leeds Castle

Covering almost 1,200 years of history, **Leeds Castle** stands on two islands in the middle of the River Len and, while the peaceful moat is the home of swans and ducks, the castle itself is surrounded by beautifully landscaped **Gardens**. Built on the site of a manor house that was owned by Saxon kings, the present castle was built just after the Norman Conquest and, when Edward I came to the throne, it became a royal palace. Beloved by Henry VIII, Leeds Castle was relinquished by the crown in the mid-16th century and, from then onwards, it has been in private hands. The last owner, an American heiress, Olive, Lady Baillie, bought the estate in 1926 and it is thanks to her vision, determination and hard work that Leeds Castle is so impressive today. It is one of the most popular visitor attractions in the country, with plenty to delight and interest the public both inside and in the gardens. Exhibits include collections of furnishings, tapestries and paintings, and it also has an idiosyncratic museum of dog collars. Many of the gardens have been restored including the maze and grotto and the informal and typically English Culpeper Garden. One new garden is particularly interesting - the Lady Baillie Garden, honouring the woman who put so much back into the castle before her death in 1974. Here are planted numerous sub-tropical species like bananas and tree palms that flourish in this south facing site.

BROOMFIELD

5 miles SE of Maidstone off the A20

This picturesque village in the Len Valley was mentioned in the Domesday Book. In the graveyard of its 12th century church lie buried several members of both the Wykeham-Martins and Fairfax families of Leeds Castle, along with Frederick Hollands, a 19th century county cricketer from Broomfield. It is also the home of a spectacular 1,000-year-old yew tree.

LOOSE

2½ miles S of Maidstone off the A229

The older part of this delightful village (pronounced Looze) lies in a narrow little valley and the cottages rise in terraces above the stream. The power of the stream, along with its purity and the availability of Fullers Earth, helped to established a flourishing woollen industry here in the 16th century. As that trade declined, some of the mills were converted to paper making, and this change of direction brought about more contact with Maidstone, just to the north. The viaduct that carries the main road from Maidstone across the Loose valley was built by Thomas Telford in 1829 and, along this stretch of road, can be seen large stones that were used, with the help of ropes, to pull heavy wagons up the steep hill.

BOUGHTON MONCHELSEA
3½ miles S of Maidstone on the B2163

On a ridge overlooking the Weald of Kent, this pleasant village was at the centre of Kentish ragstone quarrying and, not surprisingly, this local building material features heavily here. The quarries, on the edge of the village, have been worked almost continuously for seven centuries but archaeologists suggest that they were used longer ago than that as both the Romans and the Saxon used the stone in their buildings. Some of these stones were used in the construction of Westminster Abbey and Henry III ordered a number of cannonballs to be made from Kentish ragstone. Naturally, the village's 13th century parish Church of St Peter was built with this readily available material. It is also home to one of the oldest lychgates in England - erected in 1470 the gate was built entirely without nails. Local artist Graham Clark designed a modern nativity scene in stained glass for the church's millenium.

To the north of the church lies **Boughton Monchelsea Place**, a beautiful fortified ragstone manor house, originally built in 1567. The house itself is little altered since the late 18th century, retaining 16th century stained glass windows, Elizabethan wall panellings, a galleried Jacobean staircase and original oak floors and marble fireplaces. To the front, it has breathtaking views of the private deer park and unspoilt countryside. The house is not open to the public.

MARDEN
7 miles S of Maidstone on the B2079

Surrounded by orchards and hop fields, the old part of the village is centred around a main street lined with attractive tile hung and weather-boarded houses. This village was, centuries ago, part of a Royal Hundred and, as it was exempt from the jurisdiction of the County Sheriff, it had its own court. This ancient court house still stands in the old square but the village stocks have been moved and can now be found on display in the porch of Marden's 13th century church.

STAPLEHURST
8 miles S of Maidstone on the A229

There was once a stronghold in the village but, today, all that can be seen is a tree covered mound and little is known of the fortification's history. In 1865, the novelist Charles Dickens was involved in a serious train accident at the point where the track crosses the River Beult, that lies to the east of Staplehurst, and he makes a reference to this in a postscript to his novel *Our Mutual Friend*.

A garden with a difference, **Iden Croft Herbs** has wonderful displays of herbs, aromatic wild flowers and plants that particularly attract butterflies, in both open and walled gardens. It is also home to the national oreganum and mentha collections.

EAST FARLEIGH

2 miles SW of Maidstone on the B2010

Standing on steeply rising ground on the side of the River Medway, East Farleigh is surrounded by orchards and overlooks a graceful 14th century bridge. It was over this superb five-arched river crossing that Parliamentary soldiers marched in 1648, on their way to capturing Maidstone from the Royalists during the Civil War. One of the most important engagements in the war, the battle left 300 of the King's supporters dead and more than 1,000 taken prisoner. In the churchyard of the village's ancient church, a cross marks the final resting place of 43 hop pickers who died of cholera while working here in 1849. Also in the churchyard can be found the graves of the artist Donald Maxwell and Barbara Spooner, the wife of the reformer William Wilberforce, two of whose sons were vicars here.

YALDING

5 miles SW of Maidstone on the B2010

This lovely village's position, at the confluence of the Rivers Medway, Beult and Teise, provides ample irrigation for the fertile soil so it is not surprising that Yalding lies in one of the largest hop-growing parishes in England. Each of the three rivers here is crossed by its own medieval bridge while the delightful high street is lined with charming weather-boarded houses that date back to the 17th century. At **Yalding Organic Gardens** visitors can see 14 individual gardens, including a Tudor garden, a

TEAPOT ISLAND

Hampstead Lane, Yalding, nr Maidstone, Kent ME18 6HG
Tel/Fax: 01622 814541
e-mail: sue.blazye@btinternet.com
website: www.teapotisland.com

The village of Yalding, on the B2162 southwest of Maidstone, is home to one of the most charming and fascinating attractions in the whole county. **Teapot Island** houses an amazing collection of over 3,500 teapots, each with its own unique history. They all have lids and they all have spouts, but there the family resemblance ends! They come in a wonderful, colourful array of designs: cottages, telephones, a Dalek, a goose with goslings, a chest of drawers, a dancing lady with champagne, a flying saucer, and Seymour Designs Golly Quartet.......The 'signature' teapot is one representing Teapot Island - a green island in the sea, a little fishing boat, the whole thing topped with a tiny gold lid. These one-off teapots are there strictly to admire, but there are also teapots to be bought, and the talented resident potter Gary Seymour is often on the premises holding pottery demonstrations.

Owner Sue Blazye has pottery available that can be bought for children to use their talent and imagination by painting the pots with their own designs; the pots are then fired, giving them a personal keepsake of their visit. After looking at the teapots on display, visitors can enjoy a cream tea, or lunch or dinner in the riverside café. Others take a stroll along the lovely river bank, perhaps finishing with a drink in the picturesque Anchor Inn across the river.

Victorian garden and a wildlife garden, that illustrate the history of gardening from medieval times through to the present day. Changing ideas and themes down the ages are also highlighted such as stewardship of resource, the importance of genetic engineering and organic horticulture.

NETTLESTEAD

5 miles SW of Maidstone on the B2015

A quiet village set on a bank above a particularly pleasant stretch of the River Medway, Nettlestead is home to two buildings that are thought to have been founded by Bishop Odo, the half-brother of William the Conqueror. The present parish **Church of St Mary** was rebuilt in 1420 and it contains some lovely stained glass windows that were greatly damaged in 1763 when a thunderstorm unleashed 10 inch hailstones on the village. Beside the church stands **Nettlestead Place**. Restored in the early 20th century, this ancient private house still retains its old stone gatehouse and medieval undercroft.

BELTRING

7½ miles SW of Maidstone on the A228

This neat little village is home to one of the county's major attractions - the **Hop Farm Country Park**. Situated on a 1,000 acre former hop farm, this agricultural complex was originally a hop-drying centre supplying this major brewery but it has grown to house a museum, a rural crafts centre and a natural trail. Visitors can learn about the history and purpose of hops in the brewing process (until the 14th century cloves were more commonly used as flavouring) and also about the brewing industry itself. Visitors, particularly children, will also enjoy meeting the famous Whitbread shire horses and the smaller animals at the

pets' corner. A collection of agricultural machinery is on display along with an interesting exhibition of rural crafts.

HADLOW

9 miles SW of Maidstone on the A26

Lying in the Medway Valley, this attractive village has a wide main street where a number of its older houses can be found. These, and the rest of the village, are, however, completely overshadowed by the curiosity known as **May's Folly**. A tower some 170 feet high, this is all that remains of Hadlow Castle that was built by the eccentric industrialist Walter Barton May over a number of years and was finally finished in the early 19th century. May built the tower so that he would have a view that extended as far as the south coast but, unfortunately, the South Downs made this particular dream of his impossible to realise.

Anyone looking for gardening ideas in the heart of the Garden of England should pay a visit to **Broadview Gardens** where the belief of the success of a garden lying in its design is firmly held. There are a wide range of gardens to see here - from subtropical, stone and water, oriental and Italian to mixed borders, cottage, bog and wildlife. Beside the more traditional gardens there are experimental areas and this is an ideal place to come to for anyone looking for gardening inspiration.

ROYAL TUNBRIDGE WELLS

Surrounded by the unspoilt beauty of the Weald, some of the most scenic areas of countryside in England, Royal Tunbridge Wells is a pretty and attractive town that has been a popular place to visit for several hundred years. However, unlike many of the major towns and cities of Kent, Royal Tunbridge Wells has no

Roman or ecclesiastical heritage and, during the Middle Ages, when many towns were establishing their trading reputations, it was little more than a forest. The secret of how this charming place gained such prominence lies in the 'Royal' and 'Wells' of its name. In 1606, the courtier, Dudley, Lord North, found chalybeate springs here and he rushed back to court to break the news of his discovery of what he declared to be health-giving waters. Soon the fashionable from London were taking the water and spreading the word of their health-restoring qualities but, for three decades, there were still no buildings beside the springs.

In 1630, Tunbridge Wells received its first royal visitor when Queen Henrietta Maria, the wife of Charles I, came here to recuperate after giving birth to the future Charles II. She and her entourage, like other visitors, camped on the grounds by the springs. However, soon afterwards, enterprising local people began to build here but the real development of the town into one of the most popular spas of the 18th and 19th centuries was due to the Earl of Abergavenny. In order to increase the popularity of the spa, Beau Nash, the famous dandy who played an important role in the development of another spa town, Bath, came here as Master of Ceremonies in 1735. With Nash at the helm, guiding and even dictating fashion, Tunbridge Wells went from strength to strength and, while royalty had always found the town to their liking, it was granted its 'Royal' prefix in 1909 by Edward VII.

The chalybeate spring that was accidentally discovered by Lord North while out riding in what was then Waterdown Forest still flows in front of the **Bath House**, which was built in 1804 on top of the original Cold Bath.

Little Petals

30 Monson Road, Tunbridge Wells,
Kent TN1 1LU
Tel: 01892 619922

Children's clothes are the speciality of **Little Petals**, a delightful shop located in one of the main shopping streets of Royal Tunbridge Wells. Sharon and Amber, partners in the business, have children themselves, so they have an excellent idea of the quality, appeal and desirability of the clothes they stock.

They source the clothes mainly from leading manufacturers such as Burberry, Tickityboo, Paper Moon, Sisco, Cavalli and Baby Graziella, but Little Petals does not stop at clothes: they also stock a funky range of Italian-made spoons and bottles, bowls and bibs; accessories by Vice Versa; soft toys and teddies; and children's jewellery by Lucia & Co - perfect for birth or christening presents. The shop has a wonderful play area to keep the little ones amused while the grown-ups do the serious work of turning out the best-dressed kids in town.

THURLWELL'S

63 High Street, Tunbridge Wells, Kent TN1 1XU
Tel: 01892 533223

Christopher Thurlwell came to Royal Tunbridge Wells in 1989 after a long and successful career as a jeweller in the West End of London. He runs **Thurlwell's** with his wife Carolyn in an elegant shop

on the corner of High Street and Little Mount Sion, where he specialises in the design and manufacture of distinctive hand-crafted jewellery. Christopher is an expert in rare stones such as padparadscha, alexandrite and tanzanite, as well as unusual pink, yellow and black diamonds; he also works with rubies, emeralds and sapphires, tourmaline, topaz and quartz, remodelling old jewellery in new ways, resetting gems to his own contemporary designs in gold, silver and platinum.

Many of the pieces are commissioned, and customers can be involved throughout the whole process, from design and stone selection to the manufacture of the finished article. Most of the stock is designed in house, but there are also contemporary watches from Scandinavia and some Italian pieces.

ROYALL FINE ART

52 The Pantiles, Tunbridge Wells, Kent TN2 5TN
Tel/Fax: 01892 536534
website: www.royallfineart.co.uk

Set in the heart of the Pantiles in the Georgian part of Royal Tunbridge Wells, **Royall Fine Art** specialises in fine-quality British watercolours, oils, sculpture and ceramics of the 19th, 20th and 21st centuries. The gallery was established in 1983

by Trevor Royall and his wife Nicola, and from the beginning its aim has been to exhibit a broad range of work of the finest quality that will stand the test of time.

Some of the foremost artists working in the UK have shown here from the start, and among many notable names are Nicholas St John Rosse, who studied under Pietro Annigoni; Paddy Burrow, who works in bronze and bronze resin; the architectural painter Jonathan Pike; and Tony Sheath, one of the country's leading landscape and genre painters. Nicola herself exhibits here and at other venues including the Society of Women Artists.

CATS EYE

80 Camden Road, Tunbridge Wells, Kent TN1 2QP
Tel: 01892 538122 Fax: 01892 664004
e-mail: m.pearson@catseyeshop.com
website: www.catseyeshop.com

Opened in 2003 in the heart of Royal Tunbridge Wells, **Cats Eye** is a wonderful little shop filled with delightful things for the home and gifts for any occasion. Rich tones of red and orange and brown predominate in the displays, which include everything from cushions to candles, figurines to artificial flowers, jugs to jewellery and glassware. Browsers are very welcome, and each visit to this lovely place is guaranteed to provide fresh ideas and inspiration.

Meanwhile, close to the original springs was a grassy promenade known as The Walks where those coming to take the waters could take some exercise. In 1699 Princess Anne visited Tunbridge Wells with her son, the Duke of Gloucester, who slipped and hurt himself along The Walks. The irate Princess complained and the town authorities tiled over the grass and so created **The Pantiles**, a lovely shaded walk, lined with elegant shops. The Pantiles were the central focal point for the hectic social life arranged by Beau Nash and there were concerts and balls throughout the season along with gambling houses. Also in this area of the town is the **Church of King Charles the Martyr**, often called the 'Jewel of the Pantiles'. Originally established as a chapel in 1678 for those coming to take the waters, the church has many interesting features, including

PANTILES ANTIQUES

31-31b The Pantiles, Tunbridge Wells,
Kent TN2 5TD
Tel/Fax: 01892 531291

Pantiles Antiques has been owned and run since the early 1980s by Erica Blackburn, and her customers come from all over the world to her lovely shop. It takes its name from its location in the elegant walk that was created for a royal princess 300 years ago. Once the social hub of Royal Tunbridge Wells, it is now filled with elegant and unusual shops, and Pantiles Antiques occupies one of the oldest premises. The stock includes

furniture in rosewood, walnut and mahogany, mainly from the Georgian to Edwardian eras; there are chairs for all occasions and a wide variety of tables - dining, writing, work, coffee, card, occasional.

Erica has one of the very best upholsterers in the business working for her, with 50 years experience of doing work for individual customers as well as for stately homes, museums and other institutions. He uses traditional materials and traditional techniques to produce work of a quality rarely seen nowadays, all done by hand as it would have been when the pieces brought here for renovation were new. A visit to Pantiles Antiques is both a delight and a privilege.

TREVOR MOTTRAM LTD

33-41 The Pantiles, Tunbridge Wells,
Kent TN2 5TE
Tel: 01892 538915
e-mail: sarahmfwood@aol.com

Created at the beginning of the 18th century, The Pantiles soon became the hectic social centre of life in Royal Tunbridge Wells. The concert halls and taverns and gambling houses have long gone, replaced by elegant shops filled with high-quality and unusual products. One of the finest of these shops is **Trevor Mottram Ltd**, a specialist cookshop with a formidable range of products covering every conceivable item connected with cooking and eating in the home. Opened in 1976, it was one of the first specialist cookshops, and it quickly gained a country-wide reputation. That reputation has continued to grow as the premises and the stock have expanded,

and since March 2000 it has flourished in the ownership of Sarah and Alan Wood, who are both enthusiastic cooks.

Sarah is a chef's daughter who grew up in hotels and restaurants, while Alan is a chartered accountant who has held management and board roles in large organisations. Between them they are extremely well qualified to run one of the leading shops of its kind in the country, and the display areas are stocked with a truly amazing range of more than 8,000 products from 150 different manufacturers and suppliers. Tableware and glassware sit beside an impressive range of electrical goods and gadgets, and the recent expansion of the premises has allowed an even larger variety of goods to be displayed, along with the creation of an area for cookery demonstrations.

The main part of the shop occupies one of the oldest buildings in the town, originally a tavern and later a seed merchants. It has retained many delightful old features, including a sack-loading door on the first-floor balcony and an ancient dumb waiter. Trevor Mottram Ltd is a must for anyone with an interest in cooking, and browsers should allow plenty of time - this really is an Aladdin's Cave of kitchen goods, and everything from a humble jelly mould to the latest food processor is highly desirable. Friendly, professional staff put the seal on this outstanding establishment, which many years ago earned its entry in the list of places that simply must be visited in Royal Tunbridge Wells.

L'ITALIA A TAVOLA

3b Monson Road, Tunbridge Wells, Kent TN1 1LS
Tel: 01892 615665 Fax: 01892 615664
e-mail: max@litaliaatavola.co.uk

Owner Max Faraone, from Riccione on the Adriatic coast, is passionate
about creating tantalising tastes for his customers. Many of the products
on mouth-watering display are exclusive to this splendid shop-around-
the-corner style delicatessen. The deli boasts hams, salamis and cheeses
in abundance as well as a chilled cabinet filled with freshly prepared
salads, stuffed peppers, marinated vegetables as well as hot foods such
as lasagne and cannelloni. The shop offers superb catering for business
and private functions as well as picnic boxes. Open for breakfast and
lunch.

a charming clock donated to the church in 1760 by Lavinia Fenton, the actress and mistress of the Duke of Bolton. The superb ceiling that was created by Henry Doogood, the chief plasterer to Sir Christopher Wren.

For a greater insight into the history and development of the town, a visit to the **Tunbridge Wells Museum and Art Gallery**, opened in 1952 is a must. Among the displays and exhibits on natural history and art, there is an exhibition of local history and a collection of Tunbridge ware - the decorative woodwork that is unique to the area.

Once part of the extensive network of railway lines in Kent and neighbouring

JOHN THOMPSON

27 The Pantiles, Tunbridge Wells, Kent TN2 5TD
Tel: 01892 547215

In his shop in the elegant heart of Georgian Royal
Tunbridge Wells, **John Thomson** brings together
his three great
interests: antiques;
architecture and
interior design; and
gardening. Examples
of his work have
featured in numerous

publications, including *Country Living* magazine. The stock on display
is mainly 18th and 19th century items ranging from simple country
pieces to the more grand; they range from porcelain, glass and decorative
items to pictures and furniture. As an adjunct, John provides an interior
design consultancy which covers advice on interior design and
decoration together with the choosing and purchasing of antiques on
commission.

The third main part of the business is a consultation service for garden
design and advice on anything from simple borders to fully landscaped
gardens. John Thompson established the business when he came to this
country from New Zealand, where he had practised law. He has built up
an extensive clientele, providing a comfortable, civilised setting in which
to discuss each customer's requirements.

RACHELTOLHURST

2 Ely Court, Royal Victoria Place,
Tunbridge Wells, Kent TN1 2SP
Tel: 01892 617440
website: www.racheltolhurst.com

Royal Tunbridge Wells is home to many elegant and stylish shops, and few are more elegant and stylish than the fashion shop **racheltolhurst**. Rachel Tolhurst fell in love with fashion design at the age of 19 while studying in Italy, drawing inspiration from the chic ladies of Florence. After excelling in her final year project at university back in the UK, she won acclaim when representing the new British fashion designers in Japan.

The first racheltolhurst shop opened here in 1997 and instantly made a name for itself selling a

stunning collection of daywear both formal and casual, knitwear and evening wear. Through great attention to detail and the choice of the finest textiles and raw materials, simple, beautifully cut garments have become the signature of the racheltolhurst collections, and her line remains chic, luxurious and timeless in both quality and style.

A second racheltolhurst shop is located at 47 Jubilee Arch, Windsor Royal Station, Windsor, Berkshire SL14 1PJ (Tel: 01753 624224).

East Sussex, **Spa Valley Railway** is a restored and preserved section of this system that was re-opened in 1996. Now running between Royal Tunbridge Wells, High Rocks and Groombridge, the trains leave Tunbridge Wells West station and take passengers on a pleasant journey through the Wealden countryside.

AROUND ROYAL TUNBRIDGE WELLS

The Pantiles, Royal Tunbridge Wells

MATFIELD

5 miles NE of Tunbridge Wells on the B2160

The village name is derived from the Anglo Saxon name 'Matta' and 'feld' meaning large clearing and appropriately at the centre of this village is one of the largest village greens in Kent. Around it old and new houses blend harmoniously including several fine tile hung, typically Kentish houses and an impressive Georgian dwelling built in 1728.

HORSMONDEN

7½ miles E of Tunbridge Wells on the B2162

It is hard to imagine that this delightful village, tucked among orchards and fields, was once a thriving industrial centre. Although little evidence of this remains today the key to the village's prosperity lies in the pond found just to the west. Known as a furnace pond, it supplied water to the ironworks that flourished throughout the Weald of Kent. Now, nature is reclaiming the pond and it will soon be indistinguishable from other expanses of water in and around the village.

Oast Houses, Goudhurst

From the village green, known as The Heath, a footpath leads to the village church, some two miles to the west. This is a walk worth making as the countryside is pleasant and, on reaching the church, visitors can see a memorial to John Read, who died in 1847, and is best known for inventing the stomach pump.

GOUDHURST

9 miles E of Tunbridge Wells on the A262

Standing on a hill and with sweeping views across the surrounding orchards and hop fields, and especially over the Weald, Goudhurst (pronounced 'Gowdhurst') is a picturesque place that draws many visitors, not least because of its main street, lined with traditional tile hung, weatherboarded cottages. The solidity of the village reflects the prosperity it enjoyed when the woollen industry was introduced here in the Middle Ages. The village church, which stands on the hilltop, begun as a chapel in 1119, dates chiefly from the 15th century and, inside, there are many memorials to the leading local family, the Culpepers. The Culpepers were at one time noted ironmasters and made guns for Drake's navy against the Spanish Armada. From the church tower it was said that 51 other churches could be seen

WEST WINCHET

Winchet Hill, Goudhurst, Kent TN17 1JX
Tel: 01580 212024 Fax: 01580 212250
e-mail: annieparker@jpa-ltd.co.uk

Annie and Jeremy Parker offer quiet, civilised Bed & Breakfast accommodation in their beautiful Victorian house with a wonderful garden and lovely views. The house has two guest bedrooms, a twin and a double, both with en suite facilities, TV and tea tray; the twin has French windows providing direct access to the terrace and garden. Guests start the day with a regal breakfast that includes home-made yoghurt, fruits and cereals, and a traditional English spread using local farm produce – a fine start to a day exploring the towns and villages, the great houses and the gardens of the Weald.

on a clear day. This may have been possible when the tower was higher, but whatever the truth of the 51 churches it is certainly possible today to see Canary Wharf Tower in London, which is 40 miles away.

Just to the southwest of the village lies **Finchcocks**, a charming Georgian manor house, with a dramatic frontage, that is named after the family who lived on this land in the 13th century. Built for the barrister Edward Bathurst in 1725, the house has managed to retain many of its original features despite having changed hands several times over the years. In 1970, Finchcocks was bought by Richard Burnett, a leading exponent of the early piano and, today, it is home to his magnificent collection of historic keyboard instruments. The high ceilings and oak panelled rooms are the ideal setting for this collection of beautiful

instruments, which includes chamber organs, harpsichords, spinets and early pianos and, whenever the house is open to the public those instruments restored to concert standard are played. Along with these instruments Finchcocks also houses some fine pictures and prints and an exhibition on 18th century pleasure gardens. Tucked away behind the elegant house are four acres of beautiful gardens, which provide a dramatic setting for outside events. The gardens are mainly of Victorian design, except the walled garden, which was designed in 1992, as an 18th century Pleasure Garden.

Further south again and adjoining the county border with East Sussex lies **Bedgebury National Pinetum** , founded jointly by the Forestry Commission and the Royal Botanic Gardens at Kew in the 1920s. Today, Bedgebury is home to the National Conifer Collection, the finest

HEARTS & FLOWERS COUNTRY STORE

West House, West Road, Goudhurst, Kent TN17 1AB
Tel/Fax: 01580 213696

Sarah Mattacks recently returned a slice of village life to Goudhurst when she re-opened a shop that had been a general store in the 1930s. **Hearts & Flowers Country Store** was the realisation of a dream for Sarah, who trained with Laura Ashley and has a passion for attractive, well-designed products for house and garden. As preparation for the opening of Hearts & Flowers, which is every bit as pretty as its name, she spent many years cultivating producers and suppliers of hand-crafted items, often with a rustic look and feel. These include hand-made furniture,

wrought-iron, old pine, country pottery and crafts, traditional toys, basketware, home accessories and a range of special gifts that are a delight to give or receive.

Many of the goods are just that little bit different and unusual, and Sarah makes many of the articles herself – her creations have become much-loved treasures in many homes in the region. All purchases are beautifully wrapped in pastel-coloured tissue and prettily bagged and gift tagged if required. Sarah is a strong believer in interacting with her customers and she is always ready with helpful advice on gift ideas and interior design.

collection of conifers in the world, where some of the most famous conifers, including large Californian redwoods are to be found.

LAMBERHURST

6 miles E of Tunbridge Wells on the A21

As this village lies on the main road between Royal Tunbridge Wells and Hastings, it once played an important role as a coaching stop but much of the village's prosperity is due to the iron industry of the Weald. The high street here is lined with attractive old houses and other buildings dating from those days. Lamberhurst produced iron railings, which are also in evidence at St Paul's Cathedral, can be seen along this road. Lamberhurst's 14th century church, set some way from the village centre in the valley of the River Teise, has been remodelled to accommodate a smaller congregation than those it

attracted during the years of Lamberhurst's heyday. Today, the village is associated with viticulture and the first vineyard was established here in 1972.

To the northwest of the village lies **Owl House Gardens** a particularly pretty little cottage whose tenants, according to records dating from 1522, paid the monks at Bayham Abbey an annual rental of one white cockerel. Later the house became associated with night smugglers or 'owlers' (hence its name) who traded English wool for French brandy and avoided the tax inspectors by giving out coded hoot calls. In 1952, the house was bought by Lady Dufferin and, while this is not open to the public, the beautiful **Gardens** that she planted can be visited. There are extensive lawns and walks through woodland of birch, beech and English oak as well as spring bulbs, roses, flowering shrubs and ornamental fruit trees. As this was once the site of

LAMBERHURST VINEYARD

The Down, Lamberhurst, Kent TN3 8ER
Tel: 01892 890412 Fax: 01892 891242

In a beautiful Wealden setting, with views of fields, orchards, vines and oast houses, **Lamberhurst Vineyard** invites visitors to take time to enjoy and learn about fine English wines. The vines were first planted here in the early 1970s and now extend over 15 acres. The Vineyard Shop sells a complete range of high-quality English wines grown here and produced at Tenterden Vineyard – Curious Grape still wines, Chapel Down sparkling wines, Lamberhurst Estate wines and fruit liqueurs. The shop also sells wine accessories, local foodstuffs and many unusual gifts.

Organised tours of the vineyards are available, or visitors can follow the various vineyard trails, and there is of course ample opportunity to sample the superb wines. The Bistro, where fresh local produce is to the fore, is open for morning coffee, snacks, afternoon teas and Sunday roasts, and the Vineyard has its own pub, The Swan at the Vineyard, selling a wide range of English wines, real ales and fine food. Children can romp to their hearts' content in the adventure playground or, new for this year, make friends with the animals in pets corner. A less expected amenity is Vino Beauty, a smart centre offering a variety of facials, massages, reflexology and many other beauty treatments.

Scotney Castle

the iron works that made some of the fitments for St Paul's Cathedral, there are also hammer ponds and these have been creatively converted into informal water gardens surrounded by willows, camellias and rhododendrons.

To the east of the Lamberhurst lies **Scotney Castle**, a massive, rust-stained tower that was built by Roger de Ashburnham in 1378 and that now incorporates the ruins of a Tudor house. However, what especially draws people to Scotney are the romantic gardens that are renowned for their autumn colours but are beautiful throughout the seasons. The water lily-filled moat around the ruins provides the perfect centrepiece to the wealth of plants found in the gardens and there are also delightful countryside walks around the estate.

GROOMBRIDGE
4 miles SW of Tunbridge Wells on the B2110

Straddling the county border between Kent and Sussex, it is generally recognised that the Kent side of this village is the prettier and more interesting as this is where the triangular village green lies,

overlooked by the tile hung cottages of the Groombridge estate. This charming village centre piece is also overlooked by **Groombridge Place**, a classical 17th century manor house that stands on the site of a medieval castle. The house is surrounded by superb parkland and **Gardens**, designed by the famous Jacobean diarist John Evelyn in a formal manner. Likened to a series of rooms, the walled gardens are complemented by extensive herbaceous borders while, high above these, there is **The Enchanted Forest** a magical and imaginative series of mysterious gardens that are a delight to explore.

RUSTHALL
1½ miles W of Tunbridge Wells off the A264

Although Rusthall lies on the outskirts of Royal Tunbridge Wells it has managed to retain some of its original rural character and not become completely engulfed by its much larger neighbour. A lovely common marks the heart of the village and some of the unusual rock structures that can be found in Royal Tunbridge Wells can also be seen here, in particular, there is **Toad Rock**, a natural rock formation, so called because of its remarkable resemblance to a giant toad balanced atop a rock.

SPELDHURST
2½ miles NW of Tunbridge Wells off the A26

This attractive chiefly residential village was mentioned as early as the 8th century and, though close to Royal Tunbridge Wells, still manages to preserve a cohesive sense of village identity and a rural atmosphere. At its heart lies the village church, built on the foundations of a much older Norman church that was struck by lightning in 1791. Great care was taken by the Victorians when the church was rebuilt and it is worth visiting to view the colourful stained glass windows, designed by Burne-Jones.

CRANBROOK

Originally a little hamlet lying in the hills close to the source of the River Crane, Cranbrook began to grow in the 11th century and by the end of the 13th century it was sufficiently well established to be granted a market charter by Edward I. However, it was the introduction of the wool weaving from Flanders, in the 14th century that really changed the town's fortunes and, for the next few centuries, Cranbrook prospered. Several old buildings date back to this period of wealth including the church and the Cloth Halls and winding streets lined with weatherboarded houses and shops. However, the industry began to decline and, by the 17th century, agriculture had taken over and, like other Wealden places, Cranbrook was transformed into a market town serving the needs of the surrounding area.

Often dubbed the 'Capital of the Kentish Weald', one of the best places to start any exploration of the town is at the **Cranbrook Museum** that is housed in a museum piece itself. Dating back to 1480, the museum is a fine example of a timber-framed building that is held together by elaborate joints. Opened in 1974, the displays and exhibitions here cover many aspects of Wealden life, from agriculture and local crafts to Victorian and wartime memorabilia. Naturally the town's reliance on the weaving industry is highlighted and, along

with the collection of prints by the 19th century Cranbrook colony of artists, there is a display of local birds, many of which are now rare.

The parish church, **St Dunstan's**, is believed to have been built on the site of first a Saxon and then a Norman church. Known locally as the 'Cathedral of the Weald' and built between the 14th and 16th centuries, the size of this church reflects the prosperity of the town at the time. Even the stone font is of impressive proportions, designed for total immersion, its base featuring wooden bosses of Green Man. Above the porch, reached by a stone staircase, is a room known as 'Baker's Jail' where, in the reign of Mary Tudor, Sir John Baker, sometimes known as 'Bloody Baker' imprisoned the numerous Protestants he had convicted to await their execution. Originally, the room was intended to hold church valuables.

Although St Dunstan's church tower is tall, the town is dominated by the tallest smock mill in England, **Union Mill**, which is around 70 feet high. Built in

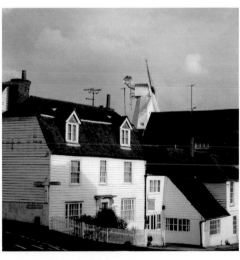

Cranbrook Town and Windmill

HARVEYS OF CRANBROOK

11-13 Stone Street, Cranbrook, Kent TN17 3HF
Tel: 01580 712345 Fax: 01580 720352
e-mail: harveysfinewines@btopenworld.com

Harveys of Cranbrook is a veritable gastronomic Aladdin's Cave situated in a listed building in a conservation area just off the High Street. Inside the double-windowed shop, Mark and Debbie preside over a mouthwatering selection of delicatessen items, with specialities from Italy featuring prominently. Just inside the front door is a large deli counter that's jam packed with delights, including a range of over 70 cheeses, salads, pasts dishes, olives and seasonal Italian produce to tempt all lovers of fine food. Hanging from hooks on the shelves behind are sausages, salamis and hams, while on the shelves themselves are various exotic olive oils, vinegars, jams, preserves and mustards.

On the deli counter is a collection of jars, bottles and tins containing preserved fruits and roasted vegetables. There's also an excellent choice of sweet goodies, including amaretto biscuits and some particularly fine local preserves and honeys. Wine is another speciality of Harveys, and fine wines from around the world include Riojas from Spain, Chianti and Prosecco from Italy, classic French reds and whites and Kentish wine and cider No serious deli deserves to survive without a decent range of coffees, and at Harveys they sell it ground or as roasted beans – they even have their own label blend. On Saturday mornings fresh fish and seafood is sold outside the shop and can be eaten in the restaurant.

At the back of the shop is a splendid coffee bar with a light, airy ambience created by a combination of warm terracotta walls, a polished wooden floor and plain, light pine tables. The prints on the wall play their part in the décor, constantly changing as customers buy their favourites. This is a perfect place to come for morning coffee or afternoon tea as a break from shopping or seeing the sights, and it's also ideal for a light lunch, relaxing in the pleasant surroundings and sampling the deli's produce. There's a superb choice of dishes both hot and cold, including panini, fish dishes, pastas and salads, meats, olives and tapas-style snacks.

The coffee bar is licensed, so the wines can be sampled as well as a selection of beers and ciders. It's best to book at peak times and is essential for the jazz evenings that have become a regular and very popular attraction. Harveys is open from 8.30 to 5 Monday to Saturday and from 10 to 2 on Sunday. Jazz nights start at 7 o'clock every other Friday.

CRANBROOK GALLERY

Stone Street, Cranbrook,
Kent, TN17 3HF
Tel: 01580 720720
e-mail: info@cranbrookgallery.com
web: www.cranbrookgallery.com

Established in 1977 and now owned
and run by Paul and Nicole Rodgers,
Cranbrook Gallery is housed in an

ancient timber-framed building. In Victorian times Cranbrook
attracted a colony of distinguished artists, so it is entirely
appropriate that the primary focus of the gallery is the work of
British artists. The range of watercolours, drawings and original
prints covers the period from 1750 to the present day. The gallery
also offers a good selection of antique maps, both of the English
counties and other countries.

Gallery hours are 9.30am to 5pm Tuesday to Saturday or at
other times by arrangement. Interested customers are welcome
to visit the gallery in person or browse through a small selection
of pictures available on the website (see above). The gallery is
able to send pictures almost anywhere in the world and numerous
testimonials from satisfied customers are a tribute to the quality,
efficiency and reliability of the service offered.

1814, the windmill was fully restored
in the 1960s and in 2003 and, wind
permitting, it still grinds corn into the
flour that is sold here.

AROUND CRANBROOK

SISSINGHURST

1½ miles NW of Cranbrook on the A262

The main street of this village is lined
with old weatherboarded houses that
have been built over a period of several
centuries. Many of the larger houses were
erected by prosperous weavers who
worked in the thriving industry that was
introduced to Sissinghurst during the
reign of Edward III.

Sissinghurst is, of course, famous for
the lovely gardens that were the creation
of the writer Vita Sackville-West and her
husband Harold Nicholson. When, in
1930, the couple bought **Sissinghurst**

Castle, it was all but a ruin. The castle
was originally built in Tudor times by Sir
John Baker, who, during the reign of
Mary Tudor, sent so many Protestants to
their deaths that he became known as
'Bloody' Baker. Such was Sir John's
reputation that local legend tells that
when two women working at the castle
heard him approaching, they hid under
the main staircase. From their hiding
place they saw that their master was being
followed by a servant carrying the body
of a murdered woman. As the men
climbed the staircase, one of the dead
woman's hands became caught in the
banisters. Impatient to continue
whatever gruesome tasks he was about to
perform, Sir John quickly hacked the
hand from the body and he and his
servant continued up the stairs.
Meanwhile, the severed hand fell into the
lap of one of the women hiding below.

Later, during the Seven Years War in

LAMBERDEN HOUSE

Rye Road, Sandhurst, Kent TN18 5PH
Tel: 01580 850968   e-mail: Margie@lamberdenhouse.co.uk
Fax: 01580 850121   website: www.lamberdenhouse.co.uk

Margie and Julian Croysdill extend a warm welcome to guests at
Lamberden House, a beautiful and immaculate conversion of a
traditional Kentish oast barn. The letting bedrooms are spacious,
bright and very comfortable, and the house has a pleasant garden
with a heated swimming pool. Bed & Breakfast guests should
definitely take up the option of an evening meal, as Margie is a superb cook who uses local organic
produce, home-grown vegetables and herbs to create meals to remember.

THE WALLED NURSERY

St Ronan's School, Water Lane, Hawkhurst, Kent
Tel: 01580 752425

Visitors to **The Walled Nursery** in Hawkhurst will find an impressive range of
plants of all sizes for all seasons, as well as pots and planters, garden accessories
and a wealth of lovely gift ideas. But the interest does not end there, as the
owners Peter and Karen Horn have the most splendid setting for their nursery
within the redbrick walls of a fine set of Victorian buildings. They have preserved
much of the Victorian look, taking visitors back to a bygone era, and inside the
beautifully restored greenhouses the original trees and climbing plants still
flourish.

CUPCAKES

The Corner Shop, Highgate, Cranbrook Road,
Hawkhurst, Kent TN18 4AB
Tel: 01580 755587 website: www.cupcakesdirect.com
Cupcakes is based in the centre of the historic weald village of
Hawkhurst. The shop carries a variety of stock ranging from a fantastic
range of cards and gift-wrap, painted furniture, gorgeous and
imaginative gifts, items for the garden and so much more. Cupcakes
also supports local craft workers and always has a range of rural crafts
in stock including handmade cards, cats, teddies, horses and garlands
using vintage fabrics, original jewellery, natural handmade soap,
handbags, children's and adults clothes, hand-painted brooms, cushions
and quilts with new ideas arriving weekly.

Christmas is a very special time when Cupcakes becomes a cosy shop
filled with the scent of
cinnamon and orange from the handmade garlands,
decorations and Christmas goodies, and with the welcoming
sight of a real Christmas tree it truly is a special time of the
year. Cupcakes has an easy-to-use website where you can
browse through most items which are available in the shop,
order gifts and even have them gift wrapped and sent directly
to your friends and relatives. However, if you can manage
to visit Cupcakes you will be greeted with a warm welcome
and will be able to browse at leisure and enjoy the unique,
friendly atmosphere of a truly different gift shop.

the 18th century, the castle was used as a prison for 3,000 French troops and, by the time they had left, only a few parts of the original building were left standing. Decades of neglect and a short time as a workhouse finally saw the castle descend to the wrecked state of the 1930s.

Restoring what they could of the castle, the couple concentrated on creating the famous **Gardens** that, today, bring so much pleasure to visitors. Laid out in the Elizabethan style, there are a series of formal gardens, or 'rooms', that each have a different theme such as the White Garden where only silver leafed, white flowering plants are grown. Away from this formality there are also woodland and lakeside walks and the estate's oast house is home to an interesting exhibition.

Sissinghurst Gardens

BENENDEN

3 miles SE of Cranbrook on the B2086

This attractive village is strung out along a ridge. It is famous for its girls' public school, also called **Benenden**, housed in a mock-Elizabethan house dating from 1859 to the west of the village centre. Benenden village itself is famous for cricket, played on most summer evenings on the large green.

ROLVENDEN

5 miles SE of Cranbrook on the A28

Surrounded by orchards and hop fields, this large village stands on the eastern fringe of the Weald and on the edge of the Isle of Oxney. A place of white weather-boarded and tile hung houses, the village is home to the **CM Booth Collection of Historic Vehicles**, centred on a unique collection of Morgan three-wheeled cars that date from 1913 to 1935. However, there is much more to discover at this fascinating museum, such as a 1904 Humber Tricar, numerous bicycles and motorcycles, toy and model

cars and a whole host of other motorcar related memorabilia.

Close to the village lies **Great Maytham Hall**, a charming country house, renovated by Sir Edwin Lutyens, which stands in glorious grounds. At the turn of the 20th century, the novelist Frances Hodgson Burnett, who spent most of her life in America, leased the house. While staying here, she fell in love with the particularly beautiful walled kitchen garden that was to inspire her to write the classic children's book *The Secret Garden*. The garden is open to the public on a limited basis.

SANDHURST

5 miles S of Cranbrook on the A268

Visitors coming here expecting to find the Royal Military Academy will be disappointed as this is located at Sandhurst, Berkshire. However, Sandhurst, Kent, is an attractive place that deserves a visit in its own right. Set in reasonably hilly terrain this feature of the countryside gave rise to the name of the local inn, The Missing Link, which refers to the practice of linking extra horses to the wagons in order to pull heavy loads up the hill.

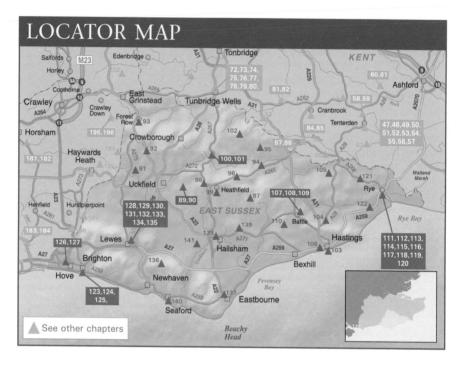

LOCATOR MAP

Salfords · Horley · Copthorne · Crawley · Crawley Down · Horsham · Haywards Heath · Henfield · Hurstpierpoint · Lewes · Brighton · Hove · Newhaven · Seaford

Edenbridge · East Grinstead · Forest Row · Crowborough · Uckfield

Tonbridge · Tunbridge Wells · Cranbrook · Tenterden · Heathfield · Battle · Hailsham · Bexhill · Eastbourne · Hastings · Rye · Pevensey Bay · Beachy Head

M23 · KENT · EAST SUSSEX · Walland Marsh · Rye Bay · Ashford

72,73,74, 75,76,77, 78,79,80, · 81,82 · 60,61 · 58,59 · 47,48,49,50, 51,52,53,54, 55,56,57 · 84,85 · 87,88 · 100,101 · 107,108,109 · 89,90 · 128,129,130, 131,132,133, 134,135 · 183,184 · 126,127 · 123,124, 125, · 111,112,113, 114,115,116, 117,118,119, 120 · 122 · 93 · 102 · 92 · 91 · 94 · 96 · 98 · 99 · 97 · 95 · 105 · 121 · 104 · 103 · 106 · 136 · 137 · 140 · 141 · 138 · 139 · 181,182 · 195,196

▲ See other chapters

ADVERTISERS AND PLACES OF INTEREST

East Sussex has been witness to some of the most momentous events in the history of England. The coastal village of Pevensey was the landing place of William, Duke of Normandy and his army in 1066 and, as every school child knows, William proceeded to defeat Harold near Hastings and claim the crown of England. Hastings and Battle, the town that grew up around the site of the battlefield, have museums and exhibitions on these history-changing events.

The victorious Normans soon set about building castles and fortifications from which to defend their new territory, as well as religious buildings, and the area is still rich in Norman architecture.

The south coast was always an obvious target for

Royal Pavilion, Brighton

invasion and, in the days before the Royal Navy, the confederation of Cinque Ports was established to provide a fleet of ships to defend the coast. Many Sussex towns, now some distance from the sea, were part of the confederation. The silting up of the harbours has changed the landscape of the East Sussex coast considerably in the last 1,000 years.

Nowadays the coast is the preserve of holiday makers, taking advantage of the generally moderate climate and the bracing sea air. The thriving resorts of Brighton and Eastbourne began life as quiet fishing villages but developed rapidly at the beginning of the 19th century. Brighton is best known for its exotic Royal Pavilion, designed in magnificent Indian style by John Nash for the Prince Regent. Eastbourne, by contrast, was carefully planned and laid out in genteel style by William Cavendish, the 7th Duke of Devonshire, close to the chalk cliffs of Beachy Head. St Leonards and Bexhill are quieter resorts and perhaps the most picturesque of all is Rye, with its many medieval buildings.

Away from the coast, on the high ridges of the Weald, is the largest area in southeast England that has never been put to agricultural use. Ashdown Forest was a royal hunting ground and its thriving population of deer made it a favourite sporting place. The network of tracks across the forest goes back to prehistoric times, the Romans built a road straight across it and the rights of commoners to gather wood for fuel, cut peat and graze cattle, were well established by

Alfriston, South Downs

Norman times. Much of the woodland has been lost, but the remaining forest is protected as an Area of Outstanding Natural Beauty and Site of Special Scientific Interest. The surrounding area is characterised by small towns and villages of weatherboarded cottages, traditional hall houses and unspoilt farmsteads.

Many artists and writers of the 19th and 20th centuries chose to live here. A A Milne set the *Winnie the Pooh* stories in Ashdown Forest and surrounding area. Virginia Woolf and her husband Leonard lived at Monk's House, Rodmell, while her sister, Vanessa Bell, was at nearby Charleston Farmhouse in Selmeston. The Elms at Rottingdean was the home of Rudyard Kipling until 1902, when he moved to Burwash, and the village of Ditchling was home to several of the leading lights of the Arts and Crafts Movement.

ASHDOWN FOREST AND THE SUSSEX WEALD

This region of East Sussex is centred around the ancient Ashdown Forest, a royal hunting ground that also provided fuel for the area's iron industry. Much of the actual woodland has been lost both as fuel and for shipbuilding, and the area is characterised by small towns and villages of weatherboarded cottages, traditional hall houses and unspoilt farms. There is evidence in ancient tracks that the area has been inhabited since prehistoric times, but the exciting discovery of a supposedly 150,000 year old skull in 1912 at the village of Piltdown was proved some 40 years later to be a clever and complicated hoax.

Over the centuries the area has been notable for many fine houses and castles. The impressive Herstmonceux Castle, home of the Royal Observatory from 1948 until the 1980s, is a magnificent medieval brick fortress, which also provided comfortable living accommodation for its inhabitants; it is set in the most glorious gardens and parkland.

Other houses here have a more personal appeal and one, Bateman's at Burwash, was the home of Rudyard Kipling from 1902 until his death in 1936. A quiet place in a secluded position, the house has been left as it was when Kipling died and is full of his personal possessions. Ashdown Forest and Hartfield are linked with another 20th century writer, A A Milne. He lived close by and wrote the *Winnie the Pooh* stories, set in the forest and surrounding area, for the amusement of his son Christopher Robin.

CROWBOROUGH

This Wealden town, on the eastern edge of Ashdown Forest, is, at over 750 feet above sea level, one of the highest towns in Sussex. Before the arrival of the railways in the 1860s, this was a small community of iron smelters and brigands centred around the parish church and vicarage. At the heart of the town is a triangular green where stands the greystone church dating from 1744.

The railways put Crowborough within easy reach of London and it was gradually transformed into the flourishing residential town it is today. A relatively peaceful place, its convenient location attracted a number of well-known late 19th century writers including Sir Arthur Conan Doyle, creator of Sherlock Holmes, perhaps the best-known detective in the world. Conan Doyle's house, high up on Crowborough Beacon, was a country house called Windlesham. Apparently he nicknamed it Swindlesham because of the amount it cost to extend and refurbish it.

AROUND CROWBOROUGH

GROOMBRIDGE
4 miles N of Crowborough on the B2110

This unspoilt village straddles the county border with Kent and, while the Sussex part of the village, which grew up around the railway station, has little to offer, the Kent side is particularly charming. The name is said to be derived from the Saxon 'Gromen', meaning man as in bridegroom. Centred around a triangular green, there are attractive 15th and 16th century estate cottages and a superb manor house **Groombridge Place**, dating from the 17th century. The

Gardens at Groombridge Place

site on which the foundations were laid is much older and there is some evidence that there was first a Saxon then a Norman castle here. Built by Charles Packer, the Clerk of the Privy Seal, who accompanied Charles I on his unsuccessful journey to Spain to ask for the Infanta's hand in marriage, Groombridge Place is a splendid redbrick house surrounded by a moat. Set within beautiful terraced gardens, the house has a small museum dedicated to Sir Arthur Conan Doyle, who was a frequent visitor to the house and the surrounding woodland known as the Enchanted Forest. This is indeed a magical place, with a wild wood area, a Celtic Forest, a North American Wood and a Jurassic Valley. The gardens and woodlands are open throughout the summer months. Groombridge Manor was the model for Birlstone Manor in Conan Doyle's *The Valley of Fear*.

HADLOW DOWN
4 miles SE of Crowborough on the A272

This handsome hamlet is surrounded by winding lanes that weave their way through some of the most glorious Wealden countryside. Just outside Hadlow Down, the **Wilderness Wood** is a living museum of woodland management that does much to maintain the crafts and techniques of woodland management. Visitors can see the woodland being tended in the traditional chestnut coppices and plantations of pine, beech and fir. The wood is then harvested and the timber fashioned, using traditional techniques, into all manner of implements in the centre's workshops. There are also woodland trails, a bluebell walk and an adventure playground for children.

WALDRON
7 miles S of Crowborough off the B2192

The 13th century village **Church of All Saints** has a lovely kingpost roof and, unusually for its age, a very wide aisle and nave, the reason for which has never quite been explained.

BUXTED
5 miles SW of Crowborough on the A272

This village has long been dominated by the great house of **Buxted Park**. This Grade II listed building was built along classical lines in 1725. Almost destroyed by fire in 1940, it was restored by the architect Basil Ionides. Although altered from its original design, it was sensitively rebuilt using numerous period pieces from other locations. There are doors and chimney pieces by Robert Adam, cabinets and pillars from grand London houses and country mansions, and a particularly fine staircase from a house in Old Burlington Street in London.

In the 19th century the house was the home of Lord Liverpool who, wishing to give himself more privacy, decided to move the village further away. The villagers were incensed and refused to move, so his lordship retaliated by declining to repair the estate cottages. Eventually the villagers gave way and moved to the village that is now Buxted. However, several buildings have remained in the old location including, at the entrance to the park gates, the half-timbered **Hogge House**. Dating back to the 16th century, the house was once the home of Ralph Hogge, who is said to have been the first man to cast guns in England, in 1543. The much-restored 13th century parish church also remains in the park's grounds and the Jacobean pulpit was once used by William Wordsworth's brother, who was vicar here for a time.

MARESFIELD
5½ miles SW of Crowborough off the A22

Before the turnpikes between London and the south coast were laid through the Weald, this was a remote place. However, in the 18th century, its position at a crossroads on the turnpike ensured its development. The tall Georgian Chequers Inn is arguably the village's oldest building and a fine example of its type. Close by is a white-painted iron milestone with the number 41 and four bells and bows in outline. One of a whole chain of such milestones that stood on the old turnpike road, this is a particularly witty one as it refers to the distance, in miles, from Maresfield to Bow Bells, London.

In the neighbouring village of **Fletching** is one of the loveliest churches in East Sussex. It was here in May 1264 that Simon de Montfort kept vigil the night before he and his troops defeated Henry III at the Battle of Lewes. It is said that some of the knights who fell in the battle are buried in full armour beneath the nave.

PILTDOWN
7½ miles SW of Crowborough off the A272

Though the village itself is not well known, its name certainly is. In 1912, an ancient skull was discovered by a Lewes solicitor and amateur archaeologist, Charles Dawson, in the grounds of Barcombe Manor. At the time, archaeologists the world over were looking for a 'missing link' between man and the ape and the skull seemed to fit the bill. It had a human braincase and an ape-like jaw. The find was believed to be about 150,000 years old, and it was not until the 1950s, with much-improved scientific dating techniques, that the skull was shown to be a fake. It was actually the braincase of a medieval man who had suffered a bone-thickening disease and the jaw of an orang-utan, both carefully treated to suggest fossilisation. The perpetrator of the hoax was never discovered.

Though the skull has been proved a hoax, the village inn, which changed its name to the **Piltdown Man** in 1912, still carries the name and an inn sign with the famous skull on one side and a stone-carrying humanoid on the other.

UCKFIELD
7 miles SW of Crowborough on the B2102

Situated in the woodland of the Weald, on the River Uck, this was once a small village at the intersection of the London to Brighton turnpike road with an ancient pilgrims' way between Canterbury and Winchester. When the stagecoaches arrived, a number of coaching inns sprang up. Before this, the village had been a centre of the iron industry thanks to its plentiful supplies of wood and water.

However, despite these advantages, Uckfield remained small until the 19th century, when a period of rapid

PURE PLANTS

Blackboys Nursery, Blackboys, Uckfield,
East Sussex TN22 5LS
Tel: 01825 890858 Fax: 01825 890878

Pure Plants opened in Spring 2003 as the culmination of a lifelong dream for Brian and Fiona. They have created a nursery dedicated to providing their customers with an array of beautiful plants to enhance their gardens. They grow a wide and ever-changing range of both usual and unusual plants including trees, shrubs, climbers, perennials, grasses and ferns.

Between them Brian and Fiona have over 25 years of nursery experience and Brian has practised as a landscape architect and a garden designer. Using these skills they have created a beautiful nursery in the heart of East Sussex with wonderful views across the countryside. They both have a passion for plants and want to share it with their customers, aiming to enthuse them with new ideas, making a visit to Pure Plants a voyage of discovery.

As they grow the majority of the plants themselves they are able to do this in a way that is sympathetic to the environment. Peat usage has been reduced by 80% by using a coir and bark based compost and wherever possible biological controls and organic pesticides are used to control pests and diseases. They are also carrying out trials of pots made predominately from wood pulp for young plants, together with a completely peat-free compost.

Brian and Fiona have many plans to continue to develop Pure Plants. Pay them a visit and you will be most welcome. They are open Tuesday-Saturday 9am-5pm and every day of Bank Holiday weekends.

JOSE MIGUEL UPHOLSTERY

Brownings Farm, Craft Workshops, Blackboys,
Uckfield, East Sussex TN22 5HG
Tel/Fax: 01825 890156
e-mail: josemi@fsbdial.co.uk

In a part of the country where traditional crafts are still to be found, **José Miguel Upholstery** represents all that is best in its field. The eponymous owner comes from the northern part of Spain and has been practising his trade for almost 30 years. For the past 10 years he has been

based among the craft workshops at Brownings Farm in the village of Blackboys, a short drive from Uckfield.

José uses traditional materials and traditional techniques in the making and upholstering of pieces of furniture, some new, others here for repair and renovation; some items are made for stock, and José also undertakes commissions to make new pieces either from customers' ideas or from photographs. Much of the work is done by hand, and it is always a delight to watch a true master at work: visitors to José's workshop can see the work in progress right up to the finished product.

expansion followed the arrival of the railway.

Several of the old coaching inns survived the move from horse-drawn to steam-powered travel, and among the Victorian buildings lies **Bridge Cottage**, a very fine example of a 15th century hall house.

SHEFFIELD GREEN

8 miles SW of Crowborough on the A275

The village takes its name from the manor house, a Tudor building that was remodelled in the 1770s by James Wyatt for John Baker Holroyd, MP, the 1st Earl of Sheffield. At the same time as creating his mansion, **Sheffield Park**, the earl had Capability Brown and Humphry Repton landscape the gardens (see panel on page 138). During his time here, the earl's great friend Edward Gibbon came to stay during the last months of his life, and it was while here that he wrote much of his epic *Decline and Fall of the Roman Empire* in the library.

A later inhabitant, the 3rd Earl of Sheffield, was a keen cricketer and was the first to organise the test tours between England and Australia. At the same time he began a tradition that the visiting team came to Sheffield Park to play their first match against the Earl of Sheffield's XI. Though the house remains in private hands, the splendid gardens belong to the National Trust and are open to the public. From the mass of daffodils and bluebells in spring to the blaze of colour from the rare trees and shrubs in autumn, there is always plenty to look at and enjoy.

Not far from the house, in the village, lies the **Sheffield Arms**, a coaching inn built by the 1st Earl in the 18th century. Local stories told of a cave behind the inn with an underground passageway to

a nearby farmhouse that was used by smugglers and, in order to test out the truth of the tales, three ducks were shut in the cave. After ten days, one of the ducks reappeared - in the cellars of the farmhouse.

The village is also the terminus of the **Bluebell Railway** and the cricketing Earl would surely have been pleased with the railway's success today as he was on the board of the Lewes and East Grinstead Railway that originally built the line.

CHAILEY

9 miles SW of Crowborough on the A275

This large and scattered parish comprises three villages: North Chailey, Chailey and South Common. Though small, Chailey has some impressive old buildings including the 13th century parish church and a moated rectory. To the north, lies **Chailey Common**, a nature reserve covering some 450 acres of wet and dry heathland where also can be found **Chailey Windmill**. Unlike many Sussex windmills, Chailey's splendid smock mill was saved from ruin just in time.

Overlooking the common is **Chailey Heritage**, which was founded in 1903 as a home for boys with tuberculosis from the East End of London. The home has become a learning centre for children with disabilities and has a worldwide reputation.

NEWICK

9 miles SW of Crowborough on the A272

The village is centred around its large green on which stands an unusual long-handled pump, erected to mark Queen Victoria's Diamond Jubilee in 1897. The actor Dirk Bogarde spent some time in the area and was given his first big acting part in an amateur production here in the 1930s.

THE NATIONAL TRUST SHEFFIELD PARK GARDEN

The National Trust

Sheffield Park, East Sussex, TN22 3QX
Tel: 01825 790231 e-mail: sheffieldpark@nltrust.org.uk
Fax: 01825 791264 website: www.nationaltrust.org.uk

This is a magnificent landscaped garden, laid out in the
18th century by Capability Brown and further developed
in the early years of the 20th century by its owner, Arthur
G. Soames. The centrepiece is the original series of four lakes.
There are dramatic shows of daffodils and bluebells in
spring, and the rhododendrons, azaleas and stream garden
are spectacular in early summer. Autumn brings stunning
colours from the many rare trees and shrubs. The short walk
towards the neo-Gothic Sheffield Park House is bordered
by several autumn foliage trees and shrubs including
maples, photinias, nyssas and fothergillas.

Even in winter there are spectacular views and many
splendid walks, the most spectacular of which, is the Big
Tree Walk with its fine specimens of North American Sequoia. The walk goes past oak and beech under
planted with hardy hybrid rhododendrons and towards the end of the first lake is a superb specimen
of the rare, Mexican Pinus Montezumae planted in 1910.

At the head of the first and second lakes
is a fine specimen of Blue Cedar. The banks
of those lakes are broken by rounded clumps
of pink, white and crimson rhododendrons.
Just past the first bridge the main path goes
through groups of deciduous and evergreen
azaleas and some fine old lime trees. Beyond
the lower bridge is a fine view of a
magnificent waterfall and in summer the lake
is covered with deep pink and white flowered
water lilies. The path continues to a large
Copper Beech and a Cedrus Atlantica, where superb views across the first lake take in a landscape full
of silver birch, oaks and conifers.

An extended tour of the gardens should include the Aucklandii Walk with its Hydrangea 'Blue
Wave', a small specimen of Eucalyptus Gunnii, some wonderful Rhododendron 'Angelo' and several
large groups of pink Japanese azaleas. The Conifer Walk, although devastated by the storm of 1987,
contains many young specimens propagated from the original trees as well as a fine Acer saccharinum.
The Gentian Walk, with its two long beds of blue Chinese gentian, leads into the Stream Garden and
the Seven Sisters Glade. The former is at its best in the late spring and early summer when its plantings
of hostas, astilbes, ferns, Siberian iris, lilies and Asiatic primulas are at their peak. The Giant Lily of the
Himalayas is undoubtedly the top attraction here with its
large scented white flowers on stems at least eight feet high.
Beyond the Glade, replanted after the storm, is a grove of
superb, autumn-coloured, Tupelo trees that have already
reached 60 feet in height.

On the bank of the fourth lake two fine specimens of
Dawn Redwood and Swamp Cypress stand in front of clumps
of the huge Brazilian Gunnera with its six-foot wide leaves.
The Cascade Bridge, which crosses the cascade between the
third and four lakes is haunted, according to legend, by a
headless woman, who vanishes when approached.

NUTLEY ANTIQUES CENTRE

Libra House, High Street, Nutley,
East Sussex TN22 3NF
Tel: 01825 713220

Liza Barnes started **Nutley Antiques** 16 years ago and has
built up a fine reputation for quality, value for money and
customer care. The two floors of her shop contain a large
selection of original painted furniture in pine, mahogany,
satinwood and oak, oils and watercolours and prints, glass,
metalware and textiles. Liza is always on hand with help
and advice for buyers, browsers and trade customers, and
Nutley Antiques is open from 10am to 5pm Monday to Saturday, and 1.30pm to 5pm Sundays.

NUTLEY

5 miles SW of Crowborough on the A22

The village is home to **Nutley Windmill**,
Sussex's oldest working windmill. It was
restored in 1968 by a group of
enthusiasts after it had stood unused and
neglected from the turn of the century.

ASHDOWN FOREST

3 miles W of Crowborough on the B2026

This ancient tract of sandy heathland
and woodland on the high ridges of the
Weald is the largest area in south east
England that has never been ploughed or
put to agricultural use. The original
meaning of 'forest' was as a royal
hunting ground and this is exactly what
Ashdown Forest was. The earliest record
dates from 1268 and its thriving
population of deer made it a favourite
sporting place. However, the area was
used long before this, and in prehistoric
times there was a network of tracks
across the forest. Later, the Romans built
a road straight across it and, by the time
of the Norman invasion, the rights of the
commoners living on its fringes to gather
wood for fuel, cut peat and graze cattle
were well established.

During medieval times it was a great
place for sport and a 'pale', or ditch, was
dug around it to keep the deer within its
confines. A famous sporting owner was
John of Gaunt, Duke of Lancaster, and

during his ownership the forest became
known as Lancaster Great Park. Henry
VIII and James I were also frequent
visitors. By the end of the 15th century
much of the woodland had been cut
down to be used as fuel for the area's
iron industry; the forest was neglected
during the Civil War and by 1657 no
deer remained.

Today, the forest is designated an Area
of Outstanding Natural Beauty, a Site of
Special Scientific Interest and a Special
Protection Area for birds. It is a place of
recreation with many picnic areas and
scenic viewpoints and open access for
walking throughout. The deer have
returned and the clumps of Scotch pines
that make prominent landmarks on the
higher points of the forest were planted
in the 19th century.

WYCH CROSS

6 miles W of Crowborough on the A275

Marking the western limit of Ashdown
Forest, local folklore has it that the
village's name is derived from a cross
that was erected on the spot where the
body of Richard de Wyche, Bishop of
Chichester, rested overnight on the
journey from Kent to its burial place in
Chichester during the 13th century. This
is the location of the **Ashdown Forest
Llama Park**, one of the top visitor
attractions in Sussex.

FOREST ROW

6 miles NW of Crowborough on the A22

This hillside village in Ashdown Forest is a popular place with walkers and also a good starting point for wonderful forest drives. The village was founded in the late Middle Ages when the forest was still extremely dense in places and provided a thick swathe of vegetation between the Thames Valley and the south coast.

Unusually, many of the village's buildings are older than the parish church, which dates only from 1836. The village is also the proud owner of a stone wall which commemorates a visit made by President John F Kennedy.

HAMMERWOOD

7 miles NW of Crowborough off the A264

Down a potholed lane lies **Hammerwood Park**, a splendid mansion that was built in 1792 by Benjamin Latrobe, the architect of the Capitol and the White House in Washington DC (Latrobe's work was much admired by Thomas Jefferson and he became Surveyor of Public Buildings in 1803). The house has had a chequered history. Divided into flats in the 1960s, it was bought by the rock group Led Zeppelin in the 1970s and was rescued from ruin in the 1980s. Extensive and meticulous restoration work has been undertaken by the present owner David Pinnegar and his family, with help from volunteers and some support from English Heritage. The dining room remains derelict and there is still a massive amount of work to be done inside and out.

HARTFIELD

4 miles NW of Crowborough on the B2026

An old hunting settlement on the edge of the Ashdown Forest, which takes its name from the adult male red deer, or

LILA GALLERY

Lower Road, Forest Row, East Sussex
Tel/Fax: 01342 826724
e-mail: info@lila-jeweller-designer.com
website: www.lila-jeweller-designer.com

In the centre of the lovely village of Forest Row in the Ashdown Forest, **Lila Gallery** opened in 2001 to present the work of jeweller Lila Stern-Shewry. Her jewellery is exotic, bold and organic, combining art and wearable sculpture, and wearing her work is to experience an adventure. Drawing on nature as a major influence, Lila's work is a blaze of colour, using around 100 varieties of semi-precious stones set in silver and gold.

From the fine texture and delicate designs of the bridal pieces through to the more substantial rings ands cuffs with large stones, closer to the Greek or Roman idea of jewellery as a visual art form, Lila's work never fails to attract attention. Granulation, reticulation and various wirework techniques form the basis of design along with the unusual stones which are faceted, polished cabochons and rough stones from all over the world. Her rings, earrings, brooches and bangles, chokers, tiaras and bracelets are on display in the gallery, which is open Thursday, Friday and Saturday from 11am to 5pm, or by appointment.

hart. The village is very closely associated with A A Milne and *Winnie the Pooh*. Milne lived at Cotchford Farm, just outside Hartfield, and he set his books, which he wrote in the 1920s, in the forest. Designed to entertain his son, Christopher Robin, the books have been delighting children ever since and, with the help of illustrations by E H Shepard, the landscape around Hartfield has been brought to millions around the world.

In the village lies the 300-year-old sweet shop to which Christopher Robin was taken each week by his nanny. Now called **Pooh Corner**, this is a special place to visit for both children and those who remember the stories from their own childhood. Full of Winnie the Pooh memorabilia, the shop caters for all tastes as long as it involves Winnie. All the famous Enchanted Places lie within the parish of Hartfield. **Poohsticks Bridge**, a timber bridge spanning a small tributary of the River Medway, was fully restored in 1979.

WITHYHAM

3½ miles NW of Crowborough on the B2110

This small village, with its church and pub, was the home of the Sackville family from around 1200. The original village church was struck by lightning in 1663. The lightning was said to have come in through the steeple, melted the bells and left through the chancel, tearing apart monuments on its route. Completely rebuilt following the destruction, the church incorporates some original 14th century features including the west tower. The Sackville Chapel was commissioned in 1677 to house a memorial to Thomas Sackville, who had died aged 13. The marble memorial incorporates life-size figures of

the boy and his parents. There is also a memorial to Vita Sackville-West, the poet and owner of Sissinghurst Castle in Kent, who died in 1962.

BURWASH

Standing on a hill surrounded by land that is marsh for part of the year, Burwash is an exceptionally pretty village, whose main street is lined with delightful 17th and 18th century timber-framed and weather-boarded cottages. Among the buildings is **Rampyndene**, a handsome timber-framed house with a sweeping roof that was built in 1699 by a wealthy local timber merchant. Between the 15th and 17th centuries Burwash was a major centre of the Wealden iron industry, which brought great prosperity to the village.

However, it is not the village that brings most people to Burwash, though it certainly deserves attention, but a house just outside. In 1902, Rudyard Kipling moved from Rottingdean to **Bateman's** to combat the growing problem of over-enthusiastic sightseers. Located down a steep and narrow lane, the Jacobean house was originally built in 1634 for a prosperous local ironmaster. With its surrounding 33

Batemans, Burwash

acres of beautiful grounds, landscaped by Kipling and his wife, it proved the perfect retreat.

Kipling and his wife lived here until their deaths - his in 1936 and hers just three years later - and during his time here the author wrote many of his famous works including *Puck of Pook's Corner*, the poem *If* and the Sussex poems. Now in the care of the National Trust, the rooms of the house have been left as they were when the Kiplings lived here, and among the personal items on display is a watercolour of Rudyard Lake in Staffordshire, the place where his parents met and which they nostalgically remembered at the time of their son's birth in Bombay. Also here is a series of terracotta plaques that were designed by Kipling's father, Lockwood Kipling, and used to illustrate his novel *Kim*. Lockwood was an architectural sculptor and went to India as the principal of an

art school; he later became the curator of Lahore Museum.

While the family lived at Bateman's the only son, John, was killed on active duty during World War I at Loos, France in 1915. There is a tablet remembering the 18-year-old in the village church.

AROUND BURWASH

Three Leg Cross

4 miles N of Burwash off the B2099

In 1975, the Southern Water Authority dammed the River Bewl to create **Bewl Bridge Reservoir**, the largest area of inland water in the south east of England. A great many buildings were lost under the water but one, the 15th century **Dunsters Mill**, was taken down, brick by brick, before the waters rose and resited above the high water level.

Church House

High Street, Burwash, nr Etchingham,
East Sussex TN19 7EH
Tel: 01435 883282
e-mail: grahamandrose@sendall.fsnet.co.uk

Rosemary Sendall offers Bed & Breakfast accommodation with a difference at **Church House**, an elegant Georgian house in the heart of Burwash. The interior decoration adds to the charm with each guest bedroom displaying its own style and character; Rudyard Kipling's links with the village provided the inspiration for one room that includes antique colonial four posters and a splendid mural.

The dining room is a particularly fine room with polished oak floor and an open fireplace lit for breakfast in winter.

During their stay guests are welcome to use Rosemary's lovely garden and visit her husband Graham's studio. Leaving a career in graphic design Graham now works full time from home on his landscape and architectural paintings of the locality.

The house, standing opposite the Parish Church in the High Street, enjoys far-reaching views towards Brightling, and the surrounding countryside provides excellent walking opportunities.

View from Church House, Graham Sendall

Another couple of timber-framed farm buildings in the valley were also uprooted and sent to the Weald and Downland Museum at Singleton.

The land around Bewl Bridge is a Country Park and has much to offer, including lakeside walks, trout fishing, pleasure boat trips and glorious countryside.

TICEHURST

3½ N of Burwash on the B2099

This ancient village is filled with attractive tile-hung and white weather-boarded buildings that are so characteristic of the settlements along the Sussex-Kent border. Among the particularly noteworthy buildings here are **Furze House**, a former workhouse, and **Whatman's**, an old carpenter's cottage with strangely curving walls. The village is also home to **Pashley Manor Gardens**, which surround a

Grade I listed timber-framed house that dates from 1550. With waterfalls, ponds and a moat, these romantic gardens are typically English, with numerous varieties of shrub roses, hydrangeas and peonies adding colour and lushness at every corner. Less formally, there is a woodland area and a chain of ponds that are surrounded by rhododendrons, azaleas and climbing roses. The gardens and house are privately owned but the gardens are open to the public throughout the summer.

ETCHINGHAM

2 miles NE of Burwash on the A265

This scattered settlement, located in the broad lush valley of the River Rother, was home in the Middle Ages to the fortified manor of the de Echyngham family. Built to protect a crossing point on the River Rother, the house, which stood where the station now stands, has long

BROWSERS BARN

New Pound Farm, Wallcrouch, Ticehurst, East Sussex TN5 7JN
Tel: 01580 200938 Fax: 01580 200885
website: www.browsers-barn.co.uk

This part of East Sussex, close to the border with Kent, is filled with interesting places to explore, but few can compare with the delights that a visit to **Browsers Barn** can reveal. Inside and out, this aptly named establishment houses an amazing range of antiques

and other desirable objects, from furniture for the house and garden to huge pots, concrete Grecian urns, lamps and lighting, barometers, tableware, pictures and picture frames.

The furniture takes up the major part of the covered space, ranging from a butler's tray and occasional tables to dining suites, Welsh oak dressers, wardrobes, cupboards and display cases. Browsers Barn is owned and run by Brian Langridge and his wife Mary; Brian has been in the business for 35 years and has been here since 1987. Down the years he has built up a large and loyal clientele, and a shipping service sends items to the USA and many other parts of the world. The stock at this fascinating place changes all the time, so browsers will always find plenty of interest on every trip. The barn is located on the B2099 about three miles east of Ticehurst.

SHANKS NURSERY

Old Orchard Nursery, Burwash Common, nr Etchingham,
East Sussex TN19 7NE
Tel: 01435 882060 Fax: 01435 882728

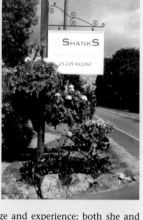

Owners David and Isobel have run **Shanks Nursery** since 2002, and their hands-on approach makes it a delight to visit at any time of the year. A lovely display of hanging baskets and a planted wheelbarrow send out a colourful welcome at the entrance, and the array of plants and flowers on display in the greenhouses and in the spacious outside areas offer a great choice. This is not a garden centre but a specialist nursery and plant centre, with thousands of plants to suit every taste and every type and size of garden, and also a good range of plant pots.

Isobel started in her parents' nursery 20 years ago and has built up an impressive store of knowledge and experience; both she and David are ready with expert advice on all aspects of plants and gardens. Browsers are always welcome at Shanks Nursery, and the charming owners put visitors under no pressure to buy. The village of Burwash Common lies on either side of the A265 a short drive east of Heathfield.

THE SWAN INN

Woods Corner, Dallington, nr Heathfield,
East Sussex TN21 9LB
Tel: 01424 838242 Fax: 01424 838525

The Swan Inn has been dispensing hospitality for 600 years, and today's hosts Di and Jane continue that tradition in fine style. The atmosphere throughout is cosy and welcoming, and the place has retained many fine original features, including oak beams and timber floors. The well-stocked bar and comfortable lounge are perfect places to relax with a drink and a chat, and

in the separate non-smoking restaurant excellent homecooked hot and cold food is served lunchtime and evening; the blackboard announces the day's choice, which might include macaroni cheese, Thai green chicken curry, sausage and mash with onion gravy and sirloin steak.

Bar snacks provide a lighter alternative, and Tuesday is take away fish & chips night. House wines are served by the bottle or in two sizes of glass, and the bar is stocked with a good range of real ales, lagers and spirits. The Swan has a really lovely garden that's perfect for alfresco dining in fine weather.

gone. Just outside the village lies **Haremere Hall**, an impressive Jacobean manor house now rented for holiday accommodation.

BRIGHTLING
2½ miles S of Burwash off the B2096

The character of this tiny hillside village is completely overshadowed by the character of one of its former residents. It is certainly not unkind to say that the Georgian eccentric, 'Mad' Jack Fuller, was larger than life since he weighed some 22 stones and was affectionately referred to as the 'Hippopotamus'. A local ironmaster, squire and generous philanthropist, 'Mad' Jack, who sat as an MP for East Sussex between 1801 and 1812, was elected only after a campaign that had cost him and his supporters a massive £50,000. Fuller was one of the first people to recognise the talents of a young painter, J M W Turner, and he was also responsible for saving Bodiam Castle from ruin.

However, it is for his series of imaginative follies that this colourful character is best remembered. He commissioned many of the buildings to provide work for his foundry employees during the decline of the iron industry and among those that remain today are Brightling Observatory, now a private house, a Rotunda Temple on his estate and the **Brightling Needle**. The 40-foot stone obelisk was built on a rise to the north of the village which is itself 650 feet above sea level.

One of Fuller's more eccentric buildings was the result of a wager. Having struck a bet with a friend on the number of spires that were visible from Brightling Park, Fuller arrived back to find that the steeple of Dallington church, which he had included in the bet, was not visible. In order to win the bet, Fuller quickly ordered his men to erect a 35-foot mock spire in a meadow on a direct line with Dallington and the monument is affectionately referred to as the **Sugar Loaf**. Perhaps Fuller's greatest structure is his **Mausoleum**, a 25-foot pyramid which he built in the parish churchyard some 24 years before his death. The story went around that Fuller was buried inside in a sitting position, wearing a top hat and holding a bottle of claret. However, despite the appropriateness of this image of his life, the parish church quashed the idea by stating that he was buried in the normal, horizontal position.

CROSS IN HAND
8 miles W of Burwash on the A267

This intriguingly named settlement lies on a busy road junction that has a post mill standing in the triangle formed by the converging roads. Certainly worth a second glance, the windmill at one time stood five miles away at Uckfield.

SPICERS B & B

21 Spicers Cottages, Cade Street, Heathfield, East Sussex TN21 9BS
Tel/Fax: 01435 866363
e-mail: travel@spicersbb.co.uk website: www.spicersbb.co.uk

In a Grade II listed beamed cottage in the hamlet of Cade Street (two
miles east of Heathfield), Valerie and Graham Gumbrell offer a warm
welcome and cosy, characterful Bed & Breakfast accommodation. The
three bedrooms - a single and a double upstairs and a ground-floor twin with level access - have en
suite or private facilities, tea/coffee tray, TV, radio-alarm and hairdryer, and central heating keeps
things snug whatever the weather. The garden and sitting room are available for guests' use, and
smokers can use the comfortable summer house at the bottom of the garden. A full English breakfast
starts the day, and evening meals are available by arrangement.

CADE STREET

5 miles W of Burwash on the B2096

This hamlet, used as a street market until
the early 20th century, is reputed to be
the place where the notorious Jack Cade,
leader of the Kentish rebellion, was killed
in 1450 by the High Sheriff of Kent,
Alexander Iden. A stone memorial marks
the spot where he fell and on it is
inscribed the moral, 'This is the Success
of all Rebels, and this Fortune chanceth
ever to Traitors'.

HEATHFIELD

6 miles W of Burwash on the A265

To the east of the town centre lies the
large expanse of **Heathfield Park**, once
owned by General Sir George Augustus
Elliot (later Lord Heathfield), the
Governor of Gibraltar and commander
of the British garrison that successfully
withstood attacks from both France and

Spain between 1779 and 1782. Despite
the wall surrounding the grounds,
Gibraltar Tower, a castellated folly
erected on his estate in his honour,
can be seen.

Heathfield remained a quiet and
undistinguished town until the arrival of
the Tunbridge Wells to Eastbourne
railway in the 19th century, after which
it grew to become an important market
town for the local area.

MAYFIELD

6 miles NW of Burwash off the A267

This ancient settlement, one of the most
attractive villages in the area, possesses
one of the finest main streets in East
Sussex, with a number of fine 15th to
17th century houses. According to local
legend, St Dunstan, a skilled blacksmith
by trade, stopped here in the 10th
century to preach Christianity to the

S F SMITHER - TRADITIONAL FAMILY BUTCHER

High Street, Mayfield, East Sussex
Tel: 01435 872335

Stephen Smither, who came from a beef farming background, trained
at Smithfield College in London and worked in several aspects of the
trade before setting up in the main street of Mayfield in 1997. **S F
Smither** is a traditional family butcher run by Stephen with his wife
Kelly and Carl Leppard, who has progressed in the shop from Saturday
lad to fully trained butcher. The shop supplies high-quality Sussex-reared beef, and also deals in lamb,
pork, free-range poultry and game, as well as cooked meats and cheeses. Other services include private
cutting, providing meat for spit-roasts and handling catering and freezer orders.

pagan people of this remote Wealden community. While working at his anvil, St Dunstan was confronted by the Devil disguised as a beautiful maiden. When she attempted to seduce the missionary, he spotted that her feet were cloven and grabbed her by the nose with a pair of red-hot tongs. The Devil gave out an almighty scream and beat a hasty retreat. But he soon returned, this time dressed as a traveller in need of new shoes for his horse. Dunstan again saw through the deception and, threatening Satan with his blacksmith's tools, forced him to promise never again to enter a house which had a horseshoe above the door.

St Dunstan became Archbishop of Canterbury in 959 and, some time later, **Mayfield Palace**, one of the great residences of the medieval Archbishops of Canterbury, was built here. Though little remains of the grand palace, a Roman Catholic Convent School

Windmill at Mayfield

THE CINNAMON GALLERY

Mayfield Chambers, High Street, Mayfield, East Sussex TN20 6AW
Tel: 01435 873773

The ancient village of Mayfield has much to interest the visitor, including the Church of St Dunstan and the remains of the Archbishops' Palace. It also has one of the finest main streets in the region, and among its many gems is **The Cinnamon Gallery**, housed in 100-year-old premises previously occupied by a bank. Interior furnishings, accessories and gifts are its stock in trade, and the owner Susan Wagland, with a lifelong interest in interior design, has filled the space with a ever-changing selection of items, all of them

personally chosen with an eye to style and individuality.

The eclectic range of homeware and gifts runs from decorative boxes, bags and baskets, picture frames, jewellery, scented candles, wooden ducks, lamps and lampshades, cushions and throws to bowls and pepper mills made by a local craftsman from wood collected around Mayfield, small items of indoor furniture and wrought-iron garden furniture in a variety of colours. The Cinnamon Gallery is open from 9.30am to 5pm Monday to Saturday.

incorporates the surviving buildings. St Dunstan also founded here a simple timber church, replaced by a stone structure in the 13th century. It was rebuilt after a fire in the 14th century and again after a lightning strike in the 17th century. The present day **Church of St Dunstan** is a conglomeration of styles, incorporating a 13th century tower, a Jacobean pulpit, a font dated 1666 and some 17th and 18th century monuments to the local Baker family.

WADHURST
5 miles NW of Burwash on the B2099

This was another great centre of the Wealden iron industry in the 17th and 18th centuries, and it was also one of the last places in Sussex to hold out against the improved coal-fired smelting techniques which had taken root in the north. Though the village **Church of St Peter and St Paul** is not quite built of

iron, the floor is almost entirely made up of iron tomb slabs, a unique collection marking the graves of local ironmasters who died here between 1617 and 1772.

Many of Wadhurst's fine buildings date from the iron industry's heyday, including the large Queen Anne vicarage on the main street, built by John Legas, the town's chief ironmaster. In the late 19th century, the village found fame when an important prize fight was held here, with many of the spectators travelling down from London to this otherwise rather obscure venue by train.

THE CINQUE PORTS AND THE EAST SUSSEX COAST

The story of this area of the East Sussex Coast is, of course, that of the events leading up to October 14th, 1066. William, Duke of Normandy came here

JACKIE MARTEL

The Market House, High Street, Wadhurst,
East Sussex TN5 6AP
Tel/Fax: 01892 784710

Jackie Martel trained as a pharmacist and worked in the family pharmacy before opening her own shop next door as a ladies fashion retailer. From the very first week three years ago **Jackie Martel** has been attracting customers from outside the area as well as building up a loyal local clientele base with quality ranges of clothes, handbags, luggage, cosmetics and jewellery. The wide frontage of the early 19th century premises provides generous display space in the windows, and the ash and navy interior has a feeling of space and light that makes browsing a real pleasure.

The clothing range includes classic Daks and Pringle, Chatham - casual and smart, colourful and very wearable by all ages - and Watercolours, Traffic and Traffic Sport which Jackie buys in Ireland. From Denmark comes the casual, well-fitting range of Elton and Junge. There are bags from England, France and Italy and cosmetics from Clarins, Floris, Crabtree & Evelyn, Elizabeth Arden and Pecksniffs. Advice and help is on hand from fully trained, professional staff, and Jackie is continually seeking new ideas to keep customers' interest.

to claim the throne of England and, after defeating Harold a few miles from the town of Hastings, this is exactly what he did. Hastings and Battle, the town that grew up around the abbey that was built on the site of the battlefield, have a concentration of museums and exhibitions on the events of the 11th century. The victorious Normans soon set about building castles and fortifications from which to defend their new territory along with religious buildings. Today this area is still rich in Norman architecture.

The South Coast was always susceptible to invasion and, in the days before the Royal Navy, the confederation of Cinque Ports was established to provide a fleet of ships to defend the coast. Many of the towns that were part of the confederation seem unlikely sources of ships today but the silting up of many of the harbours has changed the landscape of the East Sussex coast considerably in the last 1,000 years.

More recently, the coast has been the preserve of holidaymakers taking advantage of a moderate climate and bracing sea air. St Leonards was created in the 1820s and went on to become a fashionable resort, while the small and more modest Bexhill-on-Sea is home to the impressive De La Warr Pavilion, constructed from steel in the 1930s.

Perhaps the most picturesque of the coastal settlements is the ancient town of Rye. Situated on a hill and once a great haunt for smugglers, the changing fortunes of the town have left it with a great number of handsome old buildings, making it a charming place to visit.

HASTINGS

Long before William the Conqueror landed on the beach at nearby Pevensey, Hastings was the principal town of a small Saxon province that straddled the county border between Sussex and Kent. Its name comes from 'Haestingas', a Saxon tribal name, and, during the reign of Edward the Confessor, the town was well known for its sailors and ships. In fact, the town became so important that it even had its own mint. Earlier, during the 9th century, when the Danes were occupying the town, the crowing of a cockerel, awoken by the movements of the townsfolk preparing to surprise their oppressors, alerted the occupying force to the uprising. As a vengence on all cockerels, the people of Hastings instituted a game called 'cock in the pot', where sticks were thrown at an earthenware pot containing a bird. Whoever threw the stick that broke the pot was given the cockerel as his prize and the game continued to be played each Shrove Tuesday until the 19th century.

Following the Battle of Hastings, which actually took place six miles away at Battle, the victorious William returned to Hastings where the Normans began to build their first stone castle in England. Choosing the

Hastings Beach

high ground of West Hill as their site, the massive structure is now in ruins and all that can be seen on the clifftop are the original motte and parts of the curtain wall. Here, too, is the permanent display - **1066 Story at Hastings Castle**. Housed in a medieval siege tent, the exhibition transports visitors back to October 1066 through clever use of audio-visual techniques.

West Hill also contains a system of elaborate underground passages, known as **St Clement's Cave**, where the naturally formed tunnel network has been extended. The caves were leased to Joseph Golding, who spent a great deal of time fashioning the sandstone into sculptures, arcades and galleries which became one of the town's first commercial sights. Used as air raid shelters during World War II, the caves are now home to the **Smugglers Adventure**, where visitors are told stories of the town's illegal trade by a grizzly old smuggler known as Hairy Jack. After the Conquest, this already important port became a leading Cinque Port, a role it played until the harbour began to silt up in Elizabethan times. Nevertheless, the fishing industry has managed to survive here and today fishing vessels continue to be hoisted on to the shingle beach by a winch. One of the town's greatest features is the cluster of tall wooden huts used for drying nets and storing fishing tackle. Dating from the 17th century, they are known as net shops or 'deezes'. The old fishermen's church of St Nicholas is now home to the **Fishermen's Museum**, which has as its centrepiece *The Enterprise*, one of the last of the town's sailing luggers. Also here, among the displays of fishing tackle, model boats and historic pictures and

St Clement's Church, Hastings

photographs, is *The Edward and Mary*, the first locally built boat to be fitted with an engine. Staying with a maritime theme, the **Shipwreck Heritage Centre** is an award-winning museum devoted to the history of wrecked ships. Exhibits on display here include a medieval sailing barge sunk on the River Thames in London, the warship *Anne*, beached near Hastings in 1690, and *Primrose*, the last Rye barge. Additional displays cover modern methods that help eliminate the possibility of a shipwreck, including radar and satellite navigation.

The old part of Hastings consists of a network of narrow streets and alleyways - or 'twittens' - which lie between West and East Hill. There are two cliff railways, one running up each of the hills. West Hill railway runs underground, taking passengers to Hastings Castle and St Clement's Caves, while the **East Hill Railway**, the steepest in England, takes passengers to the clifftop and the beginning of **Hastings Country Park**. This 500-acre park is unlike the clifftops around Eastbourne as the drop here is not sheer but is split by a series of sloping glens over-hung with trees.

The best way to discover the town's many interesting old residential buildings, inns and churches is to take a walk up the High Street and All Saints Street. **St Clement's Church**, in the High Street, has two cannonballs embedded in its tower, one of which was fired from a French warship, while the **Stag Inn**, in All Saints Street, has a concealed entrance to a smugglers' secret passage and a pair of macabre 400-year-old mummified cats.

Occupying the old Town Hall, which was built in 1823, the **Museum of Local History** is an excellent place to find information on this historic town. Going right back to the Stone Age, and with a considerable section on the Norman Conquest, the museum also covers the more recent past, including displays on the rise of the Victorian resort, its life as a Napoleonic garrison and its role as a Cinque Port. By contrast, the **Hastings Museum and Art Gallery** covers a wider range of exhibits that also take in the county's ancient crafts. Hastings also contains a variety of attractions that are typical of a traditional seaside resort. The 600-foot pier was completed in 1872 and had to be repaired after World War II when, like many piers, it was deliberately holed in two places to prevent it being used as a landing stage for Hitler's forces. According to local legend, the Conqueror's Stone at the head of the pier was used by William the Conqueror as a dining table for his first meal on English soil. The town also has its own version of the Bayeux Tapestry, the **Hastings Embroidery**, made by the Royal School of Needlework and completed in 1966.

TRINITY WHOLEFOODS

3 Trinity Street, Hastings, East Sussex TN34 1HG
Tel: 01424 430473

Conveniently situated in the centre of Hastings, **Trinity Wholefoods** is a splendid workers' co-operative owned and managed by local people. It was set up to promote the gospel of wholefoods and to provide high-quality produce in a fair and ethical trading environment.

The shelf units and chill cabinets are filled with all manner of good things, including dairy-free and gluten-free produce, Trinity's own bagged dried fruits, nuts, rice and cereals, organic wines and ready-made meals and a fine selection of fresh organic fruit and vegetables. Also in stock are environmentally friendly cleaning materials and toiletries, and books covering all aspects of healthy eating and living.

AROUND HASTINGS

WESTFIELD

3½ miles N of Hastings on the A28

This modern redbrick village on the edge of Brede Level has at its old centre weatherboarded cottages and a Saxon church, with a beautiful Norman arch.

Vineyards in this country are still something of a novelty, but the gentle rolling slopes of the South Downs and the high mineral content of the soil are ideal. At **Carr Taylor Vineyards**, visitors can follow the Vineyard Trail from the vines, to the massive presses which crush two tons of grapes in one load, right through to the bottling plant to see the fascinating process of turning grapes into wine.

BREDE

5 miles N of Hastings on the A28

Situated to the north of the River Brede, this compact village has a long history, shrouded in myth and tales of the supernatural. One particular legend is that of the Brede Giant, based around the 16th century owner of Brede Place, Sir Goddard Oxenbridge. At over seven feet tall he was certainly a giant and, by all accounts, he was a god-fearing gentleman of the parish. However, some time after his death, stories spread that he was a child-eating monster who was eventually killed by a band of Sussex children who, having got him drunk, sawed him in half - the children of East Sussex holding down one end of him with the children of West Sussex securing the other.

CARR TAYLOR WINES LTD

Wheel Lane, Westfield, nr Hastings,
East Sussex TN35 4SG
Tel: 01424 752501 Fax: 01424 751716
e-mail: sales@carr-taylor.co.uk
website: www.carr-taylor.co.uk

Carr Taylor Wines has been a family business from the start, founded in 1971 by David and Linda Carr Taylor and now in the hands of Alexander, the second-generation wine-maker. The 37-acre estate produces high-quality English still, sparkling and fruit wines, and after many years of successful

growing they have developed a truly English style that is crisp, aromatic, fresh and very appealing. The quality comes from the soil, a combination of rich iron ore minerals and a light layer of clay shale; the unique maritime climate in the region provides a long and cool growing period which infuses a complex range of flavourings in the wines.

The Carr Taylor use of the classic, traditional method of bottled fermentation, along with advanced modern machinery, has resulted in a stunning range of award-winning wines, and a visit to the vineyard is guaranteed to be a memorable occasion. The shop is stocked with the wines, and also wine-related items, preserves, honey, mustards and chutneys, gift packs and hampers, and visitors can follow the vineyard trails or join a guided tour (groups of 20 or more). Light refreshments are always available, with picnics by the pond and a glass of chilled wine.

Tombs of the Oxenbridge family can be seen in the small Norman village church, as can a wood carving of the Madonna created by a cousin of Sir Winston Churchill who died, aged 84, in 1970. This remarkable woman travelled to America, where she learnt to carve in wood while staying for six months on a Native American reservation. In the aftermath of the Russian revolution, she journeyed to Moscow and, staying for two months at the Kremlin, she carved busts of both Lenin and Trotsky.

Oast Houses at Tufton Place, Northiam

NORTHIAM

9½ miles N of Hastings on the A28

In this large and picturesque village, characteristic white weatherboarded cottages and a number of fine 17th and 18th century buildings overlook the triangular green at its heart. Elizabeth I is known to have dined and rested on this green under a great oak tree on her journey through Kent and Sussex in 1573. Her green high-heeled shoes must have been particularly uncomfortable as she took them off here and left them to the villagers, who saved them as a memento of her brief visit. Unfortunately, the vast oak tree, which was said to be over 1,000 years old and was held together by chains and clamps, has died and all that remains of it is its giant stump.

Of the memorable buildings in the village, **Brickwall House** is one of the finest. This imposing 17th century gentleman's residence was the home of the Frewen family, an old local family who had been living in Northiam since 1573 when the first Frewen came to the village as rector. Well known for its splendid plaster ceilings, it also has a comprehensive series of family portraits from the 17th century. On display in the house are also Elizabeth I's famous green shoes and a sedan chair that belonged to Martha Frewen, who burnt to death in her bedroom in the 1750s. Several members of the family were strict Puritans and one family named their two sons Accepted and Thankful. Despite the

Great Dixter House and Garden

timber-framed rooms in the country. Many of the original rooms are filled with antique furniture, and there are some very fine examples of 18th century needlework.

However, it is the gardens that make Great Dixter so special. The imaginative design was laid out by Lutyens and various new features were added such as the sunken garden, the topiary lawn and the meadow garden. Begun by Nathaniel Lloyd and his wife, Daisy, the gardens were added to by their son Christopher. A regular contributor on gardening to magazines, Christopher's lively and inventive approach to horticulture obviously stems from working in the gardens. A mixture of formal and wild, there are many rare plant specimens on display here and the gardens are open to the public.

Northiam Station is also on the **Kent and East Sussex Railway**, which was restored in 1990 and has steam trains running on a track between Tenterden in Kent and Bodiam during the summer months. At one time too, the River Rother was navigable to this point and barges were brought upstream to be unloaded at the busy quay. This must have been an ancient port as in the 1820s the remains of a Viking long ship were found in the mud by the river where they must have lain hidden since the 9th century.

handicap of these unusual names, Accepted went on to become first the president of Magdalen College, Oxford and then the Archbishop of York, while Thankful is remembered for having donated the communion rails to the church in 1683. The church is also home to an impressive 19th century family mausoleum. Brickwall House, so named because the house and grounds are surrounded by a high stone wall, has some splendid topiary in the **Gardens**, as well as an arboretum and chess garden. Now a private school, the house and grounds are open by appointment only.

Just three miles northwest of Northiam lies **Great Dixter House and Gardens**, one of the finest examples of a late medieval hall house, surrounded by a very special garden. Built in the 1450s, the manor house was purchased in 1910, by Nathaniel Lloyd, who then employed Sir Edwin Lutyens to renovate and extend the property. He restored the house to its original medieval grandeur, as well as adding suitable domestic quarters for an Edwardian household. The Great Hall, constructed of Wealden oak and moved here from nearby Benenden to be incorporated into the building, is one of the largest surviving

BODIAM

10½ miles N of Hastings off the B2244

Situated in the valley of the River Rother, this attractive village, whose name is pronounced 'Bodjem', is home to one of the most romantic castles in the country. In the 1380s, Richard II granted Sir Edward Dalyngrygge a licence to fortify his manor house in order to defend the upper reaches of the then navigable River Rother. Thankfully, Dalyngrygge chose to interpret the licence liberally and thus one of the last great medieval fortresses in England was built. Construction on **Bodiam Castle** was begun in 1385, when the technology of castle building was at its peak and before the use of gunpowder. Completely surrounded by a wide moat, the arrow slits, cannon ports and aptly named murder holes (through which objects were thrown at attackers below) were never used in anger. However, there was a minor skirmish here in 1484, and during the Civil War the castle surrendered without a shot being fired.

Bodiam Castle and Moat

A long period of decay followed in the 17th and 18th centuries until, in 1829, plans to dismantle the castle were thwarted by 'Mad' Jack Fuller of Brightling and a programme of restoration begun. This was started by George Cubitt at the end of the 19th century, and completed by Lord Curzon in 1919. On his death in the 1920s, Lord Curzon left the castle to the National Trust and they continued the restoration programme, including replacing the floors in the towers so that visitors can climb to the top of the battlements and gain a real feel of the security that Bodiam must have offered its inhabitants over the centuries.

GUESTLING THORN
4½ miles NE of Hastings on the A259

With no real village centre and an isolated ancient church found down a small lane, it is hard now to believe that this was probably the meeting place for the important governing body of the Cinque Ports. However, as it lay on neutral territory and was not controlled by any of the ports, is would have been suitable to all the parties concerned.

PETT
4 miles NE of Hastings off the A259

Situated on top of a hill the village overlooks, to the south, **Pett Level**, a vast expanse of drained marshland that now consists of watercourses and meadows. Dotted with small lakes the area provides a suitable sanctuary for wildfowl.

FAIRLIGHT
3 miles NE of Hastings off the A259

Separated from Hastings to the west by its country park, this village is a small settlement of, chiefly, old coastguard cottages. The 19th century greystone church occupies a magnificent position overlooking the coast and its tower can be seen for miles out to sea. So much so, in fact, that when the weathervane blew down the villagers were inundated with requests from anxious sailors asking for it to be replaced. In the churchyard, among a number of elaborate tombstones, is the rather neglected final resting place of Richard D'Oyly Carte, the founder of the opera company linked with the works of Gilbert and Sullivan.

To the west of the village lies **Fairlight Glen**, an attractive place where a gentle stream approaches the sea through a steep side woodland valley. The Lovers' Seat placed here is said to be in memory of a girl who waited on this spot for her lover to return to her from his ship. Unlike many similar tales, this one had a happy ending as, not only did the girl's lover return from overseas unharmed, but her parents also consented to their marriage.

ST LEONARDS
1 mile W of Hastings on the A259

St Leonards was created in the 1820s as a fashionable seaside resort by the celebrated London architect, James Burton, who was also responsible for designing much of Bloomsbury. The centrepiece of Burton's plans was the Royal Victoria Hotel, which, although still standing, is now rather overshadowed by the vast **Marina Court**, built in the 1930s to resemble an ocean liner. Assisted by his son, Decimus, a talented architect in his own right who later designed the Wellington Arch at Hyde Park Corner, London, James Burton went on to create a model seaside town that was designed to attract wealthy and aristocratic visitors.

In its heyday, the town's formal social activities took place in the Assembly Rooms, behind the Royal Victoria Hotel, a classical building that had a tunnel running between the two so that the hotel could provide suitable refreshments for the wide variety of functions. The rooms are now the Masonic Hall. During the Victorian era, this well-organised town even had its own services area. Mercatoria was the tradesmen's quarters and Lavatoria the laundrywomen's.

The delightfully informal **St Leonards Gardens** stand a little way back from the seafront and were originally private gardens maintained by subscriptions from the local residents. Acquired by the local council in 1880, they form a tranquil area of lakes, mature trees and gently sloping lawns that can now be enjoyed by everyone.

In the churchyard of the parish church, which was destroyed by a flying bomb in 1944 and rebuilt in a conservative modern style in the 1960s, lies James Burton's curious tomb - a pyramid vault where he and several other family members are buried.

BULVERHYTHE
3 miles W of Hastings on the A259

A port during the Middle Ages, in the 19th century the noise made by the shingle as it was washed by the tide was called the 'Bulverhythe Bells' and their sound was seen as an indicator of bad weather by local fishermen. Just off the

WINDSOR HOTEL

9 Warrior Square, St Leonards on Sea, East Sussex TN37 6BA
Tel: 01424 422709 e-mail: enquiries@thehotelwindsor.com
website: www.thehotelwindsor.com

This Regency building has been providing guest accommodation since 1855, and friendly Norwegian owner, Hilde Swendgaard, continues the tradition in fine style. Overlooking both St Leonards seafront and the grandeur of Warrior Square, the hotel is a short walk from central Hastings. Open all year round, The Windsor offers comfortable, practical accommodation with a pleasant licensed bar-lounge. Rooms are individually decorated and most are en-suite.

coast, at very low tides, the remains of the wreck of the Dutch East Indiaman *Amsterdam* are clearly visible.

BEXHILL-ON-SEA

5 miles W of Hastings on the A259

This small seaside resort became a popular resort in the 1880s thanks in part to the influential De La Warr family, who lived at the original village of Bexhill, just a mile from the coast. The old Bexhill was an ancient place, with its roots well established in Saxon times, when the land around 'Bexlei' was granted to Bishop Oswald of Selsey by Offa, King of Mercia. Fortunately a good many of the older buildings have survived the late 19th century development including old weatherboarded cottages, a 14th century manor house and also the part Norman parish church.

Among the many late Victorian buildings, the **De La Warr Pavilion** stands out. Built in the 1930s by Erich Mendelsohn and Serge Chermayeff, it is a fine example of art deco, a style that was becoming fashionable at the time. Looking rather like an ocean going liner, with its welded steel frame, curves, abundance of glass and terraces, the Grade I listed building is currently undergoing a restoration and refubishment programme due for completion in Spring 2005. As well as live performances, new galleries will present major exhibitions of the works of new artists.

For what would appear today to be a relatively conservative resort, Bexhill was the first seaside town to allow mixed bathing on its beaches - in 1900! A very progressive move then, the gently sloping shingle beaches still offer safe and clean bathing as well as facilities for a range of watersports. The town has another first: in 1902, it played host to the birth of British motor racing when a race and other speed trials were held here. The huge Edwardian cars - nine-litre engines were not uncommon - flew along the unmade roads around Galley Hill and stopping was a matter of applying the rear wheel brakes, brute force and luck. Among the competitors were some of the best-known names of early motoring, including H S Rolls, Herbert Austin and Baron Rothschild. The anniversary of this first race was celebrated here each year until quite recently.

To discover more about the history of this seemingly modern but truly ancient settlement a visit to the **Bexhill Museum** is a must. As well as a range of exhibitions on local wildlife, history, geology and archaeology, there are also dinosaurs exhibits and even a Great Crab from Japan.

NINFIELD

7 miles NW of Hastings on the A269

To the north of this village, straggled along a ridge, lies Ashburnham Place, a redbrick house that is much less impressive than it once was. The house has been subject to many alterations over the years, including the addition of a new block in the 1960s. However, the landscaped **Ashburnham Park** has survived much as it was conceived by Capability Brown in the 18th century, though a large number of trees were lost in the hurricane of 1987.

Close to the house lies the parish church where there are several monuments to the landowning Ashburnham family. One member of the family, John Ashburnham, was a supporter of the monarchy in the Civil War and he followed Charles I on his last journey to the scaffold in London. Imprisoned in the Tower by Cromwell, the late king's possessions that he was wearing on the day of his death - his shirt, underclothes, watch and the sheet in which his body was wrapped - came into the hands of the Ashburnham family. These relics were kept in the church following the restoration of Charles II to the throne and for many years were believed to offer a cure for scrofula, a glandular disease called King's Evil.

BATTLE

6 miles NW of Hastings on the A2100

This historic settlement is, of course, renowned as being the site of the momentous battle, on 14th October 1066, between the armies of Harold, Saxon King of England, and William, Duke of Normandy. The Battle of Hastings actually took place on a hill, which the Normans called 'Senlac', meaning 'lake of blood', and even today some believe in the myth that blood seeps from the battlefield after heavy rain. However, any discolouration of the

water is, in fact, due to iron oxide present in the subsoil. The battle was a particularly gruesome affair, even for those times, and it was not until late in the afternoon that Harold finally fell on the field. However, what happened to Harold's body remains a mystery. One story tells how it was buried by his mother at Waltham Abbey in Essex, while another suggests that William the Conqueror wrapped it in purple cloth and buried it on the clifftop at Hastings.

After the battle and subsequent victory, William set about fulfilling his vow that, if he were victorious, he would build an abbey. Choosing the very spot where Harold fell, **Battle Abbey** was begun straight away and was consecrated in 1094. Throughout the Middle Ages the Benedictine abbey grew increasingly more wealthy and powerful as it extended its influence over wider and wider areas of East Sussex. This period of

BLACKSMITH'S RESTAURANT

43 High Street, Battle, East Sussex TN33 0EE
Tel: 01424 773200

Owner-chef Martin Howe has built up a loyal following at **Blacksmith's Restaurant**, since being established by him in 1981. The attractive black-and-white exterior is adorned with lovely floral displays while inside the look is charmingly traditional, with beams, carpets, pristine linen and sparkling silver and glass. Martin's menu draws its inspiration from Britain and Continental and Eastern Europe, and typical dishes include wild cherry soup; oak-smoked haddock fishcake; veal escalope with a creamed mushroom sauce; and fillet of beef filled with goose liver wrapped in Parma ham, served on a toasted brioche with a Marsala sauce.

TOLLGATE FARMHOUSE

59 North Trade Road, Battle, East Sussex TN33 0HS
Tel: 01424 777436
website: www.tollgatefarmhouse.co.uk

In a pleasant setting a short stroll from historic Battle Abbey, **Tollgate Farmhouse** is a delightful choice for a Bed & Breakfast break. It has earned a 4 diamond award from the English Tourist Council so guests can be assured of quality from this family run establishment. Its tastefully appointed bedrooms include en suite double and twins and a family suite; all have television, radio-alarm, tea trays and hairdryers. Breakfast is served in the sun lounge overlooking the garden and swimming pool.

THE GEORGE HOTEL

23 High Street, Battle, East Sussex TN33 0EA
Tel: 01424 775512 Fax: 01424 775527
e-mail: georgebattle1066@aol.com website: www.thegeorge-battle.com

For over 300 years, **The George Hotel** has been at the centre of life in the historic town of Battle, and today's guests can look forward to modern comfort and amenities combined with a well-preserved sense of the past. The 23 en suite bedrooms all have TV, tea-making facilities and hairdriers, and two rooms boast splendid four-posters – one also with a Jacuzzi. A full English breakfast starts the day, and excellent lunches and dinners are served in the newly opened Ostlers Restaurant.

prosperity, however, came to an abrupt end in 1537 when Henry VIII dissolved the monasteries. The abbey buildings were granted to Sir Anthony Browne and, during a banquet to celebrate his good fortune, a monk is said to have appeared before Sir Anthony announcing that his family would be killed off by fire and water. The prophecy was forgotten as the family flourished until, some 200 years later, in

1793, the home of Sir Anthony's descendant, Cowdray Hall near Midhurst, burnt to the ground. A few days later another member of the family was drowned in the River Rhine in Germany.

Although little of the early Norman features remain, Battle Abbey has much to offer the visitor. The most impressive part is the Great Gatehouse, a magnificent medieval abbey entrance

FARTHINGS FARM

Catsfield, Battle, East Sussex TN33 9BA
Tel: 01424 773107
e-mail: penny.Rodgers@btopenworld.com
website: www.farthingsfarm.co.uk

Peace, comfort, excellent hospitality and lovely views are among the attractions of a stay at **Farthings Farm**, an Edwardian farmhouse set half a mile from the road in 70 acres of rolling countryside. It is the home of Penny and John Rodgers, who offer guest accommodation in three en suite rooms furnished with a mixture of antique and modern pieces. The oak-floored guest lounge has plenty of books, music and games and a woodstove fire in winter, and when the weather is warmer guests are welcome to sit or stroll in the garden. Penny is an accomplished cook, and days on the farm start with a superb breakfast, cooked or uncooked, taken in the dining room or out on the terrace.

The uncooked choice includes fruit and fruit juices, homemade muesli and homemade bread and preserves, while the cooked version using local produce when possible adds all the traditional items

that make up an English breakfast, with other options such as kippers, smoked haddock, kedgeree or pancakes with maple syrup and bacon; vegetarians are well looked after with the likes of homemade meatless sausages and cashew & coriander burgers. Evening meals are available by arrangement and are equally memorable using home-grown vegetables and fruit. The house faces south, overlooking woodland, fields and a lake. Battle is a 20-minute walk away on the 1066 footpath, and there are many attractions, both scenic and historic, in the countryside or on the coast, within an easy drive.

Battle to Bexhill

Distance: 5.3 miles (8.5 kilometres)

Typical time: 150 mins

Height gain: 60 metres

Map: Explorer 124

Walk: www.walkingworld.com
ID:206

Contributor: Jacky Rix-Brown

Having crossed small streams in the early part of the walk you come to the low marshy lands formed by the streams which gather into the Coombe Haven. The latter part of the walk takes you through the quiet residential streets of Bexhill. It ends at a car park beside a park in which are a museum and the ruins of a manor.

Features:

River, Sea, Toilets, Museum, Church, Castle, Wildlife, Birds, Flowers, Great Views

Access Information:

Battle is on the main railway line from Hastings to London, and Bexhill is on the railway line between Hastings and Eastbourne. Bus service 328 runs between Battle and Bexhill, and other buses connect each town with Hastings. Parking in Battle may be tricky, but the walk finishes at a large car park in Bexhill so best advice is to park there, walk to Bexhill Town Hall Square and take the bus to Battle.

Additional Information:

In 1066 William, Duke of Normandy, landed at Pevensey. King Harold marched south to defend his land, but was defeated by William in the Battle of Hastings, which was fought at Senlac Hill. William founded a monastery there, and round it grew the town of Battle. The 1066 Country Walk connects Battle with Pevensey, Rye, Hastings and Bexhill. These five historic towns abound with interesting places to visit, In this section:Battle - Abbey, Museum, ancient church, pubs and eating places, shops, tourist information centre. Crowhurst – Fore Wood nature reserve, ancient church, 1,000 year Yew tree. Bexhill – Museum, ancient church, beach, shops, pubs, eating places and tourist information centre.

Description:

Appropriately for the scene of the Battle of Hastings in 1066, the town of Battle is the hub of the 1066 walks. The main walk is from Pevensey to Rye via Battle. This spur takes you from Battle almost due south to the seaside town of Bexhill-on-sea. It begins on Senlac hill where Battle Abbey marks the place where King Harold fell. But before you start the town is well worth exploring, with many interesting places to visit.

The walk takes you out through rolling hills, passes through a woodland nature reserve and the sleepy village of Crowhurst with its ancient church and centuries old yew tree.

Walk Directions:

1 From the front of Battle Abbey, walk west past the Pilgrims Rest restaurant (formerly the Abbey hospice). The road ends in a track and the 1066 walk symbol points the way along the track beside a wood.

2 Where the ways divide be careful as 2 routes are both 1066 walk! Ignore the right fork to Pevensey and take the left to Bexhill. Initially this stays alongside the wood. Continue over a hill, across a stream and on until meeting a tarmac track near a road.

3 On reaching the track cross straight over (as shown by arrow of 1066 symbol) and over a stile onto a path that runs between fence and hedge, parallel to a road. Be careful! The stile from the path leads straight onto a road which can be quite busy, as well as being on a blind bend with another road leading off and a drive alongside – quite a road safety hazard. Cross the main road and go down the side road directly opposite the end of the path.

4 Soon leave the side road (Talham Lane), taking the right fork towards Peppering Eye Farm (private road). Continue past the farm and other houses, ignoring paths to right and left, and go up hill towards woods.

5 At major junction of paths, near cottage, at start of woods, go left then keep right (effectively forking, rather than turning, left) as shown by 1066 symbol. On emerging from wood, turn left downhill with the footpath. (The track ahead here is not a right of way). Cross the stream and enter another wood. On entering this wood bend right on the main track, going south. Keep your eyes skinned, this is the Fore Wood Nature Reserve. There was an Elephant Hawk Moth larvae beside the path when we were there! Stay on the main track through the wood.

6 Here the map doesn't fully match the ground. In the wood just past a pond on the left (not on map) you reach this fork in the path. Keep right and go to the stile at the edge of the wood, where the familiar 1066 symbol directs you forward. Cross the field and bear left up the hill on the obvious track and continue to the road.

7 Turn right onto the road through Crowhurst village. Here I suggest deviating from the 1066 walk to go through the village. Go right into the church and pass its ancient yew. Go right round the church and leave the churchyard at the bottom gate and turn right down the hill. Cross

the stream and up the other side (on road) past the millennium memorial garden. Keep left at the fork. Ignore the first footpath on the right. Where the road bends sharp left go right over a style onto the footpath beside a stream. You are now back on the 1066 way. Continue on this path by the stream for about a kilometre.

8 Just past the track to Adam's Farm, the main track curves left beside the stream. Turn right, as shown by 1066 sign, to follow a zig-zag path to the bridge. The ground is marshy so keep to the path even though it takes you right then left. There are actually 2 bridges across adjacent watercourses. From the bridges continue south across the marshland, noting the embankments where a railway line used to cross on a long viaduct.

9 As you approach the stile it is hidden in a corner under a tree. Once over it, continue up a dry valley beside the hedge with the railway embankment to your left, then on across an open field, rising to cross the course of the old railway. Follow the track up, past Little Worsham farm, where it is more of a road.

10 At the T-junction turn right and pass a low building with a red tiled roof. After about 400m at another junction turn left toward Upper Worsham Farm. Continue about 150m.

11 Look out a fork, where the main track continues south and another track forks right to the farm. In the angle of the fork, almost hidden by the hedgerow, and just to the right of a telegraph pole, there is the stile. Climb this and continue on a well-walked path across the field, over a stream and on beside a hedge until you come to a busy road, the A2036.

12 With care, cross the main road directly, and enter an enclosed footpath between gardens. Follow this for about 300m until it meets a road at right angles.

13 On emerging onto a residential road, do not take the continuation of the path between gardens, but turn left along the pavement (as signed 1066). Continue to the next road junction and turn Right (another 1066 sign). Follow this road to its end.

14 Take the footpath which leaves the end of the road going left up onto a bridge across a very busy trunk road, A259. On the far side of the bridge the footpath takes you back to the right to the end of another road. This road leads you straight to the car park where the walk ends on the opposite side of another road.

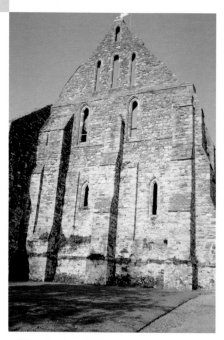

Abbey Remains, Battle

built around 1338. The **Prelude to Battle Exhibition** introduces visitors to the site and its history. This is followed by a video on the Battle of Hastings. Other on-site attractions are a children's themed play and picnic area and an educational Discovery Centre.

There is more to Battle than the abbey and the battlefield, and any stroll around the streets will reveal some interesting buildings. The **Battle Museum of Local History** is an excellent place to discover more about the lives of those living in East Sussex through the ages and there is also a replica of the Bayeux Tapestry. Opposite the abbey, and housed in a 600-year-old Wealden hall house, is **Buckleys Yesterday's World**, where more than 50,000 objects are displayed in authentic room settings, which cover the period from 1850 to 1950. There are even replicas of a Victorian kitchen, a

1930s country railway station and a bicycle shop.

SEDLESCOMBE
6½ miles NW of Hastings on the B2244

This former flourishing iron founding settlement is a now a pleasant and pretty village, stretched out along a long sloping green, where the parish pump still stands under a stone building of 1900. The interior of the village church, on the northern edge of the village, retains its seating plan of the mid-17th century, which lays out the hierarchy of this rural society in no uncertain terms. The front pew was retained for the Sackville family, with the other villagers seated behind; right at the back, the last few pews were kept for 'Youths and Strangers'.

To the southeast of the village, centred around an adapted 19th century country house, is the internationally renowned **Pestalozzi Children's Village**. Founded in 1959 to house children from Europe who had been displaced during World War II, the centre follows the theories of the Swiss educational reformer, Johann Heinrich Pestalozzi. This influential gentleman believed that young people of all nationalities should learn together and took into his care orphans from the Napoleonic Wars. The village now takes children from Third World countries, who live here in houses with others from their country under the care of a housemother of the same nationality. After studying for their first degree, the young adults return to their own countries where their newly learnt skills can be put to excellent use in the development of their homelands.

ROBERTSBRIDGE
10 miles NW of Hastings off the A21

Situated on a hillside overlooking the valley of the River Rother, the village's name is a corruption of Rothersbridge. In the 12th century an annexe to a Cistercian Abbey was founded here by the river, and today some of the buildings can still be seen, now part of a farm. The unusually high pitched roof protects the remains of the abbot's house and there are other ruins in the garden. Robertsbridge has long been associated with cricket and, in particular, the manufacture of cricket bats. The village establishment of Grey Nicholls has made bats for many of the sport's famous names, including W G Grace, who once stayed at The George Inn in the village.

Hurst Green

12 miles NW of Hastings of the A21

Set in four acres of gently sloping Weald farmland, close to the village, **Merriments Gardens**, is a place that never fails to delight its visitors. A naturalistic garden, where the deep borders are richly planted according to the prevailing conditions of the landscape, it nurtures an abundance of rare plants. By contrast, there are also borders that are planted in the traditional manner of an English garden and colour themed, using a mix of trees, shrubs, perennials and grasses.

RYE

This old and very picturesque town was originally granted to the Abbey of Fecamp in Normandy, in 1027, and was only reclaimed by Henry III in 1247. It became a member of the confederacy of the Cinque Ports, joining Hastings, Romney, Hythe, Dover and Sandwich as the ports which were a key part of the south coast's maritime defence and became a full Head Port in the 14th

Forget-Me-Not

72 Church Square, Rye, East Sussex TN31 7HF
Tel: 01797 222330

June O'Sullivan, landscape gardener and designer, and Lester Hewitt, artist, combine to offer an amazing selection of high-quality goods and gifts at their lovely shop in an historic setting in the town of Rye. Included in this impressive range stocked by **Forget-Me-Not** are Gabriella Miller pottery – all the pieces are individually handmade and finished in cream or gentle pastels; Antique Designs exclusive bed and table linen; Lothantique perfumes, soaps, sprays and linen fresheners; Bristol China – tea sets, trinket boxes, clocks; and Anne Cotterill's fine limited edition prints and greetings cards – she is a member of the Society of Botanical Artists.

There are cushions and soft furnishings made especially for June, pieces of original French furniture, and something unexpected but very charming – a range of Baby Pure first shoes, sizes 1 and 2, made from the softest of materials and available in a choice of colours. Forget-Me-Not stands just a few steps from the magnificent parish church of St Mary, which celebrated its 900th anniversary in 2003. The church is just one of many places of historic interest in Rye, which overlooks both the Rother estuary and Romney Marshes from its hilltop position.

FLETCHER'S HOUSE TEA ROOMS

2 Lion Street, Rye, East Sussex TN31 7LB
Tel: 01797 222227
e-mail: thelowes52@yahoo.co.uk

Named after the Elizabethan dramatist born here in 1579, **Fletcher's House** is a very popular tea room located at the top of Lion Street next to the parish church of St Mary. It has been in business since 1932, and is run by Peter and Jeanette Lowe, who are trained chefs with over 30 years experience. Behind the half-timbered and Sussex peg tile frontage the look in the three tea rooms is charmingly traditional, with a woodstrip floor, exposed brickwork, heavy old oak beams, open fires, brass and copper ornaments, and a prominent painting of John Fletcher himself, one of the leading playwrights of his day and best known for his collaboration with Shakespeare and Francis Beaumont.

Home cooking, with Jeanette at the helm, is the order of the day, and the food ranges from light snacks and lunches to cakes, pastries and splendid Sussex cream teas. The lunchtime choice is particularly tempting, and many of the dishes have a contemporary ring: wild mushroom soup, Moroccan filo parcels, parmesan chicken, Kent hop sausages, salmon fish cakes flavoured with lemon grass and coriander. Fletcher's House, which has seats for 50, with a further 20 in the secret walled garden, is open Wednesday to Sunday, and on Bank Holiday Mondays from 10am-5pm (5.30pm in season).

MARTELLO BOOKSHOP

26 High Street, Rye, East Sussex TN31 7JJ
Tel: 01797 222242 Fax: 01797 227335
e-mail: martbook@aol.com

This High Street site has been a booksellers since at least 1894, having a series of owners that include A. Whiteman, publisher of Whiteman's Almanac and Gouldens of Rye, founded by Fran Goulden in 1929. That family business continued as stationers and booksellers until taken over by the Reavells in 1975. They renovated the shop and renamed it **Martello Bookshop** after the Martello Towers that are such an important feature of the East Sussex coastal landscape. Terry and Wendy Harvey, the present owners, took over from the Reavells in 1996 and have continued to expand the business. Theirs is a magnificent general bookshop, with a wide range of paperbacks and sections on

mind, body and spirit, art, photography, crafts, cookery, gardening, sports, reference and dictionaries and children's books.

This is the best place to find books on local history, maps and wildlife, and it also stocks an outstanding selection of cards and calendars. The bookshop holds regular signings by prominent authors, and exhibitions of photography and local crafts. Terry and Wendy formed the Martello Reading Club in 1999, and twice a month, on a Monday and a Wednesday, members read a chosen book and discuss it in detail at the next meeting.

century. Over the years, this hill top town, which overlooks both the Rother estuary and the Romney Marshes, was subjected to many raids, including one by the French in 1377, which left no non-stone building standing. As a result, the rebuilt town is one of the prettiest in England, with timber-framed houses, some with jettied upper storeys. The harbour suffered the same fate as many ports along the south coast as it silted up and the harbour was moved to further down the estuary. **Rye Harbour Nature Reserve**, on the mouth of the River Rother, is a large area of sea, saltmarsh, sand and shingle which supports a wide range of

The Quay, Rye

both plant, animal and bird life.

Rye's prominent hill top position was a factor, which made it a strategically important town from early times. A substantial perimeter wall was built to

CINQUE PORTS POTTERY

The Monastery, Conduit Hill, Rye, East Sussex TN31 7LE
Tel: 01797 222033 e-mail: cppottery@aol.com
Fax: 01797 222400   website: www.cinqueportspottery.com

Cinque Ports Pottery enjoys the most atmospheric of settings in an Augustinian friary founded in 1379 and commonly known as the Monastery. This magnificent building, with stone walls over two feet thick and Gothic arched windows, is situated in a steep cobbled way leading from the High Street. Stairs lead up the outside of the building into the ancient chapel, which now houses potters. Next door is the casting section, where goods are sponged, fettled and dried. Downstairs are the glazing and painting departments. Every item is hand-painted, either for stock or for individual commissions.

The viewing gallery enables visitors to follow the whole fascinating process of creating pottery from beginning to end, finishing in the showroom, where all the end products can be bought. These

include commemorative pieces, house name plaques, hand-painted studio ware by local artists, tiles to customise a bathroom or kitchen, and many collectables designed in house by James Elliott. The Country Gentlemen animal series is as popular as ever, including Sir Freddy Fox in his green or red hunting jacket and his wife Felicity. Visitors can also make a booking to paint their own pottery, creating a unique piece to keep or to give as a present. Once the piece is chosen, help is on hand to plan the colours and design and paint the pot, which will be glazed and fired ready for collection or for sending out a week later.

GRAHAM CHINA & GLASS SPECIALISTS

91 High Street, Rye, East Sussex TN31 7JN
Tel: 01797 222357 Fax: 01797 321149
e-mail: csanyal@graham-of-rye.co.uk
website: www.graham-of-rye.co.uk

Graham China & Glass Specialists has been a family business
for more than 40 years, and the well-appointed shop in the
High Street is in the more than capable hands of owner
Sheelagh Jenkinson and her daughter Christine (with a little
help from dog J). Behind the black-and-white, glass-fronted
exterior, the well-lit display rooms hold an impressive array
of china and glass tableware, figurines, miniatures and collectables.

Graham Specialists are the sole agents in town for Royal Doulton, Spode, Royal Worcester, Royal
Crown Derby, Wedgwood and Waterford, and other
famous names represented on the shelves and in the
display cabinets include the Walt Disney Collection,
Border Fine Arts and Lilliput Lane Collectable
Cottages. Most of the major suppliers have collectors'
clubs and Christine is happy to assist with any club
business for existing or new members. The ancient
Cinque Port town of Rye is well worth taking time to
explore, and anyone looking for a special gift to take
away from a visit should certainly make a point of
taking time to browse at Graham China & Glass
Specialists.

THE GLOBE INN

Military Road, Rye, East Sussex TN31 7NX
Tel: 01797 227918
e-mail: info@theglobe-inn.com
website: www.theglobe-inn.com

Having previously opened a delicatessen on the main
street of Rye, the brother-and-sister team of Dezi Dalton
and Javed Khan turned their attention to breathing new
life into **The Globe Inn** on the town's northeastern edge.
They totally refurbished the white weatherboarded inn
and opened it in January 2004. It has quickly become
one of the most popular spots in the area for relaxed drinking and great eating, functioning equally
brilliantly as convivial local and a fine restaurant.

The two resident chefs put a major emphasis on
fresh local produce, organic wherever possible, and
their menus change constantly. Some dishes have
become firm favourites, including moules marinière,
potted shrimps and the Rye Deli platter for starters;
pan-fried duck with chilli jam, braised lamb shank and
plaice fillets stuffed with prawn and leek mousse for
main courses; and tarte au citron and crème brûlée
among the desserts. The Globe holds regular
gastronomic evenings and charity dinners, and in fine
weather barbecues are organised in the award-
winning garden.

defend the northern approaches and one of its four gateways, the **Landgate**, still survives today. This imposing structure is all that remains of the fortifications erected by Edward III in the 1340s.

Found in the heart of this ancient town, **Durrant House Hotel** is a charming, spacious Georgian residence that also has a part to play in the history of Rye. Built for a local gentleman in the 17th century, the house was, like so much of the town, at the centre of the smuggling trade. However, in the 18th century the property was bought by Sir William Durrant, a friend of the Duke of Wellington, and gained respectability. During the Napoleonic Wars, it was an operations centre for the defence of the Channel port and a relay station for carrier pigeons bringing news of the victory at Waterloo.

The town grew prosperous in the late medieval period due to the activities of its fishermen and the merchant fleets that traded with continental Europe. But the loss of the harbour through silting denied Rye the chief means of earning a living and the town fell into decline. Visitors today very much benefit from this turn of events as Rye still retains a large number of medieval buildings which would undoubtedly have made way for new structures if the town had been more prosperous.

Naturally, being a seafaring town, there is an abundance of old inns, and the **Mermaid Inn**, an early timbered building down a cobbled street is one of the most famous. Rebuilt in 1420 after the devastating French raid over 40 years before, the inn was the headquarters of the notorious Hawkhurst Gang in the 18th century. The most infamous band of smugglers on the south coast in their day, they reputedly always sat with their

The Golden Fleece

16 Lion Street, Rye, East Sussex TN31 7LB
Tel: 01797 224271
e-mail: promotions@thegoldenfleece.co.uk
website: www.thegoldenfleece.co.uk

Occupying a prominent site on Lion Street, looking up towards St Mary's Church, **The Golden Fleece** specialises in traditional high-quality British country and outdoor wear. Owners Michael and Patricia Fassum have been established in Rye since 1980, having previously been in Canterbury, and they are members

of the Guild of Master Craftsmen. The Golden Fleece is the sole agent in Rye for outdoor wear by Barbour, Regatta and Target Dry, and other lines include woollen sweaters and knitwear; leisure wear by Alice Collins, Grenouille and Tulchan; and fashion wear by Gina Minetti, Concept, Slimma, Double Two and East.

The double front of the shop has well-laid out window displays of the clothes and accessories, and the carpeted interior is bright and roomy, with lots of display space, changing rooms and plenty of room for wheelchairs. The same owners also run **Goldens Rye Traders** at 86 High Street, Tel: 01797 223229. The range of clothes and accessories is equally impressive, including Wek dresses and tops; Sloggi, Poppy and Emrico casual wear; Triumph, Playtex and Caressa lingerie; Invicta, Wolsey and Oakman for men; Triumph, Beachcomber and Solar swimwear; and towels, sheets and haberdashery.

RYE LODGE HOTEL

Hilders Cliff, Rye,
East Sussex TN31 7LD
Tel: 01797 223838 Fax: 01797 223585
e-mail: info@ryelodge.co.uk
website: www.ryelodge.co.uk

The picturesque town of Rye has a great deal to attract and interest the visitor, and there's no finer base than the **Rye Lodge Hotel**. Standing in a commanding and unique position on the East Cliff, it offers stunning panoramic views across the Romney Marshes and the Rother Estuary to the sea. Before it receded, the sea actually lapped the walls of this ancient Cinque Port town, and access by land could only be gained through the Landgate, a monument built in 1329 and now standing just a few steps away from the hotel.

All Rye Lodge's 18 rooms are beautifully furnished and decorated, with en suite bath or shower

and all the modern amenities, including direct-dial telephone, satellite TV, radio, hospitality tray, mineral water and hairdrier. The De Luxe rooms are even more regally appointed, with bathrobes and slippers, mini-bar fridges, video machines, room safes and valet centres. Hands-on owners, the de Courcy family, pride themselves on the high level of personal service they offer guests, and one of the great features of the room service is breakfast in bed.

The elegant surroundings of the marble-floored Terrace Room Restaurant makes a meal an occasion to savour, and the superb

food served by candlelight is accompanied by a well-chosen selection of wines from around the world. Specialities include the renowned Romney Marsh lamb and plaice from Rye Bay. One of the jewels in the crown of this widely acclaimed hotel (AA and RAC 3 star, RAC Dining Award, ETC Silver Award) is the Venetian Leisure Centre with its heated swimming pool, sauna, spa bath and an aromatherapy steam cabinet; beauty treatments, massage and reflexology are available to sooth, relax and pamper the weary holidaymaker.

pistols close to hand in case of a sudden raid by the excisemen.

Another interesting building is the handsome Georgian residence, **Lamb House**, built by a local wine merchant, James Lamb, in 1723 and now in the care of the National Trust. The family was well known in the town and not without a certain influence. Not long after the house was built, the family were involved in a famous murder when, in 1743, a local butcher named Breads killed James Lamb's brother-in-law by mistake. His intention had been to murder James, then the town's Lord Mayor, against whom he held a grudge. Tried and found guilty, Breads was hanged on a gibbet and his bones were stolen to be used as a cure for rheumatism. Only his skull remains and it can be seen, along with the gibbet, in Rye Town Hall.

More recently, Lamb House was the home of the novelist, Henry James. He saw it in 1896 and fell in love with it; he rented it for a while, then bought it for £2,000 and lived in it until his death in 1916. Many of his personal possessions are on show in the house, including his massive French writing desk and a painting of him by Burne-Jones. Upstairs is the panelled bedroom where George I spent his first nights in England on arriving from Hanover for his coronation in 1726. His ship had struck trouble on Camber Sands and James Lamb, the Mayor at the time, offered him shelter. Henry James was also responsible for laying out the gardens and he invited many of his friends to the house, including H G Wells, Rudyard Kipling, G K Chesterton and Joseph Conrad. The literary associations do not end there as, in the 1920s, the property was leased to E F Benson, who is best remembered for

ANN LINGARD

Rope Walk, Rye, East Sussex TN31 7NA
Tel: 01797 223486 Fax: 01797 224700
e-mail: ann-lingard@ropewalkantiques.freeserve.co.uk
website: www.annlingard.mysite.freeserve.com

What started as a hobby quickly developed into a thriving business when **Ann Lingard** opened her shop Rope Walk Antiques in 1977. The spacious showrooms are contained in a handsome 18th century redbrick building that has been a rope-maker's shop serving Rye's once-important fishing industry, a sweet shop, a cycle shop and a Salvation Army chapel. The chapel is now

the light, bright main showroom, where the largest items are British antique pine furniture ranging from dressers and wardrobes to tables, display cabinets and bookcases.

The rest of the stock covers an amazing and eclectic range of antiques, bric-a-brac and collectables that includes chinaware and glassware, stone jars and bottles, chopping boards and kitchen scales, enamel pots and pans, cutlery boxes, mixing bowls, coal scuttles, candlesticks, old model boats – even some rare old books. This is certainly one of the most fascinating places in Rye, a paradise for browsers and full of bargains - and as the stock is constantly changing, every visit is guaranteed to surprise and delight. The showrooms are open from 10am to 5pm Monday to Saturday, with a short break for lunch.

CADBOROUGH COTTAGES

Cadborough Farm, 172 Udimore Road, Rye,
East Sussex TN31 6AA
Tel: 01797 225426 e-mail: info@cadborough.co.uk
Fax: 01797 224097 website: www.cadborough.co.uk

In the grounds of a 24-acre farm on the western edge of Rye, **Cadborough Cottages** provide excellent self-catering accommodation. Recently converted from late-19th century brick farm buildings, they offer space, comfort and privacy in a number of cottages designed for two. Brandy's Cottage stands in its own terraced courtyard with a seating area, barbecue and entrance by a gate into the field. It has a king-size double bed, large en suite bathroom and an open-plan living and kitchen area with French doors opening on to the courtyard.

Dairy Cottage is similar, with a double bed that can be split into twin beds. The Dairy Studios, Buttercup and Daisy, are located in the old dairy, off an inner hall, and the Stables cottage has its own little garden. All the cottages are decorated and furnished to a very high standard, and all have central heating, fully equipped kitchens and televisions. The historic town of Rye is a 15-minute walk away (or just two minutes in the car), and there are many pleasant walks leading from the farm along the cliff path. The cottages are all non-smoking and are not designed for children.

FLACKLEY ASH HOTEL

Peasmarsh, nr Rye, East Sussex TN31 6YH
Tel: 01797 230651 Fax: 01797 230510
website: www.flackleyashhotel.co.uk

The **Flackley Ash Hotel** is set in five acres of beautiful grounds in a quiet village four miles northwest of Rye. Guests have a wide choice of well-appointed en suite accommodation, including four-poster beds, de luxe rooms and suites, and among the hotel's amenities are a swimming pool, sauna, whirlpool bath and gym. An excellent breakfast starts the day, and

evening meals served by candlelight put the emphasis on the best and freshest of ingredients, including fish from local waters.

Customer service takes high priority at Flackley Ash, making it a very comfortable, civilised base from which to explore the wealth of attractions in the vicinity, including the historic Cinque Port town of Rye itself, Romney and Walland Marshes, the Kent & East Sussex Railway and the smallest town in England – Winchelsea.

his Mapp and Lucia novels, which include descriptions of the town, thinly disguised as 'Tilling'. He was also for a time the Mayor of Rye. (The cartoon character Captain Pugwash was also conceived in Rye.) One of the town's oldest surviving buildings is **Ypres Tower**, which forms part of the **Rye Castle Museum**, the other part being in East Street. The collection concentrates on the town's varied past and includes exhibitions on smuggling, law and order and the iron industry. On the second site, there is an old fire engine, pottery made in the town, nautical equipment and much more that tells the full history of Rye. Combining the traditional craft of model making with the latest electronic techniques, the **Rye Heritage Centre** presents a model of the town, complete with light and sound, that transports visitors back through the ages.

AROUND RYE

PLAYDEN
1 mile N of Rye off the A268

This smart hamlet has a rather battered old 12th century church, with a shingle broach spire. Inside there is an unusual memorial to a 16th century Flemish brewer, Cornelius Roetmans. A refugee from Spanish persecution in the Low Countries, he settled in the area along with a community of Huguenots and carried on his trade as a brewer. After his death, he was remembered in the church by a memorial slab carved with beer barrels and mash forks - the tools of the brewing trade. In the chancel is a memorial to the men of *HMS Barham*, sunk in 1941. The country lanes to the northeast of Playden lead to the start of the **Royal Military Canal**, an unusual waterway built in 1804 as part of the defences against a possible invasion by Napoleon. A 20-mile towpath between Rye and Hythe offers easy and attractive walking along the fringes of

the now drained **Walland and Romney Marshes**.

CAMBER
3 miles SE of Rye off the A259

Camber is a small village lying on the western edge of Romney Marsh and is best known for its beach of golden sands.It was known as a good place for smugglers; goods were landed on Camber beach, the dunes of which provided cover for those taking part. The Excise built a Watch House in the early 1800s which is now adjacent to the Lydd Ranges. The village has seen a lot of development since World War II with the building of bungalows on the sand dunes.

WINCHELSEA
2½ miles SW of Rye on the A259

Though Winchelsea lies only a short distance from Rye, there could be no greater contrast. While Rye is a place of tourist bustle, Winchelsea is a quiet place that time seems to have forgotten. An ancient Cinque Port and one of the smallest towns in England, Winchelsea lay several miles to the south until the 13th century. This site was engulfed by the sea after a series of violent storms. The 'new' Winchelsea stands on a hill and it was built to a rigid grid pattern laid out by Edward I. The ambitious rectangular plan of 39 squares - a feature which can still be seen some 700 years later - became the home of some 6,000 inhabitants, nearly 10 times the number of residents here today.

For a short time in the 14th century, Winchelsea prospered as the most important Channel port, but again nature took its toll and the town lost its harbour. As a result of the Black Death and constant raids by the French, the town declined into almost complete obscurity. It was not until the mid 19th century that a successful recovery plan was put together to restore the town to something like its former grandeur and historic beauty.

THE TEA TREE

12 High Street, Winchelsea,
East Sussex TN36 4EA
Tel: 01797 226102
website: www.the-tea-tree.co.uk
Open: 10am-5pm Feb-Dec. (Closed Tuesdays)
Courtyard Garden: Non Smoking: No Dogs:

Easy to find on Winchelsea's High Street, **The Tea Tree** is a classic English tea shop in a classic English setting. The quaint double-fronted premises date from the 15th century, and exposed beams and an inglenook fireplace are among the delightful original features. The menu offers a choice of sandwiches, salads, hot home-cooked dishes, home baking and tempting sweets. Giant meringues and carrot cake are great favourites, and many regulars come for the splendid afternoon cream teas.

Spike Milligan was a frequent teatime visitor; he loved the Tea Tree and he loved Winchelsea. He is buried nearby in Winchelsea churchyard. The Tea Tree is a family business, a member of The Guild of Tea Shops winning awards for quality and service and the range of fresh coffee and teas available. Winchelsea has much to offer the visitor with its peace and tranquillity, ancient buildings, museum and the spectacular views towards the sea and the Brede Valley. The Tea Tree is just the place to take refreshment in what is truly a magical location in a small town with a big history.

Winchelsea Court Hall Museum illustrates events that led to the town's prosperity, culminating in it being made a Head Port of the confederation of Cinque Ports, and its gradual decline. The museum is housed in one of the oldest surviving buildings; by the ruins of a 14th century **Franciscan Friary**.

Just to the east of the town lies **Camber Castle**, a fine example of the coastal defences built by Henry VIII in the 16th century. The fortress, reached by a walk across the sands, seems rather far inland today but when it was built, it held a commanding position on a spit of land on one side of the Rother estuary.

BECKLEY

4½ miles NW of Rye on the B2088

When Alfred the Great died in 900, he referred to lands at 'Beccanleah' in his will and there was certainly a Saxon church here. A medieval building with a Norman tower, now stands on the site. Inside there are two grotesque stone heads with leaves protruding from the mouths that were known as 'jack in the greens'. On still nights, it is said that Sir Reginald Fitzurse can be heard riding furiously to the church for sanctuary after taking part in the murder of Thomas à Becket.

BRIGHTON AND THE EAST SUSSEX DOWNS

This coastal area of East Sussex centres around the thriving resorts of Brighton and Eastbourne. Both began life as quiet fishing villages but, following Royal visits, they developed rapidly at the beginning of the 19th century. Brighton, the favoured holiday resort of the Prince Regent, is best known for the lavish Royal Pavilion, a splendid monument to exotic architecture and design. However, its Lanes, the narrow streets and alleyways of the old village are a real treat for antique lovers.

Eastbourne has none of the grand architecture of its rival. Carefully planned and laid out by William Cavendish, the 7th Duke of Devonshire, this is a genteel resort close to the spectacular chalk cliffs of Beachy Head.

The county town of Lewes dates back to Saxon times and it benefited greatly just after the Norman Conquest, when both a great castle and the important St Pancras Priory were founded here by the Norman William de Warenne. Another coastal village, Pevensey, was the landing place of William, Duke of Normandy and his army.

Although many of the inland towns and villages have their roots in Saxon England they are also linked with artists and writers of the 19th and 20th centuries. Virginia Woolf and her husband Leonard lived at Monk's House, Rodmell, until Virginia's death in 1941, while her sister, Vanessa Bell, maintained her eccentric household at nearby Charleston Farmhouse, in Selmeston. The Elms at Rottingdean was the home of Rudyard Kipling until his success as a novelist forced him to move to a more secluded location in 1902, and the village of Ditchling was home to a group of artists and craftsmen at the centre of the Arts and Crafts Movement.

BRIGHTON

Before Dr Richard Russell of Lewes came here in the 1750s, this was an obscure little south coast fishing village called Brighthelmstone, dating back to medieval times. Dr Russell, a believer in the benefits of sea air and water, published a dissertation on *The Use of Sea Water in Diseases of the Glands*. Russell set about publicising the village as a place for taking sea air, bathing and even drinking sea water in order to gain relief from ailments and diseases. He also promoted the medicinal virtues of the mineral waters of St Ann's Well at Hove. By the time of the Prince Regent's first visit to the village, at 21 years of age in 1783, it was already becoming a popular place but still remained concentrated around the old village of Brighthelmstone. The effect of royal patronage on the village was extraordinary and the growth here was rapid. By the time of the Prince Regent's last visit to Brighton, some 47 years after his first, the place had been completely transformed.

The Prince Regent, later to become George IV, was so taken with the resort that he first took a house here and then built his extraordinary **Royal Pavilion** (see panel on page 175). The small farmhouse on the site was transformed in 1787 by architect

Brighton Marina

Henry Holland into a neoclassical building with a dome and rotunda. (Henry Holland was a partner of Capability Brown and married his daughter.) John Nash was employed to rebuild and enlarge Holland's building in a magnificent Indian style; based on a maharajah's palace, complete with minarets, onion-shaped domes and pinnacles, the Royal Pavilion has been the best-known Brighton landmark for almost 200 years. The interior of the palace is one of the most lavish examples of Regency chinoiserie in the world. The detail in the decoration is astonishing, with imitation bamboo everywhere. Even the kitchens have flamboyant cast-iron palm trees.

The gardens surrounding this seaside pleasure palace are also the work of John Nash, though one ancient oak tree here is said to be the one in which Charles II hid after the Battle of Worcester. Although this is an unlikely claim, the tree certainly predates Nash's splendidly laid-out grounds. Beginning life as the Royal Pavilion's stables and once housing a riding school, **The Dome**, dated 1805, is now a superb concert hall. Another part of the complex has been converted into the **Brighton Museum and Art Gallery**. Opened in 1873, this outstanding museum houses collections of both national and international importance. Among the marvellous displays are art nouveau and art deco furniture, decorative art, non-western art and culture, archaeology from flint axes to silver coins, paintings by both British and European masters, musical instruments, costume and design.

The creation of the Royal Pavilion and the almost permanent residence of the Prince Regent in the resort certainly sealed Brighton's fate as a sought after seaside location and the town rapidly expanded - westwards until it met up with Hove and eastwards to **Kemp Town**, laid out by Thomas Reid Kemp, a local lord of the manor in the 1820s. Another notable feature of Brighton is **Royal Crescent**, an early example of town planning . Built in the late 1790s, this discreet row of little houses was built to face the sea rather than have their backs turned towards the coast as was the norm at the time.

For many visitors to Brighton a visit to **The Lanes**, the warren of narrow streets that represent what is left of the old village, is a must. Today, these tiny alleys are the preserve of smart boutiques, antique shops and restaurants. The old **Parish Church** standing outside the old part of Brighton is shown in ancient pictures as an isolated building. It has long since been engulfed. In the churchyard is a curious gravestone to

Phoebe Hessel. Born in 1713, she served in the army as a private and, after her retirement, she came to Brighton where she died, aged 108, in 1821.

Another church worth visiting is the Roman Catholic **Church of St John** in Kemp Town. However, it is not for any ancient feature that visitors make their way here but to see the last resting place of Mrs Fitzherbert, who died in 1837. Maria Anne Fitzherbert, twice a widow, was secretly married to the future George IV in London in 1785. They honeymooned in Brighton, where Mrs Fitzherbert took a house, said to be linked to the pavilion by an underground passage. Their marriage had to remain a secret as it was completely in breech of the Royal Marriages Act. Eventually, the Prince Regent, who could not acknowledge her publicly without renouncing the throne, broke off their affair in 1811. The Church of St Bartholomew has one of the highest naves in the country, and the Church of St Michael contains fine windows by Burne-Jones, Webb, Morris and Kempe.

Just a short distance from the seafront lies **Preston Manor**, a delightful old house, now restored and refurbished in the style of an Edwardian gentleman's residence. Beginning life as a 13th century manor house, set within beautifully landscaped grounds, the manor was rebuilt in the 1730s and extended in 1905. Laid out on four floors, there are some 20 rooms to explore, from the attics and nursery on the top floor to the servants' quarters at ground level. The dining room is dominated by a case filled with an amazing collection of Buddhist Chinese lions. Within the pleasant grounds are a walled garden, a pets' cemetery and a croquet lawn.

Another lesser known place of interest in Brighton is **Stanmer Park and Rural Museum**, a 200-acre country park centred around the fine early 18th century mansion that was once the home of the Earls of Chichester. The park now contains a large municipal nursery as well as glasshouses where flowers are grown. Behind Stanmer House is a unique collection of agricultural implements, including

THE ROYAL PAVILION

Brighton, East Sussex BN1 1EE
Tel: 01273 292822 Fax: 01273 292821
e-mail: visitor.services@brighton-hove.gov.uk
website: www.royalpavilion.org.uk

The Royal Pavilion is one of the most exotically beautiful buildings in the British Isles. Indian architecture contrasts with interiors inspired by China in this breathtaking Regency palace. Built for King George IV the Pavilion was also used by William IV and Queen Victoria. Originally a farmhouse, in 1787 architect Henry Holland created a neo-classical villa on the site. It was transformed into Indian style byJohn Nash between 1815 and 1822.

A £10 million restoration scheme has returned the palace to its full Regency splendour with lavish decorative schemes. The centrepiece of the Banqueting Room is a huge chandelier held by a silvered dragon illuminating a table laid with dazzling Regency silver gilt. The Music Room is equally stunning, with lotus-shaped lanterns hanging from a high domed gilded ceiling.

The Pavilion is open daily, except 25th and 26th December and has a good range of facilities including a tea room and gift shop.

JEREMY HOYE

22a Ship Street, Brighton, Sussex BN1 1AD
Tel: 01273 777207 FAX: 01273 736870
e-mail: sales@jeremy-hoye.co.uk
website: www.jeremy-hoye.co.uk

Jeremy Hoye has been established as a contemporary jeweller in Brighton for 10 years. This cutting edge store leads where others follow, showcasing collections designed and manufactured in the Jeremy Hoye workshops in Brighton. Jeremy trained as a goldsmith in London before branching out with his own

collections, working in platinum, 18ct gold and silver. His signature collection is Carved, based on a mythical theme, that could have been inspired from the past or present; a very wearable collection. The Carved diamond solitaire is the most popular engaement ring, with matching band rings for men and women.

The more avant-garde collections are Finn, based on General Motors concept cars from the 50's, and Trinity, with its heavy cross theme with a feel of the film 'Matrix'. If you are looking for something simple, there is the blue collection - a collection of rub-over

set diamond rings and band rings. With strong lines its design is a truly contemporary classic.

For the more discerning customer Jeremy Hoye provides a commission service, working in his own style only in platinum or 18ct gold, providing you with the opportunity to own a personalised item of jewellery. This service can also cover the incorporation of your own diamonds from old mounts.

The store has a relaxed feel with knowledgeable, friendly staff who are willing to help and customer care is a priority, so feel free to browse. There is also an excellent after sales service, including free cleaning and refinishing for all jewellery bought from the store. Free valuations are given on all platinum and 18ct jewellery.

Jeremy Hoye showcases some of Englands finest contemporary designers, including Shaune Leane and Diana Porter, and sells the work of jewellers who are just starting out and have flair and individuality in the making of stylish, innovative jewellery. Over the years Jeremy has collaborated with other companies including Diesel, Daewoo and more recently, Grande Marnier and O2.

blacksmith's and wheelwright's tools. The late-17th century well house that was designed to supply water to the house and was originally powered by oxen can also be seen here.

For those wishing to take a step back into their childhood the **Brighton Toy and Model Museum**, under the arches of Brighton station, is the place. A fascinating display of trains, dolls, teddy bears, planes and much more will delight all members of the family - young and old. The world of natural history can also be discovered in Brighton, at the **Booth Museum of Natural History**, the creation of Edward Booth, a Victorian ornithologist. His original collection of some 500 species of bird, assembled between 1865 and 1890, has been extended by displays of butterflies, fossils and animal skeletons. **The Sea Life Centre** concentrates very much on live creatures and has the longest underwater viewing tunnel in Europe. The tunnel winds through a series of underwater habitats where both fresh and sea water creatures can be viewed. Although this is a an up to the minute centre, some of the original 19th century display cases are still in use in this Victorian building.

The Brighton **Pier** is open every day of the year to amuse and entertain. For those looking for more refinement, the **Theatre Royal**, founded in 1774, remains one of the country's best and loveliest provincial theatres. The arts certainly flourish in Brighton, and the annual Brighton Festival held each May is one of the biggest in the country. A popular feature on the seafront is the Volks railway, the first electric railway in the country. It was designed by Magnus Volk, Brighton Corporation's Electrical Engineer, and opened on August Bank Holiday 1883.

Naturally, Brighton also has a whole wealth of places to stay, from small bed and breakfast establishments to splendid five star hotels. Side by side on the front, are two superb hotels that symbolise Victorian holiday luxury, the white painted **Grand Hotel**, built in the 1860s and its neighbour, the **Metropole Hotel**, completed in 1890. In 1984, during the Conservative Party Conference, an IRA bomb blew the Grand Hotel apart. Several people lost their lives in the tragedy and a great many more were injured. The hotel too suffered as the bomb had been strategically placed in its centre. However, just under two years later the hotel was once again fully open for business with no scars to show.

AROUND BRIGHTON

HOVE
W of Brighton on the A259

Nestling at the foot of the downs and now joined to Brighton, Hove is a genteel resort with Regency squares - such as Brunswick and Palmeira - and broad tree-lined avenues. An interesting project that is still in progress is the restoration of **13 Brunswick Place**, a Regency house dating from 1820. The work is being carried out by a group of enthusiasts called the Regency Town House. A former fishing village, major development of Hove took place in the early 19th century when the seafront was built with its distinctive terraces. As well as the usual spoils of the seaside town, Hove is home to the Sussex County Cricket Club and hosts teams from all over the world at their ground.

The **Hove Museum and Art Gallery** (see panel on page 178), outside which stands the splendid wooden pavilion, **Jaipur Gateway**, an elegantly carved

structure that was transported to
England from Rajashtan in 1886,
contains a whole host of exhibits
on the history of the town.
There is also a superb collection
of 20th century paintings and
drawings and 18th century
furniture. For history of a
different kind, the **British
Engineerium**, housed in a
restored 19th century pumping
station, has all manner of
engines - from steam powered to
electric. Many of the model and
life size displays still work and
the museum's working beam
engine is powered up on a regular basis.

Beach Huts, Hove

Meanwhile, there is the Giant's Toolbox,
a hands on display of gears and levers,
cylinders and pistons that visitors can
discover for themselves.

For one of the most spectacular views
of the South Downs a visit to **Foredown
Tower** is a must. Housed in a beautifully
restored Edwardian water tower, there is
a viewing gallery with Sussex's only
operational camera obscura and a mass
of computers and countryside data that
tell the story of the local flora and fauna
as well as the geography of the night sky.

Also in Hove, and rather out of place
with the grand Regency squares and

HOVE MUSEUM & ART GALLERY

19 New Church Road, Hove, East Sussex BN3 4AB
Tel: 01273 290200

Hove Museum & Art Gallery is housed in a Victorian
villa, built during the 1870s for John Oliver Valtance.
The architect Thomas Lainson designed the house in
an Italianate style made popular by Queen Victoria's
Isle of Wight residence, Osbourne House. John Oliver
died in 1893, but his widow continued to live in the
villa until 1913. During the First World War the
building was used to house German Prisoners of War
and in 1923 it was converted into flats. Finally in 1926

it was purchased by the Hove Corporation for use as a museum. The museum opened to the public on
2nd February 1927.

The new **Toy Gallery** is a magical Wizard's Attic where highlights include dolls, teddies, a working
train set, a workshop for broken toys and a bedroom split by time. Hove's role in the birth of cinema
is explored in the new interactive **Film Gallery**. Visitors find out how film was invented through a
display of working optical toys, magic lanterns and cameras. Visitors are able to learn about the Hove
Pioneers of Film through displays of rare apparatus.

The story of Hove and Portslade from prehistoric times to the present day is explored in the new
Local History Gallery. Displays feature Hove's famous prehistoric Amber Cup and investigate the
Roman settlement at West Blatchington, Norman manors and churches, Hangleton's early medieval
village, the Regency development of Brunswick and the growth of Victorian and 20th century Hove.

DRESSWELL OF HOVE

115 Church Road, Hove, East Sussex BN3 2AF
Tel: 01273 738120

In a Grade II listed building adjacent to Hove Town Hall, **Dresswell of Hove** offers an excellent choice of clothes for the well-dressed lady. The shop has been in the same family for nearly 40 years and in Church Road for the last ten, and sisters Maureen and Heather Armstrong and their mother uphold in fine style the shop's reputation for style, quality, customer service and personal attention. The range

of clothes on display in the long, well-laid out shop run from smart casual through essential business wear to outfits for special occasions in the Mother of the Bride collection.

The Armstrongs source their clothes from the UK, Ireland, the USA and throughout Europe, and among the leading names are Lucia, Bäsler, Gerry Weber, Frank Usher, Verpass and Joseph Ribkoff. There's also an excellent selection from top milliners such as the Hat Studio, Victoria Ann and Condici. Dresswell is open from 9.30 to 5.30 Monday to Friday and from 9.30 to 5 on Saturday.

avenues, is **West Blatchington Windmill**. Built in the 1820s and still with all its original machinery working on all five floors, the mill has been restored fully. As well as watching the fascinating milling process, visitors can view an exhibition of agricultural equipment, which includes an oat crusher and a threshing machine.

DITCHLING

6 miles N of Brighton on the B2116

This historic village, known as 'Diccelingas' in Saxon times, has records going back to 765. Once part of a royal estate belonging to Alfred the Great, it was passed on to Edward the Confessor and then to the Norman William de Warenne. The oldest building here, the parish **Church of St Margaret of Antioch**, dates from the 13th century though details from before the Norman Conquest can still be seen in the nave.

Close by the village green and opposite the church, stands **Wings Place**, an unusual Tudor house, also known as **Anne of Cleves' House**. There is no record that the fourth wife of Henry VIII ever stayed here but she is thought to have acquired the property as part of her divorce settlement.

At the beginning of the 20th century, this pretty village, at the foot of the South Downs, became the home of a lively group of artists and craftsmen including Eric Gill, Sir Frank Brangwyn and Edward Johnston. Today it remains a thriving artistic community with many studios and galleries.

To the north of the village lies **Ditchling Common Country Park**, a splendid nature reserve and beauty spot, with a lake, stream and nature trails. Meanwhile, south of Ditchling lies the 813-foot summit of **Ditchling Beacon**, the third highest point on the South

Downs. Once the site of an Iron Age hill fort and almost certainly occupied by the Romans, the beacon was used as a vantage point from which fires were lit to warn of the coming of the Spanish Armada. A magnificent place from which to view much of this area - southerly over the coast and northwards over the Weald - the beacon was given to the National Trust in memory of the owner's son, who was killed during the Battle of Britain in 1940.

Visitors wanting to discover more about the locality's long and interesting history should make a point of calling in at the superb **Ditchling Museum**, which is located in the Victorian former village school. From the Iron Age there has been evidence of settlement in this area and the museum's Attree Room shows archaeological finds from prehistoric sites nearby and remains of Roman pottery dug up to the east of the village. Here is also the history of the parish church and more recently of 17th century non-conformist worship in the village. As this remarkable village has an important place in the English Arts and Crafts movement, the museum features an important collection of work by 20th century artists and craftspeople, including stone carver and typographer Eric Gill, calligrapher Edward Johnston, painter and poet David Jones, weaver Ethel Mairet, silversmith Dunstan Pruden and artist Frank Brangwyn. The village school itself opened in 1838 and the schoolmaster's garden is stocked with fruits, flowers and vegetables as it would have been in the days of the first schoolmaster, George Verrall. Life in the village, at home and on the farm, is shown in the schoolmaster's cottage.

PLUMPTON
6 miles NE of Brighton on the B2116

The village is divided in two by the railway line: the modern Plumpton Green and the old village of Plumpton. **Plumpton Green**, to the north, grew up around the railway station and is the home of the popular **National Hunt Racecourse**. Spectators arriving by train should look out for the Victorian signal box, which has been designated a listed building following the valiant efforts of local railway enthusiasts to preserve it.

Old Plumpton is centred around its flint built church which dates from the 12th century. The elegant moated 16th century **Plumpton Place** was substantially remodelled by Sir Edwin Lutyens in the 1920s. The then owner, Edward Hudson, was a wealthy magazine proprietor who had already commissioned Lutyens to renovate his other country property, Lindisfarne Castle, off the Northumberland coast. A previous Tudor owner, Leonard Mascall, was a great cultivator of apples, a tradition that is still maintained at the East Sussex Agricultural College here in Plumpton.

The site of an early Bronze Age settlement can be found up a footpath opposite the college and, nearby, is a sandstone block, which commemorates the Battle of Lewes, where Simon de Montfort defeated Henry III in 1264.

HAMSEY
8 miles NE of Brighton off the A275

This must have once been an important place for, in 925, King Athelstan held a meeting of his counsellors at Hamsey Manor. Today, though, all that remains of this hamlet is the old church that is reached through the yard of a 400-year-old farm.

BARCOMBE
9 miles NE of Brighton off the A275

On the banks of the River Ouse, which is tidal as far as this point, Barcombe is a tranquil place that was a favourite picnic place with the Edwardians. As well as fishing and picnicking, artists would come here to paint the dilapidated mill buildings in this splendid Ouse Valley setting. There is evidence that the Romans were here and the village was described as having a church and three and a half mills in the Domesday Book. The half mill was one that spanned the river and the other half was accredited to the village of Isfield.

The parish church of St Mary once lay at the heart of the village but, as the Black Death came to the area, the village was devastated and those who survived rebuilt their houses a mile away to the north. There are marvellous views of the South Downs from the churchyard.

RINGMER
9½ miles NE of Brighton on the B2192

This spacious village, familiar to anyone arriving at Glyndebourne by car, is one of the earliest recorded settlements in Sussex. Though nothing remains of the Saxon church that once stood close to the village's enormous green, there has been a place of worship here for over 1,000 years. The present church was built in 1884 by William Martin after fires in the 16th and 19th centuries had burnt down the previous buildings. Inside the church is a poignant memorial to the village's cricket team. During World War I they joined up en masse to fight at the front and, of the 34 club members who went to France, only six returned alive.

During the 17th century, this rural village played, in a roundabout manner, an important part in the history of America. Two young women of the parish married men who

went on to become influential figures in the birth of the United States. Guglielma Springett, the daughter of Sir William, who supported Parliament during the English Civil War, married William Penn, the founder of the State of Pennsylvania, while Ann Sadler married John Harvard, the founder of Harvard University.

Ringmer's most famous inhabitant was Timothy, a tortoise. He belonged to the aunt of the 18th century naturalist Gilbert White. During his visits to see his aunt, White became fascinated by Timothy's activities. After his aunt's death, White continued to study the tortoise and, in *The Natural History of Selbourne* he describes the tortoise's lethargic movements. Timothy's carapace can be seen in the Natural History Museum in London.

LEWES
7 miles NE of Brighton on the A27

The county town of East Sussex, Lewes is an historic settlement that occupies a strategically important point where the River Ouse is crossed by an ancient east to west land route. Much of the town's street plan dates from Saxon times. It

The Grange Gardens, Lewes

DAVID SMITH JEWELLERY

51 High Street, Lewes, East Sussex BN7 1XE
Tel: 01273 477255 Fax: 01273 477559
e-mail: davidsjewels@mistral.co.uk
website: www.davidsmithjewellery.com

Craftsmanship of the highest order can be seen in the windows and display cases of **David Smith Jewellery**, which was opened by the eponymous owner in 2002. He started in the business in 1982 and traded elsewhere in Lewes from 1997 until moving to this 18th century listed building in the High Street. In the workshop on the premises David and his assistant Alexis design and make a range of jewellery, some for stock, some to supply other shops and some to carry out individual commissions. They work in platinum, silver

and the various colours of gold, and many of the pieces are set with either diamonds or the increasingly popular, high-quality freshwater pearls.

The range includes engagement and wedding rings, bangles and bracelets, brooches, earrings, necklaces and tiaras, and besides their own creations they also stock jewellery made by a variety of independent craftsmen. Tiaras can be hired as well as bought, and the shop offers a bespoke repair and alteration service. Opening hours are 10am to 5pm Monday to Saturday. In August 2004 a second David Smith shop opened in Haywards Heath, at 128 South Road.

RENWICK CLARKE

178 High Street, Lewes, East Sussex BN7 1YE
Tel/Fax: 01273 487277
e-mail: daphne.culligan@btopenworld.com

The High Street of Lewes is filled with shops of quality and interest, but for fashion-conscious ladies the one that really counts is **Renwick Clarke**.

Owner Daphne Culligan worked in designer clothes shops in Edinburgh before she opened her own shop in Lewes in 1996, naming it after her mother. Behind the elegant blue-and-white blinds and the stylish double window display, the shop is stocked with a wide range of clothes for all ages and occasions. Many come from Danish

designers, including In Wear, In Touch, CCDK, Part Two, Sandwich, Stills and Noa Noa. The Steilman range comes from Germany, Avoca from Ireland, Gerard Davel from Paris. In addition to the clothes, Renwick Clarke sells a complementary selection of shoes and boots, scarves, handbags, baskets and jewellery, and also offers a bespoke alteration service. A second Renwick Clarke opened in 2001 in Haywards Heath (15 The Broadway, Tel: 01444 473788).

was one of the Saxon capitals visited by Alfred the Great and it was considered important enough to be allowed to mint currency. The Norman invasion in the 11th century and William the Conqueror's success at Battle, however, really saw Lewes grow in stature.

Because of their closeness to the English Channel, William gave the Sussex estates to his most trusted barons, and the lands around Lewes were granted to his powerful friend, William de Warenne. De Warenne and his wife Gundrada began the construction of **Lewes Castle** and founded the great **Priory of St Pancras**. Today, a substantial part of the castle remains, including a section of the keep and two towers dating from the 13th century. During the early 19th century, the castle was owned by the Kemp family and they are responsible for the elegant Georgian façade to the **Barbican House**. Overshadowed by the Barbican Gate, the house is now home to the **Barbican House Museum** where relics found in the area, from prehistoric times through to the Middle Ages, are on display. Here, too, is the **Living History Museum**, with

The Gateway, Lewes

its superb scale model of Lewes set at the end of the 19th century. There are also splendid views over the town available to anyone climbing to the roof of the keep.

Little remains of the Priory of St Pancras. Built on the foundations of a small Saxon church, the priory and a

Lewes Castle and Barbican House Museum

169 High Street, Lewes, East Sussex BN7 1YE
Tel: 01273 486290
e-mail: castle@sussexpast.co.uk

William the Conqueror instructed his loyal lieutenant, William de Warenne, to build a castle in the Lewes area. Building began soon after the Conquest of 1066 and continued for nearly 300 years. Today the romantic outline of the castle dominates the town. Climb to the top and you'll see outstanding views of the river and downs. Imagine how Norman soldiers might have lived. See how the town grew around the castle. Leave yourself time to explore and understand more about the past of Lewes and enjoy the beauty of the present.

Opposite the castle, in **Barbican House Museum**, you'll find an interactive touch screen, 'A Touch of Lewes', and a sound and light show, 'The Story of Lewes Town'. Both will help you see Lewes in times gone by. Following a visit to the museum rooms, you'll leave knowing much more about the historic town and its buildings.

W F BRUCE ANTIQUE CLOCKS

5 North Street, Lewes, East Sussex BN7 2PA
Tel: 01273 473123
e-mail: lewesclocks@btopenworld.com

One of the leaders in its specialised field, **W F Bruce Antique Clocks** was founded by William Bruce in 1980. William moved to South East England over 20 years ago, since when many high-quality clocks and barometers have passed through his hands. Behind the cheerful green-and-white frontage in a brick building on the north side of town, the grandfather clocks, long-case clocks, carriage clocks, mantle clocks and wall clocks are beautifully displayed in spacious, traditional surroundings. In addition to the impressive range of timepieces and barometers, W F Bruce offers a full service of repair and restoration of dials, cases and movements.

William Bruce learnt his trade at West Dean College and the Edward James Foundation, earning distinctions in all 3 years.

GALLERY NINETEEN

19 Cliffe High Street, Lewes, East Sussex BN7 2AH
Tel/Fax: 01273 487287
e-mail: peartreedesigns@yahoo.co.uk
website: www.gallerynineteen.co.uk

Easy to find in the middle of Cliffe High Street, **Gallery Nineteen** was opened in 2001 by Nigel Graham. Nigel has been in the jewellery trade since 1975, designing and making his own distinctive pieces, and he has now been joined in the business by his daughter. Working in a variety of precious metals and stones, they produce a wide range of items, and the attractive display in the shop ranges from rings, earrings, brooches, bangles, pendants and necklaces to gold spoons, decorative clocks and tags for wine and spirit decanters.

Also on show is a striking collection of ceramic pots from the 1960s, 70s and 80s. Nigel and his daughter are happy to accept individual commissions, and also offer a full restoration, repair and remodelling service. Lewes, the county town of East Sussex, has plenty to attract the visitor, from the castle to museums and historic houses, but anyone who appreciates beautiful jewellery and outstanding craftsmanship should certainly add Gallery Nineteen to their list of places not to miss.

FIFTEENTH CENTURY BOOKSHOP

99-100 High Street, Lewes, East Sussex BN7 1XH
Tel: 01273 474160

On the main street of the historic town of Lewes, the **Fifteenth Century Bookshop** is a paradise for book-lovers and browsers. Susan Mirabaud had known and loved the shop for years when she bought it in 1988, and the constantly changing stock ensures that every visit reveals new treasures. Children's and illustrated books are the speciality, but most interests are catered for among the thousands of second-hand and collectors' books, and telephone enquiries are welcome.

great deal of land were given to the abbey of Cluny in Burgundy. At its height, the priory had a church as large as Chichester Cathedral, with outbuildings to the same scale, but all were destroyed at the time of the Dissolution in the 16th century.

During the 14th century, a feud developed between the 4th Earl de Warenne and Lord Pevensey. In order to settle their differences the two met, one May morning, under the walls of Lewes Castle. As they fought, Lord Pevensey cornered de Warenne and, as he was about to drive home his sword, Lady de Warenne began to pray to St Nicholas to save his life and she vowed that, should her husband be spared, her first-born son would not marry until he had placed St Nicholas' belt on the tomb of the Blessed Virgin in Byzantium. At that moment, Lord Pevensey slipped and, as he fell, de Warenne drove home his sword. Years

went by before the earl's eldest son, Lord Manfred, became engaged to Lady Edona and, halfway through a banquet to celebrate the 21st anniversary of de Warenne's victory, a vision of the combat appeared to all the guests. Understanding at once that the vow must be fulfilled before their son's wedding, the earl and his wife sent Manfred to Byzantium. For over a year Lady Edona waited for him to return and, finally, his ship was sighted off Worthing. A welcoming party gathered and then, with every one watching, the ship struck a hidden rock and sank with all hands. Lady Edona, watching the ship go down, gave out a sigh and sank to the ground dead. A plinth stands in memory of Lady Edona, who was buried where she fell.

Beside the priory ruins is a bronze memorial by the sculptor Enzo Plazzottia that was commissioned to commemorate

SAY CHEESE

Riverside, Cliffe High Street, Lewes BN7 2RE
Tel/Fax: 01273 814723

Life long foodies, David and Eleanor Robins have been cheesemongers since 1989 and they love introducing people to different cheeses. They specialise in the farm cheeses of Sussex, Kent and Surrey, together with the best of the rest of the world. Fine teas, coffees and a wide range of hard to find ingredients are also a feature. **Say Cheese** is situated in a delightful 18th century warehouse alongside the River Ouse, in company with a butcher, fishmonger, chocolate shop, brasserie and sandwich bar. Talks, tasting and mail order service available.

THE WORKSHOP

164 High Street, Lewes, East Sussex BN7 1XU
Tel/Fax: 01273 474207

The Workshop is owned and run by Jonathan
Swan, a distinguished jeweller with many years'
experience. He was made a Freeman of the

Goldsmiths'
Company in
1989 and has
won several
prestigious
awards, the
most recent being the Goldsmiths Craft & Design Award for
Innovation in 2003. The Gallery is recommended as among the
countries best by the Crafts Council and is a showcase for his
work and for the work of more than 70 contemporary jewellers.
The Workshop also accepts commissions, identifying and
developing exactly what the customer requires. They also run
jewellery classes spread over 4 evenings a week in the workshop
behind the gallery.

The Workshop is easily identified with its bold blue frontage
on the High Street. The earliest part of the building dates from
around the 9th or 10th century, making it some 300 years older
than its near neighbour the Castle. The Workshop is open from
9.30 to 5 Monday to Saturday.

the 700th anniversary of the **Battle of
Lewes**. Fought on Offham Hill, the
Battle of Lewes took place in May 1264,
between the armies of Henry III and
Simon de Montfort. The night before
the battle, de Montfort and his troops
were said to have kept vigil in the church
at Fletching, while Henry and his men
had a wild, and in some cases drunken,
evening at the castle. Whether this was
the reason for the king's defeat or
whether it was down to bad military
tactics is open to debate.

Another monument in the town is the
Martyrs' Memorial erected in 1901 in
memory of the 17 Protestant martyrs
who were burnt to death on Lewes High
Street during the reign of Catholic Mary
Tudor. The mainly Protestant
inhabitants of Lewes found an outlet for
their resentment at this treatment after
the foiling of the Gunpowder Plot and
the **Bonfire Celebrations**, which still

take place here are elaborate affairs.

Like Ditchling, Lewes has an **Anne of
Cleves' House**, in this case an early 16th
century Wealden hall house which,
again, formed part of Henry VIII's
divorce settlement with his fourth wife.
Also like the house in Ditchling, it is
unlikely that the queen ever set foot in
the building. Today, the house is open
to the public and the rooms are
furnished to give visitors an idea of life
in the 17th and 18th centuries.

GLYNDE

9½ miles NE of Brighton off the A27

Situated at the foot of Mount Caburn,
this small and attractive village is home
to a splendid house and an ancient
church. Overlooking the South Downs,
Glynde Place was built in 1579 for
William Morley from flint and
Normandy stone that was brought across
the Channel in barges. The most notable

family member was Colonel Herbert Morley, a Parliamentarian who was also one of the judges at the trial of Charles I. Fortunately for the family, Morley did not sign the king's death warrant and so, at the Restoration, the family was able to gain his pardon from Charles II. The house passed by marriage into the Trevor family and, in 1743, it was inherited by the Bishop of Durham, Richard Trevor. He left the exterior of the house untouched while turning the interior into classical 18th century residence.

At the gates to the house stands the church built by the bishop in 1765 to the designs of Sir Thomas Robinson. Having recently visited Italy, Robinson was very enthusiastic about Renaissance architecture and, as a result, the church has a coved rococo ceiling, box pews and a gallery.

The village is also home of the black-faced Southdown sheep, first bred here by John Ellman, who lived here between 1753 and 1832. A benevolent farmer, he built a school for his labourers' children and, when they married, he gave the couple a pig and a cow. He even allowed the single labourers to lodge under his own roof. However, Ellman would not allow a licensed house in the village, though he didn't mind if his men brewed their own beer at home.

The distinctive **Mount Caburn**, to the west of Glynde, can be reached along a footpath from the village. Many thousands of years ago, this steep sided chalk outcrop was separated from the rest of the Downs by the action of the River Glynde. This process created a mound about 500 feet in height whose natural defensive properties have not gone unnoticed over the centuries. The earthwork defences of an Iron Age hillfort can still be made out near the summit and there is evidence of an earlier Stone Age settlement.

GLYNDEBOURNE
9½ miles NE of Brighton off the B9192

Glyndebourne, a part Tudor, part Victorian country house, just a mile north of Glynde village, is now the home of the world famous **Glyndebourne Opera House**. In the early 1930s, John Christie, a school master, music lover and inheritor of the house, married the accomplished opera singer Audrey Mildmay and, as regular visitors to European music festivals, they decided to bring opera to England and their friends. In the idyllic setting of their country estate, they built a modest theatre and, in 1934, Glyndebourne first opened with a performance of Mozart's *Marriage of*

Picnic on the Lawn at the Opera, Glyndebourne

MIDDLE FARM

Firle, nr Lewes, East Sussex BN8 6LJ
Tel: 01323 811411 Fax: 01323 811622
e-mail: info@middlefarm.com
website: www.middlefarm.com

Visitors of all ages and interests can spend many happy hours among the varied attractions at **Middle Farm**, which stands on the main A27 Lewes-Eastbourne road between the villages of Firle and Selmeston. It is a 625-acre working farm, where Helen and Rod Marsh and their team offer a warm country welcome and plenty for every member of the family to enjoy. Middle Farm is home to many kinds of farm animals and domestic pets, including cows, calves, pigs, goats, sheep, rabbits, donkeys, Shire horse, guinea pigs, fieldmice and a collection of umpteen chickens, ducks and geese. The herd of pedigree Jersey cows has won many awards, and visitors can watch the daily milking between 3 o'clock and 5.

A unique attraction is the National Collection of Cider and Perry, where over 250 examples of the cidermaker's art range from traditional farmhouse scrumpy to the wine-like elegance of fine table cider; there are meads,

perries, cider brandies, fruit liqueurs, English wines, Sussex ales and their own daily pressing of local apples for the purest, freshest juice. The Middle Farm Shop sells the very best food and drink, much of it organic, carefully sourced from small-scale producers in Sussex and beyond - cheeses, eggs, fruit and vegetables, ice cream, chocolate, home-prepared pickles and preserves, and milk from the Jersey cows. The traditional butchery specialises in additive-free British meat reared to the highest standards, including beef from the farm's pedigree organic Sussex herd, game in season and the 25 varieties of superb homemade sausages. Much of this wonderful produce goes into the delicious farmhouse dishes served in the flint-walled Plough Monday Restaurant, from home-baked cakes with morning coffee to traditional country lunches and sumptuous Sussex cream teas.

"For Gardeners..." offers those of a green-fingered disposition a wide variety of well cared for herbs and vegetables, annuals and perennials, shrubs and topiary, pots and paraphernalia. Skies & Scarecrows is a delightful gift shop stocked with a cornucopia of stylish, timeless gifts inspired by the countryside and country living, including traditional games and toys, ceramics, colourful picnic rugs, willow baskets, paintings by local artists and books on many aspects of rural life.

Figaro. Audrey sang the role of Susanna, lady's maid to the Countess Rosina. Their scheme was not an overnight success: on the second night, when *Cosi fan Tutte* was performed, the audience was very sparse. However, by the outbreak of World War II, the owners had extended the theatre to accommodate 600. The opera house re-opened after the War with a performance of Benjamin Britten's *Rape of Lucretia*, and in 1947 the premiere of Britten's *Albert Herring* was staged, with Britten himself conducting. Since those days, Glyndebourne has gone from strength to strength and, as well as extending the theatre further, the repertoire has also been widened. Today, each summer season, from May to August, sees opera-lovers venturing here dressed in evening gowns, laden with picnic hampers to enjoy a wide range of opera in a unique setting and to eat their picnics in the grounds during the long interval.

WEST FIRLE
10 miles E of Brighton off the A27

Though the village is known as West Firle, there is no East Firle - or any other Firle - in the area. A feudal village of old flint cottages at the foot of the South Downs, it is dominated by **Firle Beacon** to the southeast, which rises to a height of 718 feet. As one of the highest points in the area, the importance of this vantage point has long been recognised. It was used by the Admiralty for a fire beacon to warn of the approaching Spanish Armada in the 16th century and remains of a Stone Age long barrow and a group of Bronze Age round barrows have been found on the summit. There was also a Roman observation point here. Today, the summit can be reached by taking a small detour off the South Downs Way and the breathtaking views make the climb well worth while.

Back in the village, and set in its own idyllic parkland, is **Firle Place**, the home of the Gage family for over 500 years. Built by Sir John Gage in the 15th century, this marvellous Tudor manor house was greatly altered some 300 years later and today it will be familiar to many who have seen it as a backdrop for major feature films or as a location for TV series. Still very much a family home, today owned by the 7th Viscount, its rooms contain a wonderful collection of European and English Old Masters as well as some rare and notable examples of French and English furniture and Sèvres porcelain. The magnificent deer park, which surrounds the house, was landscaped by Capability Brown in the 18th century and it features a castellated tower and an ornamental lake. It is open to the public in the summer.

RODMELL
7 miles E of Brighton off the A26

This little village of thatched cottages is thought to have got its name from 'mill on the road' and, though no mill can be found here today, there is a Mill Road and, in the small 12th century church there is a reference to the village's old name 'Rodmill'.

However, the village's main claim to fame is that it was the home of Virginia and Leonard Woolf from 1919 until her death in 1941. The couple, escaping the confining intellectual world of the Bloomsbury set in which they were influential figures, settled at **Monk's House**, a delightful early 18th century farmhouse that is now in the hands of the National Trust and open briefly in the summer. The garden, which is lush with hollyhocks, dahlias and hydrangeas, gives good views over the downs across the River Ouse.

During her time here, Virginia wrote many of her best remembered works, but throughout her life she suffered great

bouts of depression and mental illness.
Finally, in 1941, she took her own life by
wading into the river with her pockets
full of stones. Surprisingly for the
disappearance of such a well-renowned
figure, her body was not discovered for
three weeks and then by some children
playing on the riverbank. Her ashes,
along with those of her husband who
stayed here until his death in 1969, are
scattered in the garden.

SOUTHEASE
7 miles E of Brighton off the A26

This tiny village, in a dip on the Lewes to
Newhaven road, was first mentioned in a
Saxon charter of 966, when King Edgar
granted the church and manor here to
Hyde Abbey in Winchester. Some 100
years later, at the time of the Domesday
Survey, this was a flourishing village that
was assessed as having 38,500 herrings as
well as the usual farm produce. Inside
the early 12th century church is a copy
of King Edgar's charter. The original is in
the British Museum, London. There is
also an unusual organ built by Allen of
Soho and installed in 1790. The only
other organs of this kind known to be
still in existence are in Buckingham
Palace and York Minster.

TELSCOMBE
6 miles E of Brighton off the A26

Telscombe was once an important sheep
rearing and a race horse training centre.
In fact, the last man in England to be
hanged for sheep stealing, in 1819, is
believed to have come from the village.
In 1902, the racing stables at Stud House
trained the winner of the Grand
National - Shannon Lass. The horse's
owner, Ambrose Gorham, was so
delighted with the win that he rebuilt
the village church and each Christmas
gave every child of the parish a book and
a pair of Wellington boots.

PIDDINGHOE
7½ miles E of Brighton off the A26

Set on a wide curve of the River Ouse,
this village - is pronounced 'Piddnoo' by
its older inhabitants - is a picturesque
place, with a host of 17th century
cottages and pleasant riverside walks. It
was a great place for smugglers in days
gone by. Today, however, the ships and
boats that tie up at the quayside below
the church belong to deep sea anglers
and weekend sailors. The golden fish
weather vane on top of the church tower
was referred to by Kipling as a dolphin
but is actually a sea trout.

NEWHAVEN
9 miles E of Brighton on the A26

Newhaven itself is a relatively new
settlement and it replaces the much
older village of Meeching. Inhabited
since the Iron Age, when a fort was built
on Castle Hill, Meeching lay beside the
River Ouse. However, in 1579 a great
storm altered the course of the river and
its outlet to the sea moved from Seaford
to near Meeching. Thus Newhaven was
established at the new river mouth and it
is now one of the county's two main
harbours (the other is at Shoreham by
Sea) with an important cross-Channel
passenger service and also a cargo
terminal.

Newhaven's rise began in the 19th
century and it grew steadily busier once
the rail link with London was established
in 1847. Two of the earliest visitors to
use the passenger steamer service to
Dieppe were the fleeing King and Queen
of France, Louis Philippe and Marie
Amelie, who stayed at the Bridge Inn in
1848 after their sea journey before
continuing to London by train where
they were met by Queen Victoria's coach
and taken to Buckingham Palace. In
order to maintain their anonymity, the

couple registered themselves at the inn under the rather original names of Mr and Mrs Smith.

Also in the 19th century, during one of the periodic French invasion scares, **Newhaven Fort** was built. Consisting of a ring of casements constructed around a large parade ground, the fort was equipped with modern guns during World War II and also received several direct hits from German bombs. Today, it is a **Museum** where visitors can explore the underground tunnels and galleries and view the permanent Home Front exhibition. The **Newhaven Local and Maritime Museum**, in Garden Paradise, contains a wealth of information relating to Newhaven's port, the town's history and its role in wartime. Here also is the **Planet Earth Exhibition**, which explores the world of natural history from millions of years ago to the present day.

White Cliffs, Peacehaven

PEACEHAVEN
9 miles E of Brighton on the A259

If nearby Newhaven is a recent town, Peacehaven must be considered just a fledgling village. The brainchild of wealthy businessman, Charles Neville, it was planned and designed during World War I and the intention was to call the new town Anzac on Sea in honour of the Australian and New Zealand troops, who were stationed here before going off to fight in the trenches. However, after the Armistice, it was renamed Peacehaven which very much caught the mood of the time. Laid out in the grid pattern and with no immediate connection with either the South Downs or the coast, it remains a quiet place off the usual South Coast tourist itinerary.

Along the cliff top promenade there is a 20-foot monument to King George V that also marks the line of the Greenwich Meridian.

ROTTINGDEAN
3 miles E of Brighton on the A259

Built in a gap in the cliffs between Newhaven and Brighton, Rottingdean was, naturally, a key place for smugglers at one time. However, more recently, it became the home of more artistic citizens. The artist Sir Edward Burne-Jones lived here for the last 20 years of his life in the rambling **North End House** by the green. During his time in Rottingdean, Burne-Jones designed seven windows for the originally Saxon parish church of St Margaret that were made up by William Morris. After his death in 1898 (he was buried in St Margaret's churchyard), his wife maintained her high profile in Rottingdean and in 1900 caused uproar when she hung anti-war banners from her windows following the

Relief of Mafeking.

Lady Burne-Jones was also Rudyard Kipling's aunt, and he lived here, at **The Elms**, for five years before moving to Bateman's in 1902. Overlooking the village pond, the gardens of The Elms are open to the public. Surrounded by old stone walls are formal rose gardens, wild and scented gardens and a wealth of rare plants. At the Museum of the Rottingdean Preservation Society, at **The Grange** in Rottingdean, there is a Kipling Room, with a reconstruction of his study in The Elms, and other exhibits devoted to his work. It was while living here that Kipling wrote the *Just So Stories*, *Kim* and *Stalky & Co*, and his feelings for his beloved Sussex are summed up in his well-known poem about the county:

> *God gives all men all earth to love,*
> *But, since man's heart is small,*
> *Ordains for each one spot shall prove*
> *Beloved overall.*
> *Each to his choice, and I rejoice*
> *The lot has fallen to me*
> *In a fair ground - in a fair ground -*
> *Yea, Sussex by the sea!*

Stanley Baldwin and Enid Bagnold, author of *National Velvet*, also spent time in Rottingdean, and another famous resident was J Reuter, a German bank clerk, who started a pigeon post to bring back news from abroad that expanded into the internationally respected worldwide news agency. He is buried in the churchyard of St Margaret.

EASTBOURNE

This stylish and genteel seaside resort, which has managed to avoid both becoming too brash or disappearing into shy gentility, takes its name from the stream, or bourne, which has its course in the old reservoir in the area of open land that is now known as Motcombe Gardens. When George III sent his children here in the summer of 1780, it was, in fact, two villages, the larger of which lay a mile inland from the coast. Slowly the villages were developed and merged but it was William Cavendish, later the 7th Duke of Devonshire, who really instigated Eastbourne's rapid growth as a seaside resort from the 1850s onwards.

As much of the land belonged to the Cavendish family, the expansion was well thought out and managed agreeably, which created the elegant town of today, well known for its delightful gardens. Among the first buildings that Cavendish had constructed are the handsome Regency style Burlington Hotel, St Saviour's Church, the town hall and the extremely elegant railway station. The classic pier was built in the 1880s and it remains one of the finest seaside piers in the country.

There are, however, several buildings, which pre-date the intervention of William Cavendish. The original parish church, inland from the coast, dates from the 12th century though it stands on the site of a previous Saxon place of worship. The excellent **Towner Art Gallery and Museum** is housed in a very sensible Georgian town house that was built by Dr Henry Lushington, a vicar of Eastbourne. It became home to the town's museum in the 1920s and it has a collection of 19th and 20th century British art, as well as displays on the history from the time of the Romans to the present day. The development of the old village into a seaside resort is told at the **Eastbourne Heritage Centre**. In the centre of Eastbourne is the **Museum of Shops** with its Victorian streets, room-settings and displays depicting shopping and social history over the last 100 years.

As a coastal town, during the scare of

French invasions at the beginning of the 19th century, Eastbourne had its own defences. The **Martello Tower No 73**, one of 103 built along the south coast, is also referred to as the **Wish Tower**. Its rather odd name comes from the Saxon word 'wisc' which means marshy place and today the tower is home to a small **Puppet Museum**. Another Napoleonic defence, the **Redoubt Fortress**, was built between 1804 and 1810 on the seafront. Now the home of the **Military Museum of Sussex**, the exhibitions here cover some 300 years of conflict on land, sea and in the air. Highlights include, relics from the charge of the Light Brigade at Balaklava and Rommel's staff car from World War II.

The sea has always played an important part in the life of the town,

Eastbourne Pier at Night

CLASSIQUE MINIATURES & COLLECTIBLES LTD

Unit 13, Burfield Park, South Road, Hailsham,
East Sussex BN27 3JL
Tel/Fax: 01323 844028
e-mail: info@classiqueminiatures.co.uk
website: www.classiqueminiatures.co.uk

Dolls houses, dolls house accessories and bespoke architectural model making are the trade marks of **Classique Miniatures and Collectibles Ltd**. Started in 2002 by Paul and Davina Bates, specialising in hand built

reproductions of clients' own properties and special commissions which are still a major, and perhaps unique, part of the business. They also design, manufacture and build dolls house kits, and supply just about everything that goes to decorate and furnish dolls houses, and if not in stock they will do their utmost to obtain your special requirements.

The available range includes lighting, wallpapers, furniture, carpets and DIY items all in miniature. The workshop and showroom, where a warm welcome awaits, can be visited for all dolls house requirements from 10am to 4pm Tuesday to Saturday, or by appointment and can be found at the above address.

DAVID & ANNE THOMPSON ANTIQUE PINE FURNITURE

Popes Farm, Windmill Hill, nr Hailsham,
East Sussex BN27 4RS
Tel: 01323 832159
e-mail: anne@popesfarm.co.uk
website: www.popesfarm.co.uk

The Thompson family have been in the antiques business here for more than 30 years, with David and Anne at the helm. The customer base of **David & Anne Thompson Antique Furniture** is drawn from far and wide, based on the knowledge that the reputation of the family for quality, service and reliability is second to none. This is very much a family affair specialising in old pine furniture and pine stripping: Keith does the restoring, Sophie

does the polishing, Peter is in charge of pine stripping, and David and Anne use their years of experience to make sure that their valued customers get exactly what they want every time.

The showroom is filled with handsome pine pieces, from cupboards and sideboards to dressers, chests of drawers, chairs and work, occasional, dressing and dining tables. Opening hours are 8.30am to 5pm Monday to Friday, 9am to 4pm Saturday, and the premises are easy to find, clearly signposted on the A271 a few miles east of Hailsham.

from its early days as a fishing village and now as a resort offering a safe beach environment. Naturally, the lifeboats have played an important role through the years and, close to their lifeboat station, is the **RNLI Lifeboat Museum**. Here the history of the town's lifeboats, from 1853 onwards are charted through a series of interesting exhibits, including photographs of some of their most dramatic rescues.

Lighthouse, Beachy Head

While the town is undoubtedly a charming and delightful place to explore and enjoy, most people wish to see **Beachy Head**. One of the most spectacular chalk precipices in England, with a sheer drop of over 500 feet in places, this very famous natural landmark lies just to the southwest of the town. The grand scale of the cliffs is brought home by the sight of the lighthouse, completely dwarfed at the cliff base. On the clifftop is the **Beachy Head Countryside Centre** which focuses on downland life, from the Bronze Age onwards, and includes numerous wildlife displays. This is also the end (or the beginning) of the **South Downs Way**, the long distance bridleway that was first established in 1972.

AROUND EASTBOURNE

POLEGATE
4 miles N of Eastbourne on the A27

The village grew up in the 19th century around a railway junction and, today, it is almost a suburb of Eastbourne. Visitors generally make for the **Polegate Windmill and Museum**, a splendid red brick tower mill, built in 1817, and one of the few tower mills open to the public (though on a limited basis). Restored as early as 1867, all its internal machinery is in working order and here, too, is a small but fascinating museum of milling.

HAILSHAM
7 miles N of Eastbourne on the A295

This market town, which first received its charter in 1252 from Henry III, is a pleasant town where the modern shopping facilities sit comfortably with the chiefly Georgian High Street. Once a thriving centre of the rope and string industry, Hailsham had the dubious honour of supplying all the rope for public executions. Now, its rope and string are put to less lethal uses. It maintains its rural roots and the three-acre cattle market is one of the largest in East Sussex.

HERSTMONCEUX
9 miles NE of Eastbourne on the A271

Herstmonceux Castle was built on the site of an early Norman manor house in 1440 by Sir Roger Fiennes, treasurer to Henry VI. This is a remarkable building on two counts: it was one of the first large scale buildings in the country to be

Herstmonceux Castle

In 1948, the Royal Observatory at Greenwich was looking for somewhere to move to away from the glow of the street lights of London. The Royal Observatory moved here and, after 20 careful years of planning and building, they opened the gigantic Isaac Newton telescope in the grounds. Although the Royal Observatory has moved on, the castle now contains the **Herstmonceux Science Centre**, where, among the domes and telescopes that the astronomers used between the 1950s and the 1980s, visitors can experience the excitement of viewing the heavens. There are also hands-on displays and an Astronomy Exhibition tracing the history and work of the world-famous Royal Observatory.

built of brick and it was also one of the first castles to combine the need for security with the comforts of the residents. As the castle was built on a lake there was added protection, and the impressive gatehouse, with its murder holes and arrow slits, presented an aggressive front to any would-be attackers.

Later, the castle passed into the hands of the Hare family, who presided over a long period of decline for Herstmonceux, which culminated in most of the interior being stripped to provide building materials for another house in 1777. The castle lay semi-derelict for 150 years before a major programme of restoration was undertaken in the 1930s under the supervision of a Lewes architect, W H Godfrey. His careful and inspired work saw the turrets and battlements restored to their former glory and, today, the castle is as when first built in its delightfully romantic setting. **Herstmonceux Castle Garden**, the 500 acres of grounds around the splendid moated castle, are open for most the summer.

PEVENSEY

4 miles NE of Eastbourne on the A259

On the coast, in the shelter of Pevensey Bay, Pevensey was the landing place for invading Roman legions and it was here they built a fortification to protect their anchorage. The fortress of Anderida, built around AD 280, was one of the first south coast defences. William the Conqueror landed here with his troops prior to the Battle of Hastings and left his half brother, Robert, here while he went off to defeat Harold. Robert built a Norman fortress here, which was joined, in the 13th century, by a stone curtain wall. **Pevensey Castle** seemed well able to withstand attack. Following the Battle of Lewes, Simon de Montfort laid siege here without success. However, the structure gradually fell into disrepair although it was brought back into service, briefly, during the advance of the Spanish Armada and again during World War II. Today, the castle is besieged only by visitors who can explore the ruins and follow its history, from the days of the Romans to the mid 20th century.

In the rest of the village there are several fine medieval buildings including the **Mint House**, a 14th century building that lies outside the castle gates. Coins have been minted on this site since 1076 and, though it is now an antiques showroom, visitors can see the priest's secret room and King Edward VI's bedroom. Any self respecting old building has a ghost and the Mint House is no exception. In the 1580s an Elizabethan woman, the mistress of the London merchant Thomas Dight, lived at the house. Coming back unexpectedly, Dight found her in bed with her lover. Incensed with jealousy, Dight ordered his servants to cut out her tongue and hold her while she was made to watch her lover being roasted to death over a fire. The lover's body was thrown into the harbour and the mistress lead to an upstairs room where she starved to death.

In the days prior to the founding of the Royal Navy, Pevensey served as one of the nation's Cinque Ports - that is to say, it was granted certain privileges by the Crown in return for providing ships and men in defence of the south coast.

Inland, lies the area of drained marshland known as the **Pevensey Levels**. At one time this was an area of tidal mudflats which were covered in shallow salt pans. Since then it has been reclaimed for agricultural use and is now covered in fertile arable fields.

WESTHAM
4 miles NE of Eastbourne on the B2191

This pretty village is home to one of the most ruggedly beautiful churches in Sussex, dating from the 14th century and much patched and braced over the years. Inside the church there is a memorial to John Thatcher, who died in 1649 and left his estate to the 'Old Brethren' in the hope that Roman Catholicism would one day be the religion of England once more.

EAST DEAN
3 miles W of Eastbourne off the A259

This charming village at the foot of the South Downs is one of the county's most picturesque, with its village green surrounded by flint cottages, a pub and an ancient church.

During the 18th century, the local parson, Jonathan Darby, is said to have made a cave in the nearby cliffs from which he could display a huge lantern on stormy nights to warn sailors of the hidden rocks. However, some say that the reason for his retreat to the caves was actually to get away from Mrs Darby.

Just south of the village, right on the coast, is **Birling Gap**, a huge cleft in the cliffs which offers the only access to the beach between Eastbourne and Cuckmere Haven. Naturally, this was a great place for smugglers who landed their contraband here before making their way up the steep steps to the cliff top. This stretch of the coast, during the 18th century, was controlled by a particularly notorious gang led by Stanton Collins. He had his headquarters in Alfriston, and on one particular night, the gang are said to have moved the lumps of chalk from the cliff path so that pursuing customs officers could not find their way. One unfortunate officer fell over the cliff edge but miraculously held on by his fingertips. The

East Dean

Distance:	6.0 miles (9.6 kilometres)
Typical time:	180 mins
Height gain:	17 metres
Map:	Explorer 123
Walk:	www.walkingworld.com ID:590
Contributor:	Martin Heaps

Access Information:

The start and end point are easily accessible from Eastbourne town centre with a bus stop only a few yards away. For the energetic the start point can be accessed by walking from the town centre along the A259 towards Brighton, but the climb up East Dean Hill can be taxing.

Description:

An easy walk on grassy downland paths and farm tracks. Navigation is straightforward and paths are well marked. The climb up East Dean Hill can be taxing but is certainly rewarding.

Features:

Sea, Pub, Toilets, National Trust/NTS, Great Views

Walk Directions:

1 The start of the walk is well-defined just a few yards from the bus stop. Walk along the grassy path towards the sea and enjoy the fine views over Eastbourne and further east towards the Pevensey Marshes and Hastings. The Royal Sovereign Light can be seen out to sea.

2 The triangulation point soon comes into view with the dew-pond nearby. Bear right towards the road and keep to the right to reach Waypoint 3.

3 Be careful when crossing the road as it does get busy, especially in summer. Pass through the gate and after a short while you are walking amongst the sheep. Please keep your dog on a lead. The path can get muddy, particularly around the gates. Continue to follow the path to the wonderfully-named Crapham Bottom and into East Hale Bottom. There is a newly-built pumping station which has been built in sympathy with the area. Walk on through the next gate and past a group of farm buildings to join a concrete track at Cornish Farm.

4 The track leads directly towards Belle Tout, a disused lighthouse and now a residential home. Follow the path to the road, cross to join the path and turn right towards Birling Gap.

5 Walk through the car park towards the toilet block and turn left onto the stony track.

6 A gradual climb to Went Hill but be careful not to miss the path on the right leading downhill towards East Dean. The path bears right to a gate and then past several houses to become a narrow road. The road emerges on to the village green and the Tiger pub is a welcome sight.

7 The Tiger has a wide range of meals and refreshments and the green can be used for picnics.

8 Facing The Tiger, walk to the left and onto the main road. At the road turn right and on the left is Downsview Lane. This track runs parallel to the road through the golf course and back to the start of the walk.

Seven Sisters

to be designated an ancient monument.

To the north and west of the village lies **Friston Forest**, 1,600 acres of woodland planted in 1927 by the Forestry Commission. Among the fast-growing pine trees slower-growing broad-leaved trees have also been planted. There is a waymarked circular tour through the forest.

gang came upon him and stamped on his fingertips, causing him to fall to his death.

To the east of the gap lie the **Seven Sisters**, huge blocks of chalk that guard the coast between Eastbourne and Seaford.

FRISTON
3½ miles W of Eastbourne on the A259

This is rather more a hamlet than a village, as only a part Norman church and a Tudor manor house can now be found around the village pond. The churchyard, however, is interesting as it contains the grave of the composer and virtuoso violin and viola player Frank Bridge, one of the pioneers of 20th century English music and also the mentor and teacher of Benjamin Britten. Born in Brighton, Bridge lived in Friston for much of his life though he died in Eastbourne in 1941 - the south door was placed here in his memory. Britten was his pupil from the age of 12 and dedicated his *Sinfonietta* to his teacher. Later, he wrote *Variations on a Theme of Frank Bridge*, which became a popular classic. The village pond, too, has a claim to fame as it was the first in the country

WEST DEAN
5 miles W of Eastbourne off the A259

Though the village is only a couple of miles from the south coast and close to Eastbourne, its position, hidden among trees in a downland combe, gives an impression that it is an isolated, timeless place. King Alfred is thought to have had a palace here, and no more idyllic spot could be found for such a place. Alfred is also said to have kept a great fleet here on the River Cuckmere, which in his day formed a much deeper and wider estuary.

The village is now the home of **Charleston Manor**, an ancient house built in 1080 for William the Conqueror's cupbearer. Recorded in the Domesday Book as Cerlestone, the house has been added to over the years and forms the centrepiece of a remarkable garden. Planted in the narrow valley, just north of Westdean's centre, the parterres and terraces give the garden something of a Continental look and feel.

SEAFORD
8 miles W of Eastbourne on the A259

Once a thriving port on the River Ouse,

Seaford was also a member of the confederation of Cinque Ports. Following a great storm in the 16th century which changed the course of the River Ouse, Seaford lost its harbour and also its livelihood to the newly established Newhaven. Traces of the old medieval seafaring town can still be seen around the old church but, overshadowed by Brighton and Eastbourne on either side, the town never gained the status of its neighbours. The building of the esplanade in the 1870s did bring some development as a modest resort but the constant pounding of the sea, particularly in winter, has kept the development small.

However, during the threat of a possible French invasion in the early 19th century, Seaford was considered important enough to be the site of the most westerly Martello Tower - this one is number 74. Today it is the home of

the **Seaford Museum of Local History** and among the exhibits in this friendly and lively museum are a World War II kitchen, radio sets and mementos from shipwrecks. From the roof of the tower there are magnificent views over the town and beyond as well as the tower's contemporary cannon.

To the west of the town lies **Seaford Head**, an excellent place from which to view the Seven Sisters. The nature reserve here is home to over 250 species of plants and the reserve supports a wealth of wildfowl on its 308 acres of mudflats, meadowland and downland.

JEVINGTON

3½ mile NW of Eastbourne off the A22

This old smugglers' village was established during the time of Alfred the Great by another Saxon called Jeva. Inside the parish church, which can be found along a tree-lined lane, there is a

MIKE SHORER FINE JEWELLERY

East Sussex
Tel/Fax: 01323 894140
e-mail: shorers-workshop@lineone.net
website: www.mikeshorerjewellery.com

Mike Shorer is a jewellery designer who offers a unique alternative to buying a mass-produced piece from a high-street jeweller; his alternative is to create something totally original and handmade. His family has been associated with the jewellery trade for over 250 years and after training at the Sir John Cass School of Art, he managed high street jewellers and ran the Theo Fennell workshop in London. He started his own business in 1990, became a Freeman of the Goldsmith's Company in 1994 and moved to East Sussex in 1995.

Mike is able to use a greater variety of traditional and modern techniques than any other single craftsman outside London's West End, and he links those skills with a selection of stones that would dazzle the Queen of Sheba. Attention to detail and quality of finish is paramount, and he always builds a relationship with his customers, discussing the design in detail and creating pieces that reflect both the customer's and his personality. As well as personal commissions he also designs and makes spectacular trophies and awards for major sporting occasions and corporate events. His pieces can accurately be described as heirlooms of the future, and some of the trophies are becoming sought-after collectors' items.

primitive Saxon sculpture and the tower dates from the 10th century. During the 18th century, when smuggling was rife in the area, the local gang brought their illegal goods up here from Birling Gap and stored them in the cellars of the village rectory. The gang used the local inn as their headquarters and conveniently their leader was the innkeeper who was also the ringleader of a group of highwaymen; he was finally caught and hanged in the 1760s.

ALFRISTON
6 miles NW of Eastbourne off the A27

Alfriston is one of the oldest and best preserved villages in Sussex. The settlement was founded in Saxon times and it grew to become an important port and market town on the River Cuckmere. The old market cross still stands in the square, one of two left in the county (the other is in Chichester). However, it has not escaped the ravages of time as it was smashed by a lorry and repaired by replacing the shaft.

One of the oldest buildings remaining in the town is the **Star Inn**, built in the early 15th century as a resting place for pilgrims on their way to and from the shrine of St Richard at Chichester. Inside can still be seen the original medieval carvings of animals on the ceiling beams. Another ancient inn, the **Market Cross**, had no fewer than six staircases and during the 19th century was the headquarters of the notorious gang of smugglers led by Stanton Collins (see also under East Dean). Though he was never arrested for smuggling, Collins was eventually caught for sheep stealing and, as punishment, was transported to Australia. It was tales of Stanton Collins and other local gangs, which inspired Rudyard Kipling, living at nearby Rottingdean, to write his atmospheric poem, *A Smuggler's Song*.

The former prosperity of this town is reflected in its splendid 14th century parish church that is often referred to as **The Cathedral of the Downs**. As recently as the 1930s, local shepherds would be buried here with a scrap of raw wool in their hand - a custom, which served to inform the keeper of the gates of heaven that the deceased's poor church attendance was due to his obligation to his flock.

Beside the church is the thatched and timbered **Clergy House**, the first building to be acquired - for £10 - by the National Trust, in 1896. A marvellous example of a 14th century Wealden hall house, its splendid condition today is due to the skilful renovation of Alfred Powell, who managed to save both its crown pot roof and the original timbers. Visitors to the house can see an interesting exhibition on medieval construction techniques. The house is surrounded by a magnificent and traditional cottage garden that includes rare flowers grown since Roman times and almost lost to cultivation.

By contrast, to the north of the village lies **Drusillas Park**, a child-friendly zoo that is certain to delight the whole family. As well as housing over 90 species in imaginative and naturalistic enclosures, it also has a creative play area, a train ride and attractive gardens.

WILMINGTON
5 miles NW of Eastbourne off the A27

This delightful village with its mix of building styles is home to the historic remains of **Wilmington Priory**. Founded in the 11th century by William the Conqueror's half brother, Robert de Mortain, as an outpost of the Benedictine Abbey of Grestain in Normandy, the priory was already in steady decline by the time of the Dissolution. Many of the buildings were incorporated into a farmhouse, but other parts remain on their own including the prior's chapel, which is now the parish church of St Mary and St Peter.

Cut into the chalk of Windover Hill is Wilmington's famous **Long Man**, which took its present form in 1874. There is much debate about the age of the Long Man and archaeologist and historians have been baffled for centuries. The earliest record of this giant is dated 1710 but this is inconclusive as it could be prehistoric or the work of an artistic monk from the local priory. However, what is known is that, at over 235 feet high, it is the largest such representation of a man in Europe. The giant, standing with a 250-foot shaft in each hand, is remarkable as the design takes account of the slope of the hill and appears perfectly proportioned even when viewed from below. Covered up during World War II as the white chalk was thought to be a navigation aid to German bombers, the Long Man was outlined in concrete blocks in 1969.

ALCISTON
7½ miles NW of Eastbourne off the A27

This quiet hamlet, which once belonged to Battle Abbey, became known as the 'forgotten village' after its inhabitants left following the ravages of the Black Death and settled close by. The villagers left, among other buildings, a 13th century church, which had been built on a hill on the foundations of a Saxon structure to avoid flooding, and 14th century Alciston Court, that was once used by the monks. During the Middle Ages, the tenant farmers paid a rent to the abbot of Battle in the form of

one tenth of their annual farm output and, at harvest time each year, this was brought to the abbey's vast medieval tithe barn which still looms in front of the church. After the village was abandoned, Alciston Court became a farmhouse. The remains of a large **Medieval Dovecote** can also be seen close by. During the winter, large numbers of pigeons would be kept here to help supplement the villagers' dreary winter diet.

SELMESTON
8 miles NW of Eastbourne off the A27

This ancient hamlet, which is sometimes pronounced 'Simson', was the site where, during the 1930s, archaeologists discovered tools, weapons and pottery fragments in the churchyard, thought to date from the New Stone Age. However, though the finds are interesting in themselves, Selmeston is better remembered as being the home of Vanessa Bell, the artist. Vanessa moved here to **Charleston Farmhouse** in 1916, with her art critic husband, Clive, and her lover, fellow artist Duncan Grant.

Over the next 50 years, the intellectual and artist group that became known as

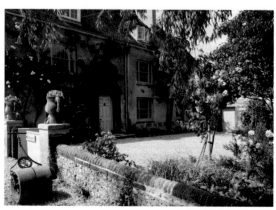

Charleston Farmhouse

the Bloomsbury set frequented the house. David Barnett, John Maynard Keynes, E M Forster, Roger Fry and Virginia and Leonard Woolf, who lived not far away at Rodmell, were all frequent visitors. During the 1930s, the interior of the house was completely transformed as the group used their artistic skills to cover almost every wall, floor, ceiling and even the furniture with their own murals, fabrics, carpets and wallpapers. They hung their own paintings on the walls, including a self portrait of Vanessa Bell and one of Grace Higgens, the valued housekeeper. The garden of the house too was not forgotten and a delightful walled cottage garden was created at the same time with carefully laid out mosaic pathways, tiled pools, sculptures and a scented rose garden. Following Duncan Grant's death in 1978, a trust was formed to save the house and garden, restoring them to their former glory. This unique task has been described as 'one of the most difficult and imaginative feats of restoration' to be carried out in Britain.

UPPER DICKER

8 miles NW of Eastbourne off the A22

This hamlet, which overlooks the River Cuckmere, is centred around a minor crossroads in an area that was once known as 'Dyker Waste'. In 1229, Augustinian canons chose this as the site for the beautiful **Michelham Priory**. Founded by Gilbert de Aquila, the Norman Lord of Pevensey, the six-acre site is surrounded on three sides by the River Cuckmere and on the other by a slow flowing moat - England's longest water-filled medieval moat. The slow moving water is still used to power an old mill where traditionally ground flour is produced in small batches. A splendid gatehouse to the priory was added in the 14th century and the priory continued to flourish until the Dissolution.

After the Dissolution the priory came into the hands of first the Pelham family and then the Sackville family who, in the 300 years of their ownership, incorporated some of the priory's buildings into a Tudor farmhouse which

MICHELHAM PRIORY

Upper Dicker, Hailsam, East Sussex BN27 3QS
Tel: 01323 844224 Fax: 01323 844030
e-mail: adminmich@sussexpast.co.uk

Michelham Priory boasts England's longest water filled medieval moat. Over a mile in length, it encircles nearly seven acres of beautiful grounds. on this picturesque island of history, you will find the impressive Gatehouse, a working watermill, and a magnificent (reputedly haunted) Tudor mansion that evolved from the former Augustinian Priory. With nearly 8oo years of history, Michelham Priory offers visitors a wealth of interesting exhibits inside and out.

In the grounds ingenious planting of the landscaped gardens offers an ever-changing display for the visitor whatever the season, from spring colour to a spectacular show of la summer herbaceous splenclour. The Physic Garden shows how our ancestors healed themselves. A recreated medieval cloister garden shows how the canons combined the practical and the pleasing with the minimum of maintenance.

Michelham Priory is situated at Upper Dicker, approx. two miles west of Hailsham and eight miles north west of Eastbourne.

went on to become the focal point of a large agricultural estate. Today, the grand Tudor farmhouse rooms are furnished with a collection of Dutch paintings, Flemish tapestries and old English furniture and the gatehouse, topped by the Pevensey coat of arms, is home to a group of brass rubbings and a reconstructed forge.

Michelham Priory Gardens are equally interesting and cover a range of styles. To the south of the house is a physic herb garden containing plants that were, and still are, grown for their medicinal and culinary benefits. There is also a recreated cloister garden, which illustrates the ability of the original monks to combine a pleasing garden with one that requires little maintenance. An Elizabethan barn can also be found in the grounds of the priory as can the working watermill, and the river and moat attract a variety of waterfowl throughout the year.

LAUGHTON

11 miles NW of Eastbourne on the B2124

This scattered village, isolated on the Glynde Levels, was once home to flourishing marble mines, potteries and a brickworks. **Laughton Place**, built in 1534, was one of the first brick buildings constructed in Sussex. The interior of the village church, which lies some way from the village centre, is dominated by a stone war memorial which features a soldier and sailor, both carved in minute detail.

HALLAND

13 miles NW of Eastbourne on the A22

Just to the south of Halland lies the interesting and fascinating **Bentley House and Motor Museum**. Covering some 100 acres of beautiful Sussex countryside, the estate cleverly combines

a wildfowl reserve, a stately home and a museum in order to provide a fun day out for all the family. Originally a modest 17th century farmhouse, Bentley was transformed into the splendid Palladian mansion by the architect Raymond Erith, who was also behind the restoration of 10, 11 and 12 Downing Street in the 1960s. Exquisitely furnished throughout, the house is particularly renowned for its Chinese Room and the Philip Rickman gallery, which contains a collection of over 150 wildfowl watercolours by the celebrated Sussex artist.

The formal gardens surrounding the house are laid out in a series of rooms, separated by yew hedges, and they often follow a colour theme. Beyond the house are the grounds and a woodland walk through the cool tranquillity of Glyndebourne Wood. The Motor Museum comprises a superb collection of privately owned vintage cars and motorcycles, which follow the history of motoring from its infancy in the Edwardian era to an elegant modern Lamborghini.

The waterfowl collection, which includes swans, geese, ducks and flamingos, was begun in the 1960s by Gerald Askew. The emphasis at the wildfowl centre is on conservation and breeding, particularly of the world's endangered birds.

EAST HOATHLY

12 miles NW of Eastbourne off the A22

Situated some 20 miles from West Hoathly, this compact village was immortalised by Thomas Turner in his *Diary of East Hoathly*. Although the village church was almost completely rebuilt in the mid 19th century, the 15th century squat tower remains from the original building. Known as a Pelham Tower, because it was built by the local

Pelham family, the structure has a belt buckle carved on it on either side of the door. This distinctive emblem was awarded to Sir John Pelham for his part in capturing King John of France at Poitiers in 1356. One of the door emblems has a deep slit in it that was supposedly caused by a bullet fired at Sir Nicholas Pelham in the 17th century. The failed murderer is said to have been a Cavalier, Thomas Lunsford, who joined the French army after being exiled for the attempted murder. He returned to Britain to fight with the king during the Civil War, then emigrated to America and died in Virginia in the 1650s.

CHIDDINGLY

10½ miles NW of Eastbourne off the A22

This small village is dominated by the 15th century spire of its church, which, at 130 feet, is a useful local landmark.

Inside the church is a impressive monument to Sir John Jefferay, Baron of the Exchequer under Queen Elizabeth, who lived at nearby Chiddingly Place - a once splendid Tudor mansion that is now in ruins.

However, his memorial is overshadowed by that of his daughter and son-in-law, who both appear to be standing on drums. Tradition has it that the Jefferay family once laid a line of cheeses from their manor house to the church door so that they would not get their feet wet. So the large discs of Sussex marble could, in fact, be a reference to those cheeses!

Curiously, the monuments have lost hands and fingers over the years as enraged locals knocked them off, thinking that the family were related to Judge Jeffries, who presided at the Bloody Assizes.

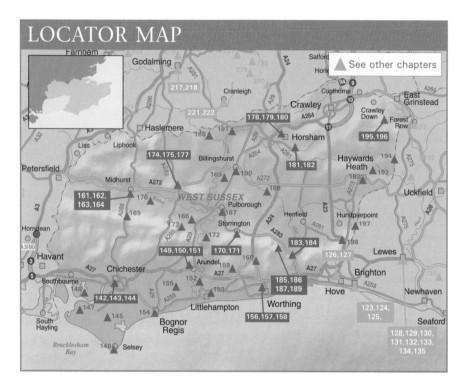

LOCATOR MAP

ADVERTISERS AND PLACES OF INTEREST

For the most part (the major development round Gatwick Airport is one of the few exceptions), West Sussex remains an essentially rural landscape dominated by the South Downs, a magnificent range of chalk hills. The South Downs Way, a 100-mile bridleway along the crest of the hills from Winchester to Beachy Head, offers panoramic views across the Weald to the north and the sea to the south. It traces the long history of this area along ancient trails, passing Bronze Age barrows and Iron Age hill forts. On the coast, Chichester, the county town, once a busy haunt of smugglers, is now a

Grounds of Wakehurst Place

thriving sailing centre, while the small fishing villages of the past are quiet holiday resorts like Littlehampton, Bognor Regis and Worthing. The ancient

woodland of the West Sussex Weald is now
a landscape of pastures and hedgerows and
small country villages. The trees were felled
for fuel to drive the furnaces of the iron
industry, which flourished here for
centuries. The legacy of this prosperous
industry can be seen in the wealth of
elaborate buildings, particularly churches,
built from the profits.

Evidence of early human habitation and
culture abound in this area. The Romans
settled in Chichester in the 1st century, and
it later became a great medieval religious
centre with a fine Norman cathedral. At
Fishbourne, the Roman remains of a
splendid palace built for the Celtic King
Cogidubnus were discovered in 1960. At
Arundel, the original Norman motte and
double bailey design of its magnificent
castle is still visible as well as the alterations

Chichester Cathedral

and additions of subsequent generations. Norman churches are everywhere,
often little altered over the centuries. In the tiny village of Sompting, there is
a Saxon church with a pyramid capped tower, unique in England. Near
Ardingly, Wakehurst Place is the striking Elizabethan mansion of the
Culpeper family, with a magnificent collection of trees and shrubs.
Wakehurst Place is also home to the Millennium Seed Bank a project, which
aims to ensure the continued survival of over 24,000 plant species worldwide.
Petworth House is an elegant late 17th century building, reminiscent of a
French château with a garden landscaped by Capability Brown. Close to East
Grinstead, the remarkable Victorian country house, Standen, has been
sensitively restored to its original Arts and Crafts Movement style.

Many great artists and literary figures have found this region inspirational.
Turner loved to paint its landscapes and harbours. H G Wells, Anthony
Trollope and Tennyson all lived here. The composer Edward Elgar wrote his
famous cello concerto at Fittleworth in 1917. And at Hurstpierpoint, at the
Elizabeth mansion, Danny, Lloyd George and his war cabinet drew up the
terms of the armistice that ended World War I.

Within easy reach of London by rail or road but not so near as to suffer too
much from commuter belt blight, served by an international airport and close
to channel ports for travel to the continent, it is no surprise that many
notable people continue to make their homes here. Few places so elegantly
combine 21st century convenience with the unspoiled charm of a rich
historic heritage.

CHICHESTER AND THE WEST SUSSEX COAST

This western, coastal region of West Sussex is centred around Chichester, the county town; Arundel, with its magnificent castle; and the resorts of Littlehampton, Bognor Regis and Worthing. Founded by the Romans in the 1st century, Chichester was an ecclesiastical centre for over 900 years. Its fine, natural harbour, once a busy place for trade and smugglers, is now a lively yachting centre with delightful old fishing villages along its inlets. Nearby, at Fishbourne, the grateful Roman conquerors built a splendid palace for the Celtic King Cogidubnus who collaborated with the invaders. The largest estate north of the Alps, the Roman remains were only uncovered this century while a new water mains was being installed.

The inland town of Arundel is home to a marvellous castle beside the River Arun and to the area's second cathedral. Built by the Roman Catholic family living at the castle, Arundel Cathedral is famous for its Corpus Christi Festival.

On the coast, the resorts of Littlehampton, Bognor Regis and Worthing, which were once small fishing villages, have much to offer visitors in an unbrash and timeless style. Finally, the small town of Selsey and Selsey Bill, the most southwesterly tip of West Sussex, is a charming place with as much history as there are pleasant walks along the coastline.

CHICHESTER

Set on the low-lying plain between the south coast and the South Downs, Chichester, the county town of West Sussex, was founded by the Romans in the 1st century AD. The invading Roman legions used the town as a base camp, christening it Noviomagus, the new city of the plain, and both the city walls and the four major thoroughfares - North, South, East and West Streets - follow the original Roman town plan. They cross at the point where a fine 16th century octagonal **Market Cross** now stands, an ornate structure built in 1501 by Bishop Edward Story to provide shelter for the many traders who came to sell their wares at the busy market.

The city walls, originally consisting of raised earthwork embankments built in an irregular 11-sided shape, were constructed around AD 200. Over the subsequent centuries alterations and improvements were made and, today, the remaining walls largely date from medieval times and large sections still form the boundary between the old and new city. After the Romans left, the Saxons arrived in about AD 500, and Chichester's modern name is derived from Cissa's ceaster after the Saxon King Cissa.

Chichester also has a long and colourful ecclesiastical history and, although St Wilfrid chose nearby Selsey as the site of the area's first cathedral, the conquering Normans, who moved all country bishoprics to towns, built a new cathedral on the present site in the late 11th century. Resting on Roman foundations, the construction work began in 1091 and the finished building was finally consecrated in 1184. A fire just three years later all but destroyed the cathedral and a rebuilding programme was started by Richard of Chichester in the 13th century. A venerated bishop who was canonised in 1262, Richard was subsequently adopted as the city's patron saint.

Lying in the heart of the city, **Chichester Cathedral**, a centre for

MECHANICAL MUSIC AND DOLL COLLECTION

Church Road, Portfield, Chichester, West Sussex PO19 4HN
Tel: 01243 372646 Fax: 01243 370299

In a former Victorian church, a mile to the east of Chichester city centre, can be found this magical collection of mechanical musical instruments. There are musical boxes, barrel pianos, organs etc. and on Wednesday afternoons in the summer visitors have the chance to hear them. Listen to the lively music of the Victorian parlours, streets and pubs, and the glorious sounds of orchestrions that filled the dance halls in the `20s. You can even take groups there by appointment for a tour any time throughout the year. Children adore these music machines, and adults sometimes remember the tunes!

Christian worship for over 900 years, is unique on two counts. Firstly, it is the only medieval English cathedral that can be seen from the sea rather than being secluded by its own close and, secondly, it has a detached belfry. The existing tower was thought not to have been sturdy enough to take the cathedral bells and another separate building was needed. In 1861, the cathedral spire

blew down in a storm and demolished a large section of the nave. The present 277-foot spire was designed by Sir Gilbert Scott, in keeping with the building's original style, and can also be seen for miles around from all directions.

Among the treasures within the cathedral is the Shrine of St Richard of Chichester along with some fine Norman arches, a set of 14th century choir stalls

THE DINING ROOM AT PURCHASE'S

31 North Street, Chichester, West Sussex PO19 1LY
Tel: 01243 537352 Fax: 01243 533397
e-mail: neil@forgehotel.com
website: www.forgehotel.com

The Dining Room at Purchase's is a gourmet haven set in a beautiful Georgian building in the heart of Chichester. It is located in the city's and the UK's oldest family run wine merchants, Arthur Purchase & Son, established in 1760. Comprising restaurant and wine bar, and open from noon right through to 11pm (last food orders 8.45pm), it caters for all tastes and appetites, and the excellent food is complemented by courteous, attentive service. Local and organic ingredients are used as much as possible, and the team of chefs under chef/proprietor Neil Rusbridger produce a wide variety of dishes, from Danish open sandwiches and hot and cold tapas to fresh fish and shellfish, seasonal game, the finest British poultry and meat, salads and many other options.

Typical delights on the main menu are Selsey crab (cold in a salad or hot with mushrooms in a cream and brandy sauce), foie gras with apple cider jelly and toasted brioche, omelette Arnold Bennett, diver-caught scallops with smoked bacon, and a vegetarian dish of pancakes filled with goat's cheese, leeks, pine nuts and fresh pear. Purchase's also serves a splendid afternoon tea, and it's one of the most popular venues for pre-theatre suppers, being only a few minutes' walk from the Chichester Festival Theatre.

and some excellent modern works of art. There is an altar tapestry by John Piper, a stained glass window by Marc Chagall and a painting by Graham Sutherland of Christ appearing to Mary Magdalene. However, the most important treasures to be seen are the Norman sculptures: *The Raising of Lazarus* and *Christ Arriving in Bethany,* which can be found on the south wall. The **Prebendal School,** the cathedral choir school, is the oldest school in Sussex and stands alongside the main building.

From the Middle Ages until the 18th century, Chichester was a major trading and exporting centre for the Sussex woollen trade, and some handsome merchants' houses were built on the profits from this trade. The city's oldest building, **St Mary's Hospital,** dating from the 13th century, was established to house the deserving elderly of Chichester. It will be closed for restoration work until Easter 2005.

The almshouses that were built into the hospital walls are still inhabited and the chapel has some unique misericords. The city's **Guildhall,** built in the 1270s as the church of the Franciscans, is also well worth seeing. Later becoming Chichester's town hall and law courts it was here, in 1804, that William Blake, poet, painter and inveterate hater of authority and the establishment, was tried with high treason for having 'uttered seditious and treasonable expressions'. He was acquitted. Today, it is home to a display telling the story of the building and the surrounding Priory Park in which it stands.

There are also some fine Georgian buildings to be found here and, in the area known as The Pallants, lies **Pallant House.** A fine example of a red brick town house, it was built in 1713 by the local wine merchant Henry 'Lisbon' Peckham and the building is guarded by a wonderful pair of carved stone dodos, which have given rise to its local nickname - the Dodo House. Another curious feature is the observation tower on the house from which Peckham would look out for his merchant ships returning laden with goods from the Iberian peninsula. Today, the house is the **Pallant House Gallery,** (closed until summer 2005), one of the finest galleries outside London, with each room reflecting a different period. The collection is mostly 20th century British, with works also by Klée and Cézanne.

One of the city's most distinctive modern buildings can be found at Oaklands Park, close by the city walls. The **Chichester Festival Theatre** was opened in 1962 and the splendid hexagonal building has since gained a reputation for staging the finest classical and contemporary drama, opera and ballet. The theatre and the cathedral are the focal points of the annual Chichester Festival. For two weeks during July, the city is alive with a myriad of cultural events. For those with quieter interests, the **Mechanical Music and Doll Collection** (see panel opposite) represents a fascinating walk through the last 100 years of mechanical music. Playing the tunes of late 19th century public houses through to genteel Victorian parlour songs, the beautifully restored instruments are put through their paces on a regular basis. Also to be seen with the collection are Edison phonographs, early horned gramophones, stereoscopic viewers and over 100 dolls spanning the years from 1830 to 1930.

The **Royal Military Police Museum** is housed in the Keep at Roussillon Barracks and is a must for anyone interested in military history (see panel on page 212).

Once a busy port, the city is now a haven for boat lovers and yachtsmen,

ROYAL MILITARY POLICE MUSEUM

Roussillon Barracks, Broyle Road, Chichester,
West Sussex, PO19 4BN
Tel: 01243 534225 Fax: 01243 534288
e-mail: museum@rhqrmp.freeserve.co.uk
website: www.rhqrmp.freeserve.co.uk

This is an essential visit for anyone interested in military history and a fascinating insight into the history and workings of the **Royal Military Police** for anyone else. Established in 1979, the present museum was formally opened in 1985 and has full registration with the Museums and Galleries Commission.

Military Police, also known as redcaps because of their distinctive headgear, have been around for a long time. Walking through the various fascinating exhibits, it is possible to trace their entire history from Tudor times to the recent conflicts in the former Yugoslavia. Display cases contain life size models of military policemen dressed in the varieties of uniforms they have used at different times and at

different points of the globe. Everything is there from full camouflage combat gear to the dress uniform worn by a mounted officer at a ceremonial occasion. Also included are maps, weapons and communications equipment the corps have used in their various theatres of operations.

Visitors can try on some of the uniforms, have their fingerprints taken and learn about the diverse role of the military police. A .22 palm pistol is part of a haul of weapons confiscated during the RMP operations, aimed at reducing weapon holding, in Republica Serbska during 1996-97. This murderous little device is lethal at close quarters and easily concealed. From the period at the end of WWII is a complicated looking illicit still recovered from a displaced persons camp in Hamburg, 1946. From the same period is the Walther P38 pistol used in the murder of Sergeant Southcott. He and two others arrested Teofil Walasek on charges of murder, rape and robbery. When they apprehended him at the railway station he was searched but they neglected to check his overcoat. Back at HQ Walasek produced the pistol, killed Southcott, wounded two others and escaped but was later recaptured and sentenced to death.

Amongst the exhibits is a ferret armoured car of the type used extensively by the Redcaps in anti-terrorist operations in Cyprus and Malaya during the 1950s. This one, which sits outside the museum, is in the livery of 17 Ghurkha Division Provost Company and was crewed entirely by RMP NCOs providing close escort to the general officer commanding the division during road moves.   A BSA motorcycle was in use from 1939-1964. Many modern exhibits are on display from theatres of operations ranging from Northern Ireland to Bosnia and Kosovo. The Northern Ireland exhibits include captured terrorist weapons, commercially and homemade, uniform items and accounts of incidents in which the RMP were involved. Outside the building are two imposing statues of Military Policemen, one standing at ease upon a large block the other on horseback. In the purpose built Broakes Room is a comprehensive collection of medals awarded to members of the RMP over the years of its existence.

with 12,000 resident boats in one of Europe's largest marinas. From the bustling harbour visitors can take a boat trip around this stretch of sheltered water with its sand dunes, mudflats, shingle and woodlands providing habitats for varied sea birds. A particularly pleasant waterside walk takes in the city's impressive canal basin, along the **Chichester Canal** to Chichester Harbour. The canal opened in 1822, taking vessels up to 150 tons from Arundel to Portsmouth. The last commercial cargo travelled the route in 1928 but now, after restoration work, this shorter stretch provides a delightful walk with a cruise boat at the other end on which to make the return journey.

Housed in an 18th century corn store, **Chichester District Museum** explores local history through displays and hands-on activities. Visitors can find out about local geology and prehistory, including Boxgrove Man, believed to have lived around 500,000 years ago. The remains, consisting of part of a human shinbone and two human feet, are the earliest remains of human-like species found in Britain. They were found during excavations in the 1990s along with bones of butchered animals and tools. Life in Roman, Saxon and medieval Chichester can also be discovered. There are displays on Chichester during the Civil War and visitors can see how the city changed during Georgian and Victorian times. The story is brought right up to date with displays on Chichester since 1900.

AROUND CHICHESTER

MID LAVANT

2 miles N of Chichester on the A286

This attractive village, along with its neighbour East Lavant, is named after the small river that flows from Singleton into Chichester Harbour. There are spectacular views from here northwards over the South Downs and it is said that these were the inspiration for the words 'England's green and pleasant land' which appear in William Blake's poem, *Jerusalem*.

GOODWOOD

3 miles NE of Chichester off the A285

This is not a village but the spectacular country home of the Dukes of Richmond, **Goodwood House**. It was first acquired by the 1st Duke of Richmond (the natural son of Charles II and his beautiful French mistress, Louise de Keroualle) in 1697 so that he could ride with the local hunt. The original, modest hunting lodge still remains in the grounds, but has been superseded by the present mansion, built on a grand scale in the late 18th century for the 3rd

'Host' by Peter Burke, Goodwood

Duke by the architect James Wyatt. At the same time the splendid stables were added. Now refurbished by the Earl and Countess of March, several rooms in this impressive house, including the state apartments, are open to visitors. The state apartments are magnificent examples of the luxury of the period with an Egyptian state dining room, grand yellow drawing room and an elegant ballroom. Among the items on display are two *Views of the Thames from Old Richmond House* by Canaletto, the *Lion and Lioness* by Stubbs, fine Sèvres porcelain collected by the 3rd Duke while he was Ambassador to Paris, gruesome relics from the Napoleonic Wars and French and English furniture.

Viewers of the BBC television drama *Aristocrats* will recognise the house as it was used as the location for the series. Not only was the drama filmed here but the story was that of the independent minded and glamorous daughters of the 2nd Duke of Richmond. The girls grew up both at Goodwood House and at the Duke's London residence, Richmond House, and the whole family were enthusiastic leaders of early Georgian society. Goodwood House was the setting for Sarah's banishment from society and it was also here that Kildare wooed Emily. On display in the house is a painting by George Stubbs which features Caroline's husband, Lord Holland, and the Meissen snuff box the couple gave to the duchess four years after their elopement.

The house is the focal point of the Goodwood Estate, some 12,000 acres of downland which also incorporate the world famous **Goodwood Racecourse**. A favourite venue with the rich, racing has taken place here for nearly 200 years and, in particular, there is the Glorious Goodwood meeting. First introduced by

the 4th Duke of Richmond in 1814, just 12 years after racing began here, this prestigious five-day meeting is one of the major events in the calendar and has long been a much anticipated part of the summer season. Further, the estate contains a golf course, motor racing circuit, children's adventure play area, sculpture park and a new Rolls Royce factory. Highlights of the year for motoring and motor racing enthusiasts are the Festival of Speed held in June and the Revival Meeting in September.

HALNAKER
3½ miles NE of Chichester on the A285

Pronounced Hannaker, this village was the seat of the influential and powerful De La Warr family. The present **Halnaker House**, designed by Edwin Lutyens in 1938, is a splendid modern country house. Just to the north lies the original Halnaker House, which was allowed to fall into decay around 1800. Built in medieval times, the old house was originally the home of the De Haye family who were also the founders of Boxgrove Priory.

Above the village, on Halnaker Hill, stands an early 18th century tower windmill, **Halnaker Windmill**, which was painted by Turner. It remained in use until 1905 when it, too, was allowed to fall into ruin. In 1912, Hilaire Belloc mentioned the windmill in a poem where he compares the decay of agriculture in Britain with the neglected mill. The exterior was restored in 1934 and the windmill was used as an observation tower during World War II. It was restored once again in 1955 by the county council.

BOXGROVE
2 miles NE of Chichester off the A27

This attractive village is home to the remains of **Boxgrove Priory**, a cell of the

Benedictine Lessay Abbey in France, which was founded in around 1115. Initially a community of just three monks, over the centuries the priory expanded and grew into one of the most influential in Sussex. However, all that remains today are the Guest House, Chapter House and the Church, which is now the parish Church of St Mary and St Blaise. Its sumptuous interior reflects the priory's former importance and, before the Dissolution of the Monasteries, the De La Warr Chantry Chapel was built like a 'church within a church' to be the final resting place of the family. Unfortunately, Henry VIII forced De La Warr to dispose of the priory and the family was eventually buried at Broadwater near Worthing. Though it is still empty, the extravagant marble chapel has survived.

A fascinating discovery was made, in 1993, by local archaeologists who unearthed prehistoric remains in a local sand and gravel pit. Among the finds was an early hominid thigh bone and, although there is still some debate over the precise age of the bone, the find has been named **Boxgrove Man**.

TANGMERE
2 miles E of Chichester off the A27

The village is still very much associated with the nearby former Battle of Britain base, RAF Tangmere and, although the runways have now been turned back into farmland or housing estates, the efforts of the pilots are remembered at the local pub, The Bader Arms (named after pilot Douglas Bader) and the **Tangmere Military Aviation Museum**. The museum, based at the airfield, tells the story, through replica aircraft,

photographs, pictures, models and memorabilia, of military flying from the earliest days during World War I to the present time. The Battle of Britain Hall tells its own story with aircraft remains, personal effects and true accounts from both British and German pilots of those desperate days in 1940. On display are two historic aircraft, each of which beat the World Air Speed record in their day. Finally, it was while at RAF Tangmere during World War II that H E Bates completed his novel *Fair Stood the Wind for France* about a bomber crew shot down over occupied France.

NORTON
6 miles S of Chichester on the B2145

One of the original communities that made up Selsey, Norton's first church was probably built on, or close to, the site of the cathedral that St Wilfrid erected when he became Bishop of the South Saxons in AD 681. Following the Norman Conquest, the country bishoprics were moved into the towns and Selsey's bishop transferred to Chichester. In the 1860s, the decision to move the medieval parish Church of St Peter from its isolated site to Selsey was taken. But, according to ecclesiastical law, a church chancel

Tangmere Military Aviation Museum

cannot be moved, so it remains here as **St Wilfrid's Chapel**.

SIDLESHAM

4 miles S of Chichester on the B2145

A pleasant village, which is home to the information and interpretation centre for **Pagham Harbour Nature Reserve**. The harbour was formed when the sea breached reclaimed land in 1910 and it is now a well known breeding ground for many rare birds. The tidal mud flats attract an abundance of wildfowl and also many species of animals and marine life. Sidlesham Ferry is the starting point for guided walks around this important conservation area.

SELSEY

7 miles S of Chichester on the B2145

Once an important Saxon town, fishing has been the main stay of life here for many centuries. However, according to accounts by the Venerable Bede, St Wilfrid, while Bishop of the South Saxons, discovered that the Selsey fishermen were unsuccessful and such was their shortage of food that they were prepared to throw themselves off nearby cliffs. St Wilfrid taught them to fish and the town has thrived ever since; at one time, only Selsey crabs were served on the liner QE2.

Now a more modest town yet still a popular resort, the main street looks much as it did in the 18th century. The **Sessions House**, where the Lord of Selsey Manor held court, was probably built in the early 17th century though it contains the exposed beams and wooden panelling of an earlier age. There are also several thatched cottages to be seen, including the 18th century cottage and the 16th century farmhouse known as The Homestead. Perhaps, though, the most impressive building here is **Selsey**

SIDLESHAM BASKET & BEDDING PLANT NURSERY

Street End Road, Sidlesham Common,
nr Chichester, West Sussex PO20 7QD
Tel/Fax: 01243 641044
e-mail: claudia@lamb64.freeserve.co.uk

South of Chichester, on the road to Selsey Bill and the sea, **Sidlesham Basket & Bedding Plant Nursery** is

undoubtedly one of the finest of its kind in the region. The owners, Chris and Claudia Lamb, certainly lack nothing in experience and expertise: Chris, who trained in horticulture, has been involved in plant growing for more than 20 years, while Claudia was brought up in a plant nursery owned by her parents.

Their friendly, helpful attitude, and that of their staff, adds greatly to the pleasure of a visit. Seasonal bedding plants are one of the nursery's specialities, and there's an impressive range of shrubs, alpines and herbaceous plants. They make a colourful display, but what really takes the eye is the lovely array of hanging baskets for which the nursery is renowned far and wide. They can be sold ready assembled or made up to customers' requirements, in either metal or wicker baskets. The Nursery also sells a range of terracotta and ceramic pots, including the top-quality guaranteed frostproof Yorkshire flower pots, proudly displayed under the 'Crafted in Britain' banner.

Windmill. Today's mill was built in 1820 as the previous late 17th century timber construction had suffered greatly from weather damage. A tower mill built from local red bricks, though it ceased milling flour in 1910, the mill continued to grind pepper into the 1920s. Now rescued and restored, it is a pleasant local landmark.

With so many of the townsfolk depending on the sea for their living, the Lifeboat Station was established here in 1860. The present building was erected 100 years later and there is also an interesting little **Lifeboat Museum**.

For many years the town's **East Beach** was a well-known site for smuggling, which, was a full-time occupation for many local inhabitants in the 18th century. In fact, while the French were in the throes of their revolution the villagers of Selsey were busy smuggling ashore over 12,000 gallons of spirits. Much later, during World War II, East Beach was used as a gathering point for sections of the famous Mulberry Harbour that was transported across the Channel as part of the D-Day landings. Just inland from the beach, now on a roundabout, is a small building called the **Listening Post**. During World War I it was used as a naval observation post, with personnel listening out for the sound of invading German airships, and as such it acted as an early warning system long before radar was established.

A gruesome reminder of Selsey's smuggling past is Gibbet Field. The bodies of two smugglers, John Cobby and John Hammond, who had been executed for their crimes in 1749, were hung in chains from the gibbet that once stood in this field, as a grim warning to others who might follow in their footsteps.

Geographically, **Selsey Bill**, the extreme southwest of Sussex, is an island,

CRAB QUAY

31 Clayton Road, Selsey, West Sussex PO20 9DF
Tel: 01243 602462 Fax: 01243 604949
e-mail: jenny@crabquay.co.uk
website: www.crabquay.co.uk

"Thank you for sharing your beautiful home." This and many similar testimonies from satisfied guests epitomise the quality of this very superior Bed & Breakfast establishment by the sea. Owner Jenny Graves likes meeting people, and from the moment they step through the door of **Crab Quay**, guests are treated like old friends. Jenny's flair for interior design is evident throughout the house, where gothic features and creative

artwork take the eye. Most striking of all are the two main bedrooms – Exotic Egypt with a king-size four-poster and Egyptian murals, and Out of Africa with its wild leafy murals. Both have en suite facilities and balconies that look out towards the Solent and the Isle of Wight. The third room is a twin with private bathroom. Guests have use of a comfortably furnished lounge, a sea-facing sunroom where breakfast is served, and an indoor pool. The lovely garden has an outdoor pool, stream, rock garden and jacuzzi.

Crab Quay is a really relaxing, romantic retreat with many outstanding features and marvellous views – a perfect spot for a honeymoon!

with the English Channel on two sides, Pagham Harbour to the northeast and a brook running from the harbour to Bracklesham Bay which cuts the land off from the remainder of the Manhood Peninsular. However, Ferry Banks, built in 1809, links the bill with the mainland. Over the centuries this part of the coastline has been gradually eroded and many of the area's historic remains have now been lost beneath the encroaching tides.

EARNLEY

6 miles SW of Chichester off the B2198

This charming small village is home to **Earnley Gardens**, a delightful five acres of themed gardens, exotic birds and butterflies. It also has a fascinating small museum of ephemera. **Rejectamenta**, the Museum of 20th century memorabilia, displays thousands of everyday items, reflecting the changes in

lifestyle over the past 100 years. There is everything here from old washing powder packets and winklepickers to stylophones and space hoppers.

WEST WITTERING

7 miles SW of Chichester on the B2179

West Wittering and its larger neighbour, **East Wittering**, both lie close to the beautiful inlet that is Chichester's natural harbour. A charming seaside village, West Wittering overlooks the narrow entrance to the harbour and this former fishing village has developed into a much sought after residential area and select holiday resort. Here, too, lies **Cakeham Manor House**, with its distinctive early 16th century brick tower that was once the summer palace of the bishops of Chichester. A splendid part-medieval, part-Tudor and part-Georgian house, it was in the manor's studio that Sir Henry Royce, of Rolls Royce, designed

FUCHSIAS GALORE

Tawny Nurseries, Bell Lane, Birdham, nr Chichester, West Sussex PO20 7HY
Tel: 01243 512168 Fax: 01243 514908
website: www.fuchsias-galore.co.uk

Tawny Nurseries, where **Fuchsias Galore** is located, was the brainchild of Derek Howell, who hit upon the name when he and his wife saw a tawny owl flying low across the ground. That was over 20 years ago, and in those years the nursery has built up an enviable reputation for the range and quality of its stock. It is now run by Derek's son Adrian and daughter Gloria, and, as the name suggests, fuchsias are the speciality, with over 1,000

varieties in the catalogue. Geraniums are also a large part of the business, with more than 250 varieties grown.

The family has won many awards over the years, particularly for the beautiful hanging baskets that can be bought ready assembled or made up to order. The gardening and display areas are very attractively laid out and a real delight to stroll around, with glorious colours and alluring scents everywhere. A popular annual event held at Fuchsias Galore is the April charity weekend, when the proceeds go to St Wilfrid's Hospice in Chichester. Adrian and Gloria also run an adjacent Caravan Club site which they plan to extend to accommodate up to 40 caravans.

many of his inventions.

Both villages have easy access to excellent sandy beaches and the headland that forms the eastern approach to Chichester Harbour, **East Head**, which is now a nature reserve. A sand and shingle spit which supports a variety of bird, plant and marine life, marram grass has been introduced to the sand dunes to help reduce the ravages of the sea and wind.

ITCHENOR

5 miles SW of Chichester off the B2179

Originally a Saxon settlement called Icenore, in the 13th century the villagers of Itchenor built a church, which they chose to dedicate to St Nicholas, the guardian of seafarers. As the village overlooks the sheltered waters of Chichester Harbour, shipbuilding was an obvious industry to become established here and, as early as the 1600s, there was a shipyard at Itchenor. The last ships built here were minesweepers during World War II but the village today is a busy sailing and yachting centre as well as being the customs clearance port for Chichester Harbour.

BIRDHAM

4 miles SW of Chichester on the A286

The setting for Turner's famous painting of Chichester Harbour (which can be seen at Petworth House), this delightful place is as charming today as it was when the views captured the great artist's imagination. Here, too, can be found the **Sussex Falconry Centre**, which was originally set up as a breeding and rescue centre for indigenous birds of prey. In 1991, the centre started to exhibit the birds to the public and, as well as viewing and watching the birds fly, visitors can also take advantage of the centre's falconry and hawking courses.

FISHBOURNE

2 miles W of Chichester on A286

This unremarkable village would not appear on anyone's list of places to visit in West Sussex if it was not for the splendid Roman remains discovered in 1960 when a new water main was cut. **Fishbourne Roman Palace** was built around AD 75 for the Celtic King Cogidubnus, who collaborated with the Roman conquerors. As well as taking on the role of Viceroy, Cogidubnus was rewarded with this magnificent palace with underfloor heating, hot baths, a colonnade, an ornamental courtyard garden and lavish decorations. This was the largest residential building north of the Alps and among the superb remains are a garden and numerous mosaic floors, including the famous **Cupid on a Dolphin** mosaic.

As well as walking through the excavated remains of the north wing, visitors can see the formal garden, which has been replanted to the original Roman plan. When the palace was first constructed the sea came right up to its outer walls and the building remained in use until around AD 320 when a fire largely destroyed the site. The history of the palace, along with many of the artefacts rescued during the excavations, can be discovered in the site museum, where there is also an exhibition area on Roman gardening.

BOSHAM

3½ miles W of Chichester off the A286

Pronounced Bozzum, this pleasant village is well known for both its history and its charm. Though it was the Irish monk Dicul who built a small religious house here, Bishop Wilfrid is credited with bringing Christianity to the area in AD 681 and Bosham is probably the first place in Sussex where he preached.

MILLSTREAM HOTEL & RESTAURANT

Bosham Lane, Bosham, nr Chichester,
West Sussex PO18 8HL
Tel: 01243 573234
Fax: 01243 573459
e-mail: info@millstream-hotel.co.uk
website: www.millstream-hotel.co.uk

In the heart of historic Bosham on the shores of Chichester Harbour, the **Millstream Hotel** combines the style and elegance of an English country house with the charm and character of an 18th century malthouse cottage. It offers the highest levels of comfort, service and hospitality and is a holder of the coveted ETC Gold Award. Each of the 35 enchanting guest bedrooms has its own individual appeal, and all are decorated and furnished to an impressively high standard. Two particularly charming rooms are suites with private gardens, located in the thatched Waterside Cottage. The cosy bar is the perfect place to unwind – perhaps to meet other guests, to have a game of cards or to enjoy a quiet read by the fire. In fine weather, afternoon tea or an aperitif on the lawn is guaranteed to put the daily grind of city life far into the background. The hotel is open to residents and non-residents for morning coffee, light and full lunches, afternoon cream teas and candlelit suppers. In the fine restaurant, overlooking the garden and millstream, a wide-ranging menu of English and European dishes is served, with the emphasis on top-quality fresh local produce. The chefs pay great attention to both preparation and presentation in dishes that range from starters such as wild mushroom and dolcelatte terrine or salmon & herb fishcake to halibut with a shellfish and dill sauce, or best end of fillet of lamb with a honey, rosemary and mustard balsamic dressing. There's always a good choice for vegetarians, and desserts like raspberry crème brûlée or hot spiced plums in a cinnamon meringue set the seal on a meal to remember.

Bosham is a lovely place to spend time discovering. Now a popular base with yachtsmen, its maritime connections go back famously to the day when King Canute found that the waves had little regard for his majesty's authority. Canute's daughter is buried in the Saxon church. The town also has plenty of interesting old buildings, shops and a craft centre, and the Millstream Hotel is the ideal base for getting to know this delightful place.

Later, in the 10th century, Danish raiders landed here and, among the items that they stole, was the church's tenor bell. As the Danes left and took to their boats, the remaining bells were rung to sound the all clear and to indicate to the villagers that they could leave the nearby woods and return to their homes. As the last peal of bells rang out, the tenor bell, in one of the Danish boats, is said to have joined in and, in doing so, capsized the boat. Both the bell and the sailors sank to the bottom of the creek and the place is now known as Bell Hole. Whether the story is true or not, Bosham certainly has its fair share of local legends as the village has strong associations with King Canute. It was here, on the shore, that the king, in the early 11th century, is said to have ordered back the waves in an attempt to demonstrate his kingly powers. King Canute's daughter is also buried in the once important Saxon parish church.

Feeding the Swans at Bosham

King Harold sailed from Bosham in 1064 on his ill-fated trip to Normandy to appease his rival, William of Normandy, for the English throne. However, Harold's plans went awry when he was taken captive and made to swear to William to aid his claim to the crown - a promise which, famously, Harold did not keep. It was the breaking of the promise that caused William to set forth with his army a couple of years later. As a result, Harold's lands in Sussex were some of the first to be taken by the conquering Norman army and Bosham church's spire can be seen alongside Harold's ship in the Bayeux Tapestry.

An important port in the Middle Ages and particularly, between the 1800s and the 20th century, when it was alive with oyster smacks, today's Bosham is a place for keen yachtsmen as well as a charming place to explore. The narrow streets that lead down to the harbour are filled with elegant 17th and 18th century flint and brick buildings among which is the **Bosham Walk Craft Centre**. This fascinating collection of little shops selling all manner of arts, crafts, fashions and antiques within an old courtyard setting, also holds craft demonstrations and exhibitions throughout the season.

WALDERTON
6 miles NW of Chichester off the B2146

Just to the west of the village lies **Stansted House**, a splendid example of late 17th century architecture, built on the site of Henry II's 11th century hunting lodge. Stansted has played host to a variety of distinguished guests, including royalty, over the centuries. The house was built on its present site in 1668 for Richard Lumley - probably by the architect William Talman. Heavily altered in the following two centuries, it was burnt to the ground in 1900 but, in

Stoughton

Distance: 4.3 miles (6.9 kilometres)

Typical time: 105 mins

Height gain: 146 metres

Map: Explorer 120/Landranger 197

Walk: www.walkingworld.com
ID:2092

Contributor: Sylvia Saunders

Access Information:

From Emsworth A27(T) take the B2148, B2147 then the B2146 turning off right to Walderton and Stoughton. You will see the sign for St.Mary's church at the green. Park at the end of the green in the marked out triangle on the road, as shown in waymark 1. Have no fear of blocking the bus stop as sadly the buses stopped running a couple of years ago.

Description:

When most people arrive at the quiet village of Stoughton they cannot resist walking in the outstandingly, beautiful Kingley Vale Nature

Reserve. However, this walk takes you up and over the hill on the opposite side of the road where the views and the woodland are just as spectacular, but much quieter. You will be unlucky if you don't spot some deer on this walk.

Features:

Hills or Fells, Pub, Church, Wildlife, Birds, Flowers, Great Views, Butterflies, Woodland

Walk Directions:

1 Take the lane to the right of the tree and village notice board. After a short distance you will see two tracks on your right hand side. The first one leads up to the church. Ignore this. Turn right up the second track, signposted "bridleway" with the telephone box on the left hand side of it. Near to the top of the hill there is a track off to your right, ignore this and follow the bridleway as indicated by the post. As you begin to drop, ignore the footpath off on your left and all other trackways, following the well signed route to the lane.

2 Cross straight over the lane and follow the bridleway uphill. After a short distance you will arrive at a set of fingerposts. Ignore the bridleway off to the left and carry straight on up the hill ignoring all other tracks. The route is clearly marked along the way with wooden posts. At the top of the hill you arrive at a T-junction with another track.

3 Turn right here taking the footpath through Lyecommon. Pass the idyllic Keeper's Cottage where you can usually find a kindly placed drink of water for thirsty dogs. After passing a couple of other cottages you will arrive at a wooden gate and stile. At the time of walking the stile was overgrown but the gate was wide open. Pass straight through and you will soon arrive at a choice of routes.

4 Take the lower track to the left as indicated by the footpath sign. Walk downhill until you come to a track bearing right. Turn right as indicated. After a short distance you will arrive at another track. Turn right here. After a short distance you will arrive at a fingerpost sign by a big beech tree. Turn left here and the track soon opens out into a field. Walk through this field with the trees on your right hand side. The main trackway bends off to the right out of this field. Carry on straight ahead still walking on the right hand side of the field edge. As you climb this gentle rise, look at the trees on the other side of the field. They look like they have all had their foliage carefully trimmed to the same length at the bottom. Study the bottoms of them carefully and you may see some deer looking at you. Look at the green open area beyond the field ahead. There is often a herd of them to be seen here as well. You may well see one of the local celebrities... an albino deer. The track leaves the field and you will shortly arrive at a fingerpost sign.

5 Turn right here. When the track bends to the left, follow it, ignoring the track on your right which leads into a field entrance. You will soon arrive at metal gates with a stile.

6 Go over the stile and turn right down the lane. After about 200 metres there is a track on the left hand side with a sign to Tumblecroft and Black Barn cottages. The bridleway fingerpost is opposite but was hardly visable when I last walked here as it was overgrown at the time.

7 Turn left here. Walk along this track, pass the cottage and ignore both footpaths. The track then opens up into fields. Carry on walking straight ahead keeping the trees on

your left hand side. Here you must be quiet. Have a good look around - there may well be deer to be seen in these fields. Walk along to the end of the field where you will find a wooden marker post. Turn right here walking through the woods. The track descends and crosses over a wide track. Soon you will get a first glimpse of the view over to Kingley Vale. Now look out for the footpath marked with a wooden post off to your right. Be careful that you don't miss it as the wooden post is tucked around the corner a little.

8 Turn right here. This path was beautiful before the devastation of the 1987 storm. For years afterwards it was decimated but now I believe it is even more lovely than it ever was. The views are better and the more open woodland has allowed a wealth of wild flowers to flourish. Carry on until the path divides with one path bending uphill to the right and another more minor path carrying straight on. Carry straight on here and in a few metres the path will bring you out into a field with more outstanding views. Walk along the top edge of this field with the trees on your right. When you reach the other side of the field you will see a fingerpost directing you into a shady track.

9 Turn left onto this track and walk downhill to the road.

10 Turn right and walk along this quiet road back through the village of Stoughton. Shortly after you pass the Hare and Hounds you will find yourself back at the starting point.

1903, the house was rebuilt to the exact plans of Richard Lumley's grand mansion.

Now open to visitors, on a limited basis, the house is home to the late Lord Bessborough's collection of paintings and furnishings, including some fine 18th century tapestries. The **Below Stairs Experience** transports visitors to the old kitchen, pantry, servants' hall, living quarters and wine cellars. The surrounding grounds are renowned for their peace and tranquillity and the **Stansted Park Garden Centre** in the original walled garden has restored Victorian glasshouses,

including a palm house, camellia house, fernery and vine house.

East Ashling

3 miles NW of Chichester on B2178

A couple of miles to the north of East Ashling lies **Kingley Vale National Nature Reserve**, which contains the largest forest of yews in Britain. The trees were protected until the mid 16th century as they were used for making long bows, England's successful weapon against crossbows. Yews are a long-lived species - 100 years is nothing in the life of a yew tree. Here at Kingley Vale, there are several 500-year-old trees, although most of the forest is made up of trees approaching their first century. Towards the summit of **Bow Hill**, the trees give way to heather and open heathland and it is here a group of four Bronze Age burial mounds, known as the King's Graves or Devil's Humps, can be found.

ARUNDEL

A settlement since before the Romans invaded, this quiet and peaceful town, which lies beneath the battlements of one of the most impressive castles in the country, is a strategically important site where the major east-west route through Sussex crosses the River Arun. It was one of William the Conqueror's most favoured knights, Roger de Montgomery, who first built a castle here, on the high ground overlooking the river, in the late

11th century. With a similar plan to that of Windsor castle, **Arundel Castle** consisted of a motte with a double bailey, a design which, despite several alterations and much rebuilding, remains clearly visible today. The second largest castle in England, it has been the seat of the Dukes of Norfolk and the Earls of Arun for over 700 years.

It was damaged in 1643 when, during the Civil War, Parliamentarian forces bombarded it with canons fired from the church tower. A programme of restoration took place during the late 18th century to make it habitable once more. A second programme of rebuilding was undertaken 100 years later by the 15th Duke of Norfolk, using profits from the family's ownership of the newly prosperous steel town of Sheffield. Unfortunately, all that remains today of the original construction are the 12th century shell

Arundel Castle

However the castle is still an atmospheric place to visit. The state apartments and main rooms contain some fine furniture dating from the 16th century and there are some excellent tapestries and paintings by Reynolds, Van Dyck, Gainsborough, Holbein and Constable on show. Also on display are some possessions of Mary, Queen of Scots and a selection of heraldic artefacts from the Duke of Norfolk's collection. The title, the Duke of Norfolk, was first conferred on Sir John Howard in 1483, by his friend Richard III. Carrying the hereditary office of Earl Marshal of England, the Duke of Norfolk is the premier duke of England.

keep and parts of the 13th century barbican and curtain wall.

Perhaps the most gruesome item to be seen at the castle can be found, not

DECOGRAPHIC COLLECTORS' GALLERY
TOYS, CAMERAS, WIRELESS, GRAMOPHONES

Arundel Antiques Centre, 51 High Street,
Arundel, West Sussex BN18 9AJ
Tel: 01243 787391

F. MARTIN: LE CAB 1903

Quentin Cox, whose background was in computers and information technology, let nostalgia take over when he started his wonderful **DecoGraphic Collectors' Gallery** in Chichester, moving in 1995 to the Antiques Centre in the main street of Arundel. His collection of **toys, wireless sets, cameras and gramophones** dates from 1880 to 1960.

The toys include early tinplate, Dinky, Hornby, Corgi, bisque dolls and Britains soldiers. **Cameras** include mahogany field models, classic bellows, 35mm and sub-miniatures. **Wireless** sets are from early crystal sets through '30s bakelite to '50s VHF and transistor radios. **Gramophones** range from Edwardian horn instruments to '30s table models to '50s radiograms.

'HMV' TRADEMARK MODEL 1898

Also in this fascinating collection are related books, period photographs and recorded music on both vintage records and remastered 78s on CDs.

Music of the '20s to '40s sets just the right tone for browsing through this remarkable collection which is housed in a 500-year-old listed timber frame town house that Quentin shares with 20 or so other dealers. In addition to selling all these amazing period collectables, DecoGraphic Collectors' Gallery provides a repair and restoration service for clients' own pieces.

Arundel Wildfowl and Wetlands Centre

Mill Road, Arundel, West Sussex, BN18 9PB
Tel: 01903 883355 Fax: 01903 884834
e-mail: info.arundel@wwt.org.uk
website: www.wwt.org.uk

Have a fantastic day out seeing, feeding, and learning about wetland birds and wildlife, and at the same time help the Wildfowl & Wetlands Trust to conserve wetland habitats and their biodiversity.

WWT was founded in 1946 by the artist and naturalist Sir Peter Scott and is the largest international wetland conservation charity in the UK. WWT Arundel is one of nine centres and it

consists of more than 60 beautiful acres of ponds, lakes and reed beds.   WWT Arundel is home to over 1,000 of the world's most spectacular ducks, geese and swans, many of which are rare or endangered. This includes the world's rarest goose, the Nene, which was saved from extinction by WWT. Also see the New Zealand Blue Ducks - WWT Arundel is also the only site in the world outside of New Zealand where Blue Ducks have successfully bred. You can enjoy an atmospheric stroll through the reed beds on the new boardwalk, or watch wild birds from one of the many hides. Kids can follow the themed Discovery trail through the grounds. WWT Arundel also features the award-winning recreation of the volcanic Lake Myvatin, complete with lava formations, waterfalls, and its native duck the common Scoter which is part of a specialist breeding programme. There is also plenty to do inside the centre - the new Eye of the Wind wildlife art gallery shows a continuous programme of local

and national wildlife artists, many of whom host art workshops at the centre. You can enjoy superb homemade food in the Waters Edge Restaurant situated in the main viewing gallery overlooking swan lake, or browse through the gift shop or In Focus (telescope and binocular specialists) shop.

Special events run throughout the year, and there are children's crafts every school holiday. Open every day except Christmas day. Less than one mile from Arundel town centre (follow the brown duck signs). Free parking. 20 minute walk from Arundel train station.

WWT Arundel – the most complete year round wildlife experience in Sussex!

surprisingly, in the armoury. The **Morglay Sword**, which measures five feet nine inches long, is believed to have belonged to Bevis, a castle warden who was so tall that it was said he could walk from Southampton to Cowes without getting his head wet. In order to determine his final resting place, Bevis, so the story goes, threw his sword off the castle's battlements and, half a mile away, where the sword landed, is a mound that is still known as Bevis's Grave.

The period of stability that the castle brought to the town in the late medieval times turned Arundel into an important port and market town. In fact, the port of Arundel was mentioned in the Domesday Book and it continued to operate until the 20th century when it finally closed in 1927 - the last Harbour Master was moved to Shoreham and the port transferred to Littlehampton.

It was also during this peaceful period that the 14th century parish Church of St Nicholas was built, a unique church in that it is divided into separate Catholic and Anglican areas by a Sussex iron screen. Despite religious persecution, particularly during the 16th century, the Fitzalan family and the successive Dukes of Norfolk remained staunch Catholics. So much so that the 15th Duke, who was responsible for the 19th century rebuilding of the castle, also commissioned the substantial Catholic Church of St Philip Heri which was designed by J A Hansom and Son, the inventors of the Hansom cab, in 1870. In 1965, this impressive building became the seat of the Catholic bishopric of Brighton and Arundel and was renamed the **Cathedral of Our Lady and St Philip Howard**. (Sir Philip was the 13th Earl of Arundel who died in prison after being sentenced to death by Elizabeth I for his beliefs.) Each June, the cathedral

hosts the two-day Corpus Christi Festival during which the entire length of the aisle is laid out with a carpet of flowers.

Other historic sites in the town include the **Maison Dieu**, a medieval hospital outside one of the castle's lodges, founded by Richard Fitzalan in 1345. Dissolved by Henry VIII 200 years later, this semi-monastic institution combined the roles of clinic, hotel and almshouse. For a greater insight into the history of the town and its various inhabitants down the ages, the **Arundel Museum and Heritage Centre** is well worth a visit. With imaginative use of models, old photographs and historic artefacts, the story of Arundel, from Roman times to the present day, is told.

Just to the north of the town, is the **Wildlife and Wetland Trust** (see panel opposite), a wonderful place that plays host to a wide variety of ducks, geese, swans and other migratory birds from all over the world. There is a trail around the various lakes and ponds and an award-winning visitor centre. The Centre is part of the Wildfowl & Wetlands Trust founded in 1946 by the artist and naturalist Sir Peter Scott.

AROUND ARUNDEL

BURPHAM
2 miles NE of Arundel off the A27

This charming and attractive downland village of flint and brick built thatched cottages overlooks the River Arun and provides excellent views of Arundel Castle. The peace and quiet found here seems far removed from the days when the Saxons built defensive earthworks in an attempt to keep the invading Danes at bay. Later, during the Middle Ages, one of the farms on nearby Wepham Down was a leper colony and the track leading down into the village is still known as Lepers' Way.

LYMINSTER

1½ miles S of Arundel on the A284

Lyminster is an ancient settlement of flint cottages and protective walls, which appears as Lullyngminster in Alfred the Great's will of AD 901. From the village there is a marvellous view of Arundel Castle across the water meadows of the lower River Arun. Local legend has it that the deep pool, known as the **Knuckler Hole**, which lies northwest of Lyminster church, was once inhabited by a savage sea dragon, whose only food was fair maidens. This monster was said to have terrorised the local population to such an extent that the King of Wessex offered half his kingdom and his daughter's hand in marriage to the man who killed the beast. The dragon was finally slain after a terrible fight though there is some

confusion regarding the identity of the brave dragon slayer. This was either a gallant young farm boy known as Jim Pulk or a handsome knight. The early Norman coffin slab in the north transept of the church is where the conquering hero was finally laid to rest and it is still known as the **Slayer's Stone**.

LITTLEHAMPTON

3 miles S of Arundel on the A284

This is a charming maritime town, at the mouth of the River Arun. Signs of Roman occupation have been discovered here and the local manor is mentioned in the Domesday Book. Following the Norman invasion, Littlehampton became an important Channel port (declining considerably in the 1500s), exporting timber from the Sussex Weald and importing stone from Caen, France. It was here, too, that Queen Matilda arrived from France, in 1139, to stake her

PINDARS

Lyminster, West Sussex BN17 7QF
Tel/Fax: 01903 882628

Situated on the A284 road between Littlehampton and Arundel, **Pindars** is a delightful, civilised base for discovering the many attractions of the Sussex countryside and coast. The house was designed and built by Jocelyne and Clive Newman 35 years ago, and the numerous artistic touches about the house include Jocelyne's decorative hand-painted furniture and paintings collected when they ran an art gallery in Arundel. The two main bedrooms face south overlooking the beautiful gardens and have private facilities, television, tea trays and hairdryers.

The high standard of furnishing and decor was recognised by the Tourist Board in awarding Pindars runner-up in Best Bed & Breakfast in the South East. There is also a standard room which can be used

in conjunction with the twin room, an ideal option for families. Guests have the use of an antique-furnished sitting room leading out to the terrace and garden. Breakfast is served in a bright breakfast room with an 18th century dresser and longcase clock. Guests can enjoy traditional bacon and eggs or try smoked fish cakes (order the night before). Home-made scones and preserves complete the perfect start to the day. The Newmans are the most welcoming of hosts, and the household is completed by the Burmese cats Bendicks and Bittermint.

unsuccessful claim to the English throne from Stephen.

Now a quiet and pleasant coastal town and a popular holiday resort, though not as fashionable as many of its larger neighbours, Littlehampton has all the ingredients for a traditional seaside break. There is a large amusement complex, a boating marina, a promenade and a harbour. **Littlehampton Fort** was built in 1854 to protect the entrance to the River Arun. Although the site is fenced off and heavily overgrown, it is visible from the path and there is a plaque with historical details. However, the town's most charming feature is, undoubtedly, the large green, which lies between the seafront and the first row of houses.

In the old manor house in Church Street, **Littlehampton Museum** tells the history of the town, including its maritime past, through a series of informative displays. The Body Shop

Headquarters lie just outside the town, which is the birthplace of both the company and its founder Anita Roddick. Another attraction, The Look and Sea Visitor Centre, is great fun for all the family with interactive dispalys, games and superb panoramic views. It takes you on a voyage of discovery showing how Littlehampton has devloped over thousands of years.

FORD
2½ miles S of Arundel off the A259

Situated on an ancient ford crossing of the River Arun, this village is dwarfed by the prison on the site of an old RAF station. This does little to spoil the splendid and isolated setting of the old **Saxon church** that stands alone by the river.

FELPHAM
5 miles SW of Arundel off the A259

This is the village to which the poet and

ROBERT CARVER'S RESTAURANT

61 Surrey Street, Littlehampton, West Sussex BN17 5BJ
Tel: 01903 719419 Fax: 01903 719519
website: www.robertcarvers.co.uk

In a neat brick and stone building on a corner site, **Robert Carver's** is a much-loved bar and fine dining restaurant. The roomy bar on the ground floor has a wood-plank floor and an arched beamed ceiling that extends up to the galleried first-floor, where the tables are set more formally; a separate non-smoking area has views of the river and marina. Both the bar menu and the restaurant menu are changed regularly to take advantage of what is best and freshest in season, and the specialities include locally caught fish fresh from Littlehampton fish market. The chefs combine classic skills with imaginative touches, and the fine food is complemented by excellent, unobtrusive service. Focaccia open sandwiches or a mixed mezze plate make excellent snacks in the bar, while main courses in the restaurant could include sea bass with chilled cucumber soup, pea purée, wilted spinach and hazelnuts, or sumac-crusted duck

breast with smoked beetroot and caramelised butternut squash. The wide-ranging wine list is one of the best in the region, and several wines are available by the glass (two sizes). The Loft Room is an ideal venue for private parties, birthdays, wedding receptions and other special occasions.

The restaurant is named in remembrance of a townsman of Littlehampton who lived here when it was a private residence. Robert Carver was born in 1769 and became the harbourmaster of the town when it was known simply as Hampton.

artist, William Blake, moved, along with his wife and sister, in 1800 to undertake some engraving work for William Hayley, a gentleman of the period. The cottage where the Blakes lived can still be seen down Blake's Road and it was here that he wrote *'Away to sweet Felpham for Heaven is there'*, which recalls the view of the sea from his window. He left the village a few years later after being acquitted of a charge of treason.

Bognor Regis

6 miles SW of Arundel on the A259

Towards the end of the 18th century Sir Richard Hotham, a wealthy London milliner, sought to transform Bognor from a quiet fishing village into a fashionable resort to rival Brighton. He set about constructing some imposing residences, including The Dome in Upper Bognor Road, and even planned to have the town renamed Hothampton.

Unfortunately, the fashionable set of the day stayed away and Hotham's dream was never realised - at least not in his lifetime. However, in 1929, George V came to the resort to convalesce following a serious illness and, on the strength of his stay, the town was granted the title Regis (meaning of the King). "Bugger Bognor" was allegedly a retort made by King George in his last illness when a courtier tried to cheer him up by saying that he would soon be well enough to travel to Bognor to recuperate. Today, the town is a pleasant coastal resort with some elegant Georgian features, traditional public gardens, a promenade and safe, sandy beaches. The large central **Hotham Park** is another feature of this charming town where visitors can enjoy concerts given at the bandstand, clock golf and tennis. The naturally planted gardens are perfect to stroll in, picnic or just watch the

The Old Priory

North Bersted Street, nr Bognor Regis,
West Sussex PO22 9OQ
Tel: 01243 863580 Fax: 01243 826597
e-mail: old.priory@btinternet.com
website: www.old-priory.com

Owners Deborah and Nigel Collinson offer a choice of guest accommodation at **The Old Priory**, which stands on the site of the original priory dating back to the time of the Domesday Book. There are still traces of older building in and around the walled garden, where the swimming pool is now situated.

The present house has been lovingly restored to blend old-world charm and up-to-date comfort, making it a perfect base for exploring Chichester, the countryside and the south coast.

The Old Priory is well known for there luxury bedrooms with four poster beds and double air baths, one of them being a waterbed. The new suites set in the straddle barn give you comfort with there own unique style. A perfect place, for that special break. So if it's champagne and roses or just a quiet getaway this could be the place for you. All rooms have TV with satellite, tea and coffee making facilities and central heating.

Bognor Regis Beach at Sunset

squirrels. The **Bognor Regis Museum**, housed in a lodge of Hotham Park, plays tribute to Sir Richard Hotham as well as telling the story of the famous bathing machine lady, Mary Wheatland. Mary Wheatland was a well known Bognor Regis character. Born in 1835 in the nearby village of Aldinbourne, she hired out bathing machines as well as teaching children to swim. She also saved many souls from drowning, for which she received medals and recognition from the Royal Humane Society. The sea air and exercise must have done the eccentric lady a great deal of good as she lived to be 89 years old.

Perhaps, more than anything else, the resort is known for its 'Birdmen' and the annual international **Birdman Rally** held in July. The competitors, in a variety of classes, take it in turns to hurl themselves off the pier in an attempt to make the longest un-powered flight and so win the coveted competition.

YAPTON

3½ miles SW of Arundel on the B2233

Set amid the wheatfields of the coastal plain, this village has a charming 12th century church, the tower of which leans at an alarming angle.

WALBERTON

3 miles W of Arundel off the B2132

Down a narrow country lane, this pleasant village has obviously been settled for centuries as the local parish church is built on Saxon foundations and it still contains an ancient Saxon tub shaped font.

FONTWELL

3½ miles W of Arundel off the A27

The village is well known to followers of horse racing as it is home to the pleasantly situated **Fontwell Park National Hunt Racecourse**. First opened in 1921, the unusual 'figure of eight' track holds 15 meetings between August and May and remains a firm favourite with jumping enthusiasts. Fontwell is also home of **Denman's Garden**, a beautifully sheltered, semi-wild, 20th century garden where the emphasis in planting has been on colour, shape and texture which can be seen all year round.

EARTHAM

5 miles NW of Arundel off the A285

The village was the home of the 19th century Member of Parliament, William Huskisson, who was famously knocked down by Stevenson's *Rocket* during its inaugural run in 1830. He thereby acquired the dubious honour of being the world's first recorded victim of a railway accident.

SLINDON

3 miles NW of Arundel off the A29

With a dramatic setting on the side of a slope of the South Downs, the name Slindon is derived from the Saxon word for sloping hill. This picturesque village has splendid views over the coastal plain

THE YARD IN BURNDELL ROAD

Yapton, nr Arundel, West Sussex BN18 0HP
Tel: 01243 551359 mob: 07714 292196
e-mail: peterhilljones@man.com

Peter Hill Jones and his wife Caroline run **The Yard in Burndell Road**, a business started by Peter's parents 50 years ago. It has various components, and Peter claims with some accuracy that his yard is 'a cross between Steptoe's Yard and the British Museum'. **Burndell**

Architectural & Reclamation provides building materials and a bewildering range of useful items for home and garden, including doors, tables, old church pews, fireplaces, bronze sculptures cast on the premises, period heated towel rails, bath tubs and an amazing collection of architectural artefacts.

Yapton Metal Co buys non-ferrous metals and undertakes casting, smithing and pine stripping, and Caroline's side of the business, **Caroline Jones**, deals in decorative furniture and antiques, furniture restoration and books. Peter also runs blacksmith and sculpture courses, usually in the form of summer schools. Visitors looking for something in particular will probably find it here, while browsers will almost certainly find something they didn't even know they needed - Caroline came here 12 years ago looking for a door and ended up marrying Peter!

to the English Channel and numerous lovely old cottages. As an excellent observation point, it has been occupied from Neolithic times and many fine examples of early flint tools have been found in the area.

The village was the estate village for Slindon House. Today, the **Slindon Estate** is owned by the National Trust and most of the village, the woodlands and Slindon House (now let to Slindon College) come under its care. The largest Trust-owned estate in Sussex, there is plenty to see here as well as excellent opportunities for walking and birdwatching. Slindon House was originally founded as a residence for the Archbishops of Canterbury. (Archbishop Stephen Langton, a negotiator and signatory of the Magna Carta, spent the last weeks of his life here in 1228.) Rebuilt in the 1560s and extensively re-modelled during the 1920s, the house is

now a private boys' school. The estate's wonderful post office is an amalgamation of two 400 year-old cottages and it is the village's only remaining thatched building. The focal point of the village is the crossroads where a tree stands in a small open area close to the village church. Dating from the 12th century, this charming flint built church contains an unusual reclining effigy of a Tudor knight, Sir Anthony St Leger, the only wooden carving of its kind in Sussex. Finally, just to the north lies the cricket field where Sir Richard Newland is said to have refined the modern game over 200 years ago.

From the village there is a splendid walk around the estate that takes in the ancient deer park of Slindon House as well as other remains such as the summerhouse. The magnificent beech trees in the woodland were once highly prized and their seeds were sold worldwide. Unfortunately, the severe storm of October 1987 flattened many of these splendid trees, some of which had stood for 250 years. Though most of the fallen trees were cleared, some were left and the dead wood has provided new habitats for a whole range of insects and fungi. Birds and other wildlife also abound in the Slindon woodlands and, in May, the woodland floor is a carpet of bluebells.

Also at the Slindon Estate is **Gumber Bothy Camping Barn**, a stone tent now fully restored by the National Trust, which provides simple overnight accommodation just off the South Downs Way. Originally an outbuilding of Gumber Farm, a secluded working farm in the folds of the South Downs, the bothy is available to anyone over the age of five who enjoys the outdoor life.

WORTHING

Worthing has been inhabited since the Stone Age and until the mid-18th century it was a small and isolated fishing community. The popularity of sea bathing in the late 18th century made Worthing an ideal location, not far from London or Brighton, but far enough away to be relaxing and unspoilt. The royal stamp of approval came in 1798 when George III sent his teenage daughter, Princess Amelia, to Worthing to rest her lame knee. Her visit initiated a period of rapid development. Few examples of Georgian Worthing survive but it is worth wandering along Warwick Street and Montague Place.

The town grew steadily throughout the 19th century until 1893 when its worst typhoid outbreak kept holiday makers away and it became a ghost town. During the 20th century, an extensive development programme was begun and the town became more residential with its boundaries expanding.

Throughout much of the 19th century, Worthing remained a popular resort with both royalty and the famous. It was here, in the summer of 1894, that Oscar Wilde wrote *The Importance of Being Earnest* and immortalised its name in the central character, Jack Worthing. **Worthing's Pier**, one of the country's oldest, was built in the 1860s as a pier was a must for any successful Victorian seaside resort. An elegant construction with a 1930s pavilion at the end, it has, during its lifetime, been blown down, burnt down and blown up. Of the more recent buildings to be found here, the **English Martyrs Catholic Church**, just west of the town centre, is a recommended stopping point as, painted on the ceiling, is a replica of Michelangelo's Sistine Chapel fresco that was completed by a local artist in 1993.

It also plays host to the **National Bowls Championships** that take place in Beach House Park.

Worthing Beach

FLOWERS IN THE WINDOW

115 Rowlands Road, Worthing, West Sussex BN11 3LA
Tel: 01903 213370
website: www.flowers-in-the-window.com

The name of the shop comes from a Travis song, but **Flowers in the Window** is definitely not a flower shop, but a purveyor of a delightful range of gifts and home accessories. Partners Jackie Adsett and Sally Langham sell a constantly changing, eclectic mix of hand-painted furniture, shabby chic, retro and vintage-style tins and containers, pictures and picture frames, mirrors, pots and vases, postcards and puzzles and much,

much more – even some flowers and plants in pots.

The country-style pieces of furniture are the stars of the show, hand-painted on the premises by Jackie and Sally. Each piece receives seven coats, including a lime waxing cover that imparts a French-style chalky finish. The partners opened the shop at the end of 2002 after finding exactly what they had been looking for – a shop with an 'old-fashioned' look and large windows to display the beautiful goods on sale. Inside, the retro look includes old oak floors and white-painted panelled walls. Flowers in the Window is always a delight to visit, and in fine weather it spills out into a pretty courtyard.

ROSEDALE HOUSE

12 Bath Road, Worthing, West Sussex BN11 3NU
Tel: 01903 233181
e-mail: rosedale@amserve.net

Resident proprietors Mr and Mrs Siriano welcome guests to **Rosedale House**, a neat terraced house with an attractive front garden. The Bed & Breakfast accommodation, available all year round, comprises six well-appointed bedrooms – three doubles, two twins and a single. All have either en suite or private bathroom, TV, hairdryer and hospitality tray, and one of the doubles is on the ground floor. Rosedale House, a non-smoking establishment, is situated in a quiet road only a two-minute walk from the seafront.

CHATSWORTH HOTEL

Steyne, nr Worthing, West Sussex BN11 3DU
Tel: 01903 236103   e-mail: hotel@chatsworthworthing.co.uk
Fax: 01903 823726   website: www.chatsworthworthing.co.uk

In a terrace overlooking Steyne Gardens and the sea, the family-owned **Chatsworth Hotel** has earned a fine reputation for comfort, service and facilities. Behind the attractive creeper-covered Georgian frontage, the interior retains a period charm while offering all the modern comforts, and each of the 98 bedrooms has a private bath or shower, television, radio, hairdryer, trouser press, direct-dial phone and hospitality tray. The hotel has roomy, relaxing lounges, a restaurant offering a choice of menus, and snooker and pool tables in the basement.

For an insight into Worthing's past a visit to the **Worthing Museum and Art Gallery** is essential. The Local History and Downalnd Gallery tells the story of the town's development over the years. The museum is also home to nationally important costume and toy collections. No visit would be complete without a wander around the museum's stunning Sculpture Garden.

As Worthing expanded it also swallowed up a number of ancient nearby settlements including Broadwater with its fine cottages and Norman church and West Tarring where the remains of a 13th century palace belonging to the Archbishops of Canterbury now double as the village hall and primary school annexe.

AROUND WORTHING

HIGH SALVINGTON
1½ miles N of Worthing on the A24

This village, now almost entirely engulfed by Worthing, is home to the last survivor of several windmills that once stood in the area. **High Salvington Windmill**, a black post mill, was built between 1700 and 1720 and its design is one that had been used since the Middle Ages - a heavy cross shaped base with a strong central upright (or post) around which the

sails and timber superstructure could pivot. The mill stopped working in 1897 but, following extensive restoration in the 1970s, it has now been restored to full working order. It is now open on a limited basis with afternoon tea available.

FINDON
3 miles N of Worthing off the A24

An attractive village, Findon's main square is surrounded by some elegant 18th century houses. Situated within the South Downs Area of Outstanding Natural Beauty, Findon is famous for being the venue of one of the two great Sussex sheep fairs - the other is at Lewes. Markets have been held on Nepcote Green since the 13th century and the Findon **Sheep Fair** has been an annual event each September since the 18th century. The village has a festival atmosphere and thousands of sheep change hands here during the fair. Despite a gap year in 2001 due to foot and mouth disease, the fair has returned to business as usual.

From Findon there is also easy access to **Cissbury Ring**, the largest Iron Age hillfort on the South Downs. Overshadowed only by Dorset's Maiden Castle, this impressive hilltop site covers an area of 65 acres and is surrounded by a double rampart almost a mile in circumference. Archaeologists have

WOODLANDS STABLES

Titnor Lane, Patching, nr Worthing,
West Sussex BN13 3UG
Tel: 01903 871339

In a woodland setting close to the South Downs, **Woodland Stables** is run by former show jumper and current British Show Jumping Association judge Avril Sirett. Qualified instructors offer tuition for all ages, and the speciality of the school is bringing young children into show jumping and pony club showing. There's an indoor school on site, and the South Downs and Angmering Park provide riding experience on the stable hacks.

MAR D'AMORE

The Square, Findon Village, West Sussex BN14 0TE
Tel: 01903 877699

On the main square in the delightful village of Findon, **Mar d'Amore** is a splendid seafood restaurant. Owner Toni Kalan has a lifetime's experience in the catering business, and since opening here in November 2001, he has won many friends with menus that are determined by the markets and the seasons. The room has comfortable seating for 40, with 30 more in the patio garden and four tables at the front - a real bonus in summer. Mar d'Amore is open for lunch and dinner; closed Sunday evening and all Monday.

estimated that over 50,000 tons of chalk, soil and boulders would have had to be moved in the fort's construction, which would indicate that this was once a sizeable community in the 3rd century BC. However, the site is much older than this as Neolithic flint mines dating back 6,000 years have also been discovered here, which makes Cissbury one of the oldest industrial sites in the country.

COOMBES

4 miles NE of Worthing off the A27

This tiny settlement of just a few houses and a farm is worthy of a visit if just to see the village church, which stands in the farmyard. An unassuming Norman church, it contains some exceptional 12th century murals in many shades of red and yellow that were only uncovered in 1949 and are believed to have been painted by monks from St Pancras Priory, Lewes. Just to the north of the hamlet lies **Annington Hill** from where there are glorious views over the Adur valley and also there is access to a section of the South Downs Way footpath.

SHOREHAM-BY-SEA

4½ miles E of Worthing on the A259

There has been a harbour here, on the River Adur estuary, since Roman times and, though evidence of both Roman

and Saxon occupations have been found, it was not until the Norman period that the town developed into an important port. At that time the River Adur was navigable as far as Bramber and the main port was situated a mile or so upstream, where the Norman **Church of St Nicholas**, with some notable Norman figure carvings, still stands today.

However, towards the end of the 11th century, the river estuary began to silt up and the old port and toll bridge were abandoned in favour of New Shoreham, which was built at the river mouth. Again, the Normans built a church, the **Church of St Mary**, close to the harbour and both churches remain key features of the town. The old town lapsed into the life of a quiet village while, during the 12th and 13th centuries, New Shoreham was one of the most important Channel ports. It was here in 1199 that King John landed with an army to succeed to the throne of England following the death of Richard the Lionheart and, in 1346, Shoreham was asked to raise 26 ships, more than both Dover and Bristol, to fight the French. Perhaps, though, the town's most historic moment came in 1651 when Charles II fled from here to France, following defeat at the Battle of Worcester, on board the ship of Captain Nicholas Tettersell.

The new port flourished until the 16th century when, once again, silting, in the form of a shingle spit, which diverted the river's course, had disastrous economic consequences. The next 200 years or so saw a period of decline in Shoreham, which was only relieved by the rise in popularity of nearby Brighton and the excavation of a new river course in 1818. To reflect its new importance, **Shoreham Fort** was constructed at the eastern end of the beach as part of Palmerston's coastal defence system. A half-moon shape, the fort was capable of accommodating six guns, which could each fire 80 pounds of shot. The fort has been restored and is now open to visitors who will also have a superb view of the still busy harbour.

The history of Shoreham-by-Sea and in particular its maritime past, are explored at **Marlipins Museum**. The museum is, itself, interesting, as it is housed in one of the oldest surviving non-religious buildings in the country. A Norman customs warehouse, an unusual knapped flint and Caen stone patterned façade was added in the 14th century and it has a single 42-foot beam supporting the first floor.

Though the town's past is, undoubtedly, built upon its port, **Shoreham Airport** was opened in 1934 and is the country's oldest commercial airport. It remains a major base for recreational flying and the delightful art deco terminal acts as a departure lounge and arrivals hall for many business passengers who are travelling to and from the Channel Islands and Western Europe. Tours of the airport can also be booked.

NORTH LANCING
3 miles E of Worthing off the A27

This attractive downland village, with its curved streets, has one of the most ancient Saxon names in Sussex. It is derived from Wlencing, one of the sons of Aella, who led the first Saxon invasion to the area in AD 477. Apart from the old flint cottages on the High Street, the 13th century church adds to the timeless atmosphere of the village. However, North Lancing is dominated by a more recent addition to its skyline - **Lancing College**. Set high up on a beautiful site overlooking the River Adur, the college was founded in 1848 by Nathaniel Woodward, whose aim was to establish a group of classless schools. By the time of his death in 1891, there were 15 such schools in the Woodward Federation. Of the buildings at Lancing College, the splendid 19th century Gothic-style chapel is the most striking and is considered to be one of the finest examples of its kind.

SOMPTING
2 miles E of Worthing off the A27

This village, the name of which means marshy ground, has, as its pride and joy, a church that is unique in Britain. Built on foundations, which can be traced back to AD 960, the **Church of St Mary** has a distinctive spire that consists of four diamond-shaped faces which taper to a point. Known as a Rhenish helm, the design was popular in German Rhineland but is not found elsewhere in this country. In 1154, the church was given to the Knights Templar who completely rebuilt it except for the spire, which they left untouched. Just over 150 years later the building came into the hands of their rivals, the Knights Hospitallers, who were responsible for the present design of the church as they returned it to its original Saxon style.

GORING-BY-SEA

1½ miles W of Worthing on the A259

Until the arrival of the railway in the mid 19th century, this was a small fishing village. However, the Victorians love of a day by the seaside saw the rapid growth of Goring and today it is a genteel place with a pleasant suburban air.

To the northwest stands the cone-shaped **Highdown Hill**, which, although only 266 feet high, stands out above the surrounding coastal plain. Its prominent nature has made a much sought after vantage point over the centuries. It has been an Iron Age hillfort, a Roman bath house and a Saxon graveyard.

Close by **Highdown Gardens** are the creation of Sir Frederick and Lady Stern, who spent over 50 years turning what was originally a chalk pit into this splendid garden. One of the least known gardens in the area, Highdown has a unique collection of rare plants and trees which the couple brought back from their expeditions to the Himalayas and China in the mid 20th century. The garden was left to the local borough council on the death of Sir Frederick in 1967 and it has been now declared a national collection.

On the south side of the main A27 is **Castle Goring**, built for the grandfather of the poet Percy Bysshe Shelley. It is not exactly a castle although the castellated frontage and the arched windows with their elaborate tracery are believed to be based on Arundel Castle. The south frontage is quite different with pillars and pediments resembling a Roman villa. The building is currently a private English language school.

THE WEST SUSSEX DOWNS

The southern boundary to this part of West Sussex is the South Downs, a magnificent range of chalk hills extending for over 100 miles. The South Downs Way, a long distance bridleway follows the crest of the hills from Winchester to Beachy Head at Eastbourne and, whether taken as a whole or enjoyed in sections, it provides splendid views of this Area of Outstanding Natural Beauty as well as a wealth of delightful rural hamlets and villages to discover.

To the north of the Downs lies Midhurst, the home of the area's most famous ruin - Cowdray Park. Though the once splendid Tudor mansion has been reduced to a shell following a fire in the late 18th century, the ruins provide a haunting backdrop to the parkland's famous polo matches. In better condition are Uppark, where H G Wells spent many hours in the great library as a boy, and Petworth House, an elegant late 17th century building that is very reminiscent of a French château.

Other great names from the world of the arts have also found this region inspirational. The novelist Anthony Trollope spent his last years at South Harting, the poet Tennyson lived under the wooded slopes of Black Down and the composer Edward Elgar visited Fittleworth several times and wrote his famous cello concerto while staying there in 1917.

MIDHURST

Though this quiet and prosperous market town has its origins in the early Middle Ages, its name is Saxon and suggests that once it was surrounded by forest. It was the Norman lord, Savaric Fitzcane, who first built a fortified house here, on the summit of St Ann's Hill, and, though only a few stones remain today, the views from this natural vantage point over the River Rother are worth the walk.

The town of Midhurst grew up at the castle gates. By 1300, when the de Bohuns (the then lords of the manor) moved from their hilltop position the town was well established. Choosing a new site by the river in a coudrier, or hazel grove, gave the family the name for their new estate - **Cowdray**. In the 1490s, the estate passed, by marriage, to Sir David Owen, who built the splendid Tudor courtyard mansion. However, due to rising debts he was forced to sell the house to Sir William Fitzwilliam, a leading figure in the court of Henry VIII and the 1st Earl of Southampton. He and his family added the finishing touches and, when complete, the magnificent house was a rival to Hampton Court. Indeed, the house played host to many notable visitors including both Henry VIII and Elizabeth I who were frequently entertained here. Even though the house is in ruins following a devastating fire in 1793, it is still a splendid monument to courtly Tudor architecture. Today, visitors can view, albeit from a distance, the roofless remains of the east side of the quadrangle court, along with parts of the west side where the turreted three-storey gatehouse still remains largely intact. However, most visitors come to **Cowdray Park** to watch the polo matches that take place every weekend and sometimes during the week from May until September.

Back in the town, on the opposite side of the River Rother from Cowdray Park, there are some impressive buildings. The 16th century timber framed **Market Hall** stands in front of the even older **Spread Eagle Inn**, an old coaching inn, dating

The Pond, Midhurst

from the 1400s, where Elizabeth I is reputed to have stayed. Nearby is the famous **Midhurst Grammar School**, founded in 1672 by Gilbert Hanniman and now a successful comprehensive school. Though the centre of the town has migrated away from its old heart around the market square and the church, the custom of ringing the curfew each night at eight o'clock from the heavily restored church continues and is said to be in memory of a legendary commercial traveller. While endeavouring to reach Midhurst, the traveller got lost in the local woods at dusk and, on hearing the sound of the church bells, was able to find his way safely to the town.

For most people visiting Midhurst, it is through the books of H G Wells that they feel that they already know the town. Herbert George's maternal grandmother came from Midhurst and his mother worked at nearby Uppark where, as a young boy, Wells spent many hours in the library. At the age of 15, H G was apprenticed to a chemist in the town and also enrolled at the Grammar School for evening classes. Though he left Midhurst for some years, Wells later returned to the school as a teacher. As

JUST BEECAUSE

York House, Knockhundred Row, Midhurst, West Sussex GU29 9DQ
Tel: 01730 810982

Just off the main street in the fine old market town of Midhurst, **Just Beecause** is a delightful little shop that specialises in candles. They come in all shapes and sizes, including the long-burning candles from St Eval and the multi-coloured, hand-dipped, 100% natural beeswax candles from E & S Churchill. Candles are by no means the only things to be found here: there are soft toys, lamps, hanging decorations, jewellery, animals in china and bronze, Staffordshire pottery that can be painted to customers' requirements, towels, cushions......in short, an Aladdin's Cave of things for the home and lots of gift ideas.

COMESTIBLES

Red Lion Street, Midhurst, West Sussex GU29 9PB
Tel: 01730 813400

A short walk from the centre, in the old part of town, **Comestibles** is an excellent provider of specialist food to enjoy on the spot or to take away. The front part is the delicatessen, stocked with English and Continental cheeses, home-cooked ham and other meats and patés, local beer and cider and splendid organic chocolate made near Petworth. There's an impressive choice of made-to-order sandwiches, and the daily changing menu in the café includes all-day breakfasts, scrambled eggs, salads, savoury flans and platters of cheese, patés and charcuterie.

CHATTERBOX

West Street, Midhurst, West Sussex GU29 9NQ
Tel: 01730 812696 Fax: 01730 814888

Starting with not much more than an empty room, Susan Davies has created a thriving business that everyone's chatting about. Behind a cheerful green awning and a double window display, **Chatterbox** is stocked with a wide range of ladies' clothes, fashion accessories, bedding, children's toys, jewellery and all kinds of gifts and knick-knacks, and the interior of the shop is a veritable kaleidoscope of colours. Ladies fashion

is the main thrust of the business, catering for all sizes and ages, and presenting a great choice in knitwear, cottons, silks and linens.

Among the featured designers are Avoca, 120% Lino and Out of Xile, and there's a large collection of the Jackpot range, which includes jackets, trousers, pullovers, cardigans, T-shirts, skirts, scarves and bags. Susan and her staff are very friendly and helpful, making it a real delight to visit Chatterbox, to browse and to choose just the right purchase from a terrific range that is growing all the time.

well as providing the inspiration for his most famous book *The Invisible Man*, Midhurst has been the setting for many of his short stories including *The Man Who Could Work Miracles*. The great novelist and science fiction writer obviously had fond recollections of his time in the town for he wrote in his autobiography: "Midhurst has always been a happy place for me. I suppose it rained there at times, but all my memories of Midhurst are in sunshine."

AROUND MIDHURST

EASEBOURNE
1 mile N of Midhurst on the A272

This delightful estate village, which has some superb half-timbered houses, was the home of an Augustinian convent of the Blessed Virgin Mary. Founded in the 13th century, the convent prospered until 1478, when the prioress and some of her nuns were accused of gross immorality and squandering the convent's funds on hunting and extravagant entertaining. All that remains today of the priory is the church now the parish church. Another interesting building here is **Budgenor Lodge**, built in 1793, it was a model workhouse and now occupied by the Christ for the Nation Training Centre.

FERNHURST
4½ miles N of Midhurst on the A286

Just to the east of this pretty village, with its assorted tile hung cottages surrounding the village green, lies **Black Down**, rising abruptly from the Sussex Weald. A sandstone hill covered in heather, gorse and silver birch, that is an ideal environment for a variety of upland birdlife, the summit is the highest point in Sussex and from here

---

EVE

2 Regency House, Rumbolds Hill, Midhurst, West Sussex GU29 9DA
Tel: 01730 815860 Fax: 01420 564493
e-mail: sales@eveco.co.uk
website: www.eveco.co.uk

Bags, hats and clothing - the total look is what **Eve** is all about. Customers can visit the shop in Midhurst or order online. Owner Emma Molyneux has over 20 years' experience in

the fashion world, including spells in some of the top stores in London. She opened her shop in a bay-windowed redbrick building in June 2003, offering an eclectic blend of fashion, classic and fun footwear, handbags and hats all of which she sources personally.

Eve is well known for its alluring windows and superb customer service and in the bright, well laid-out interior you can find occasion wear by Satsuma with stunning dresses and pashmina's, shoes by Fiorelli and Franco Banetti, hats for all occasions, bags in vibrant colours made from silk, sisal, straw or printed cottons for the beach or a special event. Eve is the local official stockist for Scholl, Cosmopolitan bags, Emreco casual wear and Adini. Other eye-catching items include jewellery by Boheme and Topazglow all complimented by French designer silk scarves there are views over the Weald and South Downs to the English Channel.

A particularly fine viewpoint lies on the southern crest and one of the footpaths up the hill has been named locally as **Tennyson's Lane**, after the famous poet who lived for 20 years in the area. At one time a Royal navy signal tower stood on Tally Knob, a prominent outcrop to the southeast of the Temple of the Winds. A development of the tried and tested system of fire beacons, in 1796 the Admiralty introduced the Shutter Telegraph here as a more sophisticated means of passing messages between Portsmouth and London. Though ingenious, the system was found to be impractical and was soon abandoned.

To the west of Fernhurst, an Augustinian priory, on a smaller scale than the magnificent Michelham Priory near Upper Dicker, was founded in the late 12th century. At the time of the Dissolution the priory became a farmhouse. One of the first floor rooms, which was originally the prior's chamber, is decorated with Tudor murals and although it is a private house, **Shulbrede Priory** is occasionally open to the public.

LURGASHALL
4½ miles NE of Midhurst off the A283

This delightful rural village has, as a backdrop, the wooded slopes of Black Down, where Tennyson lived at **Aldworth House**. The village's largely Saxon church has an unusual loggia, or porch, outside where those who had travelled from afar could eat and rest before or after the service.

LODSWORTH
2½ miles E of Midhurst off the A272

Situated on the River Lod, a small tributary of the River Rother, this old community

has some fine buildings including a 13th century manor house and an early 18th century Dower House. The whitewashed village Church of St Peter lies on the outskirts of Lodsworth, and just to the north is **St Peter's Well**, the water of which is said to have healing qualities.

TILLINGTON
5 miles E of Midhurst on the A272

Dating back to the days before the Norman Conquest, the village appeared in the Domesday Book as Tolinstone. Tillington lies beside the western walls of Petworth House. The local landmark here, however, is **All Hallows' Church** and, in particular, its tower. Built in 1810, the tower is topped by stone pinnacles and a crown that is very reminiscent of the lower stage of the Eiffel Tower. Known as a Scots Crown, the church and its tower have featured in paintings by both Turner and Constable.

DUNCTON
5 miles SE of Midhurst on the A285

Sheltered beneath Duncton Hill, beside Burton Park, the main building of St Michael's Girls' School, stands a small church on the wall of which can be seen the Royal Arms of Charles I dated 1636.

SINGLETON
5½ miles S of Midhurst on the A286

Lying in the folds of the South Downs, in the valley of the River Lavant, Singleton, owned by Earl Godwin of Wessex, father of King Harold, was one of the largest and wealthiest manors in England. Little remains here from Saxon times, except an ancient barn on the village green, though the 13th century church was built on the foundations of its Saxon predecessor. Inside the church, in the south aisle, is a memorial to Thomas Johnson, a huntsman of the nearby Charlton Hunt who died in 1744. There are also two interesting monuments to two successive Earls of Arundel who died within two years of each other in the mid 16th century.

Singleton is also the home of the famous **Weald and Downland Open Air Museum**, which has over 40 historic rural buildings assembled from all over southeast England. All

Weald and Downland Open Air Museum, Singleton

the buildings in the Museum, which was founded by J R Armstrong in 1971, were at one time under threat of demolition, before being transported here and reconstructed.

The buildings vividly demonstrate the homes and workplaces of the past and include Titchfield's former Tudor market hall, farmhouses and agricultural buildings from the 15th and 16th centuries, hall houses, a Victorian tollhouse from Bramber, a schoolroom

---

Moonlight Cottage Tea Rooms

Chichester Road, Cocking, West Sussex GU29 0HN
Tel: 01730 813336
website: www.moonlightcottage.co.uk

Moonlight Cottage is a lovely redbrick building dating from the early 19th century with a wealth of greenery and beautifully kept lawns. Run by three generations of the same family, it is the perfect spot for morning coffee, a light lunch or afternoon tea, and once a week it is open for bistro-style suppers.

Regular customers return time after time for the splendid traditional teas with scones or toasted

teacakes, jam and cream, or for the high tea which also includes dainty smoked salmon and cucumber

sandwiches. But food is not the only reason to visit Moonlight Cottage, which also has a lovely little shop-cum-gallery selling collectables, antiques and contemporary arts and crafts, including paintings and wood turning by talented local artists. This charming place is very difficult to leave, and for those who want to linger in the relaxed, civilised surroundings the family offer Bed & Breakfast accommodation in three elegant, traditionally appointed bedrooms and a chalet that can sleep up to six guests.

from West Wittering, labourers' cottages, a working blacksmith's forge and the watermill from Lurgashall which produces flour every day for sale in the shop and use in the lakeside café. Several interiors have been furnished as they may have been during the building's heyday and visitors can take a look at the Tudor farmstead, with its fireplace in the middle of the hall, traditional farmyard animals and gardens, and the Victorian schoolroom is complete with blackboard, benches and school bell. To complement the buildings, five historic gardens have been carefully researched and planted, using traditional methods, to demonstrate the changes and continuities in ordinary gardens from 1430 to 1900.

This enchanting and unusual collection is situated in a delightful 50-acre park on the southern edge of the village. The museum also arranges demonstrations of rural skills and children's activities' days where traditional games, trades and crafts of the past, such as basket making and bricklaying, can be enjoyed.

WEST DEAN
6 miles S of Midhurst on the A286

Just to the south of this pretty community of flint cottages, the land rises towards the ancient hilltop site known as **The Trundle**. One of the four main Neolithic settlements in Sussex, the large site was fortified during the Iron Age, when massive circular earth ramparts and a dry ditch were constructed. Named after the Old English for wheel, the site now enjoys fine views over Chichester, Singleton and Goodwood Racecourse.

Amidst the rolling South Downs, **West Dean Gardens** reproduces a classic 19th century designed landscape with its highly acclaimed restoration of the

walled kitchen garden, the 16 original glasshouses and frames dating from the 1890s, the 35 acres of ornamental grounds, the 40 acres St Roche's arboretum and the extensive landscaped park. All the areas of this inspiring and diverse garden are linked by a scenic parkland walk. A particular feature of the grounds is the lavishly planted 300-foot Edwardian pergola, designed by Harold Peto, which acts as a host for a variety of climbers including roses, clematis and honeysuckle. The beautifully restored Victorian glasshouses nurture vines, figs and soft fruits as well as an outstanding collection of chilli peppers, aubergines, tomatoes and extensive floral displays.

CHILGROVE
6 miles SW of Midhurst on the B2141

To the north of this village, which is situated in a wooded valley, lies **Treyford Hill** where a line of five bell-shaped barrows, known as the **Devil's Jump**, can be found. Dating back to the Bronze Age, these burial mounds - where the cremated remains of tribal leaders were interred in pottery urns - received their descriptive name as a result of the local superstitious habit of attributing unusual, natural features of the landscape to the work of the Devil.

WEST MARDEN
9 miles SW of Midhurst off the B2146

This picturesque place, much loved by artists, is the largest of the four Marden hamlets, which are all linked by quiet country lanes. **North Marden**, itself only a tiny place, is home to the Norman Church of St Mary which is one of the smallest in the county, while **Up Marden**'s minute 13th century church, which stands on the ancient Pilgrims' Way between Winchester and Chichester, is only a little bigger. It is quite plain and simple apart from its Victorian Gothic pulpit. Of the four Mardens, **East Marden** is the most village-like and, on the village green, there is a thatched well house with a notice reading, 'Rest and be Thankful but do not Wreck me'. As the well is still very much in existence, the advice has been heeded down the centuries.

COMPTON
8 miles SW of Midhurst on the B2146

A tranquil settlement of brick and flint buildings, Compton lies under the steep slope of **Telegraph Hill**. Close to the hill is a grassy mound, which is, in fact, a Neolithic long barrow, known locally as **Bevis's Thumb**. This mysterious burial site was named after a local giant, Bevis (the same Bevis who threw his sword from the battlements of Arundel Castle), who had a weekly diet of an ox washed down with two hogsheads of beer.

SOUTH HARTING
6 miles W of Midhurst on the B2146

One of the most attractive villages of the South Downs, South Harting has ancient thatched cottages and elegant redbrick Georgian houses. The spire of the local church is, famously, covered in copper shingles, the bright verdigris hue of which can be seen from several miles away, acting as a signpost to this handsome place. Outside the church stand the ancient village stocks, along with a whipping post, and inside, there are several monuments including a set of tombs of the Cowpre family and one commemorating the life of Sir Harry Fetherstonhaugh of Uppark. In the churchyard is a memorial by Eric Gill to the dead of World War I.

South Harting can boast of being the home of the novelist Anthony Trollope for the last two years of his life. Though here only a short time before his death

in 1882, Trollope wrote four novels while in South Harting and his pen and paper knife can be seen in the church.

The village stands at the foot of **Harting Down**, beneath the steep scarp slope of the South Downs ridge, which is traversed by the South Downs Way. This spectacular long distance footpath and bridleway stretches for nearly 100 miles, from Winchester to Beachy Head and, here, the path skirts around **Beacon Hill**. At 793 feet above sea level, the hill is one of the highest points on the Downs.

Just south of the village lies the magnificent house, **Uppark**, a National Trust property that is superbly situated on the crest of a hill. However, the climb up to the house was so steep that, when the house was offered to the Duke of Wellington after his victories in the Napoleonic Wars, he declined as he considered the drive to the mansion would require replacing his exhausted horses too many times. The house was built in the late 1680s for Lord Grey of Werke, one of the chief instigators of the Duke of Monmouth's rebellion of 1685. Lord Grey was let off with a fine and he retired from his none too illustrious military career and concentrated on building his house to the latest Dutch designs. As well as being a splendid house architecturally, the building of the house on this site was only made possible with the help of a water pump invented by Lord Grey's grandfather which brought water up to the hill top from a low lying spring.

It was a mid-18th century owner, Sir Matthew Fetherstonhaugh, who created the lavish interiors by decorating and furnishing the rooms with rare carpets, elegant furniture and intriguing objets d'art. At his death in 1774, Sir Matthew left his estate to his 20-year-old son, Sir Harry, who, with his great friend the Prince Regent, brought an altogether

Sussex Farm Foods

The Old Forge, Bury Gate, Pulborough, West Sussex RH20 1NL
Tel: 01798 831985 Fax: 01798 831001

Sussex Farm Foods is located in a former village forge run by partners Gilly Stuart-Smith and Di Robertson. Gilly, who was responsible for the interior design, also masterminded the design of 10 Downing Street when Mrs Thatcher was in residence. She opened the shop in 1996, converting it from its previous incarnation as an antique shop. The interior has the original black-beamed apex ceiling and a traditional wooden floor, and the display areas are in a style sympathetic with the age and character of the room - the exception being the glass chill cabinets required by food hygiene laws. The stock includes goods that are hard to track down elsewhere, and many of the most popular items are either produced or sourced locally.

There's lovely freshly baked crusty bread, all kinds of cakes and biscuits (the mini iced fruit cakes make a wonderful children's treat), local honey, fresh seasonal fruit and vegetables (some grown by friends) and shelf after shelf of pickles and oils, sweets and preserves. A recent and very well received addition is a range of locally made frozen meals such as haddock, prawn & spinach gratin, blue cheese & broccoli pasta or venison, red wine & juniper casserole joining old favourites like coq au vin, or meat balls in a herby tomato sauce. This exceptional farm shop is open seven days a week (except Sundays in January and February). It is located on the main A29 three miles south of Pulborough, at the junction with the B2138 Fittleworth road.

Murrells Nursery & Garden Centre

Broomers Hill Lane, Pulborough, West Sussex RH20 2DU
Tel: 01798 875508 Fax: 01798 872695

Murrells Nursery & Garden Centre was established over 30 years ago by the Murrell family on a six-acre site that was previously a farm. The original family is no longer involved, but the current owners adhere to the friendly and attentive ethos on which its reputation has been built. The quality of the produce is first-class, and much of it is grown and nurtured on site. The large greenhouses and surrounding grounds are bursting with a colourful display of plants, trees and shrubs. Murrells stocks an extensive range of alpines, bamboos, conifers and ferns; there are ivies, bedding plants, fuchsias and geraniums.

Hanging baskets are a speciality and can be bought ready made or made to order. Heathers and ornamental grasses of every hue abound, and the roses range from the favourites of yesteryear to newly propagated varieties. For gardeners interested in growing their own supply of fresh food the centre has an excellent

choice of fruit trees and bushes, and a full range of vegetables ready to transplant into their own plots. The staff are never obtrusive, being very happy to let visitors browse to their heart's content, but they are always there to assist customers in making the right choice and to offer advice on the particular soil and climatic conditions preferred by the various plants. Open seven days a week, Murrells Nursery and Garden Centre is situated on the outskirts of Pulborough just off the A29 or A283.

different atmosphere to the house. He installed his London mistress, Emma Hart (who later married Sir William Hamilton and became Lord Nelson's mistress), and carried on a life of gambling, racing and partying. However, in 1810, Sir Harry gave up his social life and, at the age of 70, he married his dairymaid, Mary Ann, to the amazement and outrage of West Sussex society. He died, at the age of 92, in 1846 and both Mary Ann and then her sister, Frances, kept the house just as it had been during Sir Harry's life for a further 50 years.

This latter era of life at Uppark would have been remembered by the young H G Wells who spent a great deal of time here as his mother worked at the house. As well as exploring the grounds and gardens laid out by the early 19th century designer Humphry Repton, Wells had a self-taught education from Uppark's vast stock of books.

After the upper floors of the house were destroyed by fire in 1989, the National Trust undertook an extensive restoration programme and reopened the house to the public in 1995. Luckily, most of the house's 18th century treasures were rescued from the fire and the fine pictures, furniture and ceramics are now on view again in their original splendid settings.

Also close to South Harting lies the site of the now demolished **Durford Abbey** - an isolated monastery founded in the 12th century by a community of Premonstratensian monks, a strict vegetarian order founded in 1120 by St Norbert at Premontre, France. Unlike other orders of their time, which grew wealthy on the income from their monastic estates, life at Durford seems to have been very much a struggle for survival. In fact, so harsh was the monks' existence here that, on the monasteries dissolution in the 16th century, is was described by a commissioner as "The poorest abbey I have seen, far in debt and in decay." Although little of the abbey remains today, the monks of Durford succeeded in leaving an important legacy in the form of two 15th century bridges over the River Rother and its tributaries. (During the medieval period it was a duty of religious houses to provide and maintain such bridges.) Both Maidenmarsh Bridge, near the abbey site, and Habin Bridge, to the south of Rogate, are worth a visit and the latter, which consists of four semicircular arches, still carries the road to South Harting.

Trotton

3 miles W of Midhurst on the A272

This pleasant village lies in the broad valley of the River Rother, once a densely wooded area known for its timber and charcoal. The impressive medieval bridge in the village dates back to the 14th century and is still carrying modern day traffic. The money for the bridge was given by Lord Camoys, who accompanied Henry V to Agincourt. Inside the parish church is a memorial to Lord Camoys, who died in 1419, and his second wife, Elizabeth Mortimer, who was the widow of Sir Henry 'Harry Hotspur' Percy. Here, too, can be found the oldest known memorial to a woman, a floor brass of Margaret de Camoys, who died here in around 1310.

PULBOROUGH

This ancient settlement has grown up close to the confluence of the Rivers Arun and Rother and it lies on the old Roman thoroughfare, Stane Street. Although it was a staging post along the old route between London and Chichester and was strategically located near the rivers, it was never developed like its rivals over the centuries. It remains today a pleasant and sizeable village, well known for its freshwater fishing. The centre of Pulborough, on the old Roman route, is now a conservation area with several fine Georgian cottages clustered around the parish church, which occupies a commanding hilltop position.

Just southeast of the village lies the **RSPB Pulborough Brooks Nature Reserve** where there is a nature trail through tree-lined lanes, leading to views overlooking the restored wet meadows of the Arun Valley.

AROUND PULBOROUGH

KIRDFORD

5½ miles N of Pulborough off the A272

This village, with its square green surrounded by stone cottages and tree-lined main street, has more the feel of a small town. Like its neighbour, Wisborough Green, Kirdford was a centre for glassmaking between 1300 and 1600 and the village sign incorporates diamonds of locally made glass. Iron smelting also prospered here for 100 years from the mid 16th century and this accounts for the rather lavish extensions to the village's original Norman church.

LOXWOOD

8 miles N of Pulborough on the B2133

This pleasant village, which lies off the beaten track and close to the county border with Surrey, is on the **Wey and Arun Junction Canal**, which opened in 1816 and linked London with the south coast. The coming of the railways saw an end to the commercial usefulness of this inland waterway and, in 1871, it was closed. However, certain stretches have been restored and it is now possible to

JOHN MURRAY & SON

2, 3 & 4 The Parade, Loxwood,
West Sussex RH14 0SB
Tel: 01403 752859
Fax: 01403 751958
e-mail: johnnythejoint@hotmail.com

Butcher and game dealer **John Murray & Son** have been trading in the village of Loxwood, West Sussex since 1986. Supplying top-quality produce to retail customers and to the catering trade. They purchase as much of their meat as possible from local farms and it is all slaughtered at a local abbatoir.

The shop also has an extensive deli counter stocked with a fine choice of salami, parma ham, olives, smoked salmon etc along with over 40 types of English and continental cheeses. John is rightly proud of the business he and his dedicated staff have developed and of the large and loyal customer base they have built up over the years.

cruise along one of the country's most attractive canals or stroll along the peaceful towpath.

The village is also associated with the Christian Dependants, a religious sect founded by preacher, John Sirgood, in the 1850s. The group were nicknamed the 'Cokelers' because of their preference for cocoa over alcohol and their chapel and burial ground can still be seen in Spy Lane.

WISBOROUGH GREEN

5½ miles N of Pulborough on the A272

This pretty Sussex village has a large rectangular green, surrounded by horse chestnut trees, around which stand half-timbered and tile-hung cottages and houses. Nearby, the village **Church of St Peter ad Vincula** is particularly interesting as the original Norman building, to which the 13th century chancel was added, has walls almost five feet thick and a doorway 13 feet high! The suggestion is that this was an Anglo-Saxon keep that was later enlarged into a church as the doorway is tall enough to admit a man on horseback. During the Middle Ages, this curious church was a centre of pilgrimage as it contained several relics including the hair shirt, comb and bones of St James and a crucifix with a drop of the Virgin's milk set in crystal.

The village is set in the undulating country of the Weald and, to the west of Wisborough Green, there are two areas of preserved woodland which give an indication to today's visitors of how most of the land north of the Downs would have looked many thousands of years ago. Looking at the countryside now it is hard to imagine that, in the 16th and 17th centuries, this area was an important industrial centre. Thanks to the seemingly limitless supply of trees for

ACORN TEA ROOM (ALDINGBOURNE TRUST)

Todhurst Site, Brinsbury College, North Heath, Pulborough, West Sussex RH20 1DL
Tel/Fax: 01798 873533
e-mail: michellewykes@aldingbournetrust.co.uk
website: www.aldingbournetrust.co.uk

The delicious home-baked cakes and pies and the wonderful, friendly atmosphere are reasons enough for a visit, although the **Acorn Tea Room** is just one of the attractions on the Todhurst site. Organic fruit and vegetables, home-grown and Soil Association registered, are sold in the Acorn shop, along with jams, preserves and gifts, and this is also the place to find some unusual herbaceous perennial plants. Through the Aldingbourne Trust, Acorn offers live work skills

training in horticulture, retail and catering for adults with learning difficulties, seeking to place them in regular work through a supported employment scheme.

'Unlocking potential' is the aim of the Trust, and The Acorn has recently introduced a Recognition of Achievement Award Scheme called 'Challenge 21'. This is to recognise students' achievements when completing challenges set at the Acorn. It is recognised within West Sussex and sponsored by Boots. Each challenge is flexible and can be adapted to the abilities of the student, meaning that everyone achieves. Each student receives a certificate for each challenge.

fuel, iron foundries and forges prospered here right up until the time of the Industrial Revolution. A plentiful supply of high quality sand from the coast supported a number of early glassworks. During the 16th century, Huguenot settlers from France and the Low Countries introduced new and improved methods of glass manufacture and the industry flourished until the early 17th century when lobbying by shipbuilders and iron smelters led to legislation banning the glassmakers from using timber to fire their furnaces.

Fishers Farm Park brings together the delights of the rural farmyard with the excitement of an adventure playground. As well as the combine harvester and pony rides, there is a whole assortment of animals, ranging from giant shire horses to goats, lambs and rabbits. For those who seek more mechanical diversions there is a merry-go-round from the 1950s and up-to-the-minute go-karts.

WEST CHILTINGTON
3 miles E of Pulborough off the A283

Built around a crossroads in the twisting lanes of the wealden countryside, this neat and compact village centres on the village green which is dominated by the delightful and relatively unrestored **Church of St Mary**. Famous for its medieval wall paintings discovered in 1882, this charming Norman church has an oak shingled spire and a roof of Horsham stone. Beside the churchyard gate are the old village stocks and whipping post.

COOTHAM
3 miles SE of Pulborough on the A283

The village is synonymous with **Parham**, the most western and the grandest of the Elizabethan mansions that were built below the northern slopes of the Downs.

Just west of the village and surrounded by a great deer park, the estate belonged in medieval times to the Abbey of Westminster and, at the Dissolution of the Monasteries, it passed into the hands of the Palmer family. As was customary, the foundation stone of the great mansion was laid by a child, in this case the two-year-old son of Thomas Palmer.

In 1601, Thomas Bysshop, a London lawyer, bought the estate and for the next 300 years it remained with that family. In 1922, the house and park were purchased by a son of Viscount Cowdray, Clive Pearson and, in 1948 Mr and Mrs Pearson opened the property to the public. The splendid Elizabethan interiors have been restored to their former glory, including the magnificent 160-foot Long Gallery (its ceiling painted by Sir Oliver Messel), the Saloon, the Great Hall and the Great Parlour, and exceptional collections of period furniture, oriental carpets, rare needlework and fine paintings are on show. The Great Room is largely dedicated to Sir Joseph Banks, the noted botanist and patron of science, who accompanied Captain Cook on his journey to the Pacific in 1768. Banks was also a President of the Royal Society and was one of the founders of the Royal Botanical Gardens at Kew. The paintings here include masterpieces by Stubbs and Reynolds.

The grounds at Parham have also been restored and contain lawns, a lake, specimen trees, fine statuary and a magnificent four-acre walled garden with an orchard, a 1920s Wendy House, and greenhouses where plants and flowers are grown for the house. The house and gardens are open to the public on certain days of the week between April and October. Parham hosts many events in the year, including the Garden Weekend held in July and the Autumn Flowers at

Parham event in September, which celebrates the tradition of flower-arranging started by the Hon Mrs Clive Pearson in the 1920s. The Garden Shop sells an impressive variety of plants, many of them unusual and all home-grown.

STORRINGTON
3½ miles SE of Pulborough on the A283

This old market town has a jumble of architectural styles from its small heavily restored Saxon church through to 20th century concrete buildings. However, from Storrington there is good access to the **South Downs Way** long distance footpath via Kithurst Hill. It was this beautiful surrounding countryside that inspired Francis Thompson to write his poem *Daisy* while he was staying in a local monastery and the composer, Arnold Bax, also lived in the area between 1940 and 1951.

The heavily restored **Church of St Mary** has, inside, a Saxon stone coffin on which is the marble effigy of a knight who is thought to have been a crusader. When the author A J Cronin moved to the old rectory in the 1930s he used this legend as the basis for his novel *The Crusaders*.

SULLINGTON
4½ miles SE of Pulborough off the A283

This hamlet is home to a 115-foot **Long Barn** which rivals many tithe barns that were such a feature of the medieval monastic estate. An exceptional building with a braced tie beam roof, the barn, which is privately owned, can be viewed by appointment. Just outside Sullington is **Sullington Warren** - owned by the National Trust this expanse of open heathland was once used for farming rabbits and it now offers superb views across the South Downs. The Warren has

SULLINGTON MANOR FARM

Storrington, West Sussex RH20 4AE
Tel/Fax: 01903 745754
e-mail: kittles@waitrose.com

On the 500-acre **Sullington Manor Farm** on the east side of Storrington, Victorian stables have been stylishly converted into comfortable self-catering holiday cottages. The five cottages form a courtyard round a shared lawn, with a vast 17th century tithe barn on one side. The self-contained, single-storey cottages - four with two bedrooms, the fifth with one - are all warm and cosy, and their facilities include central heating, a gas cooker, microwave, fridge-freezer, TV and video, and they share a laundry room and a patio with garden furniture and a barbecue.

Other amenities comprise an outdoor swimming pool, a hard tennis court and a table tennis table; the South Down Way runs through the grounds, providing excellent walking and great views, and the Saxon Church of St Mary is next to the farm. Grahame and Gail Kittle run it as a working (mainly beef) farm, and apart from the cattle there are several other creatures on the premises, including two retrievers and a labrador, Clarissa the Tamworth pig and the peacocks Percy and Peter.

SAWYARDS

Manleys Hill, Storrington, West Sussex RH20 4BT
Tel: 01903 742331   Fax: 01903 742795

In a fine stone and brick building dating from 1730, **Sawyards** serves classical French cuisine in a quintessential English setting. The three carpeted dining areas are beautifully decorated and furnished, with pristine linen, gleaming silver, sparkling crystal, fresh flowers and candle light. Old wooden pillars and beams are a striking feature in two of the rooms, and one has a fine brick inglenook fireplace. When the weather is really kind, meals can be taken on the lovely south-facing lawn. Prime fresh ingredients, many of them locally sourced, are handled with skill, flair and respect by the head chef in the superb dishes that make up the daily changing two- or three-course menu, with five choices for each course.

Starters might include seared scallops with a butternut squash purée and squid ink sauce, or terrine of roast chicken, foie gras and wild mushrooms, while typical main courses could include brill with a lemon grass sauce, rack of lamb served pink with thyme jus, or ratatouille millefeuille with aubergine crisps. Desserts such as caramelised lemon tarte with red fruit coulis end a meal in style, and the fine food is complemented by an excellent selection of wines. Sawyards is open for lunch and dinner Tuesday evening to Sunday lunch. Smoking in the bar only.

AMBERLEY VILLAGE POTTERY

Church Street, Amberley, West Sussex BN18 9ND
Tel: 01798 831876
e-mail: john@v8man.com

Amberley Village Pottery is a working studio where Caroline Seaton, Barbara Ward and David Berry produce a range of pottery using traditional materials and techniques. They make a wide range of domestic pots to complement food and drink, including plates,

cups and saucers, bowls, cooking pots, jugs and wine goblets. They also produce their own one-off pieces - large floor jars, platters, vases and lamp bases to sit in odd corners, fireplaces or conservatories. Every piece is hand made using traditional Studio Pottery skills. The glazes are developed and mixed by them to produce a range of colours to suit every home..

Their aim is to provide useful pots at affordable prices. Caroline, Barbara and David do not give demonstrations as such but are happy for visitors to watch and chat while they work.

Open daily all year from 10am-5pm except Wednesdays.

nine prehistoric round barrows, all listed as Ancient Monuments.

AMBERLEY

4 miles S of Pulborough on the B2139

An attractive village of thatched cottages situated above the River Arun, Amberley is an ancient place whose name means 'fields yellow with buttercups'. Lands in this area were granted to St Wilfrid by King Cedwalla in around AD 680 and the village church of today is thought to stand on the foundations of a Saxon building constructed by St Wilfrid, the missionary who converted the South Saxons to Christianity. Later, in the 12th century, Bishop Luffa of Chichester rebuilt the church and it still has a strong Norman appearance.

At around the same time as the church was being rebuilt, a fortified summer palace for the Bishops of Chichester was also constructed. During the late 14th century, when there was a large threat of a French sea invasion, Bishop Rede of Chichester enlarged the summer palace and added a great curtain wall. Still more a manor house than a true castle, **Amberley Castle** is said to have offered protection to Charles II during his flight to France in 1651

During the 18th and 19th centuries, chalk was quarried from Amberley and taken to the many lime kilns in the area. Later, large quantities of chalk were needed to supply a new industrial process, which involved the high temperature firing of chalk with small amounts of clay to produce Portland cement. Situated just to the south of Amberley and on the site of an old chalk pit and limeworks is **Amberley Museum**, which concentrates on the industry of this area. This is very much a working museum, on a site of 36 acres, and visitors can ride the length of the museum on a workmen's train and see

the comprehensive collection of narrow gauge engines, from steam to electric. The history of roads and road making is also explored, and in the Electricity Hall is an amazing assortment of electrical items from domestic appliances to generating and supply equipment. In the workshop section, there are various tradesmen's shops including a blacksmith's, pottery, boatbuilder's and a printing works.

To the north of Amberley there is a series of water meadows known as the **Amberley Wild Brooks**. Often flooded and inaccessible by car, this 30-acre conservation area and nature reserve is a haven for bird, animal and plant life. The trains on the Arun Valley line cross the meadows on specially constructed embankments, which were considered wonders of modern engineering when the line was first opened in 1863.

HARDHAM

1 mile SW of Pulborough on the A29

This tiny hamlet, on the banks of the River Arun, is home to the Saxon **Church of St Botolph**, which is famous for its medieval wall paintings. Considered some of the finest in England, the oldest of the paintings dates from around 1100 and among the scenes on view are images of St George slaying the dragon and the Serpent tempting Adam and Eve. The murals are thought to have been worked by artists based at St Pancras Priory in Lewes, who were also responsible for the paintings at Coombes and Clayton.

At one time Hardham had a small Augustinian monastic house and the site of **Hardham Priory** can be found just south of the hamlet. Now a farmhouse, the priory's cloisters have been incorporated into a flower garden. From here a footpath leads to the disused **Hardham Tunnel**, a channel, which was

Houghton

Distance:	4.3 miles (6.9 kilometres)
Typical time:	150 mins
Height gain:	25 metres
Map:	Explorer 121
Walk:	www.walkingworld.com ID:76
Contributor:	Nicholas Rudd-Jones

Access Information:

North Stoke, South of Amberley Station and B2139 from Storrington. Can start walk from Amberley station if no car (on Pulborough line from London). In North Stoke, park near phone box

Additional Information:

Note the River Arun is tidal and very prone to flooding. Check before you start.

Description:

A circular walk based around the River Arun, taking in delightful villages of North & South Stoke. A good walk for kids.

Features:

River, Pub, Church, Wildlife, Great Views

Walk Directions:

1 Take footpath to right of small road next to phone box and post box. Climb two stiles, cross track and continue on grassy path downhill. At bottom of field path becomes gravelled.

2 Cross footbridge; path swings right. Climb stile and turn left at river.

3 Climb stile & cross bridge; follow track past houses and St Leonard's Church in South Stoke. Join road; swing left past barn on right.

4 Turn right off road and take bridleway behind barn. At next bridleway signpost turn left. Follow stony track (glimpses of river below to right). Pass through gate and turn right at field; follow path around field edge.

5 Pass gate back into woods. Continue past a metal gate on left: this is the entrance to Arundel Park, an interesting diversion if you have time, and a possible link to ww1001 - Houghton Forest and Bignor Hill. Follow path along river, passing under white cliffs.

6 At end of path, pass through metal gate and join road uphill into Houghton village. There is a path marked along the river's edge straight to Houghton bridge, but when we walked it was completely flooded and impassable — could be worth exploring as a short cut in drier weather. At the crossroads, George & Dragon pub is a short walk along the road to left: lovely garden. Cross B2139 and take minor road signed to Bury (marked Houghton Lane on map) across fields.

7 Turn right when South Downs Way crosses road. On reaching the river, follow round to the right, until you reach Amberley bridge on west bank. Turn left over the bridge. Take footpath halfway across the bridge on the right, heading south.

8 Cross a subsidiary bridge, then turn right back alongside the river.

9 Climb a stile & shortly afterwards take path to left.

10 On reaching the North Stoke Road, turn right, and return to the car.

built to provide a short cut for river barges wishing to avoid an eastern loop of the River Arun.

BIGNOR

5 miles SW of Pulborough off the A29

The main thoroughfares of this pretty village are arranged in an uneven square and, as well as a photogenic 15th century shop, there are some charming ancient domestic buildings to be seen. In 1811, a ploughman working on the east side of the village unearthed a **Roman Mosaic Floor** , which proved to be part of a villa built at the end of the 2nd century AD. This is one of the largest sites in Britain with some 70 Roman buildings surrounding a central courtyard. It is thought that the find was the administration centre of a large agricultural estate. The villa, being the home of a wealthy agricultural master, was extended throughout the time of the Roman occupation and the mosaic decoration of the house is some of the finest to be seen in this country.

Unlike the Roman excavations at Fishbourne, this remains relatively undiscovered by tourists and, charmingly, the exposed remains are covered, not by modern day structures, but by the thatched huts that were first built to protect them in 1814. The 80 foot long mosaic along the north corridor is the longest on display in Britain and among the characters depicted on the mosaics are Venus, Medusa and an array of gladiators. The **Bignor Roman Villa Museum** (see panel below)houses a collection of artefacts revealed during the excavation work and a display on the history of the Roman settlement and its underfloor heating system or hypocaust.

FITTLEWORTH

2½ miles W of Pulborough on the A283

An acknowledged Sussex beauty spot, this village has retained much of its charm despite its position on the main Pulborough to Petworth road. Its narrow roads wind through woods passing an old mill and bridge, lovely old cottages and lanes leading to the surrounding woods and heath. This rural idyll has been popular with artists over the years, particularly around the turn of the century. In the Swan Inn, the local hostelry, there is a number of paintings of local views, supposedly left by artists

---

BIGNOR ROMAN VILLA

Bignor, Pulborough, West Sussex RH20 1PH
Tel/Fax: 01798 869 259
e-mail: bignorromanvilla@care4free.net
website: www.bignorromanvilla.co.uk

Bignor Roman Villa is situated in a superb rural setting to the north of the South Downs. Only one mile from the South Downs Way. The mosaic floors, discovered in 1811, are some of the finest in Britain, and they are displayed under cover. The 24m (80ft) long mosaic in the north corridor is the longest on display in the country and there are many other mosaics including the famous Venus & Cupid Gladiators, Medusa and Ganymede.

The museum, which contains many interesting artefacts found on site during excavations, tells the story of the Villa over the years. You can also see how the hypocaust under floor heating system worked. Free car and coach parking areas, well-stocked gift shop, cafeteria supplying tea, coffee and light snacks, free picnic area for visitors to the Roman Villa and facilities for the disabled are all available on site. Guided tours and special party rates by arrangement with the curators.

in return for their lodgings.

Well known too among anglers, the village has excellent fishing on the River Rother and further downstream, where it joins the River Arun.

In the middle of woodlands is **Brinkwells**, a thatched cottage, once home to the village's most famous visitor, the composer Edward Elgar. He first came here in 1917, when he wrote his much-loved cello concerto, and returned for the last time in 1921. Appropriately, the Jubilee clock in the village church has a very musical chime.

STOPHAM

1 mile NW of Pulborough off the A283

This charming place, where a handful of cottages cluster around the early Norman church, lies on the banks of the River Rother. The family home of a distinguished local family who can trace their ancestry back to the Norman

invasion, **Stopham House** is still here, as is the splendid early 15th century bridge which the family were instrumental in constructing. The impressive **Stopham Bridge** is widely regarded as the finest of its kind in Sussex and, though the tall central arch was rebuilt in 1822 to allow masted vessels to pass upstream towards the Wey and Arun Canal, the medieval structure is coping well with today's traffic without a great deal of modern intervention.

PETWORTH

5 miles NW of Pulborough on the A283

This historic town, though now a major road junction, still has many elements of an ancient feudal settlement - the old centre, a great house and a wall dividing the two. Mentioned in the Domesday Book, where it appeared as *Peteorde*, this was a market town and the square is thought to have originated in the 13th

SOANES RESTAURANT

Grove Lane, Petworth,
West Sussex GU28 0HY
Tel/Fax: 01798 343659

Vanessa and Edward Portman welcome guests to **Soanes Restaurant**, which is situated in a redbrick former farmhouse in idyllic open countryside. Beams, candlelight, pristine linen and sparkling glass and silver make a romantic setting for enjoying Edward's excellent cooking, which features locally sourced ingredients as much as possible. His style is traditional English with a European twist, and everything from the bread to the ice cream is

made on the premises. His menus make mouthwatering reading, and results on the plate never disappoint. Lunchtime starters or snacks - the menus change constantly - might include pan-fried mackerel with horseradish cream, wild mushroom risotto or chestnut and sage polenta; open sandwiches are made with homemade bread, and even the omelettes are very special, with interesting fillings such as chorizo, olive and potato or roasted Mediterranean and feta cheese.

Main lunch and dinner dishes run from salmon fishcakes with dill cream sauce and pan-fried monkfish with a scallop coral sauce to pigeon breast with black pudding, chicken breast stuffed with rocket and pine nuts on olive risotto, or fillet of beef Wellington with a red wine gravy. Desserts like mango crème brûlée or banana-stuffed pancakes with a warm toffee sauce keep the enjoyment level sky high to the end, and the fine food is complemented by a well-chosen wine list featuring Old World reds and New World whites.

century and its street fair dates back to 1189. Between the 14th and the 16th centuries this was an important cloth weaving centre and a number of fine merchants' and landowners' houses remain from those days. **Daintrey House**, which has a Georgian front façade and Elizabethan features to the rear, has magnificent iron railings around the front garden. Another house, **Leconfield Hall**, dating from 1794, was the courthouse and council meeting place before becoming a public hall. The garden of **Lancaster House**, close by, is said to have been used as a hiding place for the church silver during the time of Cromwell.

As well as taking time to wander the streets here and see the many interesting houses, cottages and other buildings, visitors should make time to take in the town's two museums. The **Petworth Cottage Museum** is housed in a 17th century cottage of the Leconfield estate, restored to the days of 1910 when it was the home of Maria Cummings. She was a seamstress at nearby Petworth House and a widow with four grown up children. The cottage recreates her domestic setting, including her bedroom, sewing room, a copper boiler in the scullery and a 'Petworth' range for cooking and heating. The unusual **Doll House Museum** has an interesting collection of over 100 doll's houses, inhabited by 2,000 miniature people, put together to capture the incidents of everyday life. Among the one twelfth size houses there are replicas of the Royal Albert Hall, a prison and a museum full of tourists.

However, what brings most visitors to Petworth is the grand estate of **Petworth House** (see panel on page 259) , now owned by the National Trust. Built between 1688 and 1696 on the site of a

---

VARCA

Unit 1, Station Business Park, Petworth, West Sussex GU28 0JF
Tel: 01798 343530 Fax: 01798 343233
e-mail: varca@varca.com website: www.varca.com

'Spain's Best Kept Secret' was introduced into the UK in 1998, when Varca sandals were first imported. Typical Menorcan sandals, 'abarcas', were worn many years ago by Spanish farmers, made in simple traditional style, with a tyre sole and leather sewn on to fit the foot and ankle. Today, the Varca sandals are made in a small Menorcan village and Varca remains a family business. The parents of partner Marianne Pope brought the sandals back from their holiday home in Menorca to friends in Britain, and the idea for the business was born.

Varca sandals are made with the same durable craftsmanship as the original, but are now with a lighter rubber sole and are available in a wide range of vibrant colours and modern designs. The secret of this amazing sandal is style combined with comfort and practicality, and they are ideal for beach wear or for strolling. The strap sits high on the heel and does not drop with wear, and the rubber soles

are made to last. The sandals come in a variety of styles for men, women and kids, and the range includes loafers in four styles made from nubuck and leather. New lines are introduced from time to time, and discontinued lines are offered at discounted prices. Varca also make bags in a choice of sizes and colours or transparent - handbags, beach bags, raffia bags, sequinned bags for evening use. Varca is predominantly a mail order business, with viewing by appointment only. Call or fax for a product list and selected retail outlets.

medieval manor house belonging to the Percy family by Charles Seymour, the 6th Duke of Somerset, Petworth House is a simple and elegant building that has more the look of a French château than an English country house. Both French and English architects have been suggested. The construction of the house was completed by the Duke's descendant, the 2nd Earl of Egremont, who had the grounds and deer park landscaped by Capability Brown in 1752.

Petworth House and Grounds

Today, the house is home to one of the finest art collections outside London and the layout of the house, with one room leading directly into another, lends itself perfectly to life as an art gallery. Among the works on view are paintings by Rembrandt, Van Dyck, Hobbema, Cuyp, Holbein, Reynolds, Gainsborough and Turner, who was a frequent visitor to Petworth House. On a less grand scale, in decoration terms, the servants' block is also open to the public and provides an interesting insight into life below stairs.

Just south of the estate is the **Coultershaw Water Wheel and Beam Pump**, one of the earliest pumped water systems, installed in 1790 to pipe water two miles to Petworth House. Restored to full working order by the Sussex Industrial Archaeology Society, it is now open to the public on a limited basis.

THE WEST SUSSEX WEALD

This area, to the north of the South Downs, is called a Weald, a word that is derived from the German word Wald, meaning forest. This would suggest an area covered in woodland and, though some areas of the great forest remain, the landscape now is one of pastures enclosed by hedgerows. From the Middle Ages onwards, until the time of the Industrial Revolution, the area was very much associated with iron working and, less so, glassmaking. The trees were

---

FITZLEA FARMHOUSE

Selham, nr Petworth, West Sussex GU28 0PS
Tel: 01798 861429

A wooded track leads to **Fitzlea Farmhouse**, a 16th century Grade II listed building set in four acres of quiet, secluded gardens and paddocks bordered by bluebell woods and farmland. Owner Maggie Paterson has lived at the farm for 30 years and offers Bed & Breakfast accommodation in three comfortable, characterful rooms with TV and tea/coffee-makers. An Aga-cooked breakfast is served in the farmhouse kitchen, and Maggie can provide snacks and packed lunches on request. Guests can plan their day in the drawing room, where an open fire adds to the cosy feel. Maggie also has a beachside cottage to let at Beesands in South Devon.

felt for fuel to drive the furnaces and streams were dammed to create hammer ponds. The legacy of this once prosperous industry can be seen in the wealth of elaborate buildings and, particularly, the splendid churches, that were built on the profits of the industry.

Those interested in visiting grand houses will find that this region of West Sussex has several to offer. Close to East Grinstead, Standen, a remarkable Victorian country house now restored to its original glory, is a wonderful example of the Arts and Crafts Movement. The low half-timbered 15th century house, the Priest House, at West Hoathly, was built as an estate office for the monks from St Pancras Priory, Lewes. Now restored it is open to the public as a museum filled with 18th and 19th century furniture. The magnificent Elizabeth mansion, Danny, at Hurstpierpoint, has a very special place in history as this is where Lloyd George and his war cabinet drew up the terms of the armistice to end World War I. In private hands today, the house is occasionally open to the public.

Near Ardingly lies Wakehurst Place, a striking Elizabethan mansion built by the Culpeper family in 1590. Now leased to the Royal Botanical Gardens at Kew, the magnificent collection of trees and shrubs in the grounds are well worth seeing. Other great gardens can also be found in this region of West Sussex, including Leonardslee at Lower Beeding which was laid out in the late 19th century by Sir Edmund Loder and Hymans, which was created with the help of the 19th century gardening revivalists William Robinson and Gertrude Jekyll.

HORSHAM

This ancient town, which takes its name from a Saxon term meaning 'horse pasture', was founded in the mid 10th

THE EARTH COLLECTION

11 Piries Place, Horsham, West Sussex RH12 1EH
Tel/Fax: 01403 261888
website: www.theearthcollection.com

The Earth Collection is a range of environmentally friendly clothes and accessories designed with environmentally friendly people in mind. The products - skirts, trousers and tops, shirts, sweaters, hats, bags, informal shoes - are all made from natural fibres - cotton, silk, ramie and hemp - all known for their comfort and strength. Even the buttons are natural, made from coconut shells and bamboo, and the environmental awareness extends to the hang tags, which are made from recycled paper and marked with water-based ink.

Simple really is beautiful at The Earth Collection, and all the clothes look as good as they feel. As more people are becoming conscious of the environment, so more are becoming aware that the Earth Collection range not only makes the wearer look and feel good but also makes a statement and helps the earth. One of the favourite fabrics in the childrens' range is natural coloured cotton used for the babywear which is very suitable for chemically sensitive skin due to the minimal use of chemicals in its production and treatment. And since there is obviously no need for dyeing, that, too, is of benefit to the environment.

PICCOLO'S ITALIAN RESTAURANT

24 West Street, Horsham, West Sussex RH12 1PB
Tel: 01403 263281
e-mail: alfredoaquilina@aol.com
website: www.piccolosrestaurant.co.uk

Alfredo Aquilina learned his culinary skills in his native Italy and brought them to London before settling in Sussex to delight the residents of Horsham and the surrounding area. **Piccolo's Italian Restaurant** is located on the first floor above retail premises in a town-centre pedestrian precinct. Cane-seated chairs set at neatly laid tables create a cosy, traditional ambience for enjoying a wide variety of cooked-to-order dishes from the classic Italian repertoire.

The menu includes an excellent selection of starters, pasta and chicken, veal, steak and seafood main courses, and Alfredo puts his individual stamp on house specials such as penne with cream, tomatoes and vodka; Piccolo's tortellini with ricotta cheese and spinach; and Piccolo's chicken breast with garlic, black and green olives, peppers and a spicy wine sauce. Wine is also taken seriously at Piccolo's, and among the decorative features are an array of wine bottles and a mural of a cherubic figure resting on wine barrel. The list includes Chianti in the famous wicker-covered flasks and the impressive Amarone made from dried grapes. Piccolo's is open for lunch and dinner Tuesday to Saturday.

century. Some 300 years later, Horsham had grown into a prosperous borough and market town, which was considered important enough to send two members to the new Parliament established in 1295. Between 1306 and 1830, Horsham, along with Lewes and Chichester, took it in turns to hold the county assizes. During the weeks the court was held in Horsham, large numbers of visitors descended on the town giving it a carnival atmosphere. Public executions were also held here, either on the common or on the Carfax, including one, in 1735, of a man who refused to speak at his trial. He was sentenced to death by compression, and three hundredweight of stones were placed on his chest for three days. When the man still refused to speak, the gaoler added his own weight to the man's chest and killed him outright. **The Carfax** today is a thriving pedestrianised shopping centre and nothing is left of the horrors of its past.

Horsham's architectural gem is **The Causeway**, a quiet tree-lined street of old buildings that runs from the Georgian fronted town hall to the 12th century Church of St Mary, where can be found a simple tablet commemorating the life of Percy Bysshe Shelley, a celebrated local inhabitant.

Here, too, can be found the gabled 16th century **Causeway House** - a rambling building that is now home to the **Horsham Museum**, a purpose for which its layout is ideal. This excellent museum has recreations of a Sussex farmhouse kitchen, a wheelwright's and saddler's shop, and a blacksmith's forge and, among the old prints and photographs, is an extraordinary drawing of a hard labour machine that was installed in Horsham Goal. It consisted of a long row of hand operated cranks, linked to a vast wind vane, which beat the air for no apparent purpose other than to exhaust the convicts. Concentrating on local history in particular, the collection is varied and includes toys, costumes, 19th century literature and aspects of town life.

Just two miles southwest of Horsham lies the famous **Christ's Hospital School**, a Bluecoat school that was founded for poor children, in Newgate Street, London, in 1552 by Edward VI. In the 18th century the girls moved to Hertford and in 1902 the boys moved here to Horsham. The girls joined them here in 1985. The present buildings incorporate some of the original London edifices. Bluecoat refers to the traditional long dark blue cloak that is still worn by the pupils.

TERRA DÉCOR

Handcross Road, Plummers Plain, nr Horsham,
West Sussex RH13 6NX
Tel: 01403 891969 Fax: 01403 891906
Website: www.TerraDecorLtd.com

A must visit. Stop in and see the most extensive range of garden pots available in the UK. As importers from around the world, they offer a full range of terracotta and glazed pots from 7cm to 1.5 metres.

Marvel at the tactile feel of pots from Crete and Shona stone carvings from Africa.

By dealing with the importer you benefit from the largest range at the lowest prices. Compare! Indoor and outdoor displays are open daily throughout the year. It is a family run business that offers quality, value and customer service.

Terra Décor is located on the B2110 between Lower Beeding and Handcross.

THE OLD POSTHOUSE

Handcross Road, Plummers Plain, nr Horsham,
West Sussex RH13 6NU
Tel/Fax: 01403 891776
e-mail: russell@oldposthouse.com
website: www.oldposthouse.com

Comfort and character are both in generous supply for overnight guests at **The Old Posthouse**, which enjoys a prime location in the tiny hamlet of Plummers Plain on the edge of the village of Lower Beeding. It stands on the B2110 almost opposite Holy Trinity Church. The property has evolved into its present form since about 1840: the east wing was formerly the village store and post office, and the oldest part, the west wing, now contains the guest accommodation. It was converted into a guest house in 1990, and the current owner, Dr Russell Crisp, has made many improvements.

The six bedrooms – two of them on the ground floor - have en suite facilities, TV and tea/coffee trays, and the central heating has individual thermostat controls. A solar energy collection system provides most of the hot water throughout the year. The tariff includes an excellent breakfast in which home-grown and local produce features prominently. The Old Posthouse has a beautiful secluded garden with lots of 'secret' pathways and an ornamental pond, where guests can while away a quiet hour or two. The village pub is only 200 yards away, and there are many delightful walks in the vicinity.

AROUND HORSHAM

RUSPER
3 miles N of Horsham off the A264

This secluded village of tile-hung and timbered cottages grew up around a 13th century priory. Rusper Priory is long gone and the only reminders of it are the medieval tower of the church and the graves in the churchyard of a prioress and four sisters. The church was rebuilt in the mid 19th century by the Broadwater family, whose wealth came from their piano manufacturing business. Lucy Broadwater, who died in 1929 and to whom there is a memorial tablet in the church, was a leading figure in the revival of English folk music.

Rusper Church in Winter

GATWICK AIRPORT
7½ miles NE of Horsham off the A23

The airport opened to commercial air traffic in 1936 when the first passengers took off for Paris. The return fare was £4 5 shillings (£4.25) and this included the return first-class rail fare from Victoria Station, London, to the airport. A month later the airport was officially opened by the Secretary of State for Air. He also opened the world's first circular air terminal here which was immediately christened The Beehive. During World War II, Gatwick airport, like all other British airports, was put under military control and was one of the bases for the D-Day operations.

After the war, the terminal buildings were extended and, in 1958, the new airport was reopened. Among Gatwick Airport's notable firsts was the pier leading from the terminal to the aircraft stands giving passengers direct access to the planes, and Gatwick was the first airport in the world to combine air, rail and road travel under one roof. Further extensions have increased the airport's capacity to a point where it handles over 30 million passengers a year flying to destinations right around the world.

Gatwick Airport Skyview gives visitors the chance to see behind the scenes of this busy airport through its multimedia theatre and there is also a real aircraft and cockpit to explore.

CRAWLEY
6½ miles NE of Horsham on the A23

A modern town, one of the original new towns created after the New Towns Act of 1946, Crawley is really an amalgamation of the villages of Three Bridges and Ifield with the small market town of Crawley. Though much has been lost under the new developments, Crawley probably dates back to Saxon times though it remained a quiet and unassuming place until the late 18th century. A convenient distance from both London and Brighton, it was used by the Prince Regent and his friends as a stopping over point as they commuted between the south coast resort of Brighton and the metropolis. However, the coming of the railways took away the need of a resting place and so Crawley returned to its quiet life. In the churchyard of the Franciscan friary is the grave of Lord Alfred Douglas, the intimate friend of Oscar Wilde. He lies beside his mother, who supported him when his father cut off his allowance during his friendship with Wilde.

MANNINGS HEATH

2 miles SE of Horsham on the A281

Just north of the village lies **St Leonard's Forest**, one of the few wooded heathland areas to survive the long term ravages of the timber fuelled iron industry of the Weald. Rising in places to around 500 feet, the forest lies on the undulating sandstone ridge that is bounded by Horsham, Crawley and Handcross. According to local folklore, St Leonard's Forest is the home of the legendary nine foot long dragon which roamed the heath and terrorised the surrounding villagers. Coincidentally, some dinosaur bones were discovered nearby in 1822 by Mary Mantell.

LOWER BEEDING

3 miles SE of Horsham on the B2110

The name of the village, along with that of its near namesake, Upper Beeding to the south, is somewhat confusing. Lower Beeding is actually situated on the summit of a hill while Upper Beeding lies in one of the lowest parts of West Sussex. However, this can be explained by looking at the derivation of the shared name. Beeding is derived from the Old

English 'Beadingas' which means 'Beada's people' and the Upper and Lower refer to the importance of, rather than the geographical positions of, the two settlements.

Just to the south of the village lies the beautiful **Leonardslee Gardens**, in a natural valley created by a tributary of the River Adur. Laid out by Sir Edmund Loder who began his task in 1889, the gardens are still maintained by the family and are world famous for the spring displays of azaleas, magnolias and rhododendrons around the seven landscaped lakes. Deer and wallabies live in the semi-wild habitat around the small lakes. There are several miles of walks around this large area as well as small gardens, including a bonsai garden to enjoy. The Loder family collection of motor vehicles dating from 1889 to 1900 is an interesting and informative display of the various different designs adopted by the earliest car constructors.

COWFOLD

4 miles SE of Horsham on the A272

This picturesque village of cottages clusters around the parish **Church of St Peter**, which holds one of the most famous brasses in Sussex. Dating back to the 15th century, the life-size brass is of Thomas Nelond, Prior of Lewes in the 1420s, and the brass, along with its elaborate canopy, is over 10 feet long.

Looking at Cowfold today it is hard to believe that is was once an important centre of the iron industry. The abundance of timber for fuel and reliable streams to drive the bellows and heavy hammers made this an active iron smelting area from medieval times through to the end of the 18th century. In order to secure a steady supply of water to these early foundries, small rivers were dammed to form mill or hammer ponds and a number of disused examples can still be found in the surrounding area.

Just to the south of Cowfold and rising above the trees is the spire of **St Hugh's Charterhouse**, the only Carthusian monastery in Britain. Founded in the 1870s, after the order had been driven out of France, the 30 or so monks of this contemplative order live cut off from the rest of the world behind the high stone walls. Each monk has his own cell, or hermitage, complete with its own garden and workshop, and the monks only emerge from their solitude for services and dinner on Sunday.

UPPER BEEDING

13 miles S of Horsham off the A2037

A sprawling village of cottages along the banks of the River Adur, during the Middle Ages, Upper Beeding was the home of **Sele Priory**, a Benedictine religious house founded in the late 11th century by William de Braose. Long since destroyed, the site of the priory is now occupied by a private house.

Though a quiet place today, in the early 19th century an important turnpike road passed through Upper Beeding and the old village toll house, one of the last in the county to remain in service, is now an exhibit at the Weald and Downland Museum, Singleton.

BRAMBER

13 miles S of Horsham on the A283

Visitors seeing Bramber for the first time will find it hard to imagine that this small, compact village was once a busy port on the River Adur estuary during Norman times but its demise came as the river silted up. The name Bramber is derived from the Saxon 'Brymmburh' meaning fortified hill, and when William

ST. MARY'S HOUSE AND GARDENS

Bramber, West Sussex BN44 3WE
Tel/Fax: 01903 816205
e-mail: info@stmarysbramber.co.uk
website: www.stmarysbramber.co.uk

This enchanting medieval timber framed house is situated in the award-winning downland village of Bramber. The fine panelled rooms of **St. Mary's**, which include the famous 'King's Room', associated with the escape of Charles II in 1651, and the unique 'Painted Room' with its intriguing *trompe Poeil* murals, give an air of tranquillity and timelessness. On open afternoons, visitors may wander history at their leisure, helped by friendly stewards. The informative guided tours for prearranged groups tell of fact and legend from earlier Knights Templar foundations to the present day.

Once the home of the real Algernon and Gwendolen so brilliantly portrayed by Oscar Wilde in his scintillating comedy, *The Importance of Being Earnest,* St. Mary's is said to be the setting for the Sherlock Holmes story, *The Musgrave Ritual,* and has served as a location for a number of TV series, including the world famous Dr. Who. The well known entertainer, Donald Swann, who gave a number of concerts in the Victorian Music Room has family connections with the house.

The formal gardens, with amusing topiary, include an exceptional example of the 'Living Fossil' tree, *Gingko biloba,* and a mysterious ivy clad 'Monks' Walk'. In the 'Secret Garden' can still be seen the original Victorian fruit wall, potting shed, circular orchard, and woodland walk.

St. Mary's is a house of fascination and mystery. Many thousands of visitors have admired its picturesque charm, and enjoyed its atmosphere of friendliness and welcome, qualities which make it a visit to remember.

THE OLD TOLLGATE RESTAURANT & HOTEL

The Street, Bramber, nr Steyning, West Sussex BN44 3WE
Tel: 01903 879494 Fax: 01903 813399
e-mail: info@oldtollgatehotel.com
website: www.oldtollgatehotel.com

Travellers passing through Bramber were once obliged to pause on their journey to pay a few pence at a tollgate before continuing on their way. Today, travellers still stop, but for many it's to enjoy the comfort, fine food, service and hospitality offered at **The Old Tollgate Restaurant & Hotel**. Located on the A283 between Brighton and Worthing, it stands on the site of the old tollhouse, and during building works over the years the older, main part of the restaurant was found to contain sections of the timber frame walls of the original building. The hotel has 31 beautifully designed bedrooms in four distinct styles, all en suite, and all with direct-dial telephones, trouser presses, mini-bars and a selection of toiletries. The lounges and bars offer plenty of space for guests to unwind, and the facilities are in keeping with the high standards set by the Best Western marketing group, of which the Old Tollgate is a member.

One of the main attractions of this outstanding hotel is its famous carvery-style restaurant, acclaimed by many as unrivalled in the region for the quality and variety of what is on offer from head chef Andrew Coburn and his team. The unique Total Tollgate Experience served every day for lunch and dinner starts with a selection from the extensive hors d'oeuvre table, followed by a main course – a choice of meats from the carvery or a mouthwatering variety of casseroles, pies, fish and vegetarian dishes. The final flourish comes from the tempting display of hot and cold puddings and an interesting cheeseboard.

The Old Tollgate produces its in-house newsletter the *Tollgate Times*, in which guests can read all the latest news of the hotel, with features on members of staff and many activities and events. This newsletter illustrates the excellent team spirit generated by hotel director Reina Alston and all the staff, some of them with many years' service here.

The ruins of a Norman castle can be seen on a hill just behind the hotel, and in the village itself is the 15th century St Mary's House. The nearby South Downs provide excellent walking, fine views and a range of activities that include golf, riding and fishing. Guests with an interest in horse-racing can hear about the hotel's sponsored horse in training locally and have a choice of racing venues within an easy drive – flat racing at Goodwood and Brighton, the all-weather track at Lingfield and National Hunt racing at Fontwell Park.

de Braose built his castle on the steep hill above the village it was probably on the foundations of a previous Saxon stronghold. Completed in 1090, the castle comprised a gatehouse and a number of domestic buildings surrounded by a curtain wall. An important stronghold while the port was active, the castle was visited by both King John and Edward I. However the castle did not survive the Civil War. It was all but demolished by the Parliamentarians. Today, the stark remains of **Bramber Castle** can be seen on the hilltop and the site is owned by English Heritage.

During the 15th century, the lands of the de Braose family were transferred to William Waynflete, the then Bishop of Winchester and founder of Magdalen College, Oxford. It was Waynflete who was responsible for constructing **St Mary's House** (see panel on page 265), in 1470, a striking medieval residence that was first built as a home for four monks who were bridge wardens of the important crossing here over the River Adur. Now a Grade I listed building, this is a classic half-timbered dwelling with fine wood panelled rooms, Elizabethan trompe l'œil paintings and medieval shuttered windows. However what remains today is only half of the original construction, which also acted as a resting place for pilgrims travelling to Chichester or Canterbury.

Following the Dissolution of the Monasteries, the house came into private ownership and was refurbished as a comfortable residence for a well-to-do family. The Painted Room was decorated for a visit by Queen Elizabeth I in 1585 and the room in which Charles II rested before fleeing to Shoreham and then France is

known as the King's Room. For a time at the end of the 19th century St Mary's House became part of the social scene when owned by Algernon Bourke, the owner of White's Club in London. His wife was called Gwendolen and their names were 'borrowed' by Oscar Wilde for two characters in his play *The Importance of Being Earnest*. Lovingly restored and with charming topiary gardens, the house was the setting for the Sherlock Holmes story *The Musgrave Ritual* and it has also featured in the *Dr Who* TV series.

Before the Reform Act of 1832 swept away the rotten boroughs, this tiny constituency returned two members to Parliament. This was despite the fact that, at one time, Bramber only had 32 eligible voters! One member of Parliament who benefited from the unreformed system was William Wilberforce, who was more or less awarded one of the Bramber seats in recognition of his campaigning work against slavery.

STEYNING

13 miles S of Horsham off the A283

This ancient market town, whose main street follows closely the line of the South Downs, was founded in the 8th

High Street, Steyning

LUCY D'AUVERGNE

56 High Street, Steyning,
West Sussex BN44 3RD
Tel: 01903 879478
website: www.lucydauvergne.com

Fine lingerie and swimwear are the stock in trade of **Lucy d'Auvergne**, an elegant shop founded by its eponymous owner. Lucy is passionate about bringing the very best of British and European designer-wear to her customers. Her staff are always happy to advise on style and size, being

committed to the perfect fit rather than a quick sale. The salon-style shop in a two-storey, medieval timbered-framed, building on the High Street, makes a stylish setting for showing off the clothes, and spacious changing rooms make personal fitting sessions easy and accurate.

Top French brand Aubade is Lucy's own personal favourite, offering superb style and fit. Her enthusiasm for Aubade is such that she is creating a museum of past collections! Other top brands include Cotton Club, Ravage, Gottex, Fantasie and Triumph.

THE WHITE HORSE INN

23 High Street, Steyning, West Sussex BN44 3YE
Tel: 01903 812347 Fax: 01903 814084
e-mail: TheWhiteHorseInn@vwood.wanadoo.co.uk
website: www.whitehorseinn-steyning.co.uk

A familiar landmark on the main street of Steyning, the **White Horse Inn** is a period red brick building adorned by a luxuriant growth of Virginia Creeper. Refurbished in 2004, inside, the look is delightfully traditional, a perfect setting for enjoying a leisurely drink or a meal in a friendly atmosphere. Owners Val and Robin Wood and their team are totally committed to making this one of the leaders in its field, a charming old pub and a top-class restaurant. Their aim is to provide the best of both worlds (smart and casual) under one roof, where in community can enjoy simply meeting for a drink or dining in the friendly, relaxed surroundings.

The Head Chef's style, of combining classic skills and contemporary flair based on seasonal produce by supporting local suppliers, is shown in the exciting dishes on the menu in Wood's Restaurant, typified

by an imaginative and varied menu of meats and fish. 'Catch of the South' is dependent on local daily supply, and seasonal shellfish is always in demand. The seasonal menu rotates during the year offering the best selection of meats available in the locality. Simpler fare, from sandwiches and salads to pub classics such as beer-battered cod and Ribeye Steak make up the bar menu. The "Platters" offer an innovative, unusual dish - a unique complete meal on one plate incorporating a tasty selection of sweet and savoury dishes. Drinks include well-kept cask ales, top-quality lagers and a varied selection of wines by the bottle or glass.

century by St Cuthman. An early Celtic Christian, Cuthman travelled from Wessex eastwards pushing his invalid mother in a handcart. On reaching Saxon Steyning, the wheel on the handcart broke as they passed Penfolds Field and the nearby haymakers laughed and jeered as the old lady was thrown to the ground. St Cuthman cursed the field and the unhelpful haymakers, and the heavens are said to have opened and torrential rain poured and spoilt their labours. To this day, it is said to rain whenever Penfolds Field is being mown. St Cuthman took his calamity as a sign that he should settle here and he built a timber church.

By the late Saxon period Steyning had grown to become an important port on the then navigable River Adur and, as well as being a royal manor owned by Alfred the Great, it also had a Royal Mint. By 1100, the silting of the river had caused the harbour to close but, fortunately, the town was well established and could continue as a market place. Designated a conservation area, there are many buildings of architectural and historical interest in the town's ancient centre. There are several 14th and 15th century hall type houses as well as Wealden cottages but the most impressive building, built in the 15th century as the home of a religious order, is the famous **Old Grammar School**, now a successful comprehensive. Steyning's large and imposing Church of St Andrew has some notable Norman carvings and a renaissance reredos of 48 carved panels. An excellent place to discover Steyning's past is at **Steyning Museum** in Church Street where there are exhibitions showing both the town's history and local prehistoric finds.

Steyning's close proximity to the **South Downs Way** and the **Downs Link**

COUNTRY HOUSE

68 High Street, Steyning, West Sussex BN44 3RD
Tel: 01903 815518

Behind the smart green and white frontage on Steyning's main street, Barbara Tyrie has created the **Country House**, an amazing shop where customers can feast their eyes on a beautiful display of ladies wear. Barbara personally selects and assembles a collection of clothes for all ages and all occasions, all of them very feminine and also very practical and wearable. The fabrics include linens, cottons, silks and wools, and to complement the clothes there is an equally stylish range of accessories to complete the ensemble, from shoes and hats and scarves to belts, bags and jewellery.

Style, elegance and sophistication are the keynotes of the Country House, where the clothes make a definite statement without having to shout it.
Barbara has established a loyal customer base at her shop, but first-time visitors can also be assured of a warm, friendly welcome and helpful advice from the owner and her staff.

THE COUNTRYMAN INN

Shipley, West Sussex
Tel: 01403 741383 Fax: 01403 741115
e-mail: countrymaninn@btopenworld.com
website: www.countrymanshipley.co.uk

With its famous smock mill, its historic old tollhouse, its pretty 12th century church and its hammer pond, Shipley packs more visitor attractions into its modest boundaries than most villages. But for lovers of good food, good drink and genuine country hospitality, **The Countryman Inn** is the number one draw. With its weatherboarded exterior and red-tiled roof, it really looks the part, and inside is equally appealing, with sturdy traditional furniture, smart carpets throughout, a copper-hooded fire in the hearth, jugs and pots and pans, ceramics and prints and pictures of local scenes. Among the more unusual eye-catching features are a framed notice about the Royal Antediluvian Order of Buffaloes and brass plates on the bar top remembering regulars

who helped organise charity events down the years.

The Countryman Inn is run by Alan Vaughan, who once controlled a group of six pubs but now devotes himself to this outstanding hostelry, which combines all the best qualities of a traditional country local and a serious restaurant.

The choice of food changes daily, with typical options ranging from dressed crab salad and Spanish quiche to paella, rack of BBQ ribs, beef jalfrezi, seasonal game and lamb & cranberry pie. The fresh fish specials, including cod, salmon, lemon sole and monkfish, are the choice of many, and the traditional Sunday roast is another guaranteed winner.

A lovely place at any time of year, The Countryman is particularly delightful in fine weather, when the large lawn, with picnic benches under parasols, comes into its own. A separate garden complete with swinging hammocks is used for private parties, for which the inn is an ideal venue.

RINGCRAFT JEWELLERY WORKSHOP

51a High Street, Steyning, West Sussex B44 3RE
Tel: 01903 879410 website: www.ringcraft.co.uk

Richard Burden has a wealth of experience in the jewellery trade. He was trained as a jobbing jeweller and diamond mounter before setting up a workshop to serve retail jewellers in 1975. He opened his own retail shop in Steyning in 1992 and moved to the present attractive High Street premises in 1995. **Ringcraft Jewellery** stocks designer jewellery from around the world, with Finland, Israel, Mexico and China among the many countries represented.

The display includes hand-made wedding and engagement rings in gold, silver and platinum; pavé, costume and silver jewellery; gold and silver necklaces, chains and pendants; a wide range of designer watches; and Caran d'Ache pens and propelling pencils. Richard and his assistants repair, renovate, alter and rebuild jewellery, they undertake watch and clock repairs, they offer a diamond mounting service and will restring pearls. An engraving service on the premises personalises christening, wedding and other gifts, including picture frames, tankards and hip flasks. Richard has always put customer satisfaction at the top of his priorities, and personal service and top-quality work have built up a large and loyal clientele.

(a long-distance bridleway which follows the course of the old railway line to Christ's Hospital near Horsham and on in to Surrey), makes this a lovely base for both walking and riding holidays.

SHIPLEY

6 miles S of Horsham off the A272

As well as its pretty 12th century village church, this pleasant village also features a small disused toll house and a distinctive hammer pond that in the 16th century would have supplied water to drive the bellows and mechanical hammers in the adjacent iron foundry. However, Shipley is perhaps best known for being the former home of the celebrated Sussex writer Hilaire Belloc. He lived at **King's Land**, a low rambling house on the outskirts of the village, from 1906 until his death in 1953 and, appropriately enough, as a lover of windmills, he had one at the bottom of

his garden. Built in 1879, **Shipley Mill** is the only remaining working smock mill in Sussex and, while being the county's last, it is also the biggest. Open to the public on a limited basis, the mill was completely restored and returned to working order after the writer's death.

Belloc is not the only connection that Shipley has with the arts, for the composer John Ireland is buried in the churchyard of the village's interesting church, built by the Knights Templar in 1125.

WASHINGTON

12 miles S of Horsham off the A24

Standing at the northern end of the Findon Gap, an ancient pass through the South Downs, this village's name is derived from the Saxon for 'settlement of the family of Wassa'. A pretty place, with a varied assortment of buildings, Washington stands between the chalk downland and the sandstone Weald. The village gets an honourable mention in Hilaire Belloc's *West Country Drinking Song*:

> They sell good beer at Haslemere
> And under Guildford Hill.
> At Little Cowfold as I've been told
> A beggar may drink his fill:
> There is a good brew in Amberley too,
> And by the bridge also;
> But the swipes they take in at Washington Inn
> Is the very best beer I know.

Just southeast of the village, and not far from the South Downs Way, lies one of the county's most striking landmarks - **Chanctonbury Ring**. An Iron Age hillfort, the site is marked by a clump of beech trees, planted in 1760 by Charles Goring who inherited the hill along with Wiston Park. Many of the trees suffered during the October hurricane of 1987, though sufficient remain to make this an eye-catching sight on the horizon. Meanwhile, the part-16th and part-19th century mansion of **Wiston House** is now leased by the Foreign Office and, though it is not open to the public, views of the house and the park can be seen from the road leading to village church.

The countryside around Chanctonbury Ring inspired the composer John Ireland who, towards the end of his life in the 1950s, bought **Rock Mill** which lies below the hill. A converted tower mill, a plaque on the wall records that Ireland lived the happiest years of his life here before his death in 1962.

BILLINGSHURST

6½ miles SW of Horsham on the A272

This attractive small town, strung out along Roman Stane Street, was, in the days before the railways, an important coaching town and several good former coaching inns, including the 16th

TACK A ROUND

41a High Street, Billingshurst, West Sussex RH14 9PP
Tel: 01403 783862 Fax: 01403 785962
e-mail: sales@tackaround.co.uk

Strung out along an old Roman road, Billingshurst was once an important stop on the coaching route, and a number of the old coaching inns survive. The stage coaches have long gone, but riding for pleasure is a popular activity in this part of the world, and riders will find all that they need for themselves and their horses at **Tack A Round** in the High Street.

This thriving centre of excellence for all things equestrian, owned and run by rider-turned-business lady Alison Sturrock, is

stocked with an impressive range of clothes and tack, including saddles, leathers, country and wet weather wear, hats, crops, bits and other essential equipment. There are also many accessories, including books and videos on riding and the care of horses. At the back of the shop is a workshop for the repair of saddles and leather equipment. Tack A Round is a qualified saddle fitter and a member of the Society of Master Saddlers.

century Olde Six Bells, can still be found in the old part of the town. The Norman parish **Church of St Mary** has a 13th century tower but most of the rest of the building dates from the 15th to 16th centuries apart from some unfortunate Victorian restoration to the east end.

ITCHINGFIELD

3 miles SW of Horsham off A264

The parish church, in this tiny village, has an amazing 600-year-old belfry tower, the beams of which are entirely held together with oak pegs. During a restoration programme in the 1860s, workmen found a skull, said to have been that of Sir Hector Maclean, on one of the belfry beams. A friend of the vicar of the time, Sir Hector was executed for his part in the Jacobite Rising of 1715 and, presumably, his old friend thought to keep his gruesome souvenir in a safe place. In the churchyard of this early 12th century building is a little priest's house, built in the 15th century as a resting place for the priest who rode from Sele Priory at Upper Beeding to pick up the parish collection.

RUDGWICK

5½ miles NW of Horsham on the B2128

A typical Wealden village of charming tile-fronted cottages, the 13th century village church has a fine Sussex marble font in which the shells of sea creatures have been fossilised in the stone.

WARNHAM

2 mile NW of Horsham off the A24

This small, well-kept village is best known as the birthplace of the poet Percy Bysshe Shelley. He was born in 1792 at **Field Place**, a large country house just outside the village, and this is where he spent a happy childhood exploring the local countryside and playing with paper boats

THE FOX INN

A281 Bucks Green, Rudgwick, West Sussex RH12 3JP
Tel: 01403 822386
e-mail: fish@foxinn.co.uk
website: www.foxinn.co.uk

Landlords Simon and Erica Godsland put a lifetime's experience in catering and brewery management to excellent use in running **The Fox Inn**, one of the most delightful country inns for miles around. The bars and non-smoking restaurant feature many lovely traditional features, and outside there are large gardens and lawns, parking for 50 cars and an area where children can romp. The Fox is not just a splendid 'local' with a fine range of Sussex ales, it's also a fine restaurant.

Food is served all day, and the printed menu and blackboard snacks offer a really mouthwatering

choice. Baguettes served with chips and salad are meals in themselves, and the main menu specialises in seafood, with dishes like Foxy's famous fish pie, crab & salmon fishcakes, traditional fish & chips in a Sussex beer batter (also available to take away), and grilled sea bass with roasted vegetables and herb butter. For those who wish to push the boat out, the mighty fruits de mer platter – 48 hours notice needed - includes lobster, crab, king prawns, mussels, oysters, cockles, winkles and whelks. Most of the wines can be ordered by the bottle or two sizes of glass.

on the lake at the house. Famously, the young poet was cast out of the family home by his father who did not approve of his profession, and while there are many Shelley memorials in the parish church Percy has no memorial. Shelley was drowned when sailing his boat in a storm in the Gulf of Spezia off the west coast of Italy. His body was washed up on the beach some days later and he was cremated on the beach in the presence of Byron, whom he had recently visited at Livorno. His ashes are buried in Rome, though his heart lies in his son's tomb in Bournemouth.

HAYWARDS HEATH

On first appearances, Haywards Heath appears to be a modern town, situated on high heathland. However, the conservation area around **Muster Green** indicates where the old settlement was originally based. A pleasant open space surrounded by trees, which is believed to takes its name from the obligatory annual 17th century custom of mustering the militia, the green was the site of a battle during the Civil War. Here, too, can be found Haywards Heath's oldest building, the 16th century **Sergison Arms** which takes its name from the landed family who once owned nearby Cuckfield Park.

The modern town has grown up around the station to which Haywards Heath owes its prosperity as the two nearby villages of Lindfield and Cuckfield both refused to allow the railway to run through them when the line from London to the south coast was laid in the 19th century.

AROUND HAYWARDS HEATH

LINDFIELD
1 mile NE of Haywards Heath on the B2028

This famous beauty spot is everyone's idea of the perfect English village: the wide common was once used for fairs and markets, the High Street leads up hill to the church and there are some splendid domestic buildings from tile-hung cottages to elegant Georgian houses. The village is also home to **Old Place**, a small timber framed Elizabethan manor house that is said to have been Queen Elizabeth's country cottage and the cottage next door is said to have been Henry VII's hunting lodge. Sited on a hill top, the 13th century village church with its large spire was a useful landmark in the days when the surrounding area was wooded. Beside the churchyard is **Church House**, which was originally The Tiger Inn. During the celebrations after the defeat of the

TUFNELLS

75 High Street, Lindfield, West Sussex RH16 2HN
Tel: 01444 483200
website: www.tufnells.co.uk

Located on the B2028 a mile northeast of Haywards Heath, Lindfield is many people's idea of the perfect English village, with some splendid old buildings and a main street leading up the hill to the church. One of the real gems in this street is

Tufnells, a delightful shop filled with lovely things for the home and garden. Owner Christine (Chrissie) White opened here in 1997, and has built up a business that wins great acclaim for the range and quality of the goods in stock.

Among the items on display are small pieces of antique furniture and some modern pieces (including Gustavian furniture from Sweden); gardeners' accessories; beautiful hand-painted boxes; lamps, lighting and tableware; velvet cushions, bags and make-up pouches; crystal and ceramics; Angela Hale jewellery; luxurious goods in leather and suede; soaps, bath gels, lotions, lavender and rose bags – and the wonderful range of candles from the Paris company Point à la Ligne – available in up to 60 different perfumes. Chrissie also offers an interior design service, with lots of colours and fabrics to choose from, and plenty of readily available help and advice.

Spanish Armada in 1588, the inn supplied so much strong ale to the villagers that the bell ringers broke their ropes and cracked one of the church bells. The inn was one of the village's busy coaching inns in the 18th and 19th centuries when Lindfield was an important staging post between London and Brighton.

ARDINGLY

3½ miles N of Haywards Heath on the B2028

Ardingly is chiefly famous for being the home of the showground for the South of England Agricultural Society. Although there is some modern building, the old part of the village has remained fairly unspoilt. **Ardingly College**, a public school, founded by the pioneering churchman Nathaniel Woodard in 1858 is a large red brick building with its own squat towered chapel. The village church, around which the old part of

Ardingly is clustered, dates from medieval times though there is much Victorian restoration work. Inside can be found various brasses to the Tudor Culpeper family while, outside, the churchyard wall was used, in 1643, as a defensive position by the men of Ardingly against Cromwell's troops who came to take the Royalist rector.

To the west of the village, a tributary of the River Ouse has been dammed to form **Ardingly Reservoir**, a 200-acre lake which offers some excellent fishing as well as waterside walks and a nature trail.

Just north of Ardingly, at the top end of the reservoir, lies **Wakehurst Place**, the Tudor home of the Culpeper family, who arrived here in the 15th century. The present house, a striking Elizabethan mansion, was built in 1590 by Edward Culpeper and the house and estate were eventually left to the National Trust in 1963 by Sir Henry Price. Over the years,

Horsted Keynes

Distance: 5.9 miles (9.4 kilometres)

Typical time: 220 mins

Height gain: 40 metres

Map: Explorer 135

Walk: www.walkingworld.com
ID:1076

Contributor: Matthew Mayer

Access Information:

By car, there is free parking at Horsted Keynes and Sheffield Park. You can reach Kingscote Station, the northern terminus of the Bluebell Railway, by bus from East Grinstead Station. Buses also run to Horsted Keynes on Saturdays and Sundays.

Additional Information:

Make sure you check the timetable if you are planning to travel using the Bluebell Railway. Phone 01825-722370 (24 hours) or visit www.bluebell-railway.co.uk

Description:

Starting from the Bluebell Railway station at Horsted Keynes, the route heads first through pretty Horsted Keynes Village. It then heads south through woodland and farmland, crossing the railway at one point. Following the West Sussex Border Path for some of its route, the walk then heads east towards Sheffield Park Station, the southern terminus of the Bluebell Railway. The railway uses original steam locomotives to give today's visitors a taste of the 'Age of Steam'. From Sheffield Park it is possible to return to Horsted Keynes by the railway for around £3.

Features:

Lake/Loch, Pub, Toilets, Birds, Food Shop, Public Transport, Tea Shop, Woodland

Walk Directions:

1 Starting from outside Horsted Keynes Station, turn left following the sign 'Car Park and Picnic Area'. Continue along the road at the rear of the car park.

2 Take the first right turn towards the wooden gates. Pass through the metal kissing-gates on the right of the wooden gates, down a wooded path. Ignore a gate on the right and instead continue over a stile, following the public footpath signs, past a field and over another stile. You reach a minor road. Turn left and cross over into the drive of the first house on the other side (Leamlands Barn).

3 Walk up the drive and take the path through the metal gate (quite heavy, lift it up to swing it). At the rear of the properties, turn right along the grassy path. At the field boundary, cross over into the next field and follow the path round to the left and over a stile. A public footpath sign confirms the route. At the crossroads, go straight on, following the public footpath sign. You cross over a small bridge and then at the end of the path, three more bridges lead onto a track.

4 Turn right along the track, passing a small lake on your left. At the crossroads take the minor path ahead, following the red arrow (High Weald Circular Walk). You cross over a farm track but stay on the waymarked path. You cross over one stile, then pass into a wide path between two fields.

5 At the end of the path, turn right into this road. At the junction go straight across past the 'No Vehicles' signs. At the top of the hill cross over the main road into Horsted Keynes. There are two pubs (the Green Man and the Crown) along the road on the left. Continuing with the walk, take the left fork down Chapel Lane, passing some tennis courts. At the junction go straight on along Wyatts Lane. The road curves to the right, following signs for 'West Sussex Border Path' (WSBP).

6 At the turnings to Wyatts and Milford Place, take the track straight ahead. You emerge onto another track to turn right and keep on the WSBP. There are a several right turns which you should ignore as you walk through a small wood. When you emerge from the wood, the path climbs a small hill. At the top of the hill, turn left along the WSBP.

7 Turn right up the road. Stick to the road until you reach a T-junction, where you should take the left fork to reach the main road.

8 Head right along the road for around 100m. Take the next left towards Kidborough Farm. Take the right fork off the path at the 'No Horses' sign and skirt along the side of the field and nta a small wood. When you emerge from the wood you pass through two fields before reaching the road.

9 Turn right along the road.

10 Just past 'Town Place', turn left into the field and skirt round it on the left-hand side. You soon pick up the footpath signs which lead you across the field. Take the stile and bridge at the corner of the field and turn right on the path onto which you emerge.

11 Just before you reach the railway line, you reach this junction. Don't take the path ahead, which ends up running parallel to the railway line. Instead look for the footpath sign in the bushes on your right. This path takes you across the railway on a bridge. Then

follow the signs across the next field. Cross over this stile at the far end of the field. Two more stiles take you to the road.

12 Turn left down the road, past the Sloop pub. Turn left down this driveway to Bacon Wish and Field Cottage, regaining the WSBP. Pass over a stile into the wood on a wide track.

13 About 120m into the wood, bear right down this smaller path, staying on the WSBP. The wide track straight on through the forest is not a public right of way. Follow the small path through the wood, over a small stile. You exit the wood over a stile at this signpost. The signpost points you diagonally left across the open space towards another wooden signpost, which you should head straight for.

14 At the three-way signpost, leave the WSBP and follow the public footpath sign left across the open space towards the wood, where there is another stile. Go over the stile and follow the path, well marked with yellow arrows, through the wood. About 500 metres into the wood, follow the arrows right down this path. Shortly afterwards, turn right onto a wider track.

15 Shortly afterwards, bear left down this path, following the yellow arrows. The path continues through the wood, descending a slight slope; watch your footing! At the end of the path cross over the stile, bringing you to the edge of a large field.

16 Turn left and make your way along the edge of the field by the trees. When you reach two small benches at the corner of the wooded area, carry on straight ahead on the track to the wooded area on the far side of the field. Carry on skirting along the wood to the corner of the field. Cross over the stile and turn right across the grass through the wooden gate. Follow the road left at the fork, past a caravan park and farm buildings. Continue until you reach the main road.

17 Turn left along the road. You pass the entrance to Express Dairies. About 100m further on on the left is the entrance to Sheffield Park station. From here, it is possible to catch a train back to Horsted Keynes station where the walk began.

Wakehurst Place

Gardens at Kew, the 500-acre gardens are open to the public throughout the year. As well as the varied and magnificent display of plants, trees and shrubs, visitors can take in the exhibitions in the house on local geology, habitats and woodlands of the area. Wakehurst Place is also home to the **Millennium Seed Bank**, a project which aims to ensure the continued survival of over 24,000 plant species world-wide.

but particularly during the 20th century, the owners of Wakehurst Place have built up a splendid collection of trees and shrubs in the natural dramatic landscapes of woodlands, valleys and lakes. Now leased to the Royal Botanic

WORTH

8 miles N of Haywards Heath off the B2036

For those with a particular interest in historic churches, the ancient settlement of Worth, which is now all but a suburb

---

THE COACH AND HORSES

School lane, Danehill, Near Haywards Hill,
Sussex, RH17 7JF
Tel: 01825 740369
e-mail: coachandhorses@danehill.biz

Set in attractive countryside, this 19th century rural pub has a relaxed and friendly atmosphere and a mix of chatty customers. It is also home to Harvey, a seven-year-old blonde retriever who is well loved and a great favourite with visitors. There's a cosy little bar with half-panelled walls, polished wooden floorboards and a wood-burning stove in the fireplace. It has an intimate atmosphere and is just the place for concentrating on a game of darts, with drinks available through the big hatch into the bar. That is where the locals gather, crowding round the wooden counter or sitting on the high bar stools enjoying the well kept Harvey's Best or guest beers like Adnams Best or Badger Best from the handpump. This is as good as the traditional English country pub gets and where the visitor can enjoy a realistic slice of village life from a bygone age.

In the summer it's a delight to sit outdoors in the large, attractive garden and enjoy the views over the South Downs, or on the newly opened terrace. Food is an important part of what the **Coach and**

Horses has to offer. Ian and Catherine Philpots, the owners, pride themselves on their bar lunches and the constantly changing evening menu. Standards like mouth watering grilled ciabatta with roasted pepper and goats cheese, appear beside fresh herb risotto and spiced salmon fish cakes with a lime mayonnaise. Old favourites appear on the main menu, like grilled pork loin with confit white cabbage, alongside daily specials such as oven roasted lobster with frites and celeriac remoulade. There's a grand selection of wines available to wash it all down.

of Crawley, is well worth a visit. Considered by many to be one of England's best churches, the Saxon **Church of St Nicholas** was built between 950 and 1050. The massive interior is dominated by three giant Saxon arches. Salvin built the tower in 1871 and also restored the chancel.

The Benedictine monastery and Roman Catholic boys' public school, **Worth Abbey**, to the east of Worth, was originally built as the country house of a wealthy tycoon. Paddockhurst, as it was known, was built by Robert Whitehead, a 19th century marine engineer, who invented the torpedo. It was greatly added to by the 1st Lord Cowdray who purchased the property from Whitehead in 1894. Using Paddockhurst as his weekend retreat, Lord Cowdray, who had amassed a fortune through civil engineering works, spend thousands of pounds on improving the house, including adding painted ceilings and stained glass. After the lord's death, in 1932, the house was purchased by the monks as a dependent priory of Downside Abbey, Somerset and it became an independent house in 1957.

EAST GRINSTEAD
10 miles N of Haywards Heath on the A22

Situated 400 feet above sea level on a sandstone hill, this rather suburban sounding town has a rich history that dates back to the early 13th century. East Grinstead was granted its market charter in 1221. Throughout the Middle Ages, it was an important market town as well as being a centre of the Wealden iron industry. The name, Grinstead, means 'green steading' or 'clearing in woodland' and, though Ashdown Forest is a few miles away today, it was once a much more extensive woodland which provided much of the fuel for the town's prosperity.

Although there is much modern building here, the High Street consists largely of 16th century half-timbered buildings and this is where the splendid **Sackville College** can be seen, set back from the road. However, this is not an educational establishment as the name might suggest, but a set of almshouses, founded in 1609 by the Earl of Dorset. A Grade I listed building, the dwellings built for the retired workers of the Sackville estates, are constructed around an attractive quadrangle. It still provides accommodation for elderly people and guided tours of the building are provided for visitors. The parish **Church of St Swithin** stands on an ancient site but it only dates from the late 18th century as the previous church was declared unsafe after the tower collapsed in 1785.

Beside the porch are three grave slabs in memory of Anne Tree, John Forman and Thomas Dunngate, Protestant martyrs who were burnt at the stake in East Grinstead in 1665.

Before the Reform Act of 1832, only the occupants of East Grinstead's 48 original burgage plots (long, narrow housing allotments) were eligible to vote - making this one of the county's most rotten boroughs. As was common practice elsewhere, the local landed family, the Sackvilles, would ensure that they acquired enough votes to guarantee a comfortable majority.

The arrival of the railways in 1855 ended a period of relative decline in the town and, today, East Grinstead is a flourishing place. Perhaps, however, the town will always be remembered for the pioneering work carried out at the Queen Victoria Hospital during World War II. Inspired by the surgeon, Sir Archibald McIndoe, great advances in plastic and reconstructive surgery were made here to help airmen who had suffered severe burns or facial injuries.

Following McIndoe's death in 1960, the **McIndoe Burns Centre** was built to further the research and the hospital remains the centre of the Guinea Pig Club, set up for and by the early patients of the pioneering surgeon.

The **Town Museum**, housed in East Court, is a fine building that was originally constructed as a private residence in 1769. An interesting place, which tells the story of the town and surrounding area, as well as the life of its inhabitants, the Greenwich Meridian passes through the town at this point.

To the south of East Grinstead lies **Standen**, a remarkable late Victorian country mansion that is a showpiece of the Arts and Crafts Movement. Completed in 1894 by Philip Webb, an associate of William Morris, for a prosperous London solicitor, the house was constructed using a variety of traditional local building materials.

Morris designed the internal furnishings such as the carpets, wallpapers and textiles. Now fully restored, the house, owned by the National Trust, can be seen in all its 1920s splendour, including details such as original electric light fittings. Open to the public, the house is set in a beautiful hillside garden with views over the Ashdown Forest and the valley of the Upper Medway. From near Standen runs the **Bluebell Railway**, which offers a pleasant journey by steam train through the Sussex Weald to Sheffield Park, the railway's headquarters, via the 1930s station at Horsted Keynes.

Nearby **Saint Hill Manor**, one of the finest sandstone buildings in the county, was built in 1792 by Gibbs Crawfurd, the grandfather of the man who brought the railway to East Grinstead in the mid 19th century. Other owners of the house include the Maharajah of Jaipur and Mrs

INGWERSEN

Birch Farm Nursery, Gravetye, East Grinstead, West Sussex RH19 4LE
Tel: 01342 810236
e-mail: info@ingwersen.co.uk
website: www.ingwersen.co.uk

The name of **Ingwersen** has been well known and respected among plant growers and gardeners in this country for almost a century, and it was in 1927 that Walter Ingwersen started his own nursery here in delightful wooded countryside at Gravetye. With his sons Will and Paul, he expanded the business

rapidly, and today it is recognised as having one of the most comprehensive collections of alpines and other hardy plants for sale in the world.

They grow about 900 different plants, mostly alpines, but also dwarf herbaceous plants, shrubs, conifers and bulbs, and their seed list runs to more than 200. They also sell a wide range of associated items, from potting soil and alpine grit to pots, troughs and HTA National Garden Gift Vouchers. Ingwersen plants can be bought at Birch Farm Nursery and at numerous flower shows throughout the UK, including the Royal Horticultural Society Shows held at the RHS Halls in Vincent Square, Westminster.

GRAVETYE MANOR

Near East Grinstead, West Sussex RH19 4HJ
Tel: 01342 810567 website: www.gravetyemanor.co.uk

This peaceful Elizabethan manor house was built in 1598. William Robinson's English garden is surrounded by forest, yet only 30 miles from London. As one of the first country house hotels it remains a shining example in its class, enjoying a Michelin starred restaurant. Visitors can relax in oak panelled sitting rooms, warmed by open log fires. Bedrooms enjoy vistas of the gardens. Dine by candlelight, savouring classical British dishes made by chef, Mark Raffan, with wines from one of Britain's finest cellars. A treat for garden lovers and gastronomes.

Neville Laskey, a generous lady who accommodated the RAF patients of Sir Archibald McIndoe. L Ron Hubbard, the author and founder of the Church of Scientology, was the house's last owner and it was he who oversaw the work to restore the manor to its former glory including the Monkey Mural that was painted in 1945 by Sir Winston Churchill's nephew, John Spencer Churchill. The house and gardens are open to the public.

WEST HOATHLY

5½ miles N of Haywards Heath off the B2028

Situated high on a ridge overlooking the Weir Wood Reservoir to the northeast, this historic old settlement grew up around an ancient crossing point of two routes across the Weald. The squat towered village church was begun before the Norman Conquest and, inside, there are a number of iron grave slabs of the Infield family from nearby Gravetye Manor. In the churchyard, on the south wall, is a small brass in memory of Anne Tree, one of the 16th century East Grinstead martyrs. Lying in woodland just north of the village is **Gravetye Manor**, a splendid stone Elizabethan house built in 1598 for the Infield family, who were wealthy, local iron masters. In 1884, William Robinson, the influential garden designer and gardening

correspondent of *The Times*, bought the house and over the next 50 years created the splendid gardens, following the natural contours of this narrow valley. Today, the manor is a first-class country house hotel.

The village's most impressive building is undoubtedly the **Priest House**, a low half-timbered 15th century house probably built as the estate office for the monks of Lewes Priory who owned the manor here. This would originally have been one vast room but, in Elizabethan times, it was altered to a substantial yeoman's house. It is now a museum belonging to the Sussex Archaeological Society, filled with 18th and 19th century furniture and a fascinating collection of kitchen equipment, needlework and household paraphernalia. The museum is set in a classic English country garden with a formal herb garden containing over 150 culinary, medicinal and folklore herbs.

BURGESS HILL

3 miles SW of Haywards Heath on the B2113

This small town, which has recently undergone much central redevelopment, owes its existence to the arrival of the railway in the mid 19th century. Compared to many of the settlements in the surrounding area, Burgess Hill is a relatively new addition to the landscape. It does, however, have a particularly spacious cricket pitch and some older buildings remaining from what was once a small settlement.

KEYMER

5½ miles SW of Haywards Heath on the B2116

Situated between two tributaries of the River Adur, this old village was once a centre of smuggling. In 1777 over £5,000 worth of goods were seized by customs. Keymer is, however, better known for its famous works that are still producing handmade bricks and tiles. Surprisingly, though, the double spire of Keymer's Church of St Cosmas and St Damian (patron saints of physician and surgeons) is covered not with tiles but with wooden shingles.

HURSTPIERPOINT

5½ miles SW of Haywards Heath on the B2116

Surrounded by unspoilt countryside, this pretty village, which takes its name from the Saxon for wood - *hurst* - and Pierpoint after the local landowning family, was mentioned in the Domesday Book. The narrow High Street here is particularly attractive with some fine Georgian buildings and a tall Victorian church, designed by Sir Charles Barry, the architect of the Houses of Parliament. Another imposing building, dominating the countryside to the north of the village, is **Hurstpierpoint College** chapel. Like nearby Lancing and Ardingly, the school was founded in the 19th century by Nathaniel Woodard.

To the south of the village lies the ancestral home of the Norman Pierpoint family. They settled here in the 11th century close to their powerful relative William de Warenne and **Danny** was, in those days, a modest hunting lodge situated below the grassy mound of Woolstonbury Hill. In the mid 15th

century, the family had to flee after the then owner, Simon de Pierpoint, deliberately murdered some of his serfs, and the house was burnt to the ground in retaliation. The site stood empty until, in the late 16th century, Elizabeth I granted the estate to George Goring who built the impressive classic Elizabethan E shaped mansion seen today.

However, the history of Danny remains a somewhat turbulent story as Goring, a staunch Royalist, was forced to give up his splendid mansion at the end of the Civil War. It was the Campion family, coming here in the early 18th century, who added the Queen Anne south facing façade as well as remodelling the interior by lowering the ceiling in the Great Hall and adding a grand, sweeping staircase.

Danny's finest hour came, in 1918, when the Prime Minister, Lloyd George rented the house, and it was here that the terms of the armistice with Germany were drawn up to end World War I. A plaque in the Great Hall commemorates the meetings held here by Lloyd George's war cabinet and, during the time that the cabinet was here, Lloyd George was known to have walked up Woolstonbury Hill to seek peace and solitude. The house also saw service during World War II when it was occupied by British and Commonwealth troops. Today, Danny is owned by the Country Houses Association and let out in 28 serviced apartments. The house is open to the public on a limited basis.

CLAYTON

6 miles SW of Haywards Heath on the A273

This small hamlet, which lay on a Roman road between Droydon and Portslade, is home to a rather ordinary Saxon church with some early medieval wall paintings, which are undoubtedly the work of the renowned group of artists from St Pancras Priory, Lewes.

Vincent Reed Furniture

103a Keymer Road, Keymer, nr Hassocks,
West Sussex BN6 8QL
Tel: 01273 845678
e-mail: info@vincentreed.com
website: www.vincentreed.co.uk

Vincent Reed, who started his career as a restorer of antique furniture in The Lanes at Brighton, has built up a loyal customer base since starting his own business in the picturesque village of Keymer. **Vincent Reed Furniture** offers a unique and comprehensive service that includes handmade oak refectory tables, antique furniture, exclusive home accessories and the restoration of both antique and modern furniture. Vincent's highly acclaimed oak tables are constructed by traditional techniques from ancient pit-sawn timbers finished with natural beeswax. Each is unique, with a character determined by two men with a pit saw, centuries of ageing and Vincent's expertise.

After many years the wood takes on a glorious patination and colour; the original surface character is maintained and is never artificially distressed. To complement the furniture, Vincent Reed sells high-quality home accessories from around the world, including hand-thrown pottery from Provence, Italian pewter, locally made metal works, hand-made designer lamps, silks, cushions and throws. Vincent is a master of all the skills associated with furniture restoration, and his work has been commissioned by English Heritage and the National Trust as well as hundreds of satisfied private customers.

The settlement lies at one end of a mile long railway tunnel, which was constructed in the 1840s to take the still busy London to Brighton track. An engineering wonder of its day, the northern end of **Clayton Tunnel** is dominated by a large Victorian folly, **Tunnel House**, built in a grand Tudor style to house the tunnel keeper.

On a hill overlooking Clayton stand two windmills, known rather unimaginatively as **Jack and Jill**. The larger of the pair, Jack, is a tower mill dating from 1896. It fell into disuse in the 1920s and, now without its sails, has been converted into an unusual private residence. Jill, a post mill that originally stood in Brighton, was brought here by oxen in 1852, has been fully restored and is still capable of grinding corn.

Pyecombe

7 miles SW of Haywards Heath on the A23

This ancient village stands on a prehistoric track that runs along the South Downs from Stonehenge to Canterbury. Home to one of the smallest downland churches, this simple, Norman building has a 12th century lead font that survived the Civil War by being disguised by the crafty parishioners in a layer of whitewash.

Pyecombe is renowned among farmers, and particularly shepherds, as being the home of the best possible shepherd's crook, the **Pyecombe Hook**. It was the crook's curled end, known as the guide, that made the Pyecombe Hook so special as it was a very efficient mechanism for catching sheep though it was hard to fashion. Throughout the 19th and early

GURNITURE THE GREEN FURNITURE CO

Pangdean Farm, London Road, Pyecombe,
nr Brighton, East Sussex
Tel: 01273 841411
website: www.gurniture.co.uk

Marcus Kilgour started by making tables for family
and friends before setting up **Gurniture - The
Green Furniture Company** in the ancient village
of Pyecombe, a short drive north of Brighton and
very close to the junction of the A27/A23.
Pyecombe was once renowned for making the very
finest shepherds' crooks, and Marcus is continuing the tradition of quality and craftsmanship in
his workshop. His young and rapidly expanding business is dedicated to the creation of affordable,
durable furniture made from reclaimed timber treated with environmentally friendly finishes, in

particular, traditional hard-wearing hemp-seed oil. The
simple designs are intended to bring out the natural
beauty of the wood which will grow in character with
wear and tear.

Most of the wood used is reclaimed pine from the
structures of old buildings which is used to make a
variety of pieces, each unique, from tables in all sizes to
bespoke kitchens, shelving, cabinets and CD racks. Using
traditional joining techniques Gurniture is made to last
a lifetime and become the heirlooms of future
generations. Pieces can be tailor-made to suit the
individual requirements of customers, who are welcome
to visit the workshop and discuss ideas with Marcus and
his staff.

20th centuries, the village forge turned
out these world famous crooks and,
though they are no longer made today,
several rare examples can be seen in
Worthing Museum.

POYNINGS

8 miles SW of Haywards Heath off the A281

Once an iron working village, Poynings
lies in a hollow below the steep slopes of
Dyke Hill on top of which is situated an
Iron Age hillfort. Just south of Poynings,
and close to the hill, is one of the South
Downs greatest natural features - the
Devil's Dyke. Local legend has it that
this great steep-sided ravine was dug by
the Devil to drown the religious people of
Sussex. Working in darkness, intent on
digging all the way to the coast, he was
half way to the sea when an old woman

climbed to the top of a hill with a candle
and a sieve. The light of the candle woke
a nearby cockerel, whose crowing alerted
the Devil. Looking up, the devil saw the
candle light through the sieve and fled
thinking that the sun was rising.

During Victorian times, the Devil's
Dyke became a popular place from which
to view the surrounding downlands. A
railway was built to connect the village
with Brighton and a cable car was
installed over the ravine. The cable car
has now gone but the site is still a
popular place with motorists, walkers
and hang gliding enthusiasts.

SMALL DOLE

10 miles SW of Haywards Heath on the A2037

Just to the north of this small downland
village, is **Woods Mill**, the headquarters

of the Sussex Trust for Nature Conservation. As well as a nature reserve and the nature trail around the woodland, marshes and streams, the site is also home to an 18th century watermill which houses a countryside exhibition.

EDBURTON

10 miles SW of Haywards Heath off the A2037

This tiny hamlet is named after Edburga, the granddaughter of King Alfred, who is said to have built a church here in the 10th century. However, the present **Church of St Andrew** dates from the 13th century and, inside, can be seen one of only three lead fonts remaining in the county. Though battered and dented from the days of the Civil War, when it was used as a horse trough, the font escaped being melted down for ammunition. On top of the steep downland escarpment, which rises to its highest point here, stands **Castle Ring**, a mound and ditch which are the remains of an 11th century fort.

CUCKFIELD

1 mile W of Haywards Heath on the A272

Pronounced 'Cookfield', this small country town dates back to Saxon times and though it would be particularly charming if the name were to have been derived from the Saxon Cucufleda meaning 'a clearing full of cuckoos', it is more likely that it means 'land surrounded by a quickset hedge'. Situated on the side of a hill, during the 11th century, Cuckfield belonged to the Norman, William de Warenne, who had a hunting lodge and chapel here.

To the north lie **Borde Hill Gardens**, a splendid, typically English garden of special botanical interest in some 200 acres of spectacular Sussex parkland and woods. Colonel Stephenson Clarke, by funding plant hunting expeditions to China, Burma, Tasmania and the Andes, established the collection of plants and trees, which is still maintained by the Colonel's descendants. With displays carefully planted to offer a blaze of colour for most of the year, this garden is well worth exploring.

HANDCROSS

7 miles NW of Haywards Heath on the B2114

Close to this little village, which stood on the old London to Brighton road, are two glorious gardens. To the southeast lie the superb National Trust owned gardens of **Nymans**. Though much of the house that stood on this estate was destroyed by fire in 1947, the empty shell provides a dramatic backdrop to one of the county's greatest gardens. At the heart of Nymans is the round walled garden, created with the help of the late 19th century gardening revivalists William Robinson and Gertrude Jekyll. Elsewhere, the gardens are laid out in a series of 'rooms', where visitors can walk from garden to garden taking in the old roses, the topiary, the laurel walk and the sunken garden.

Just northeast of Handcross is another smaller, though no less glorious garden, **High Beeches Gardens**. Here, in the enchanting woodlands and water gardens, is a collection of rare and exotic plants as well as native wild flowers in a natural meadow setting.

LOCATOR MAP

▲ See other chapters

A329(M) | M4 | Old Windsor
Bracknell
Ascot
Staines ①
Chertsey
Richmond 200
Kingston upon Thames 199
Croydon
Crowthorne
Sandhurst
Camberley
Woking 205
M25
Cobham
Leatherhead
223,224
Sutton 203
Epsom
Caterham
Limpsfield
M25
Aldershot
208,209,210
Guildford
A31 A323 220 216
Farnham 207
Godalming 211
214
213
215
Haslemere
217,218
221,222
Cranleigh
East Horsley
SURREY
Dorking
229
230
178,179,180
Redhill
Oxted
Reigate
233,234
Salfords
M23
Horley
Copthorne
Crawley
Crawley Down
Edenbridge
East Grinstead
Forest Row
Horsham
195,196
181,182
Liss Liphook
Petersfield

ADVERTISERS AND PLACES OF INTEREST

SURREY 4

Surrey's proximity to the capital and its transport links have defined much of its history. The Thames winds through Surrey and many of the present-day villages and towns developed as riverside trading centres in the medieval period or earlier. As the Thames led to the development of medieval and earlier villages, the arrival of the railway in the mid-19th century saw new villages spring up, while others expanded out of all recognition. Rail lines and major roads fan through the whole area from London with the latest contribution to the transport theme being the M25.

However, Surrey is full of historical traces. Great houses, as well as royal and episcopal palaces,

Winkworth Arboretum

were built here from medieval times, and many villages have evidence of Saxon, Celtic, Roman and even late Stone Age settlements. The site of one of England's defining moments, the signing of the Magna Carta in 1215, is at the riverside meadow of Runnymede. The most impressive of all buildings along the Thames is Hampton Court, where Henry VIII expanded Cardinal Wolsey's already magnificent palace.

Farnham, with its lovely Georgian architecture and 12th century castle, is the largest town in southwestern Surrey, while Guildford, the ancient county town of Surrey, is an obvious base for travellers interested in exploring Surrey. Guildford has been the capital of the region since pre-Norman times and the

remains of Henry II's castle
and keep provide
commanding views over the
surrounding area. The old
Georgian cobbled High Street
incorporates the Tudor
Guildhall, with its distinctive
gilded clock. Woking, like
many Surrey towns, was
transformed by the arrival of
the railway in the 19th
century. The Victorian
influence is evident in many
of the larger houses built by
Norman Shaw and other
proponents of the Arts and
Crafts style. The more ornate
style of Victorian
architecture, designed to
reflect the prosperity of a
confident imperial power, is
also represented in the two
massive buildings funded by
Thomas Holloway - the Royal
Holloway College and the
Holloway Sanatorium, which
are near Egham in the north.

Guildford Cathedral

The best of Edwardian architecture is well represented throughout Surrey by
the work of Sir Edwin Lutyens, often working in partnership with the
eminent gardener Gertrude Jekyll.

This varied architectural heritage belies the notion that Surrey is nothing
more than a collection of anonymous suburbs of London. Much of Surrey is
indeed the capital's commuter belt and conurbations like Kingston and
Croydon spread out into a vast hinterland of suburbia. However, around
Guildford and Dorking and near the Sussex border there are small towns and
wayside villages amid rough Down and Weald uplands or thickly wooded
hillsides. The countryside is varied, from the well-maintained plantation of
Kew Gardens, possibly the most famous gardens in the world, to numerous
parks, greens, heaths, commons and open land. Rich farming areas give way
to expanses of heath and woodlands with networks of paths for walkers and
cyclists. The famous Hog's Back section of the A31 is one of the most scenic
drives in the Southeast, with excellent views north and south as it follows the
ridge between Farnham and Guildford through some of Surrey's most
unspoilt countryside.

NORTHEAST SURREY

Surrey's proximity to London often leads people to assume that it is nothing more than a collection of anonymous suburbs extending south and west from the capital. Indeed much of what had originally been (and which steadfastly continues to consider itself) Surrey was absorbed by London in the boundary changes of 1965. Growing conurbations such as Kingston and Croydon house and employ thousands. Rail lines and major roads fan through the area from London.

However this northeast corner of Surrey is also full of historical traces, some well known and others truly hidden gems. Great houses, as well as royal and episcopal palaces, were built here from medieval times, and many villages have evidence of Saxon, Celtic, Roman and even late Stone Age settlements. The countryside is varied, from the well-maintained plantation of Kew Gardens to the rough Down and Weald uplands to the south and numerous parks, greens, heaths, commons and open land in between. The sound of birdsong ringing through the woods and the click of a cricket bat on a village green are as much a part of this stretch of Surrey as the whirring suburban lawnmower.

KINGSTON-UPON-THAMES

The first impression most people have of Kingston is of high-rise office blocks and its famous by-pass, giving it the sense of being totally urbanised and something of a modern creation. However Kingston has been a thriving market town since the Middle Ages, the first of only four Royal Boroughs in England and Wales. In 838 AD it was referred to as 'that famous place called Cyningestun in the region of Surrey'. **The Guildhall**, built in 1935, is solid and functional, but nearby beside the 12th century Clattern Bridge over the River Hogsmill stands the Coronation Stone, said to have been used in the crowning of up to seven Saxon kings. Records show that Kingston was a prosperous town in Anglo-Saxon times. In the Domesday survey of 1086 it is recorded as having a church, five mills and three salmon fisheries.

Kingston has been a river crossing place since medieval times, the present stone bridge replacing the old wooden bridges in 1828. Regular street markets have been held on a site by the bridge since the 17th century, and around the market a well-preserved medieval street plan can be explored. Kingston parish church was completely rebuilt in neo-Gothic style in the 19th century, but its interior still contains many medieval monuments. On the London Road, however, is a real medieval relic - the chapel of **St Mary Magdalene**, dating from the 14th century.

Guided walks of Kingston's historical heritage start from the Market Place every Sunday in summer.

The district of **Coombe**, to the east of Kingston, was rebuilt by prosperous Victorians. Large houses, built in a variety of architectural styles, came to symbolise the solid financial standing of their owners. Unfortunately, few of these houses survive apart from their impressive gate lodges, but there are a few exceptions such as Coombe Pines in Warren Cutting.

John Galsworthy began the development of Coombe Hill, and two of his own houses survive - Coombe Leigh, which is now a convent, and Coombe Ridge, today a school. Galsworthy's son was the famous novelist and set Soames Forsyte's house in Coombe.

HERMES HOTEL

1 Portsmouth Road, Kingston-upon-Thames, Surrey KT1 2LU
Tel/Fax: 020 8546 5322
e-mail: hermeshotel@btopenworld.com
website: www.hermeshotel.co.uk

Family owned and run, **Hermes Hotel** is a listed 17th century redbrick building on the A307 Portsmouth Road, just across the road from the River Thames. Ten bedrooms - six singles and four twins/doubles - provide comfortable, practical Bed & Breakfast accommodation, and there's a cosy residents' bar. Kingston town centre, with a plethora of shops, pubs and restaurants, is a short walk along the river, and the hotel offers easy access to the A3 and M25.

AROUND KINGSTON

TWICKENHAM
4 miles N of Kingston on the A310

Lying on the west side of the Thames just a few miles north of Hampton Court Palace, Twickenham is a thriving community that makes the most of its riverside setting. Perhaps more than anything else Twickenham is renowned as the headquarters of Rugby Union Football in Britain, a role it has played since 1907. The recently rebuilt stadium plays host to England home internationals as well as the annual Varsity match between Oxford and Cambridge. The **Museum of Rugby** allows visitors to savour the history and atmosphere of the sport (see panel below). Running through the players tunnel is enough to get many people's blood rushing, and the museum provides a full account of Twickenham right up to its latest renovations.

Montpelier Row and Sion Row, wonderfully preserved 18th century terraces, are some of the fine old houses in the heart of Twickenham. At **Strawberry Hill**, just to the south of Twickenham, is the villa bought by the author Horace Walpole in 1749 and remodelled into a 'gothic fantasy', which has been described as 'part church,

THE MUSEUM OF RUGBY

Twickenham Stadium, Rugby Road, Twickenham, TW1 1DZ
Tel: 020 8892 8877 Fax: 020 8892 2817
website: www.rfu.com

Few would dispute that sport has an appeal that crosses gender, age and racial barriers. But few people would connect the thrills and spills of top level competition with the standard museum environment.

How can a museum compete with the drama, excitement and appeal of live sport? The answer is simple: today's sports museums with their hands on exhibits and interactive screens and sounds are more than just testaments to facts and figures, but living breathing ways of connecting with the unrivalled excitement that only sport can provide.

You can find out all about rugby, its history and its star players by visiting **The Museum of Rugby**, Twickenham. The word's finest collection of rugby memorabilia is housed at the Museum of Rugby, which takes visitors through the history of the sport from 1823 to the present day. The Museum also offers fans a tour of Britain 's most famous Rugby Stadium.

castle, monastery or mansion'. It is internationally recognised as the first substantial building of the gothic revival. Strawberry Hill is now St Mary's University College, a teachers' training college, but it is open for pre-booked tours, any day except Saturday, in summer. Those eager to pursue other historical associations from that era can find the tomb of the poet Alexander Pope in the Twickenham churchyard.

Richmond Park

Orleans House and Gallery, which houses one of the finest art collections outside of London's national collections, enjoys an enviable location in a woodland garden on the Riverside between Twickenham and Richmond.

On the opposite riverbank, accessible by passenger ferry for most of the year, is **Ham House**, built in 1610 and enlarged in the 1670s. Now in the hands of the National Trust, Ham's lavish Restoration interiors and magnificent collection of Baroque furniture provide a suitable setting for the popular summer ghost walks. It has extensive grounds including lovely 17th century formal gardens. Next door is **Marble Hill House**, a Palladian villa designed by Roger Morris and completed in 1729 for George II's mistress, Henrietta Howard. Visitors can walk in the 66 acres of riverside grounds, take a look at the furniture and paintings displayed in the house, or enjoy a cream tea in the café.

RICHMOND

5 miles N of Kingston on the A307

Richmond is an attractive shopping centre with the usual chain stores and a number of small specialist and antique shops. However the lovely riverside setting along a sweeping curve of the Thames and the extensive Richmond Park help to retain a strong sense of its rich and varied history.

A good place to get acquainted with old Richmond is **Richmond Green**, a genuine village green, flanked on the southwest and southeast edges by handsome 17th and 18th century houses. The southwest side has an older, and more royal, history. It was the site of Richmond Palace, built in the 12th century and passing into royal possession in 1125, when it was known as Shene Palace. The palace was destroyed by Richard II in 1394 but subsequent kings had it rebuilt in stages. The site, right by the green, made it an ideal spot for organising jousting tournaments. The rebuilding and extensions reached their peak under Henry VII, who renamed the palace after his Yorkshire earldom. Elizabeth I died in the palace in 1603. Sadly the only surviving element of the palace is the brick gatehouse beside the village green.

Just off the northeast flank of the green is the **Richmond Theatre**, an imposing Victorian building with an elaborate frontage facing the street. **Richmond Riverside**, a redevelopment scheme dating from the late 1980s, stretches along the Thames. It comprises pastiche Georgian buildings complete with columns, cupolas and facades and includes houses, offices and commercial premises. Among the modern buildings, however, there remain a few of the original Georgian and Victorian houses, including the narrow, three-storey Heron House, where Lady Hamilton and her daughter Horatia came to live soon after the Battle of Trafalgar. The riverside walk ends at Richmond Bridge, a handsome five-arched structure built of Portland stone in 1777 and widened in the 1930s. It is the oldest extant bridge spanning the Thames in London.

Richmond's Old Town Hall, set somewhat back from the new developments at Richmond Bridge, is the home of the **Museum of Richmond**, a fascinating privately run museum that provides a unique perspective on Richmond's history and special significance in English life. The museum's permanent displays chronicle the story of Richmond, Ham, Petersham and Kew - communities that grew and prospered along the Thames downstream from Hampton Court. The collections of the Museum of Richmond concentrate on different aspects of this history, detailing the rich heritage from prehistoric times through to the present.

Special features and detailed models focus on some of the most noteworthy buildings, such as the Charterhouse of Shene, which was the largest Carthusian Monastery in England. The information about Richmond Palace is a bit of English history in microcosm. Built by Henry VII - and like the town named after his Yorkshire Earldom in 1501 - the Palace was later a favourite home of Elizabeth I.

A number of displays concentrate on the luminaries who have made Richmond their home over the years. Among the roll call of the great and the good are Sir Robert Walpole, Sir Joshua Reynolds, Lady Emma Hamilton, George Eliot, Virginia Woolf, Gustav Holst and Bertrand Russell.

The steep climb of Richmond Hill leads southwards and upwards from the centre of Richmond. The view from Richmond Terrace has been protected by an Act of Parliament since 1902. The Thames lies below, sweeping in majestic curves to the west through wooded countryside. Turner and Reynolds are among the many artists who have tried to capture the essence of this scene, which takes in six counties. A little further up the hill is the entrance to Richmond Park. These 2,400 acres of open land, with deer roaming free, were first enclosed by Charles I as a hunting ground. Set amidst this coppiced woodland is the Isabella Plantation, noted for its azaleas and rhododendrons.

KEW AND KEW GARDENS

7 miles N of Kingston off the A310

Kew, lying just a couple of miles North of Richmond, on a pleasant stretch of the Thames, is a charming 18th century village, favoured by the early Hanoverian kings. They built a new palace here and the handsome 18th century houses, which still surround Kew Green, were built to accommodate the great and the good of the royal circle. The **National Archives** in Kew holds the national archive, 900 years of historical records, including the Domesday Book. The painter Thomas Gainsborough is buried in **Kew Church**.

However, Kew is best known for the **Royal Botanic Gardens**, arguably the most famous gardens in the world. Princess Augusta, mother of George III,

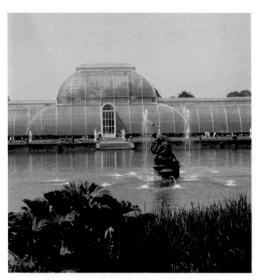

Kew Gardens

laid out an eight-acre botanical garden on the grounds of Kew Palace in 1759. Tranquil and spacious, this garden, now extending over 300 acres, has become an important botanical research centre. Over a million visitors a year are attracted to view the 40,000 species of plants and 9,000 trees which grow here in plantations and glasshouses. The most famous and oldest glasshouse, built in 1848, is the Palm House, which houses most of the known palm species. Nearby is the Water Lily House, full of tropical vines and creepers overhanging its lily pond. The Princess of Wales Conservatory, which opened in 1987, houses plants from 10 different climatic zones, from arid desert to tropical rainforest.

Kew houses Britain's smallest royal residence. The three-storey Kew Palace built in 1631, sometimes nicknamed the Dutch House because of its Flemish-bond brickwork, measures only 50 feet by 70 feet. Queen Caroline acquired it for her daughters in 1730. The only king to have lived in this tiny royal residence was George III, confined here from 1802 during his infamous madness. Behind the palace is a restored 17th century garden, with labels identifying the herbs and their uses.

Another Kew landmark is the octagonal, 10-storey **Chinese Pagoda** standing 163 feet high. Originally, the building was flanked by the Turkish Mosque and the Alhambra, all designed by Sir William Chambers, Princess Augusta's official architect. The ground floor is 50 feet across, with each storey reducing in size until the tenth storey is 20 feet by 10 feet. Built as an exotic folly in the fashion of the times, it now serves a more practical purpose as a landmark for visitors. The co-founder and director of the gardens, Sir William Jackson Hooker and his son Sir Joseph Dalton Hooker, are both buried in the churchyard of St Anne, Kew Green. Here, too, lie the artist Thomas Gainsborough and the portrait painter John Zoffany.

MORTLAKE

7 miles N of Kingston on the A205

Mortlake is best known as the finishing point of the Oxford and Cambridge Boat Race. Although it was once an attractive riverside village, it is now dominated by the large brewery building. However a series of handsome 18th century houses stand along Thames Bank, towards Chiswick Bridge and the famous Victorian explorer Richard Burton is buried in an unusual tent-shaped tomb in the cemetery.

WIMBLEDON

3 miles E of Kingston on the A219

To most people Wimbledon is synonymous with the **All-England Lawn**

Tennis Championships held each year at the end of June and in early July. However, the grounds of the All England Lawn Tennis and Croquet Club are open throughout the year and the Wimbledon Lawn Tennis Museum has a range of exhibits from the languid era of long flannel trousers to nail-biting tie-breaks and disputed line calls. However there is more to Wimbledon than tennis. In fact, the Championship fortnight is a time to avoid Wimbledon, since tennis fans throng the streets and every route in and out is clogged with traffic.

The centre of Wimbledon is a thriving commercial area, with stores lining the High Street. Here, cheek by jowl with anonymous 1960s buildings, are a few gems. Eagle House, just west of the National Westminster bank building, was built in 1613. Its Jacobean appearance, with three large bay windows by its central entrance, still conveys a harmonious grandeur, which in its day would have dominated its neighbours. From Wimbledon itself, Wimbledon High Street climbs steeply to the west towards Wimbledon Village, which has more of a boutique and bistro feel to it. Handsome residential streets lead off the High Street on its climb, and there are expansive views looking east across South London.

Further above Wimbledon Village is **Wimbledon Common**, covering more than 1,000 acres, criss-crossed by walking and riding trails, home of the Wombles and one of the capital's largest areas of public access. At the southwest corner is an Iron Age mound, called **Caesar's Camp**, although it is not Roman, but dates from around 250 BC. Archaeological evidence indicates that people have occupied this area since the Paleolithic era, some 3,000 years ago. However it did not become common land with legal public right of access until the Wimbledon and Putney Commons Act of 1871, after local residents opposed Earl Spencer's intention to enclose it.

New Malden

2 miles S of Kingston on the A2043

Just a few miles east of Hampton Court and just south of both Richmond Park and Wimbledon Common is New Malden. Excellent road and rail connections link this neat suburb with Central London as well as points south. New Malden makes a good base for exploring the nearby sights, particularly easy by public transport, avoiding traffic and parking problems.

There are a few surprises lurking in this corner of suburbia. Just by the church on Church Road is the red-brick Manor House, dating from the late 17th century. Further along, to the northeast, is a duck pond, flanked by the Plough Inn. This pub seems modern but its core was built more than 500 years ago.

Surbiton

1 mile S of Kingston on the A307

Surbiton is a well-heeled suburb adjoining Kingston, which escapes much of the traffic and commercial build-up that bedevils its northern neighbour. Handsome properties and good transport connections to London and the south coast make Surbiton one of the most desirable locations in the London commuter belt. Surbiton was called Kingston New Town and Kingston-on-Railway as it developed in the early 19th century. Most of the public buildings date from this period and the architecture of churches such as St Andrew and St Matthew are good examples of the Gothic Revival that was so dominant at the time.

The A307 follows the course of the Thames through Surbiton, with lovely views of Hampton Court Park on the opposite bank of the river. Hampton Court Palace is just over a mile away from Surbiton.

KINGSTON TO CROYDON

CHEAM
5 miles E of Kingston on the A217

Roughly equidistant between Kingston and Croydon, Cheam is one of the prettier suburbs of this area, retaining a green and leafy feel, largely due to the number of substantial houses with large gardens. Several houses in Cheam open their gardens as part of the National Gardens Scheme Charitable Trust.

As with so many other parts of Surrey where London has encroached, Cheam has lost much of its overtly medieval elements, but careful detective work can lead to some pleasant surprises. St Dunstan Church, built in the 1860s, is a large and uninspiring Victorian building but its courtyard contains the surviving portion of the medieval parish church - the **Lumley Chapel**, which was the chancel of the old church. The roof inside was remodelled in 1582 by Lord Lumley, who also commissioned the three finely carved marble and alabaster tombs. A series of delightful and well-preserved brasses commemorates Cheam notables from the 15th and 16th centuries.

Whitehall is a timber-framed building built around 1500. The history of the house and of those who lived in it over its 500 years is chronicled within.

CARSHALTON
6 miles E of Kingston on the A232

The heart of old Carshalton is clustered around two ornamental ponds, which were created in the 18th century from the old mill pond and an adjoining area of wet land. The Portland Stone bridge was probably designed by the Italian architect Giacomo Leoni for Thomas Scawen, who owned nearby Stone Court. Part of his estate, remains as Grove Park, bought by the council in the 1920s "to preserve it as an open space ... and to obtain control of the beautiful ornamental waters which form such an attractive centre to the area". Around this area are several fine old houses with grounds that are open to the public.

One of them, **Carshalton House**, now Saint Philomena's School, was finished in 1713 for Sir John Fellowes, a governor of the South Sea Company. The house is imposing, especially when first seen on the road from Sutton. It is a solid affair of red and yellow brick standing two storeys high, with an attic storey above the cornice. The harmonious, yet restrained look of the house is exactly the effect that so appealed to architects at the time of Queen Anne. The porch, built about 50 years later, with its Corinthian columns reflects a renewed love of classical embellishment. Outside is an impressive early 18th century water tower, which blends in with the architecture of the main house. It housed a water-powered pump, which lifted water from the river into a cistern, which fed the house.

Honeywood, now the **Honeywood Heritage Centre**, stands beside the upper pond. The original building is 17th century but was considerably extended at the turn of the century. Inside it is furnished in Edwardian style including the paint colours and has displays on local history including stucco and pottery from Nonsuch Palace.

Two miles south of Carshalton, on the downs, is a public park with some majestic trees. These formed part of the grounds of a stately home, The Mansion, which was destroyed in an air raid in 1944. It was the home of the 12th Earl of Derby, founder of the famous horse race that bears his name.

BEDDINGTON

7 miles E of Kingston off the A235

Croydon Airport, which was located east of Beddington village, closed down in 1959, leaving room for the development of several housing estates, which tend to dominate the village. However, traces of Beddington's past are visible in its Church of St Mary, a large building, which was probably begun in the 11th century. The local landowner Sir Nicholas Carew left money for rebuilding the church in the late 14th century, and the **Carew Chapel** bears his name. He, along with many of his descendants, is commemorated in brasses in this chapel and in the chancel of the church. One of the most attractive later additions is the organ gallery, built in 1869. The player's space is screened like a minstrel's gallery.

CROYDON

9 miles E of Kingston on the A23

Looking at the high-rise flats and offices, one-way systems and traffic lights and trams, it is hard to imagine that Croydon was not much more than a large village less than two centuries ago. That historic past seems to have been obliterated in a headlong rush to development.

Yet, as with so many other large British towns, first impressions can be deceptive. Nestling beneath some of the most modern high-rises are some much older buildings, including some brick almshouses built in 1599 and now overshadowed by their modern neighbours. More intriguingly, and certainly worth seeking out, are the remains of the palace that was the summer residence of the Archbishops of

Canterbury. The palace was built in the 11th century by Archbishop Lanfranc. It was considerably altered and expanded in subsequent centuries but remained an official residence until 1757. **The Palace** is now part of the Old Palace School for girls but the public can see some of the oldest surviving elements, including the Norman undercroft and the 15th century banqueting hall.

St John the Baptist Church is the largest parish church in Surrey, with a two-storey porch and fine tower. Its enormous size puts it in a league with St Mary Redcliffe in Bristol and St Martin in Salisbury. The 15th century church burnt down in 1867 but was rebuilt by 1870 on the old foundations in a style that largely matches the earlier church. Some original elements of the medieval church remain in the restored tower and the south porch.

Croydon also has a handsome arts complex, the **Fairfield Halls**, which flank one edge of a modern flower-filled square in the heart of Croydon. It comprises a main concert hall, the Peggy Ashcroft Theatre, the Arnhem Art gallery and a general-purpose lounge which doubles as a banqueting hall. **Waddon Caves**, along Alton Road, were the site of late Stone Age and Iron Age settlements, which were inhabited until the 3rd or 4th century AD.

EPSOM

The old market and spa town of Epsom is a prosperous residential centre which lies on the edge of London's southwestern suburbs. In the early 17th century, it was observed that cattle were refusing to drink from a spring on the common above the town and subsequent tests revealed the water to be high in magnesium sulphate, a mineral believed to have highly beneficial medicinal properties. As the fashion for 'taking the waters' grew towards the end of the century, wealthy people from London came in increasing numbers to sample the benefits of Epsom salts and the settlement grew from a small village to a town with its own street market, a charter for which was granted in 1685.

The Derby, Epsom

By the end of the 18th century, the popularity of Epsom's spa was on the decline, but by this time, the town's pleasant rural location within easy reach of the City of London was already starting to attract well-to-do business people; a number of substantial residential homes were built in and around the town during this period, several of which survive to this day. A lively street market continues to be held every Saturday in **Epsom High Street**, a wide and impressive thoroughfare, which contains some noteworthy old buildings, including a **Victorian clock tower**.

Epsom's other main claim to fame is as a horse racing centre. Each year in early June, the Downs to the southeast of the town take on a carnival atmosphere as tens of thousands of racing enthusiasts come to experience the annual Classic race meeting and the colourful fun fair,

HORTON COUNTRY PARK

The Ranger Service, Epsom & Ewell Borough Council, Town Hall, The Parade, Epsom KT18 5BY
Ranger Service   01372 741191
Horton Children's Farm   01372 743984
Equus Equestrian Centre   01372 743084
Horton Country Club   020 8393 8400

Horton Country Park is a rural landscape of fields, hedgerows, woods and ponds of great wildlife and historical interest. This range of habitats supports wildlife which is numerous and varied including many trees and flowers, a plethora of insects, many birds including the Park's emblem, the green woodpecker, and also mammals such as deer, foxes, and water voles.

Good tracks and horse rides, most with gentle or no gradient, allow you to explore the Country Park, and many of the hard surfaced rides follow the route of the old Horton Light Railway.

There is also a children's farm, Equus Equestrian Centre, and the Horton Park Country Club (with an 18 hole golf course), occupying sites within the Country Park. Other facilities include two rooms for public hire. One is used as a field studies centre, often used by the Ranger Service and schools for environmental education. The other room is used for band practices, parties and other events.

which accompanies it. Informal horse racing took place on **Epsom Downs** as long ago as 1683 when Charles II is said to have been in attendance. Racing was formalised in 1779 when a party of aristocratic sportsmen led by Lord Derby established a race for three year old fillies which was named after the Derbys' family home at Banstead, the Oaks; this was followed a year later by a race for all three year olds, the **Derby**, which was named after the founder himself, although only after he won a toss of a coin with the race's co-founder, Sir Charles Bunbury. (Had Lord Derby lost, the race would have become known as the Bunbury.)

The Oaks and the Derby were a great success and soon achieved classic status along with the St Leger at Doncaster, the earliest to be established in 1776, and the 1,000 Guineas and 2,000 Guineas at Newmarket, established in 1814 and 1809 respectively. The Derby family has maintained its connection with the Derby and the Classics down the years, and in 2004 the 19th Lord Derby won the Oaks with Ouija Board, his only horse in training.

AROUND EPSOM

EWELL
2 miles N of Epsom on the A240

It comes as something of a surprise to find shades of Xanadu in this leafy town lying just north of Epsom. **Nonsuch Park** is a reminder of a grand plan that Henry VIII had to build the finest palace in Christendom. The magnificent Nonsuch Palace was almost finished at Henry's death. Unfortunately it was demolished in 1682 and all that remains is the fine park, which surrounded it, noble in stature and perspective but singularly lacking its intended focal point.

A few other historical attractions make Ewell worth visiting. There is an ancient spring, which was discovered in the 17th century. The 18th century **Watch House**, on Church Street, was once the village lock-up. It is shaped like a small cube, with two narrow doorways under an arch. Its mean and spartan appearance alone must have deterred would-be felons.

Ewell Castle, now a school, is not a medieval fortification. It was completed in 1814 in what was known as the Gothic style. Crenellated and stuccoed, it gives the appearance of a real castle, but the effect is somewhat lessened by its location so close to the road. In addition **Bourne Hall Museum** is well worth a visit (see panel opposite).

BANSTEAD
3 miles E of Epsom on the A217

Banstead is one of the many small towns of Surrey that alert travellers from London that they are entering the real countryside. With the expansion of the Southeast, particularly since the last war, new suburbs have emerged and even towns that were themselves once suburbs have now created their own ring of smaller satellites.

Banstead is one of the exceptions to this creeping urbanisation, and the Green Belt Act of 1938 has helped it retain much of its original country feel. It stands at the edge of the rolling green downs that provide ideal riding country. The high street has its fair share of nationally known outlets, but there is still a sense of local flavour and pride in its locally run firms.

All Saints Church is a small, flint and stone parish church, which was built in the late 12th century and early 13th

BOURNE HALL MUSEUM

Spring Street, Ewell, Surrey KT17 1UF
Tel: 020 8394 1734 Fax: 020 8786 7265

If you visit Ewell village, you will soon find **Bourne Hall**. Overshadowed by the trees of a Victorian park, it is a low lying, circular modern building. For the 1960s, when it was built, this was a revolutionary design. Entering Bourne Hall, you look up to the brightly lit mezzanine floor to see a museum. The galleries, which are open plan, have displays drawing on a collection of over 5,000 items acquired over the years through the generosity of local people. After your visit, you can enjoy lunch or a coffee in the newly refurbished restaurant next to the museum.

century. It has a squat appearance, with a low, broad tower and a shingled spire. Like many Surrey churches it was renovated in the 19th century. In this case the Victorian intervention was restrained, and the church now looks much as it must have in the late Middle Ages. Just north of the church is the circular well, with its large roof. The well had formed something of a focal point in medieval times.

The Downs near Banstead are ideal for rambling. Traces of late Stone Age huts were found on the Downs, and the **Galley Hills** are formed by four bowl barrows from that same period.

CHIPSTEAD

7 miles E of Epsom on the A23

A mixture of architectural styles give Chipstead an unusual appearance, as it constitutes a mixture of Victorian model village combined with a few older houses and a good measure of suburban development. Some handsome cottages border a crossroads and there is a pretty ornamental pond in the centre. For a taste of real Victoriana though, it is worth making a short detour about half a mile south to view **Shabden**, a mansion built in the French Renaissance

style but with a large timber porch added. The overall effect is a jarring mixture of styles that contrives to make an unattractive house out of potentially attractive ideas.

COULSDON

7 miles E of Epsom on the A23

Coulsdon is a pretty village that has managed to keep recent housing developments - notably Coulsdon Woods - discreetly removed from the traditional centre. There are pretty cottages in the heart of the village and some of the more substantial farmhouses nearby can be traced to the 15th century. **St John the Evangelist Church**, on the corner of the village green, was built in the late 13th century. The tower and spire were built more than 200 years later but the interior has some well-preserved elements from the original church. Most notable of these is the sedilla, with its circular piers and pointed arches. A sedilla was a seat for (usually three) priests and always located on the south side of the chancel.

The countryside around Coulsdon has more than its share of history. Traces of a 2nd century AD Romano-British settlement have been found on the ridge along **Farthing Down**, and 14 barrows on the ridge are the evidence of a 6th century Saxon burial ground. A number of iron knives, swords and other weapons have been dug from the site. Coulsdon Common, on the way to Caterham, is a tranquil and largely undeveloped spot. Since Saxon times it has been common land given over to grazing, its soil deemed too poor for cultivation.

The **Downlands Circular Walk** conveniently begins and ends at The Fox, an attractive pub which faces Coulsdon Common.

CHALDON

8 miles E of Epsom off the A23

It is well worth making the detour to Chaldon, two-and-a-half miles to the west of Caterham, to have a look at the 11th century church of St Peter and St Paul which stands within striking distance of the old Pilgrim's Way. An unassuming flint-built structure with little to commend it (other than, perhaps, its south tower and shingled spire), the interior contains one of the most outstanding medieval wall paintings still in existence in Britain. Executed in creamy white on a deep red-ochre background, the mural covers the entire west wall of the church. It is believed to have been painted around 1200, but was covered over during the Reformation and remained undiscovered until 1870. The Chaldon Doom, as it has become known, depicts gory scenes from the Last Judgement; a 'Ladder of Salvation' can be seen reaching up to the Kingdom of Heaven from purgatory, a place where horrific punishments are meted out by fork-wielding devils to those guilty of having committed the Seven Deadly Sins. Realistic looking cauldrons, manned by infernal kitchen staff, await the wicked.

CATERHAM

8 miles E of Epsom on the B2031

The route into Caterham town centre from the south passes close to Foster Down, a section of the North Downs Way, which incorporates the impressive **Tupwood Viewpoint**; good views can also be enjoyed from the nearby 778 feet Gravelly Hill.

Caterham itself is a modern and prosperous residential town, which at first glance seems to have little to offer the casual visitor. On the other hand, the town is something of a time capsule. Until 1856 Caterham was a remote Downs village. The arrival of the railway in that year changed everything and the town developed around it and the barracks, which were built in the 1870s. The railway was never extended, so Caterham is a terminus rather than a through station. As such, the 19th century town plan remains unchanged. Near Caterham Railway Station is the **East Surrey Museum** in Stafford Road, which offers an interesting insight into the natural history and archaeology of the surrounding area as well as a collection of objects, which recall the area's rural past.

WARLINGHAM

8 miles E of Epsom on the B269

Successful enforcement of Green Belt policy since the Second World War has helped Warlingham retain much of its green and leafy look, and it is hard to imagine that it lies just a few miles south of bustling Croydon and its built-up suburbs. Warlingham's real fame stems from its church, All Saints, or more specifically two historic events that took place in it. The new English prayer book, authorised by Edward VI, was first used in the parish church. Its compiler, Archbishop Cranmer, attended the service. Four centuries later Warlingham parish church was chosen to host Britain's first televised church service. The church itself was restored and enlarged in Victorian times but dates from the 13th century. It still contains many old elements, including a 15th century wall painting of Saint Christopher and a 15th century octagonal font.

Modern housing has replaced most of the traditional cottages in the heart of Warlingham but there are a few survivors from past centuries. The **Atwood Almshouses**, a two-storey cottage flanked by single-storey cottages, were built in 1663. The vicarage nearby was built in the same year.

TATSFIELD
10 miles E of Epsom off the B269

Tatsfield, high up on the Downs, is something of a curiosity as well as a testament to the enduring power of hyperbole in advertising. In the 1920s a group of small, unassuming cottages sprang up in the wooded landscape just north of the old village green. The verdant setting, combined with the hilly location, led to a promotional campaign urging prospective house buyer to "Come to London Alps".

South of the green is St Mary's, the parish church which dates from about 1300. It stands on its own, commanding panoramic views south over the Weald.

WALTON ON THE HILL
5 miles S of Epsom off the A217

The Hill referred to in the name of this village is one of the many rolling hills that comprise the North Downs. Travellers heading south from London have a real sense of space by the time they reach Walton, and the upland farms strengthen this impression. Buildings -

both residential and commercial - have the harmonious red brick look so typical of this part of Surrey. They were built mainly in the Victorian era, but some of the earlier buildings were constructed from flint, hanging tile and weatherboarding.

Walton Manor is a good example of the tile-hung style and it was built in the 1890s. Its appearance shows the influence of the decorative Arts and Crafts movement, typified by architects such as Norman Shaw. Embedded in one end, however, are the walls of a stone-built manor house of the 14th century; a two storey hall and chapel protrude from the east of the house.

The view south from the centre takes in the extent of the Downs, with the North Downs Way - the traditional **Pilgrim's Way** to Canterbury - running along the ridge on the other side of the broad valley. In the foreground are the rolling grounds of the championship golf course.

NORTH SURREY

The Thames winds through Surrey to the north of Weybridge and many of the present-day villages and towns developed as riverside trading centres in the medieval period or earlier. Romans marched through this part of Surrey during their conquest of Britain, possibly following the trail of the Celts who were already ensconced there. Saxons left their mark later, bequeathing a number of place names, which duly entered the Domesday Book in the 11th century. The most impressive of all buildings along this - and perhaps any - stretch of Thames is Hampton Court. Here England's most larger than life monarch acquired and substantially expanded Cardinal Wolsey's palace until it was fit to match his own personality.

The human mark is much in evidence on this landscape, and for every area of suburban sprawl there also seems to be a corresponding architectural gem. It might be a sensitively preserved church, as in Thorpe, or even an unlikely high street survivor such as the Salvation Army Youth Centre in Sunbury-on-Thames, the newest incarnation of an impressive mansion.

Just as the Thames led to the development of medieval and earlier villages, so too did the arrival of the railway in the mid-19th century. New villages sprang up, while others expanded out of all recognition. The 20th century's contribution to the regional transport theme is the M25, which provides the western and southern border for the area covered in this chapter.

Relatively compact, yet full of interesting detail and constant surprises, this north-central section of the county is a microcosm of Surrey itself.

WEYBRIDGE

Although in many people's minds the epitome of a comfortable and modern commuter belt settlement, Weybridge is a surprisingly long-established settlement. The town takes its name from the bridge over the River Wey on the highway to Chertsey, and there is evidence of such a bridge existing as early as 1235. Tradition also links Weybridge with Julius Caesar, and many historians believe he crossed the Thames near here in 55 BC.

The town once possessed a palace, **Oatlands Park**, in which Henry VIII married his fifth wife, Catherine Howard, in 1540; 110 years later, the building was demolished and the stone used in the construction of the Wey Navigation.

Weybridge stands at the northern end of this historic inland waterway, which was one of the first examples of its kind when it was completed in 1670. It extends for almost 20 miles southwards to Godalming and incorporates large sections of the main river.

The middle of the 17th century, during the interregnum, also saw a remarkable development in Weybridge. **The Diggers**, a radical left-wing group, attempted to build a commune on St George's Hill, although they were thwarted by angry commoners.

Elmbridge Museum, situated in the library in Church Street, is an excellent source of information about the history - and prehistory - of Weybridge. A wide range of exhibits takes in archaeological artefacts, old maps, photographs and paintings of the district. The costume collection is particularly interesting, as it consists of clothes worn by local residents from the late 18th century to the present day.

In 1907, the worlds first purpose-built motor racing track was constructed on the **Brooklands** estate near Weybridge, and in the years which followed, this legendary banked circuit hosted competitions between some of the most formidable racing cars ever made. The Campbell Circuit was designed by record-breaking driver Malcolm Campbell in the 1930s. With the outbreak of World War II, racing came to an end; the track fell into disrepair and Brooklands never again regained its once-pre-eminent position in British motor racing.

In recent years, the circuit has undergone something of a revival with the opening of the **Brooklands Museum**, a fascinating establishment centred on the old Edwardian clubhouse, now restored to its pre-war elegance. There is a collection of the famous cars which raced here, and archive film and

Vintage Cars at Brooklands Museum, Weybridge

was a settlement here during the Saxon period. Walton appears as Waletona in the Domesday Book when the town was recorded as having a church, a fishery and two mills.

In 1516 Henry VIII granted the residents two fairs a year, and these continued until 1878. Walton's relations with Henry were ambivalent. However, in 1538, Walton along with surrounding communities, became incorporated with Henry VIII's Chase of Hampton Court, into what amounted to a private royal hunting preserve. Walton was outside the perimeter fence but it was forced to comply with forest law, which had a detrimental effect on cultivation. Luckily for the residents of Walton, this arrangement was discontinued when Henry died.

Until 1750 the Thames could only be crossed by ferry or ford, but in that year the first bridge was built. This original structure, a wooden toll bridge built by Samuel Dicker, was replaced by several other bridges until the present iron bridge one was built in 1864.

The part-Norman **Church of St Mary** stands on the highest point of the town. It contains a remarkable memorial to Richard Boyle, the Viscount Shannon, which was sculpted by Louis Roubiliac in the mid-18th century.

In Manor Road is the handsome and imposing **Manor House** of Walton Leigh, a timber-framed brick building that dates from the medieval period. Old records indicate that John Bradshaw, President of the Court that sentenced Charles I to death, lodged here.

memorabilia of the circuit's hey day. Bicycles also raced on this circuit and a display of Raleigh bicycles and accessories charts the company's story from its inception in 1886 to the present day. The Wellington Hangar, built across the finishing straight of the track, houses a collection of Brooklands built aircraft including a World War II Vickers Wellington, salvaged from Loch Ness and carefully restored.

AROUND WEYBRIDGE

WALTON-ON-THAMES
2 miles NE of Weybridge on the A244

Standing almost directly opposite Shepperton on the other side of the Thames is Walton-on-Thames. This unassuming London suburb has a surprisingly long and varied pedigree. As with many of the riverside communities along this stretch of the Thames, Walton has a claim to be the site where Julius Caesar forded the Thames during his second invasion of Britain. Hard archaeological evidence for this claim is scant, but there is ample proof that there

EAST & WEST MOLESEY

3 miles NE of Weybridge on the B369

Molesey can trace its history to the 7th century, when grants of land were made to Chertsey Abbey. Among the abbey's estates was 'Muleseg', which meant Mul's field or meadow. The identity of Mul is lost in the mists of time, but his name is commemorated in two riverside communities.

The prefixes east and west, relating to Molesey, were not used until the beginning of the 13th century. In the Domesday Survey Molesey was recorded as comprising three manors tenanted by knights who had arrived with William the Conqueror. East Molesey was originally part of the parish of Kingston-upon-Thames but its growing independence led to its separation from Kingston under a Special Act in 1769.

East Molesey's location just opposite Hampton Court Palace provided a valuable source of income for residents, and ferries did good business until the first bridge spanned the Thames in 1753. The Bell Inn, one of the loveliest inns in Surrey, dates from the 16th century, right at the beginning of Molesey's links with Hampton Court. Matham Manor, about four centuries old, is another link with the past. The Old Manor House, although handsome and impressive, is something of a misnomer. It originally served as the parish workhouse and was never a manor.

West Molesey is a continuation of East Molesey. It is much larger than its parent, but it occupies an even prettier stretch of the Thames. The parish church stands on a site where there has been a church since the 12th century. The present church is largely a legacy of the Victorian era, although the 15th century tower remains. Inside are some other artefacts from the medieval era,

including the piscina. This is a small basin in a wall niche by the altar and was used for cleaning sacramental vessels.

Molesey Hurst, a low, open stretch of land, lies along the Thames in the north of the parish. The land was once used for sporting activities such as archery, cricket, golf and even illicit duelling. It can also claim a cricketing first. It was here, in 1795, that a player was first given out leg-before-wicket.

HAMPTON COURT

4 miles NE of Weybridge on the A309

Hampton Court Palace occupies a stretch of the Thames some 13 miles southwest of London. In 1514 Thomas Wolsey, the Archbishop of York took a 99-year lease on the buildings at Hampton Court. Wolsey created a magnificent residence with new kitchens, courtyards, lodgings, galleries and gardens. Until 1528 Wolsey maintained Hampton Court as his home as well as for affairs of state. However at that point he had fallen from favour with Henry VIII, and found himself forced to appease the monarch by giving him his house. Henry comprehensively rebuilt and extended the palace over the following ten years to accommodate his wives, children and court attendants. Although much of Henry VIII's building work has been demolished over the years, the Great Hall and the Chapel Royal survive, the latter still in use as a place of worship. The Great Hall, which Henry had completed in 1534, having forced the builders to work night and day, has mounted stag heads and fine tapestries lining the walls beneath the intricate hammerbeam roof. It was the scene of theatrical productions during the reigns of Elizabeth I and James I, and among the performing troupes was that of William Shakespeare. Also intact are the enormous Tudor Kitchens, with the huge fireplaces and assortment of

Hampton Court

ancient cooking utensils that would have been used in the 16th century to prepare a feast fit for a king. During the 17th century the Stuart kings lived there both as monarchs and prisoners. James I enjoyed the hunting in the park, while Charles I, was imprisoned here after the Civil War. Charles II built accommodation for his mistress at the southeast corner of the palace.

Approached through Trophy Gate, Hampton Court gives an immediate impression of grandeur and scale. The courtyards and buildings to the left still contain a number of grace and favour apartments. Two side turrets contain terracotta roundels with the images of Roman emperors, which date from Wolsey's time. Anne Boleyn's gateway, opposite Base Court, is carved with the initials H and A, for Henry and Anne. The many courtyards and cloisters cover six acres in a mixture of Tudor and Baroque styles, with fascinating curiosities such as Henry VIII's Astronomical Clock.

William III and Mary II made the first major alterations to the palace since Tudor times. They commissioned Sir Christopher Wren to rebuild the king's and queen's apartments on the south and east sides of the palace, although the queen's apartments were left unfinished at the queen's death. King William III's Apartments remain one of the most magnificent examples of Baroque state apartments in the world. Almost destroyed in a terrible fire in 1986, there followed an ambitious restoration project which returned the apartments to the way they were when they were completed for William III in 1700. They can now be seen in their original glory, still furnished with the fine furniture and tapestries of 1700. An exhibition under the colonnade in Clock Court near the entrance to the King's Apartments details the history of the state rooms including the restoration.

The grand Queen's Staircase leads to the Queen's Guard Chamber. The Queen's state rooms run along the east wing of Fountain Court, and include the Queen's Drawing Room and the Queen's Bedroom. The Queen's Gallery contains ornate marble fireplaces with mantelpieces decorated with images of doves and Venus. Gobelins tapestries, on the theme of Alexander the Great, hang from the walls. Life-sized marble guardsmen flank the main chimneypiece. Hampton Court Palace contains a large part of the Royal Collection of art works, including many 16th, 17th and early 18th century pieces.

There are over 60 acres of gardens to explore at Hampton Court including the Great Vine and the newly restored Privy

Garden. Shrubberies that were allowed to grow in the Privy Garden in the 19th century have been removed to reveal the ancient formal beds and pathways. An exhibition on the East Front tells the story of the gardens and explains the restoration of the Privy Garden, opened in 1995. From the Privy Garden you can visit William III's magnificent Banqueting House and the Lower Orangery where Andrea Mantegna's *Triumphs of Caesar* are displayed. The Broad Walk runs from the Thames for half a mile past the east front and is lined with herbaceous borders. Just off the walk to the left and inside is the Tudor Tennis Court, a Real Tennis court built by Henry VIII, who was a keen player. To the north of the Palace is the famous Maze, planted in 1714 within William III's 'Wilderness' of evergreen trees. **The Maze** is extremely popular and can be surprisingly difficult to negotiate.

THAMES DITTON
4 miles E of Weybridge on the A309

Thames Ditton is one of the two Dittons that lie along the Thames south of Hampton Court. The name probably derives from the 'dictun', or farm by the dyke, and there were already a Saxon church and five manors in the area at the time of the Domesday Book. The heart of Thames Ditton dates mainly from the 19th century, but the harmonious blend of red brick and occasional black-timbered buildings along the High Street helps put visitors in mind of the town's earlier history.

A flower-decked path leads to **St Nicholas' Church**, which was first mentioned in the 12th century - roughly the time when Ditton was divided into two parishes. The building is of flint and stone and the interior contains a font decorated with mysterious motifs that still puzzle historians.

Thames Ditton benefited from its proximity to Hampton Court Palace and the church contains the grave of Cuthnert Blakeden, "Serjeant of the confectionary to King Henry the Eighth".

LONG DITTON
5 miles E of Weybridge on the A309

There is a peculiar lack of logic in the naming of the two Dittons; Thames Ditton is actually longer than Long Ditton but this more easterly village has a longer history than its neighbour. St Mary's Church, in the heart of Long Ditton, is a relative newcomer, having been built in 1880 but it stands close to the site of a Saxon church built long before the Dittons separated into two parishes.

Long Ditton is a scattered parish, with only a few vestiges left of its extensive history. Much of its history, however, can be gleaned from a close look inside St Mary's. The interior of the church features monuments to the Evelyn family, who put Long Ditton on the map in the 16th and 17th centuries. George Evelyn, grandfather of the famous diarist John Evelyn, acquired the local manor in the late 16th century and set about establishing gunpowder mills in the area. Business for gunpowder was booming, so to speak, in this turbulent period and the Evelyns amassed a huge fortune, eventually spreading their business further afield within Surrey.

OATLANDS
1 mile E of Weybridge on the B374

'The land where oats were grown' gave its name to the Tudor palace in Oatlands Park. This was already an established residence when Henry VIII forced its owner to cede him the title in 1538. Henry was in a rush to build a palace for his new queen, Anne of Cleves, although Ann never lived at Oatlands. However, the palace did become the home of subsequent monarchs, including Elizabeth I, James I and Charles I. In fact it was Charles who is said to have planted the proud cedar tree that stands beside the drive of what is now the Oatlands Park Hotel; he was celebrating the birth of his son, Prince Henry of Oatlands.

HERSHAM

2 miles E of Weybridge on the A307

Anglo-Saxons were the likeliest first settlers of Hersham, although prehistoric flint tools have been found on what is now Southwood Farm. In the 12th century the village was spelt Haverichesham and probably pronounced 'Haverick's Ham'. Two major events have shaped Hersham's history. The first occurred in 1529 when Henry VIII acquired Hampton Court from Cardinal Wolsey. Henry decided that his new estate lacked one of its necessities - a deer park - so he set about buying adjacent land and encircling the area with a perimeter fence. Other villages, including Weybridge and Esher, were on the edge of the park and escaped being enclosed, but Hersham was not so lucky. Not surprisingly, Hersham had a well-developed anti-royalist streak by the time of the Civil War and one of Cromwell's prominent aides, Captain John Inwood, lived there.

Politics and warfare apart, Hersham continued largely untouched by the outside world until the 19th century. Until 1804, when it was enclosed by Act of Parliament, much of the land around Hersham Green was open heathland. The arrival of the railway in 1838 led to a huge rise in Hersham's population. Development accompanied this boom

and much of Hersham's original appearance was altered completely. Local residents, however, would not let the process rip the heart out of their village and Hersham Green was actually enlarged in 1878. Despite extensive redevelopment of the centre in 1985, the charm of the village has been maintained in many of the older buildings around the village green. The village green is still used for a variety of local functions including a popular **Summer Fayre** with traditional entertainment.

CLAYGATE

4 miles E of Weybridge off the A3

Standing on a rich geological seam where dense London clay meets Bagshot sand, Claygate is well named. For many years this rich earth provided a living for many local men, who would have to bear the brunt of jibes from neighbouring villagers about working in the Claygate 'treacle mines'. Taunts notwithstanding, Claygate did supply the raw material for countless bricks and fireplaces.

Claygate can trace its origins to the Saxon times when it was a manor within the parish of Thames Ditton. In the early Medieval period the estate passed into the ownership of Westminster Abbey, which retained possession until Henry VIII dissolved the monasteries. Henry simply added it to his estates in Hampton Court.

Constrained for centuries by monastic, then royal control, Claygate remained largely unchanged as a tiny community until the 19th century. In 1838, however, **Claygate Common** was enclosed, enabling residents to enlarge the village considerably. One of the first orders of business was to erect their own church, Holy Trinity, to save the two-mile walk to Thames Ditton.

Ruxley Towers is an interesting building that dates from around the same period. It has a Gothic tower, built in 1830 and is decorated with a frightening display of gargoyles.

ESHER

4 miles E of Weybridge off the A3

Esher's recorded history goes back to Anglo-Saxon times. During the reign of Henry VIII, Hampton Court dominated all the surrounding manors including Esher. The railway arrived in Esher during the 19th century, after which it quickly became a popular residential area for wealthy city businessmen.

Esher is well known as the home of **Sandown Park**, where high-class horse racing is staged all year round. Created in 1875 by Sir Wilfred Brett, it soon attracted all the great and good of the racing world including the royal family.

The part of Surrey nearest to London is well supplied with racecourses, with Kempton Park, near Sunbury, Epsom and Sandown.

Near here, and well worth a visit is the beautiful National Trust-owned **Claremont Landscape Garden**, which lies on the southern side of the A307 Portsmouth road within a mile of the town centre. Begun in the 1715, this is believed to be one of the earliest surviving examples of an English landscape garden. Later in the century, it was remodelled by William Kent, whose work was continued by Capability Brown. Over the years some of the greatest names in garden history including Sir John Vanbrugh and Charles Bridgeman were involved in its creation. The grounds were designed to include a number of striking vistas and contain a grassed amphitheatre, grotto, lake and an island with a pavilion. Nearby **Claremont House** was designed in the

GARSONS

Winterdown Road, West End, nr Esher, Surrey KT10 8LS
Tel: 01372 460181
e-mail: info@garsons.co.uk
website: www.garsons.co.uk

Peter Thompson is one of the fourth generation in charge of **Garsons**, a garden centre and farm shop located a few minutes from the heart of Esher. One of the largest of its kind in Surrey, and certainly one of the best, it stocks an impressive range of garden supplies ranging from indoor and outdoor plants, seeds and hanging baskets to gas and charcoal barbecues, garden furniture and ornaments, log cabins, conservatories and swimming pool maintenance. The Farm Shop is a treasure trove for lovers of 'real' food, specialising in traditionally produced British fare.

The mouthwatering selection includes free-range meat, smoked fish from Scotland, home-baked cakes and bread, pickles and preserves, cheeses and dairy produce. Another of the many delights for visitors to Garsons is picking their own fruit and vegetables from the 150 acres that produce over 30 different crops, making this the largest PYO farm in Britain. The crop calendar starts in early May with asparagus and lasts until early October, with crops ranging from apples, plums and all kinds of berries to broad beans, broccoli, peas, spinach, tomatoes and sweetcorn. Garsons also has a restaurant specialising in home-style cooking, a gift shop and a children's play area.

1700s by Vanbrugh and substantially remodelled in 1772 for Clive of India. Capability Brown, Henry Holland and John Soane all had a hand in this work, which Clive had little opportunity to enjoy, as he died by his own hand in 1774. In 1816 the house was acquired for the Prince Regent's daughter and her husband, the future King of the Belgians. Queen Victoria was a regular visitor, and worshipped at St George's Church on the estate. The part-16th century church has an unusual three-tier pulpit, a very grand pew designed by Vanbrugh for the Duke of Newcastle and a marble monument to Princess Charlotte of Wales. The Princess was George IV's heir and would have succeeded him had she not died in childbirth at the house in 1817.

Cobham

COBHAM

4 miles SE of Weybridge off the A3

Cobham, now a busy residential town, with densely settled residential streets, is found in the Domesday book as 'Coveham'. However, it does possess some fine period buildings, which dominate a bend of the River Mole on the southeastern side of Cobham. An impressive 19th century water mill stands on the site of earlier mills dating back to the middle ages. The red brick building has now been restored to full working order. Cobham is also home to the **Cobham Bus Museum**, which houses the largest collection of London buses in the world. **Cedar House**, built in the mid-18th century, is a solid and well-proportioned brick building, which actually changes height halfway along its front. To the rear is a medieval section,

which includes a large tracery window. About a mile north of Cobham is **Foxwarren Park**, a bizarre house with eerie gables and multi-coloured bricks. It was built in 1860, and contemporary Victorian architects were known to introduce a bit of macabre humour into some of their designs. In this case it is hard to decide whether the intended effect was self-mocking or whether the gloomy appearance conformed to the owner's tastes.

One mile west of Cobham is **Painshill Park**, a white 18th century house with a fine setting on a hill. The house is impressive but Painshill is more noted for its grounds (see panel on page 310), which were laid out by the Hon. Charles Hamilton, son of the Earl of Abercorn, in the 1740s. These grounds were a talking point in the mid-18th century and were praised by luminaries such as Horace Walpole. Hamilton had let his imagination conjure up a series of landscapes and ornaments that created a profoundly Romantic atmosphere. An ornamental lake lay in front of a Gothic brick abbey, while on an island in the lake were various tufa sculptures and perpendicular cliffs leading down to the water. Hamilton even built a hermitage,

PAINSHILL PARK

Portsmouth Road, Cobham, Surrey KT11 1JE
Tel: 01932 868113 Fax: 01932 868001
e-mail: info@painshill.co.uk website: www.painshill.co.uk

This once barren heathland was transformed by the celebrated plantsman and designer, the Hon Charles Hamilton, into one of Europe's finest 18th Century landscape gardens. **Painshill** was one of the earliest 'naturalistic' gardens ever created, Hamilton conjured up a mysterious and magical place in which to wander- the equivalent of a 20th century theme park - where fashionable society could wander through a landscape theatre, moving from scene to scene. Staged around a huge serpentine lake with surprises at every turn. A Gothic Temple, Chinese Bridge, Ruined Abbey, a Grotto, Turkish Tent, Gothic Tower and the most magnificent waterwheel all disappear and reappear as the walk proceeds.

But Hamilton eventually ran out of money and to discharge his debts sold the estate in 1773. Since then it has been in the possession of many owners but was eventually fragmented and sold off in lots in 1948 and the gardens, which had been well-maintained for nigh on two centuries, were allowed to deteriorate. By 1981 they lay derelict and overgrown and it seemed that what had been a

national treasure would be lost for all time. However Elmbridge Borough Council, conscious of the importance of Painshill, purchased 158 acres and formed the Painshill Park Trust with a view to restoring the gardens and opening them to the public. The subsequent ongoing restoration has been one of the great success stories of garden conservation. Most of the principal features of the garden are open for viewing and the restored planting schemes are steadily maturing. The restoration has been a slow process. It's not simply a matter of clearing undergrowth and repairing features. Lots of detailed and painstaking research is required. Archaeological excavation, documentary research and the identification and dating of trees, tree stumps and historic paths. From this, detailed plans and maps are created to show what the estate would have looked like in the 18th century and all the later stages to the present day.

Now there are a variety of walks which allow visitors to explore Hamilton's idyll. The historic circuit is a signposted two-mile long route that an 18th century visitor would have followed to view all the attractions of the garden. A shorter path round the lake passes delights such as the ruined abbey, boat house and crosses the Chinese bridge. A vineyard flourished at Painshill from 1740 to 1812. This has been replanted with Pinot noir, Chardonnay and Seyval blanc grapes and once again wine is being produced at Painshill. Painshill is not allowed to call their sparkling white wine champagne but when Charles Hamilton was making wine here in the 18th century the French ambassador of the day, mistook Hamilton's product for the champagne of his native land. In a tribute to the man who made it all possible, the Painshill trust have named the new visitor centre restaurant Hamilton's. It's open from early morning serving breakfasts, coffee, light lunches and splendid afternoon teas. The shop is a cornucopia for present and souvenir buyers containing everything from trugs and dibbers to umbrellas, food, china, books, honey and beeswax candles and, of course, Painshill wine. Open March to October Tuesday to Sunday and Bank Holidays 10.30am - 6.00pm; November - February: Wednesday to Sunday and Bank Holidays 11.00am - 4.00pm. Closed Christmas Day.

and then went one stage further by installing a hermit in it. The mounting catalogue of expenses took its toll on Hamilton, however, and he eventually went bankrupt. Although many of the features in the grounds are gone it remains an amazing spectacle. The walk around the lake, takes in a Gothic temple, Chinese bridge, a ruined abbey, a Turkish tent, and a waterwheel. The planting at Painshill makes it a gardener's delight as it changes with the seasons. The landscape is enhanced by cedars and original 18th century plantings, including tiers of shrubs, flowerbeds and a vineyard.

OXSHOTT
4 miles SE of Weybridge off the A3

Taking its name from the Old English for Occa's Wood, Oxshott's history as a settlement stretches back thousands of years. A flint found on **Oxshott Heath** is believed to date back to 8000 BC, making it the oldest tool ever discovered in the area. Another fascinating find in **Oxshott Woods**, now displayed in the British Museum is an intricately carved Anglo-Saxon bronze brooch of the early tenth century. Oxshott remained a small hamlet set in woods and heather until the 1880s, when the completion of the Surbiton to Guildford Railway ushered in an era of growth and development. Some stretches of woodland have withstood the tide of new roads and houses, notably Oxshott Heath and Princes Coverts, which is a woodland owned by the Crown Estate. In the middle of Princes Coverts is a square red-brick building which was erected in the 18th century over a medicinal spring known as **Jessop's Well**. The mineral content of the spring water was said to compare with that of Cheltenham, but despite the Royal connection and the salubrious waters, Oxshott somehow never achieved true spa status.

Perhaps Oxshott was considered a bit too dissipated because for many years it was mildly notorious for having two public houses but no church. This imbalance between sacred and profane was partly offset in 1912, when St Andrew's Church was erected.

STOKE D'ABERNON
5 miles SE of Weybridge off the A3

Like Cobham, the northern part of Stoke d'Abernon is undistinguished; however, the older southern part, which reaches down to the River Mole, contains a fine mid 18th century part-Palladian, part-baroque manor house and an exceptional parish church, which is believed to be among the oldest in the country.

The south wall of **St Mary's Church** is believed to date back to the days of St Augustine in the 7th century, and indeed it has been found to contain brickwork and cornices belonging to a Roman structure, which once stood on the site. There are also traces of an early Saxon lord's gallery and one of the oldest monumental brasses in Britain, that of Sir John d'Abernon who was buried in 1277. The church, with its wonderful mixture of styles is part-medieval with the magnificent walnut pulpit dating back to the early 17th century.

About half a mile south of Stoke d'Abernon is **Slyfield Manor**, which was built in the 17th century but incorporated a late medieval timber-frame building. Garden walls, with original archways, blend with the painstaking brickwork of the house to create an effect that reminds many visitors of the work of Inigo Jones, particularly in Covent Garden.

WHITELEY VILLAGE
2 miles SE of Weybridge on the B365

A mile-and-a-half to the southwest of Weybridge, and close to the St George's

Hill residential area much-favoured by famous media personalities, lies the remarkable Whiteley Village. This unique 230-acre model village was founded on the instructions of the proprietor of a famous Bayswater department store, William Whiteley, who was shot in 1907. He left one million pounds in his will to house the elderly poor. The charitable community was designed to be entirely self-contained with its own churches, hospital and shops, and was laid out in an octagonal pattern around a green containing a memorial to the project's benefactor. The buildings are Grade II listed and of great architectural interest. The site has been planted with a great many trees and flowering shrubs, and is at its best in late-spring and summer. It is a private estate and not open to the public.

CHERTSEY
3 miles NW of Weybridge on the A320

Chertsey is an ancient riverside town, which has altered almost beyond recognition over the centuries. The town once boasted a formidable abbey, whose influence stretched over a wide area of southern England. When it was demolished following the Dissolution of the Monasteries, its stone was used to build Hampton Court Palace and later, the River Wey Canal.

One of the abbey bells now hangs in the parish church, St Peter; at one time it was used to sound the evening curfew and it is associated with a local romantic legend concerning Blanche Heriot, a young Chertsey woman who, on hearing that her lover was to be executed at the sound of the curfew bell, climbed into the tower and clung onto the tongue until his pardon arrived. This heroic action was commemorated in the ballad *The Curfew Must Not Ring Tonight* by the American poet Rose Hartwick Thorpe.

Chertsey Museum, housed in a fine Regency building near the Thames, has a large collection of items of both local and national interest including a 10th century Viking sword and a fascinating costume display exploring 300 years of high fashion. The museum closed for a time recently for a programme of renovation and extension.

Despite the upheavals that Chertsey has undergone, it still manages to preserve some lovely woodland scenery, with a number of green fields and commons including Chertsey Mead. A well-proportioned, seven arched bridge spans the River Thames in the centre of the town.

THORPE
6 miles NW of Weybridge off the M25

Many of the streets in Thorpe are walled, screening residential buildings and small parks, and planning authorities succeeded in preserving this feature - unique in Surrey - despite a postwar building boom. There are some ancient elements in St Mary Church, including a plain 12th century chancel arch. An 18th century monument to Elizabeth Townsend features a praying cherub. On closer inspection this cherub has an unusual, almost Mongol appearance - an effect that was something of a trademark of its designer, Sir Robert Taylor. Old brick cottages line Church Approach. Some of the larger buildings in Thorpe betray its farming background. Spelthorne St Mary, on Coldharbour Lane, is a solid 18th century residence with a half-timbered barn dating from a century earlier. The Village Hall, to the east of Church Approach, was converted from a 17th century brick barn.

SHEPPERTON
3 miles N of Weybridge on the B376

Over the centuries Shepperton has capitalised on its strategic riverside location, and today's thriving market town is testimony to the entrepreneurial spirit of previous generations. It grew from its origins as a straggling collection of homesteads to become a bustling way station for west-bound traffic from London. This status was firmly established by the 15th century, and many of the lovely houses around the Church Square Conservation Area date from that period, or shortly afterwards.

This century brought a new wave of development, as the famous **Shepperton Film Studios** were built in the 1930s. Handy for London's Airport, first at Croydon then at Heathrow, Shepperton presented itself as an ideal site for a film venture. International stars were collected from their transatlantic flights or from their Mayfair flats. Moreover, Shepperton's position at the edge of the Green Belt meant that "rural" location shots could be managed just a few miles from the studios themselves. Recent films to made here include *Shakespeare in Love* and *Hilary and Jackie*.

STAINES

6 miles N of Weybridge on the A30

The ancient town of Staines stands at the point where the old Roman road from London to the South West crossed the Rivers Thames and Colne, and in the 17th and 18th centuries, it became an important staging point on the old coaching routes to the West Country. When walking beside the Thames, look out for the London Stone which was erected in 1285 to mark the boundary of the city's authority over the river. The old part of Staines contains some noteworthy buildings, including the part 17th century church of St Mary and the town hall built in Flemish-style on the Market Place.

The Spelthorne Museum, located in the old fire station of Staines, tells the story of Staines and its extensive history. Archaeological excavations in the 1970s confirmed that Staines stood on the site of the Roman settlement of Pontes.

The museum contains Iron Age and Roman artefacts and archaeological evidence as well as re-creations of life in Roman times, and provides a useful chronology for the successive riverside settlements on this site. There is a re-creation of a Victorian kitchen, a collection of brewing and bottling equipment and the Staines Linoleum display devoted to the company which first made linoleum.

The M25 to the south of Staines passes close to **Great Thorpe Park**, a 500-acre leisure park which has been built on an area of reclaimed gravel pits. The park incorporates a shire horse centre, a series of historic reconstructions of life in ancient Britain, and a permanent theme

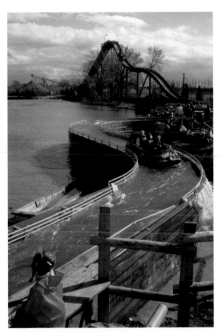

Loggers Leap at Thorpe Park

park containing some of the latest roller coaster rides and fairground attractions.

LALEHAM
5 miles N of Weybridge on the B376

Located only a few miles from bustling Staines and only minutes north of the M3, Laleham sits on the banks of the Thames, with one of London's larger reservoirs backing onto it. A triangular green lies near the river, reached by Ferry Lane. It is a pretty village with many 18th and 19th century houses. Facing the green is a pair of early 18th century houses, **Muncaster House** and **The Coverts**.

Parts of All Saints Church at Laleham are 16th century but it is said to stand on the site of a Roman temple. Laleham's best-known son is Matthew Arnold, who is buried in the churchyard. **Laleham Riverside Park** was formerly the grounds of Laleham Abbey, which belonged to the Lucan family. Water understandably plays a large part in activities here, with boat hire available just a few hundred yards west of the trim Victorian centre.

LITTLETON
5 miles N of Weybridge on the B376

Littleton has undergone a number of dramatic changes in the last four decades and today it is hard to find much of the original village lying south of the huge reservoir serving the capital. New houses, car parks and a school have replaced what had been a harmonious medieval ensemble of church, rectory, manor farm and manor house.

Luckily, of this group the church remains intact. St Mary Magdalene is built of brick and dates back to the 13th century. The brick is a 16th century addition, the original nave and chancel had been made of ragstone and flint rubble. This modification constituted a decided visual improvement. The west

tower was built at a later date; like the earlier modifications it is of brick, giving the church a cohesive appearance. Inside there are a number of curiosities, including a late medieval locker and a complete restored set of pews from that same period. The ornate choir stalls are said to have come from Winchester.

SUNBURY-ON-THAMES
3 miles N of Weybridge off the M3

With its high-rise office blocks and modern shopping precincts, today's Sunbury-on-Thames seems a far cry from its origins as a 10th century 'burgh' built by the Saxon Lord Sunna. However it developed as a medieval market town for a riverside district stretching from Chertsey all the way to Kingston and these bastions of commerce have simply kept in step with the passing of time. The local inhabitants seem happy enough to have retained the town's trading essence, even if it does mean that many of Sunbury's period buildings have long since been replaced.

A few of the town's period buildings remain, including the **Salvation Army Youth Centre**, which had been Sunbury Court, an 18th century mansion with Ionic decoration. A yew tree in the churchyard of the 18th century St Mary Church featured in *Oliver Twist* by Charles Dickens. Between Sunbury Court and the church are some handsome Georgian residences.

NORTHWEST SURREY

The northwest corner of Surrey, lying to the west of the M25 and stretching westwards to the Berkshire and Hampshire borders and given a southern limit by the A3, shows the county's countryside coming into its own. Rich farming areas give way to expanses of heath and dotted woodlands, once the haunt of highwaymen but now safe for ramblers - as long as they steer clear of the well-marked military areas.

Woking is the principal town in this area, like many Surrey towns an established centre that was transformed by the arrival of the railway in the 19th century. The Victorian influence is strong throughout this part of Surrey, evident in many of the larger houses built by or under the auspices of Norman Shaw and other proponents of the Arts and Crafts style, which blossomed as a reaction against poor-quality, mass-produced building materials.

The more ornate style of Victorian architecture, which seemed to be the embodiment of a prosperous nation flexing its imperial muscle, is also represented in the two massive buildings funded by Thomas Holloway, the Royal Holloway College and the Holloway Sanatorium, which are near Egham in the north. That same northern extremity contains the site of one of England's defining moments, the signing of the Magna Carta in 1215 at the riverside meadow of Runnymede.

WOKING

Woking is a commuter town on the main railway line to Waterloo. In fact it was the railway that defined the present appearance - and location - of Woking. The original village was what is now called Old Woking, and when the railway arrived in 1838 the station was built two miles away in what was then open heathland. Most of the heart of Woking dates from the middle of the 19th century, but among these Victorian-era buildings is an unexpected 'first'. The first purpose-built mosque to be founded in Britain - **Shah Jehan Mosque** - can be

found in Woking's Oriental Street. The construction of this unusual onion-domed structure was largely financed by the ruler of the Indian state of Bhopal who visited the town in 1889. Woking was involved in another first, the beginnings of science fiction. H G Wells' Martians, in his 1898 novel *War of the Worlds*, landed on Horsell Common in Woking. The impressive Martian sculpture in the town centre was raised to commemorate the centenary of the book. Standing seven metres tall, the alien sculpture dominates its location. Even the paving around it is patterned to represent shock waves from the impact of the alien pod landing.

Old Woking is a former market town, which is now incorporated into the southeastern suburbs of its more modern neighbour. This is an old settlement, dating from the Saxon period and mentioned in the Domesday Book. Old Woking had the good fortune to be listed as a personal possession of the king and therefore it did not need to pay taxes. Its streets contain some noteworthy old buildings, including the 17th century old Manor House, and the part-Norman parish church of St Peter which has a late-medieval west tower. On the western edge of Woking is the largest cemetery in the country. **Brookwood Cemetery** was opened in 1854 by the London Necropolis and National Mausoleum Company to relieve the overcrowded cemeteries of London. It was served by special funeral trains which ran from Necropolis Station, next to Waterloo Station. This station was bombed in 1941 and was never rebuilt. Brookwood is a good place for spotting famous graves: among its many thousands of occupants are Margaret, Duchess of Argyle, the society beauty who was the subject of Cole Porter's song *You're the Top*; the bandleader Carroll Gibbons; the painter

John Singer Sargent; the writers Rebecca West and Dennis Wheatley; and the murderess Edith Thompson.

AROUND WOKING

PYRFORD

1 mile E of Woking on the B382

Located roughly midway between Woking and Byfleet is Pyrford, which manages to retain many aspects of its village character despite being no more than a couple of miles from its larger neighbours. It is set in meadows along the River Wey, with most of its original red-brick cottages still forming a core near the church. This parish church, the largely Norman **Church of St Nicholas**, has been preserved over the centuries

without being the victim of intrusive restoration work. The south wall of the nave contains some unusual wall paintings of the Flagellation and Christ's Passion, which were painted around 1200. Research work carried out in the 1960s uncovered some even earlier murals beneath these paintings. The murals depict horsemen as well as a mysterious procession of men carrying staves.

About half a mile along the B367, to the south of Pyrford, is **Newark Priory**, an evocative ruin set in fields along the banks of the Wey. The priory was a house of Austin Canons who founded it in the 12th century. Like other monastic settlements it was a victim of the Dissolution under Henry VIII. Unlike others, however, it was never

RHS GARDEN WISLEY

Woking, Surrey, GU23 6QB
Tel: 01483 224234 Fax: 01483 211750
website: www.rhs.org.uk

The Royal Horticultural Society's garden at Wisley has 240 acres of beautiful and practical garden ideas. A gardener's paradise, the richly planted borders, luscious rose gardens and exotic glasshouses are a joy to wander through. But the garden also provides a test bed for countless cultivation methods and in a series of model gardens various growing conditions are applied. When the RHS was given Wisley in 1903, only a small part of the estate was cultivated as a garden, the remainder being woods and farmland. George Ferguson Wilson designed the original garden in 1878 as the 'Oakwood experimental garden' to try to grow difficult plants. Over the years as the garden expanded it has remained true to the original concept.

Recent developments include the Walled Garden (West) planted with tender perennials, shrubs and climbers. The rich selection of plants from around the world has been chosen for their foliage.

Cascades of water, streams and pools, terracotta pots and wrought iron work set against mellow York paving add to the architectural planting. Wooden seating designed by Julian Chicester allows visitors to enjoy the sights and scents of this unusual garden. The Temperate Glass House has been recently re-organised with a section of dry bright conditions, a central section for temporary displays and the remaining part designed around a waterfall and pools with damp, shady conditions. A new feature for Wisley is a bonsai collection in a minimalist Japanese style garden. It is on the site of the former Garden for the Disabled and is easily accessible for wheelchairs.

converted into a private residence. Instead its walls were broken down for use in local buildings, although some of its features - including the east window - are said to have been taken to Ockham. Today only the walls of the south transept and those of the presbytery still stand, and visitors must use their imagination to work out where in the surrounding corn fields there might once have been the remainder of the monastic buildings.

WISLEY

3 miles E of Woking off the A3

The Royal Horticultural Society's internationally renowned **Wisley Garden** lies on the north side of the A3, one mile to the northwest of Ockham (see panel opposite). As well as containing a wide variety of trees, flowering shrubs and ornamental plants, this magnificent 250-acre garden incorporates the Society's experimental beds where scientific trials are conducted into new and existing plant varieties. Wisley also acts as a centre for training horticultural students, and offers a wide range of plants, books, gifts and gardening advice at its first-class plant centre and shop.

RIPLEY

2 miles E of Woking off the A3

Just a mile or so to the southwest of Wisley is the attractive village of Ripley, a former staging post on the old coaching route between London and Portsmouth. The main street contains a number of exceptional brick and half-timbered buildings, including the charming Vintage Cottage with its unusual crown post roof.

Most of the attractive houses lie on the gracefully curving High Street. Unusually, the long and wedge-shaped village green lies beside the street on the west side. The village seems to have grown away from the green rather than around as in most English villages.

SUTTON PLACE

2 miles SE of Woking off the A3

Sutton Place was the creation of Sir Richard Weston, a protégé of Henry VIII who was a Knight of the Bath, a Gentleman of the Privy Chamber and eventually Under-Treasurer of England. He had accompanied Henry to France for the famous meeting at the Field of the Cloth of Gold in 1520, so in every respect he had the right to expect to live in sumptuous surroundings that reflected his high standing.

The house he had built, after receiving the grant of the Sutton estate in 1521, is seen by many critics as one of the most important English houses to be built in the years after Hampton Court was completed. It was built to describe almost a perfect square, with sides measuring about 130 to 140 feet surrounding a central courtyard. The north side was demolished in the 18th century, so today's house appears to comprise a two-storey, redbrick central building with two long projections. Symmetry is important in Sutton Place, as English architects were busy putting to use the elements of the Italian Renaissance in their buildings. Doorways and windows are balanced in each wing.

The Italian influence is particularly evident in the terracotta ornamentation of the windows and even more dramatically in a series of terracotta panels depicting cherubs over the entrance. Terracotta had been first used as an architectural feature, mainly as faience, in Hampton Court in 1521. Sutton Court was built probably no more than a decade later - records show that Henry VIII was a guest in 1533 - so it was obviously at the forefront of this style of ornamentation. It is the exterior, with its strict adherence to Renaissance tenets, that makes Sutton Place so fascinating. Inside there have been alterations and additions that make the effect less wholly linked to one period.

Sir Geoffrey Jellicoe, the most renowned British landscape gardener of the century, partially completed visionary garden for Sutton Place's then owner, the oil tycoon Stanley Seeger. Inspired by the philosophy of Carl Jung, Jellicoe created a series of symbolic gardens round the grand Elizabethan house. The most notable survival is the yew-enclosed garden which contains a vastly enlarged marble abstract 'wall' sculpture based on a small maquette by Ben Nicholson. The yew walk is one of the garden's finest features.

WORPLESDON

3 miles SW of Woking on the A322

Worplesdon retains a sense of its rural past in its setting on the edge of heaths, despite the threat posed by the expansion of Guildford which is just a couple of miles to the south. A number of brick houses dating from the early 18th century surround the triangular green, which is up on a hill. One of these houses displays a brick front, of around 1700, tacked on to a timber frame, creating an unusual effect.

St Mary's Church, standing above the village, was mentioned in the Domesday book. Although clumsily restored in the Victorian era, the oldest part is 11th century and it retains a number of interesting features from the medieval period. Chief among these is the late 15th century tower, which is compact and well proportioned. At its base is a tower arch over an intricately carved door.

PIRBRIGHT

3 miles W of Woking on the A324

Pirbright is a village that is first recorded in 1166 as Perifrith, a compound of the two words 'pyrige' (pear tree) and 'fryth' (wooded country). It remained a hamlet of scattered homesteads until the 19th century when the railway's arrival in 1840 led to a boom in the population and a corresponding burgeoning of new construction.

Despite the rapid increase in the village population, and thanks also to the enlightened Green Belt policies of this century, Pirbright has managed to keep most of its rural aspect. The huge village green, which forms its core is in fact a wedge of the surrounding heathland. Pirbright contains many listed buildings, including several medieval farmsteads. Information about these, as well as a selection of excellent walks, is contained in a lovingly produced booklet available from the vicarage.

FARNBOROUGH

7 miles W of Woking off A331

Farnborough lies just over the border in Hampshire and although it is largely a commercial and shopping - rather than historical - centre, it is worth visiting for its links with the Royal Aircraft Establishment. These ties are explained fully at the **Farnborough Air Science Museum**, with its inter -active displays and historical material. Other attractions include the bi-annual Air Show, a working monastery and the tombs of Napoleon III, his wife and his son.

FRIMLEY

7 miles W of Woking off the M3

Frimley is an extremely old village on the Hampshire border and a site of several important prehistoric and Roman finds which are displayed at the Surrey Heath

Museum in Camberley. Much of the more recent history, unfortunately, has been less well-preserved and the old sense of the village's coaching significance has been erased with a series of housing developments over the last four decades. The area around **Frimley Green**, however, gives some indication of what Frimley looked like in the late medieval period. Cross Farmhouse is one of the oldest surviving houses, its timber and brick structure containing elements dating from the 15th century. The parish church of St Peter dates only from 1825 but its churchyard contains the graves of many famous people. Among them is Francis Bret Harte, the American novelist whose wanderings around the world led him to settle eventually in England.

Just south of Frimley, and also hugging the Hampshire border, is the village of **Mytchett**, which has also suffered from some unthinking urban planning.

The **Basingstoke Canal Visitors Centre**, which lies just east of Farnborough and only five minutes from the M3, offers a tranquil and relaxing way in which to discover the charming countryside. Visitors can take a leisurely trip on a narrowboat, gaining a fascinating insight into the points of interest from the informative guide. The Canal Exhibition provides an in-depth account of how barge skippers lived a century ago and how the Basingstoke Canal, and its wildlife habitats, have been conserved more recently.

CAMBERLEY
7 miles W of Woking off the M3

Prior to 1807, when the famous **Sandhurst Royal Military Academy** was relocated nearby, the substantial town of Camberley did not exist, and indeed its oldest part, the grid-patterned York Town, was constructed to house the academy's first instructors. (Lying just across the Berkshire border, Sandhurst Academy is set around a group of buildings designed in neoclassical style by James Wyatt.)

Although now resembling many other large towns with its High Street chains and modernised pubs, Camberley still displays much of the care and attention that marked its development in the mid-Victorian era. Unlike other towns, which sprang up willy-nilly, usually with the advent of the railway, Camberley had a measured growth and the town expanded along the lines of the grid shape of York Town. Shops and workers' houses predominated north of the railway line while to the south were the larger houses of prosperous merchants set among stands of mature trees. These latter houses, many of which are good examples of the Arts and Crafts style of architect Norman Shaw and his followers, still stand although recent housing developments have encroached on much of the wooded areas.

The story of the development of Camberley and the surrounding area is well told at the **Surrey Heath Museum** on Knoll Road. Most of the exhibits have been designed to tell this story from a child's point of view, but adults will also enjoy seeing some of the curiosities and original documents from the 19th century. There are also displays on heathland crafts, the archaeology of the area and the notorious highwaymen who preyed on unwary travellers.

BISLEY
3 miles W of Woking on the A322

Surrounded by farmland and heaths, Bisley remains resolutely small-scale and unassuming. It is within easy reach of Camberley to the west and Woking to the east, but luckily much of the traffic comes in the form of ramblers who are equipped with the well-marked books of pub walks in the vicinity. Bisley's contribution to the pub supply is the Fox Inn, which stands opposite Snowdrop Farm, where a well-marked trail crosses the A322. Having crossed the A322, the trail cuts southwestwards across **Bisley Common**, where annual marksmanship competitions are held on the rifle ranges, past the pretty little Stafford Lake and into Sheet's Heath. Even making this short walk, which in fact is part of one of the longer pub trails, gives a good indication of the native landscape. Here the land is more or less in its natural state, with scrubby low bushes and bracken indicating why it was the more fertile soil east of the A322 that was more sought after for cultivation.

The attractive church of **St John the Baptist** likewise stands to the west of most houses in Bisley, giving it an almost lonely appearance. It is built of local sandstone with a short tiled spire topping its wooden tower.

LIGHTWATER
7 miles W of Woking off the M3

For many Londoners, Lightwater represents the first taste of countryside outside the metropolis. It has the advantage - from the visitor's point of view - of lying within easy reach of the M3. By turning south off the motorway, instead of north to Bagshot, drivers soon enter a countryside defined by heaths and scattered woodlands. Bagshot Heath, once a rough area peopled by highwaymen and duellists, begins at the western edge of Lightwater, and the village of **Donkey Town** lies just to the south, its name providing some confirmation of the area's rural nature.

Lightwater Country Park is over 57 hectares of countryside with two colour-coded trails guiding walkers across open areas of natural heath, and through pine and birch woodlands. There is also a Trim Trail fitness circuit set among pine woods. The steep climb to the summit of High Curley is rewarded by panoramic views of the surrounding countryside. Heathland Visitor Centre has a fascinating collection of exhibits about the history and natural history of this stretch of West Surrey countryside.

BAGSHOT
7 miles W of Woking on the A30

On the western edge of Surrey, on the Berkshire border lies the ancient village of Bagshot, which Daniel Defoe described as "not only good for little but good for nothing". Bagshot today largely bears out Defoe's description, but the village centre and the Church Road area are now Conservation Areas. The village was on the main coaching route from London to the west and was a bustling post stop, catering for thousands of travellers every year. In 1997 two wall paintings, dating from the turn of the 17th century, were discovered in a 14th century building. The paintings, which had been concealed behind wall panels, cover two walls and are now protected behind glass.

WINDLESHAM
7 miles NW of Woking on the A30

Windlesham, lying in a setting of heath and meadow, is far prettier than its larger southern neighbour Bagshot. Victorian brick buildings - including some larger examples of the 'prosperous merchant' variety - line the heath, and one of the most attractive houses in Windlesham is **Pound Cottage** on Pound Lane. This timber-framed, 17th century cottage has a lovely thatched roof, which comes down in hips to the ground floor ceiling.

Like much of Surrey Heath, Windlesham was once part of Windsor Great Forest and developed as a traditional farming community centred around several manors and the church. Like Bagshot, Windlesham contains two conservation areas.

CHOBHAM
3 miles NW of Woking on the A3046

Enjoying a peaceful location just five minutes drive from Woking town centre is the attractive community of Chobham. The village is a Conservation Area and the High Street has developed over the centuries into an attractive and generally harmonious stretch of buildings, the oldest dating back to the 16th century. The street itself curves up a hill, with the parish church of St Lawrence punctuating the row about halfway along. The original church was built in the 11th century but a

restructuring in 1170 was the first of many alterations, including the tower, added around 1400, and the Victorian extension of the side aisle, that have left the church of St Lawrence more of an assembly of disparate elements than a harmonious whole.

VIRGINIA WATER
7 miles N of Woking on the A30

From Camberley, the A30 runs along the northeastern border of the county to Virginia Water, a surprising diversion, which lies in the heart of the Surrey stockbroker belt. The 'water' referred to is a mile-and-a-half long artificial lake which is set within mature woodland at the southern end of **Windsor Great Park**; it was created by Paul and Thomas Sandby, two accomplished Georgian landscapers who were also known for their painting. The picturesque ruins standing at the lakeside are genuine remains of a Roman temple which once stood at Leptis Magna in Libya. **The Valley Gardens** also contain an unusual 100-foot totem pole which was erected here in 1958 to mark the centenary of British Columbia. A little further to the north, the Savill Garden is renowned as one of the finest woodland gardens in the country covering around 18 hectares. Begun by Eric Savill in 1932, it has continued to develop with various additions over the years, including herbaceous borders, a bog garden and a temperate glasshouse.

Holloway Sanatorium, now renamed **Crossland House**, was designed by the Victorian architect W H Crossland for the eminent businessman and philanthropist Thomas Holloway. It was built to house middle-class people, afflicted with mental disease. Holloway Sanatorium looked to the continent for inspiration, to the architecture of Bruges and Ypres. The result was a brick and stone Gothic structure that stood as the epitome of high Victorian fashion, ironically constructed after the popularity of that overblown style had begun to ebb. This Grade I listed building had fallen into dereliction until 1998, when it was sensitively restored as part of a prize-winning housing development at Virginia Park.

ENGLEFIELD GREEN
8 miles N of Woking on the A30

The green that gives Englefield Green its name is large and attractive, flanked by a number of interesting houses, including some several centuries old. The aptly named Old House dates from 1689, and most of it is a tribute to the red brick symmetry so beloved of that period. Next to it is **Englefield House**, built in the late 18th century. This is more of a curiosity, since it seems that the architect

was unclear whether his brief called for something classical, neo-Gothic or Venetian. Castle Hill is the largest building around Englefield Green. Extended in the 19th century, the original building was a 'Gothic' structure, built for Sir John Elwell. When the common lands were enclosed in 1814, the green survived as open land on account of the wealth and influence of its surrounding residents.

EGHAM
8 miles N of Woking on the A30

Skirted by the River Thames and the historic fields of Runnymede, Egham is near a number of points of real interest. The centre of Egham is not particularly noteworthy, although the area by the Swan Hotel at the Staines Bridge, is attractive with a pretty row of old riverside cottages.

The Swan Sanctuary at Egham took over an area of disused land at Pooley Green in 1989 and consists of nursing ponds, rehabilitation lakes, and various facilities for cleaning and caring for injured swans. All birds are returned to the wild as soon as they are fit.

Between Egham and Englefield Green is one of Surrey's more memorable buildings, the **Royal Holloway College**. It is a huge Victorian building, modelled on the Chateau du Chambord in the Loire Valley in France. Opened by Queen Victoria in 1886, it was one of the first colleges for women in the country. Like the Holloway Sanatorium at Virginia Water, it was designed by W H Crossland for Thomas Holloway. Holloway made his fortune from 'Holloway's Patent Pills' in the 1870s. He was an entrepreneur and philanthropist, his wife a passionate believer in women's education. Holloway's generous ideas on lodging - each student was allocated two rooms -

dictated the enormous size of the building. In the form of a double quadrangle, it measures 550 feet in length and 376 feet across. Inside, the formal rooms include a remarkable library and a picture gallery, housing a collection of Victorian paintings by artists such as Millais, Landseer and Frith. It is now part of the University of London.

Runnymede
10 miles N of Woking on the A30

A meadow beside the River Thames to the north of Egham is where King John sealed the **Magna Carta** in 1215. The historic Runnymede Site and nearby Cooper's Hill are contained within a 300-acre tract of land which is now under the ownership of the National Trust. Runnymede was an open space between the King's castle at Windsor and the camp of the rebel barons at Staines. The king was forced to agree to protect the barons from certain injustices but the important principle was established that the king, as well as his subjects, could be governed by the law.

The area contains three separate memorials: a domed neoclassical temple which was erected by the American Bar Association to commemorate the sealing of the world's first bill of democratic rights, a memorial to John F Kennedy, and the **Air Forces Memorial**. Many come to see the memorial commemorating the men and women of the Commonwealth Air Forces killed in World War II, who have no known grave. From its position on Coopers Hill, above the river, it commands splendid views over the Thames Valley and Windsor Great Park. The river below is populated by slow-moving motor cruisers and pleasure craft, and river trips to Windsor, Staines and Hampton Court can be taken

from Runnymede, daily between May and October, and at weekends during winter. The nearby **Runnymede Pleasure Ground** offers a range of children's leisure activities in a pleasant riverside setting.

FARNHAM AND THE WEST

Farnham, with its lovely Georgian architecture and battle-worn castle, is the largest town in southwestern Surrey, where the heel of the county extends westwards into Hampshire. Apart from Farnham, however, there are no large towns in this corner of the county, and its charms lie more in the array of attractive villages, scattered farmhouses, woodlands and open heaths in some of the hilliest parts of the southeast.

History plays an important role in this area, with Civil War battle cries still almost audible from the walls of Farnham Castle and the hint of plainsong hanging in the still air around the ruins of Waverley Abbey. "Stand and deliver" would seem to be a more appropriate sound to hear in the wilder sections of the southern extremity, and the Gibbet Memorial on Hindhead Common is a tangible reminder of the fate that awaited those highwaymen who had the misfortune to meet the long arm of the law.

The famous Hog's Back section of the A31 forms the northern edge of the area covered in this chapter. This lovely stretch of road is one of the most scenic drives in the Southeast, affording excellent views north and south as it traverses the ridge between Farnham and Guildford. Indeed, looking south from the Hog's Back provides an aerial perspective of many of the sites covered in the following pages, or at least the countryside surrounding them. The

The PACKH🏠USE

ANTIQUES, INTERIORS & INSPIRATION

The Packhouse is based in a beautiful 400 year old Grade II listed Hop Kiln on the outskirts of Farnham, Surrey and provides a stunning showroom for over 100 dealers offering an eclectic mix of **antiques, interiors and inspiration.**

The Packhouse team believe there should be no set rule as to how to furnish and accessorise your home. Whether it be a revived passion for antiques that are worn and well-loved or a desire for more quirky original pieces, they hope to give you the inspiration to decorate your home with an array of treasures that together combine to create a look that is absolutely now.They have an ever-evolving stock of traditional and contemporary finds, including English, French, Italian, European and Eastern antiques and interiors.In addition to furniture The Packhouse also offers a vast selection of home accessories, from mirrors, soft furnishings, lighting, pictures and frames, clocks, ceramics, china and glassware to brass and copper. Also one off finds such as armaments, silver centre pieces, garden accessories and water features. A range of services are on offer and include the Terrace Café, where freshly made snacks, lunches and afternoon tea are served daily from 10am to 5pm, in the relaxed indoor surroundings and in summer on their outside terrace. A UK home delivery / assembly service is offered to all customers for items purchased from The Packhouse. Worldwide shippers can also be recommended.

The Packhouse are also delighted to offer access to recommended 'home service' experts and the companies that they have aligned themselves with complement and add value to their antique and interior offering. The companies include an interior design, curtain making and upholstery service (all based at The Packhouse), as well as an excellent restorer, an architectural salvage merchant who can match bricks and tiles, plus a painter and decorator.Reputed as the largest centre in the South East, they guarantee no two visits will ever be the same. Open seven days a week they look forward to welcoming you (closed Xmas Day and Boxing Day only).

Payment methods: Cash, cheque, all major credit cards and interest free credit is available on items over £500.

Tel: 01252 781010   website: www.packhouse.com
Opening times: Mon - Fri 10.30am – 5.30 pm   Sat & Sun 10.00 am – 5.30 pm
The Packhouse, Hewett's Kilns, Tongham Road, Runfold, Farnham, Surrey GU10 1PJ

panorama is best viewed from the grassy verge by the side of the A31 at one of the many lay-bys.

FARNHAM

The most westerly town in Surrey is Farnham, a market town of particular architectural charm with its 12th century castle overlooking Georgian houses in the river valley below. This fine old settlement stands at the point where the old Pilgrims' Way from Winchester to Canterbury crosses the River Wey, and it has long been an important staging post on the busy trading route between Southampton and London. Remains of Roman, Saxon and Stone Age dwellings have been found within its boundaries. The town first became a residence of the Bishops of Winchester during Saxon times, and following the Norman conquest, the new Norman bishop built himself a castle on a pleasant tree-covered rise above the centre of the town. The castle is a blend of the fortified and residential. It underwent a number of alterations, most notably in the 15th century when the decorated brick-built tower was added, and it remained in the hands of the Bishops of Winchester from the 12th century until 1927.

Farnham Castle has been visited on a number of occasions by the reigning English monarch and was besieged during the English Civil War. Today, it is approached along Castle Street, a delightful wide thoroughfare of Georgian and neo-Georgian buildings which was laid out to accommodate a traditional street market. The old Norman keep, now owned by English Heritage, is open to the public at weekends during the summer and guided tours of the Bishops Palace take place on Fridays.The residential part of the castle is now occupied by Farnham Castle International Briefing and Conference Centre.

Farnham contains a number of other interesting historic buildings, including a row of 17th century gabled almshouses. The informative **Farnham Museum** is housed in an attractive Grade I listed townhouse dating from 1718, known as Willmer House in West Street. The house has many original features including a pleasant walled garden at the rear. As well as some fine wood panelling, carvings and period furniture, the museum contains some interesting archaeological exhibits and a unique collection of 19th century glass paperweights.

Farnham Maltings in Bridge Square is a thriving arts and community centre which is housed in a listed early 18th century building, thought to have been a tanyard. The writer and agriculturalist William Cobbett (*Rural Rides*) was the

TILFORD WOODS

Tilford Road, Farnham, Surrey GU10 2DD
Tel: 01252 792199 Fax: 01252 797040
e-mail: bookings@tilfordwoods.co.uk
website: www.tilfordwoods.co.uk

Tilford Woods is a private complex of purpose-built luxury timber lodges situated on the outskirts of the picturesque village of Tilford. The lodges are furnished and decorated to a very high standard and provide an ideal base for exploring the wonderful surrounding countryside and the many attractions in the region. There are four types of lodge, sleeping from two to six

guests, and all have a warm, inviting ambience and the latest in modern amenities.

The fully equipped kitchens include oven, hob, fridge-freezer, microwave and dishwasher, and the lounge areas have nicam TV, video-recorder and midi hi-fi. All the lodges have their own decking veranda with furniture and at least one of each type of lodge has facilities for disabled visitors. The complex has a splendid bonus in the shape of the Duke of Cambridge pub, which serves excellent home-cooked meals every day of the week. Fresh fish is the house speciality, and the food is complemented by wines from a well-chosen and well-annotated list.

FARNHAM MALTINGS

Bridge Square, Farnham, Surrey GU9 7QR
Tel: 01252 726234 Fax: 01252 718177
e-mail: info@farnhammaltings.com
website: www.farnhammaltings.com

Over 300,000 people visit **The Maltings** every year. They come to Performing and Visual Arts events, courses and workshops; visit the monthly markets, trade fairs; or belong to one of the 40 or so societies which meet regularly there. But, whilst the Maltings has built up its reputation as an arts and community centre since 1975, its history stretches back to the 18th century.

The earliest surviving document relating to the Maltings is dated 1729, but there is evidence of two previous owners. In those days it was a tanyard. In 1830 Robert Sampson set up as a maltster in the then separate East Wing. He was succeeded in business by his son, Sampson Sampson, whose sign can still be seen on the end of his cottage at 18 Bridge Square. Meanwhile, the tanyard was sold to John Barrett, who converted it into a brewery.

The building stood empty for 12 years before it was turned ino an arts and community centre. The conversion so far comprises the Great Hall, the Barley Room, Malt Room, Tannery, Main Bar, Forum, Maltings Gallery & Studio, Long Kiln Room, Dance Studio, South West Kiln, the East Wing Studios, Dressing Rooms and Playgroup Studio. In1991 fully retractable theatre-style raked seating in the Great Hall was installed.

son of a Farnham labourer. He was born in a hostelry - now named after him - on Bridge Square and is buried beside his father in the churchyard of St Andrew.

AROUND FARNHAM

WAVERLEY ABBEY

2 miles E of Farnham on the B3001

Lying within easy striking distance of Farnham are the atmospheric ruins of Waverley Abbey. Dating from the 12th century, this was the first Cistercian abbey to be built in England. The first church was completed in 1160 and destroyed during the dissolution of the monasteries. Its monumental floor plan was only revealed after excavations this century. There is little in the way of architectural detail remaining at the site apart from some frater arches. However architectural historians have suggested that this early church might well have inspired the famous Gothic churches of Tintern, Fountains and Rievaulx abbeys.

The Abbey remains are open during daylight hours and are said to have

provided the inspiration for Sir Walter Scott's romantic novel, *Waverley*, published in 1814 during his stay at the nearby Waverley Abbey House, whose imposing structure was built with stone taken from the abbey in 1723.

TILFORD

3 miles E of Farnham off the B3001

A lovely two mile riverside walk from Waverley Abbey leads to Tilford, an attractive village which stands at the confluence of the two branches of the River Wey. The monks of Waverley are believed to have been responsible for rebuilding Tilford's two medieval bridges following the devastating floods of 1233 during which the abbey itself had to be evacuated. At the heart of Tilford stands a triangular village green which features a 900 year-old oak tree with a 25 foot girth which is known as the King's or Novel's Oak; a pleasant early 18th century inn can be found nearby. Tilford's parish church of All Saints hosts a regular spring festival of early church music. In Reeds Road to the southwest of Tilford is the **Rural Life Centre and Old Kiln Museum** (see panel below).

RURAL LIFE CENTRE

Old Kiln Museum, Reeds Road, Tilford, Farnham, Surrey GU10 2DL
Tel: 01252 795571 Fax: 01252 795571
e-mail: rural.life@lineone.net
website: www.rural-life.org.uk

The **Rural Life Centre** is a museum of past village life covering the years from 1750 to 1960. It is set in over 10 acres of garden and woodland and housed in purpose-built and reconstructed buildings, including a chapel, village hall and cricket pavilion. Displays show village crafts such as wheelwrighting, of which the centre's collection is probably the finest in the country. An historic village playground provides entertainment for children, as does a preserved narrow gauge light railway that operates on Sundays. There is also an arboretum with over 100 species of trees from around the world where walks can be enjoyed.

The centre is open 11am-5pm, Wednesday to Sunday and Bank Holidays from March until October and during winter months it is open 11am-4pm, Wednesday and Sunday only. Picnic areas can be found around the site and there is also a cafe and a gift shop.

RUNFOLD

2 miles E of Farnham on the A31

Runfold marks the beginning of the large tracts of woodland that dominate much of the landscape between Farnham and Guildford. A well-marked turning off the A31 indicates the small road that winds south into the village. Runfold, like its immediate - and even smaller - neighbour **Seale**, was essentially a mixed farming community in the medieval period, and this way of life is displayed in Manor Farm, which lies between the two villages.

TONGHAM

2 miles E of Farnham on the A31

Tongham lies at an important junction, where Surrey meets Hampshire. Aldershot lies just west across the border which is marked by the A331. With the busy A31, linking Farnham and Guildford lying just to the south, Tongham is hard pressed to retain any sense of the country. That it manages to is to the credit of the planners, who have ensured that many of its timber-framed cottages are still seen to good effect. Look out for the distinctive curved braces (the timbers linking walls and roof) on some of these cottages. Tongham boasts its own brewery called the **Hogs Back Brewery** which can be seen after the hill to the east of the town and the stretch of the A30 that continues to Guildford. It is famous for its TEA (or Traditional English Ale) and is based in an 18th century barn, where they brew the beer in the traditional way.

HOG'S BACK

4 miles E of Farnham on the A31

The Hog's Back is the name given to the ridge which dominates the landscape between the level ground surrounding

SEALE NURSERIES

Seale Lane, Seale, Farnham, Surrey GU10 1LD
Tel: 01252 782410
website: www.sealesuperroses.com

The May family has been growing roses at Seale Nurseries since 1948. In the post-war years the enthusiasm for roses really blossomed, and now the beauty of the rose is delighting yet another generation. David and Catherine grow a wide range of wonderful varieties with a particular focus on fragrant climbing roses to suit all sorts of gardens. Always innovative, David has made a major breakthrough in production by devising a way of growing roses in pots so the roots are never damaged by the lifting process of the conventionally grown rose. He was recently granted a patent for his growing system, the first in UK rose growing for over 30 years.

These hand-raised Seale Super Roses have exceptionally fibrous roots so they establish quickly in the garden, grow away rapidly and perform superbly. An added bonus is they can be planted at any time of the year.

David also offers a "Rose Rescue" service. The gardener brings grafting material from treasured plants or varieties no longer available and David grafts it for them. David and Catherine exhibited at the at Hampton Court Palace Flower Show for the first time in 2002 and formally launched the Seale Super Roses, winning a silver medal. Many other awards have followed including most recently a prestigious Grower of the Year Award in 2004.

Guildford (looking north) and the wooded, more undulating terrain looking south towards Hindhead. Motorists refer to this stretch of the A31 as the Hog's Back, and the four-mile stretch between Tongham and Compton is well served with picnic stops and the occasional lay-by to stop and admire the views.

The hamlet of Wanborough on the northern side of the A31 contains one of the smallest churches in Surrey. Built by the monks of Waverley Abbey, it stands in the shadow of a massive monastic tithe barn.

The old manor house was constructed between the 15th and 17th centuries on the site of pre-Norman manor and was used during World War II to train secret agents.

PUTTENHAM

5 miles E of Farnham off the A31

The Hog's Back village of Puttenham lies stretched out along the route of the old Pilgrims' Way. An attractive mixture of building styles, the village contains a restored part-Norman church, several fine 15th and 16th century cottages, an 18th century farm with a number of period outbuildings and oast houses, and an impressive Palladian mansion, Puttenham Priory, which was completed in 1762.

The mixture of building styles arose because of Puttenham's location, where chalk gives way to sandstone. Cottages use one or other, or both these materials, and the effect is enlivened with brickwork, usually dating from the 18th century.

ELSTEAD

5 miles E of Farnham on the B3001

The attractive village of Elstead lies surrounded by farmland and crossed by the River Wey. In fact it is this crossing that makes Elstead noteworthy. Its rough stonework bridge dates from the medieval period, crossing the river in a series of five graceful arches. It has a brick parapet, making the overall effect one of solidity and strength. Unfortunately, the medieval effect is lessened somewhat by the modern bridge that runs parallel to it on the north side. Nevertheless, the bridge marks a delightful entrance to the village itself.

On the lane leading from the old bridge to the village green is the **Old Farm House**, a large timber-framed building that was completed in the 16th century. The green itself is compact and triangular and a small cul-de-sac leads from it to the 14th century **Church of St James**, which was overly restored in the 19th century.

Just west of the centre is **Elstead Mill**, an 18th century water mill. It stands four storeys high, its brick structure topped with a Palladian cupola. Six classical columns support a small lead dome at the very top. It is

Elstead

FRENSHAM GARDEN CENTRE

The Reeds Road, Frensham, nr Farnham, Surrey GU10 3BP
Tel: 01252 792545
e-mail: info@frensham-gardencentre.co.uk
website: www.frensham.co.uk

Robert Tyler opened **Frensham Garden Centre** in 1993 and hasn't looked back since. Trained in horticulture at Writtle College, Robert ensures that his staff are also trained and knowledgeable about all aspects of gardening and about the wide range of products stocked. Customers will find everything they need for their garden here, whether they are experienced or professional gardeners or enthusiastic amateurs. Many of the plants for sale are grown in the centre's own nursery, and other products are sourced from a wide variety of suppliers to ensure the best possible combination of high quality and very reasonable prices.

In a beautiful woodland setting, Frensham Garden Centre invites customers to browse among the displays of plants, terracotta pots, wooden barrels and ornaments. They can try out the garden furniture,

investigate the barbecues and weigh up a spade or fork. All the well-known quality names are here, including Spear & Jackson and Wilkinson for tools and Swan Hattersley, Denewood and Alexander Rose for garden furniture. The centre, which is open every day, has several other interesting and more unusual sections. At Camping World there is a wide selection of camping, hiking and skiing equipment, including the largest display of tents in the South. The Gift Box has a collection of craft items and lots of gift ideas, and the Coffee Shop is a pleasant spot for a drink and a snack.

THE MARINERS HOTEL

Millbridge, Frensham, Surrey GU10 3DJ
Tel: 01252 792050 Fax: 01252 792649
website: www.themarinershotel.co.uk

Carlo Genziana and Melita have been running the **Mariners Hotel** in Millbridge since 1982. The hotel, which enjoys a peaceful location in the Surrey countryside, has 21 comfortable en suite bedrooms with all the usual facilities. The rooms include a sumptuous and romantic bridal suite, family rooms for guests with younger children and ground-floor rooms for those who require easy access. Laundry and ironing services are available. The comfortable lounge bar is inviting on a chilly evening, with a blazing fire reflected in the gleaming brass and copper ornaments and a warm redbrick chimney breast.

On warm summer days, guests can move outside to enjoy the fresh air and the pleasant scenery sitting at one of the garden tables. Inside or out, guests can choose from a good selection of real ales

and well-chosen wines to accompany traditional lunches and suppers. For something a little bit different, the bistro-style restaurant with colourful maritime decor specialises in Italian and fresh fish dishes. The hotel is a popular venue for functions, including wedding receptions, dinner dances and club weekends, and it is an equally good choice for business meetings, with faxing and photocopying facilities available. Whatever the reason for a visit, Carlo and Melita will ensure that their guests enjoy a warm welcome and high standards of service and hospitality.

now a restaurant, and much of the machinery, including a working water wheel, is displayed within.

PEPER HAROW

6 miles E of Farnham off the A3

Peper Harow is a small village lying just west of the A3 in completely rural surroundings. It has a number of interesting cottages reinforcing its rustic charm as well as one of the best collections of Surrey farm buildings at **Peper Harow Farm** just outside the centre of the village. Of particular interest is the large granary, built around 1600. It stands - resting on its 25 wooden pillars - at the centre of a quadrangle at the heart of the farm.

The **Church of St Nicholas**, in the centre of the village, was built in Norman times but was massively restored in the 19th century. The restoration, however, was conducted by A W N Pugin, and there is great care evident throughout. St Nicholas represents something of a find for students of architecture since it appears to be one of the few churches where Pugin sought to create a Neo-Norman effect, rather than the higher-flown Gothic style. The ancient yew tree in the churchyard is probably more than 600 years old.

The other big attraction in the village is **Peper Harow House**, a Grade I listed building dating from 1768 and now converted into flats. It is a cube-shaped manor house, the bottom two storeys soberly classical. An extra floor was added in 1913 along with some Baroque ornamentation that clashes with the style of the original building. The outbuildings are almost as impressive as the house itself, in particular the three-sided stables. The park surrounding the house was designed by Capability Brown in 1763.

FRENSHAM

3 miles SE of Farnham off the A28

St Mary's Church was moved in the 13th century from its previous site on low ground beside the River Wey. The chancel walls were part of the original building. The tower is 14th century, with massive diagonal buttresses, but the whole church was subject to a major restoration in 1868.

The village of **Millbridge** lies just to the north of Frensham, and like Frensham it is set in heaths with occasional farmland dotted around it. The A287 to the south of the village runs between Frensham's Great and Little Ponds, two sizeable National Trust-owned lakes which provide good bird-watching and recreational facilities. These are now contained within a 1,000-acre country park which incorporates four prehistoric bowl barrows and the Devil's Jumps, three irregularly shaped hills whose origin, like many other unusual natural features, is attributed to Satan.

THURSLEY

6 miles SE of Farnham off the A3

Thursley is an exceptional village, which takes its name from the Viking god Thor and the Saxon word for field, or lea. The settlement was once an important centre of the Wealden iron industry and a number of disused hammer ponds can still be seen to the east. These artificial lakes provided power to drive the mechanical hammers and bellows in the once-bustling iron forges. Today, the village is a tranquil place arranged around a green containing an acacia tree which was planted as a memorial to William Cobbett, the Georgian traveller and writer who is best remembered for his book describing riding tours of England, *Rural Rides*, which was published in 1830. Thursley is also the birthplace of the

Frensham Common

Distance:	5.8 miles (9.3 kilometres)
Typical time:	180 mins
Height gain:	45 metres
Map:	Explorer 145
Walk:	www.walkingworld.com
	ID:1059
Contributor:	Tony Brotherton

Access Information:

Car parking is at Frensham Great Pond car park, entrance at SU 843406. Access is from lane to west of pond: signs from A287 for Frensham Great Pond are unobtrusive but signs for Frensham Pond Hotel are rather less so. Car park is extensive in its woodland setting and it may be possible to park facing the pond.

Additional Information:

Frensham Great and Little Ponds were created some 800 years ago as fish ponds. The surrounding lowland heath supports rare creatures such as the Dartford warbler, sand lizard and silver-studded blue butterfly. The entire area of Frensham Common is an SSSI.

Description:

Frensham Common and the Surrey Hills. This is a truly satisfying walk of great variety, embracing water features, rolling green hills and National Trust heathland, with glorious views.

Features:

Hills or Fells, River, Lake/Loch, Pub, Toilets, National Trust/NTS, Wildlife, Birds, Flowers, Great Views, Butterflies, Food Shop

Walk Directions:

1 From car park walk downhill to bottom right-hand corner to locate sandy waterside path. Follow path with Frensham Great Pond on left, to reach lane. Lane bends left. At stream and sign 'Bacon Lane', cross to bridleway.

2 Follow bridleway through woods, with first lake, then River Wey to left. At fork, either take lower, or keep to higher path - they merge further on. Proceed as far as arched bridge.

3 Cross river and continue along path to stile at minor road. Turn right along road as far as pair of cottages, then take bridleway on left and follow path winding gently uphill. Path eventually joins lane at Orchard End, then continues as bridleway, still rising, to reach The Blue Bell pub.

4 Continue walk to road at Batts Corner. Turn right, then right again along gravel drive at 'Highlands' sign, as far as footpath signed to the right over a stile.

5 Cross couple of paddocks before entering woods via stile in corner. Proceed along woodland path with fields to right, emerging onto open ridge with fine views of wooded Surrey Hills.

6 Follow line of trees to re-enter woods, now on descending path. At stile, enter field and go left to near corner and further stile at entrance to woods.

7 Enter woods once more, to exit by stile into field. Keep to right-hand side around field until just past house, cross stile and pass through wooden latch-gate onto drive and lane, to reach crossroads.

8 Cross here and go ahead. Road becomes track then footpath leading to bridge over stream. Now climb bank and bear half-right into field to reach three-way signpost. Go ahead on path into next field, with barbed-wire fence on left; and at ninth and last stile, descend through wooded strip to main A287 road at The Mariners pub.

9 Resume walk by crossing road and walking downhill to bridge over river. Continue along to Priory Lane. Walk down lane until it bends sharp left; here turn right into sandy car park leading onto Frensham Common.

10 At top of small rise, turn right to follow orange arrows denoting Two Ponds Way Trail.

11 For climactic finish of this walk, follow path across common with Frensham Little Pond coming into view on left. With Great Pond now visible to right, continue along main or parallel subsidiary path through heather and gorse until, at highest point of common, you reach sign for 'Path 43' on right.

12 Descend on 'Path 43' then go left along 'Path 1' which runs alongside main road. Cross with care to reach path across common leading to refreshments and information room by Frensham Great Pond.

13 Car park is now close by.

celebrated architect Sir Edwin Lutyens, who at the age of only 19 converted a row of local cottages into a single dwelling now known locally as the Corner.

Thursley's two principal thoroughfares, the Lane and the Street, contain a wide variety of noteworthy domestic buildings. The latter leads to **St Michael's Church**, a part-Saxon structure which was heavily restored by the Victorians. The spire and belfry are 15th century and are supported by massive timber posts with tie-beams and arched braces, a good example of late-medieval engineering.

The churchyard contains the grave of a sailor, who was murdered on Hindhead Heath in 1786 by three men he had gone to help. Although the villagers never discovered the victim's name, they gave him a full burial and erected an inscribed stone over his grave.

Two interesting old buildings stand near the church, the half-timbered and tile-hung Old Parsonage and the part timber framed Hill Farm, both of which date from the 16th century.

THE DEVIL'S PUNCHBOWL

7 miles S of Farnham off the A3

The Devil's Punchbowl, probably Surrey's best-known natural feature, is a steep-sided natural sandstone amphitheatre through which the busy A3 Guildford to Petersfield road passes four miles to the southeast of Frensham Great Pond. As usual, Lucifer's name is invoked in the place name but the origins might have more to do with real events than with superstition. The deep valley provided excellent cover for thieves and highwaymen, and even in coaching days passengers would look on the natural wonder with a mixture of awe and apprehension. On one of the paths is a memorial to the brothers of W A Robertson, both killed in the First World War. The Robertson family gave the Devil's Punchbowl to the National Trust to commemorate the men's sacrifice.

HINDHEAD

7 miles S of Farnham on the A28

Hindhead stands near the top of a ridge and at 850 feet above sea level, is the highest village in Surrey. Perhaps surprisingly, it has only been in existence since the late 19th century. Before that the site was known primarily as a site for highwaymen planning their next heist while taking cover in the steep wooded countryside. Good stands of fir trees still surround Hindhead.

The town grew up along the Portsmouth Road (now the A3) and the buildings date mainly from a concentrated period in the 1890s. Shops were built along the Portsmouth Road and a number of comfortable residences were dotted through the surrounding woodlands. Most of these houses still enjoy leafy settings even if today the appearance is somewhat tamer. The late-1890s construction date means that these residences betray the influence of the Arts and Crafts movement. Most of them derive from the designs of Norman Shaw, the movement's great proponent.

One of the best examples of this style is Thirlestane on the Farnham Road. Making the most of the south-facing situation, as well as the height, this V-shaped house faces southwest so that most of it acts as a suntrap. A deliberately rough exterior, combined with the hanging tiles, typify the attention to quality materials while the deliberately asymmetrical nature of the two wings suggests the freedom of spirit associated with that period.

HINDHEAD COMMON

7 miles SE of Farnham off the A3

Lying just to the east of Hindhead itself is Hindhead Common, comprising a largely untamed collection of wild heathlands, pinewoods and steep valleys. The National Trust owns 1,400 acres of Hindhead Common and maintains a series of trails and paths that takes visitors through evocatively

HEALTHWISE FOODS

Grayshott Health Food Stores, Headley Road, Grayshott, Surrey GU26 6LE
Tel: 01428 604046 Fax: 01428 609400
e-mail: ken@healthwisefoods.co.uk
website: www.healthwisefoods.co.uk

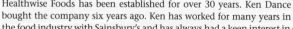

Healthwise Foods has been established for over 30 years. Ken Dance bought the company six years ago. Ken has worked for many years in the food industry with Sainsbury's and has always had a keen interest in quality whole food. **Grayshott Health Foods** is situated in a parade of shops in the main street. Providing a wide range of products, the shop caters for people with all sorts of special diets. There are sugar-free jams for diabetics, wheat and gluten-free products for coeliacs and dairy free foods for vegans or those with allergic reactions and a variety of frozen vegetarian dishes. There is even ice cream suitable for coeliacs, diabetics or vegans. For health conscious parents there are organic baby foods to give youngsters the best possible diet from the start. The emphasis of the shop is on quality.

For those who would rather restrict their caffeine intake or eliminate it from their diet entirely,

there are numerous decaffeinated teas as well as fruit and flower teas including such delightful concoctions as elderdown and lemon, apple and ginger, wild fennel, blackcurrant and gurana. The shop also carries a full range of cereals, pulses and dried fruit. In the herbal section there is a selection of natural remedies and vitamin and mineral supplements. Advice can be sought from the Therapy Centre, where specialists in homeopathy, nutrition, reiki, chiropody, counselling and reflexology provide alternative therapies for maintaining a healthy mind in a healthy body.

named sites such as Polecat Copse, Golden Valley, Hurt Hill and Stoatley Green. On the summit of Gibbet Hill is a granite monument marking the spot where the gibbet stood. The glorious views across both the North and South Downs was the last earthly memory of the thieves and murderers who were executed here.

GUILDFORD AND THE SOUTH

Guildford, with its prominent setting on a hill visible from the A3, is an obvious base for travellers interested in exploring the southwestern section of Surrey that extends down to and then, traces the West Sussex border. Like the area around Farnham, this area contains some of Surrey's most unspoilt countryside. Rough, hilly, thickly wooded in places, the landscape comes as close as anywhere in the county to fitting the descriptive term 'wild'.

The interaction between landscape and human society provides the background for some of the most interesting sights covered in the following pages. From time-worn remnants of prehistoric hill forts to medieval bridges along the Wey Valley and even including some of the modern architecture to be found among Guildford's hilly streets, the imprint of necessity-driven design is everywhere. Is it any wonder that Sir Edwin Lutyens cut his teeth, architecturally speaking, with his designs for houses occupying hilly sites or tucked in narrow valleys?

The settlements become decidedly smaller and more scattered as the Sussex border is neared. It is in these villages, many no more than hamlets, that visitors can appreciate just how even the earliest settlers scraped a

living, and how later inhabitants developed crafts that exploited the rich natural surroundings.

GUILDFORD

The route into Guildford from the northwest passes close to **Guildford Cathedral**, one of only two new Anglican cathedrals to have been built in this country since the Reformation (the other is Liverpool). This impressive redbrick building stands on top of Stag Hill, a prominent local landmark which enjoys panoramic views over the surrounding landscape. The building was designed by Sir Edward Maufe with a superb high-arched interior and was begun in 1936. However, work was halted during World War II and members of the local diocese had to wait until

Guildford Castle in Winter

1961 for the new cathedral to be finally consecrated. Guided tours and restaurant facilities are available all year round. In 1968, the **University of Surrey** relocated from London to a site on a hillside to the northwest of the cathedral. Pleasant and leafy, the campus contains a number of striking buildings including the university library and art gallery.

From the university, it is only a mile to the heart of Guildford, the ancient county town of Surrey. Guildford has been the capital of the region since pre-Norman times and in the 10th century, it even had its own mint. Henry II built a **Castle** here on high ground in the 12th century which later became the county jail. Today, the castle remains and the ruined keep provide a fascinating place from which to view the surrounding area. Those visiting the town for the first time should make straight for the old

High Street, a wonderful cobbled thoroughfare of Georgian and older buildings which rises steeply from the River Wey. Perhaps the most noteworthy of these is the **Guildhall**, a Tudor structure with an elaborately decorated 17th century frontage which incorporates a belltower, balcony and distinctive gilded clock.

Abbot's Hospital, a little further along, is an imposing turreted almshouse which was built in 1619 by the Guildford-born Archbishop of Canterbury, George Abbot; at the top of the High Street, the Royal Grammar School dates from the early 1500s and was subsequently endowed by Edward VI.

A number of interesting streets and alleyways run off Guildford High Street, including Quarry Street with its medieval St Mary's Church and old Castle Arch. The latter houses the Guildford Museum,

THE BEAR GARDEN

10 Jeffries Passage, Guildford, Surrey GU1 4AP
Tel: 01483 302581 Fax: 01483 457393
e-mail: bears@beargarden.co.uk
website: www.beargarden.co.uk

The **Bear Garden** is the brainchild of Andrew Colborne-Baber, who decided to open his own bear business after originally searching high and low in

Guildford for a teddy bear to give his mother as a present. Since its opening in 1992, it has gone from strength to strength and has become one of the leading teddy bear shops in the country. It is one of the top Steiff stockists and the largest Dean's stockist in the south of England. Robin Rive, Merrythought, Steiner and Hermann bears are all strongly represented, along with bears from leading bear artists, Hantel Victorian pewter miniatures from Scotland and many other desirable animals. A mailing list is available, there's a quarterly house magazine, and there's always something of interest on their fantastic website!

In October 2000 another Bear Garden opened in Kingston-upon-Thames (1a Crown Arcade, Tel: 020 8974 6177). This shop incorporates a Steiff shop-in-shop area, making it one of the most specialised Steiff shops in the UK.

an informative centre for local history and archaeology which also contains an exhibition devoted to Lewis Carroll, the creator of *Alice In Wonderland* who died in the town in 1898. He is buried in Mount Cemetery. A charming bronze memorial to Lewis Carroll (real name Charles Lutwidge Dodgson), which is composed of a life-sized Alice chasing the White Rabbit into his hole, can be found on the far bank of the River Wey, midway between the two footbridges. The well-known Yvonne Arnaud Theatre stands in a delightful riverside setting at the foot of the castle mound on the town side of the river. As well as offering top quality productions, the theatre has an excellent bar, coffee lounge and restaurant which remains open throughout the day. In summer, rowing boats and guided pleasure boat trips are available at the nearby Guildford Boat House.

AROUND GUILDFORD

CLANDON PARK
5 miles E of Guildford on the A247

Set in the farming countryside east of Guildford and south of Woking is the National Trust-owned property Clandon Park. This magnificent country mansion was designed in the 1730s by Giacomo Leoni, a Venetian architect, who combined Palladian, Baroque and European styles to create one of the grandest 18th century houses in England. The interior is renowned for its magnificent two-storey marble hall, sumptuous decoration and fine Italian plasterwork depicting scenes from mythology. The Gubbay collection of furniture and porcelain is also housed here, along with the Ivo Forde collection of humorous Meissen figures. The surrounding parkland was landscaped by Capability Brown in characteristic style and includes a parterre, grotto and brightly painted New Zealand Maori house.

GOMSHALL
5 miles E of Guildford on the A25

This once industrialised community has a Victorian heart and was once an important centre of the tanning and leather-working industries. The old packhorse bridge over the River Tillingbourne dates from the 1500s and the manor house at the southern end of the village from the early 1700s. Gomshall is now known for its fine craft and antique shops, several of which are concentrated in an ancient and beautifully converted water mill, the **Gomshall Mill and Gallery**. This working water mill dates back to 1086 and now houses a variety of attractive and unusual shops, a tea room and a licensed restaurant.

SHERE
6 miles E of Guildford off the A25

Shere is one of the loveliest, and consequently most visited, villages in Surrey. Thankfully now bypassed by the A25, it lies at the foot of the North Downs in the river valley which is particularly known for the growing of watercress, a plant that requires a constantly flowing supply of fresh water. The village **Church of St James** dates from the 12th century and was tastefully restored in the 1950s. Among its many noteworthy features are the 13th century Purbeck marble font, the St Nicholas Chapel, and an unusual hermit's cell built in the 14th century for a local woman who asked to be confined there for life.

The churchyard is entered through an impressive lych gate designed by Lutyens and close by stands the White Horse Inn, one of the many fine 16th and 17th century buildings to be found in the village. The **Shere Museum** in the Malt House contains an interesting collection of local artefacts, and the Old Farm behind the church is an open farm, which, at weekends, offers hands-on demonstrations of traditional farming techniques.

ALBURY
4 miles E of Guildford on the A28

Albury dates largely from the last century and was constructed in fanciful neo-Gothic style as an estate village for nearby **Albury Park**. This large country mansion was built on the site of a Tudor manor house in the early 18th century and was much altered by Pugin in the 1840s. (Pugin also designed the south transept chapel in the Church of St Peter and St Paul which stands on the estate. It was a mortuary chapel for Henry Drummond, the estate's owner.) The most eccentric feature of the house is its collection of chimneys, 63 of them built for only 60 rooms in an amazing variety of shapes and sizes. Although the mansion has now been converted into flats, the estate gardens are open to visitors and are well worth a look. They were laid out by the diarist John Evelyn at the turn of the 18th

century and feature a series of terraced orchards which rise above the house to the north. A number of smaller communities nestle around Albury.

CHILWORTH
3 miles E of Guildford on the A28

Chilworth is a former munitions and paper-making centre whose church, **St Martha on the Hill**, had to be rebuilt in 1850 following an explosion in the nearby gunpowder works. The result is a genuine success and shows great flair and sensitivity. There was no attempt made to copy the original exactly but the resulting reconstruction remains true to the Norman spirit of the destroyed church. On the hill to the south of the church are five circular banks, each about 100 feet in diameter, which have been identified as early Bronze Age henge monuments.

Chilworth Manor was built in the 1600s on the site of a pre-Norman monastic house. The exterior is a medley of styles but its 17th century gardens are complete, running up the side of the hill in terraces.

SHALFORD
3 miles S of Guildford on the A281

The residential community of Shalford contains a fascinating **Water Mill** which operated from the early 1700s right up to the World War I. Once powered by the waters of the Tillingbourne, this exceptional tile-hung structure retains most of its original machinery. During the 1930s, it was bought and restored by Ferguson's Gang, a secretive group of conservationists who hid their identities behind eccentric *noms de plume* and

The Old Post Office, Albury

who eventually donated the water mill to the National Trust.

Shalford stands near the northern entrance to the **Wey and Arun Junction Canal**, an ambitious inland waterway constructed in 1816 to connect the Thames with the English Channel. Conceived during the Napoleonic wars as a way of avoiding attacks on coastal shipping, unfortunately it opened too late to fulfil its function and was soon superseded by the railways. A towpath providing some delightful walks runs along almost two-thirds of the canal's 36-mile length, a significant proportion of which has now been fully restored by enthusiastic teams of volunteers.

About a mile south of Shalford is **Great Tangley**, one of the finest 16th century half-timbered houses in Surrey. The exterior is made up of roughly square panels each with four curved diagonal braces. This combination creates a star shape for each panel, which is repeated across the sides of the house.

BLACKHEATH
4 miles SE of Guildford off the A248

Set in the hills above Albury, this tidy Victorian hamlet gives the visitor a sense of remoteness despite being within easy striking distance of Guildford. Blackheath has some fine late-Victorian buildings. One of the most interesting is Greyfriars, a Franciscan monastery built in neo-Gothic style in 1895. The church and dormitories of this stone-built structure are contained under one roof. Another Victorian curiosity is the somewhat austere timbered residence, the Hallams.

WONERSH
4 miles SE of Guildford off the A248

Wonersh is a former weaving centre with a fine 16th century half-timbered inn, the Grantley Arms, located along the high street, which presents a cheerful and harmonious appearance with its medley of brick, stone, tile-hanging and half-timbered buildings. An imposing Lutyens house, **Chinthurst Hill**, is just a few minutes' walk northwest of the heart of the village. Lutyens used the local Bargate stone to create a Tudor effect, the work being completed in 1895, before he had developed his own distinctive style. The house occupies a lovely hillside site and the terraced garden was planted by Gertrude Jekyll.

BRAMLEY
3 miles SE of Guildford off the A248

Despite being largely Victorian, Bramley has some attractive Georgian and Regency residential buildings. These appear somewhat haphazardly through the long winding street that forms the nearest thing to a core of the village. There are two Lutyens houses in Bramley. The small, L-shaped **Millmead**, a National Trust property, is located south of Gosden Green. It was built for the gardener Gertrude Jekyll between 1904 and 1907 and traces of her original garden survive. About half a mile north is **Little Tangley**, a late-19th century house to which Lutyens added a porch and staircase hall in 1899. The Stables, which is now a private house called Edgton, was one of the architect's first works.

GODALMING
5 miles S of Guildford on the A3100

The old market town of Godalming was once an important staging post between London and Portsmouth and a number of elegant 17th and 18th century shops and coaching inns can still be found in the High Street. A market was established here in 1300 and the town later became a centre for the local wool and textile industries. Perhaps the most

Guildford to Godalming

Distance:	5.0 miles (8.0 kilometres)
Typical time:	180 mins
Height gain:	50 metres
Map:	Explorer 145
Walk:	www.walkingworld.com ID:31
Contributor:	Daisy Hayden

Access Information:

Train from Waterloo to Guildford 40 mins. Return from Godalming to Waterloo 50 mins. 2 or 3 trains per hour.

Description:

This is a beautiful, relaxing and easy walk along the River Wey including the Godalming navigations. The open valley is National Trust Land, and the scenery is varied and unspoilt. There are plenty of pubs and tea shops for refreshments in Guildford and Godalming, and toilets 2/3 of the way along the walk at Farncombe Boatyard. Wear boots or wellies as the path is muddy.

Features:

Toilets, National Trust/NTS, Birds

Walk Directions:

1 Turn right out of Guildford Railway station (you only need to cross over the line if arriving at Guildford on the train towards London). Walk 200 yards down Park Street, crossing Farnham Road to arrive at the church seen in the distance.

2 Turn left into High Street and pass in front of the church, to reach a pub, The White Horse on your right. Turn right down steps in front of the pub (the steps are just before this bridge). Go through the beer garden, and take the riverbank path to the right (behind pub

sign & evergreen tree pictured) Continue along the riverbank for 100 yards until you reach a white bridge. Cross this bridge towards Millmead Lock.

3 Do not cross Millmead Lock. Stay on the path, following the sign to the right (sign says Godalming 4½m) Pass the Jolly Farmer pub on the opposite bank. Cross this bridge, past the boathouses, and follow the path. Here the river loops to the left, then curves right (along line of trees on horizon). Follow the path on the right to join the river by a bridge, or take the longer way round, following the bend of the river to end up at the same bridge. Turn right to cross this bridge (weir to right of picture) to follow the path along the riverbank.

4 Continue along the path on the right. This part of the walk is particularly peaceful and charming, and only 15 minutes from Guildford town centre. Path gets muddy here.

5 Continue over this bridge and along the path Looking back towards Guildford at St Catherines Lock. Cross the bridge to visit the nature reserve, otherwise continue on the riverside path.

6 The Gomshall line crosses the river here on this impressive bridge. Continue on the path under the bridge.

7 Not a very pretty view, but a landmark anyway. Cross over the A248 at Broadford bridge and keep following the path ahead. Beware: fast traffic!

8 Opening Unstead lock. Children may want to watch or help boatpeople operate the lock gates.

9 Cross the road over a bridge to follow this footpath sign. Caution; fast traffic!

10 Continue past this old brick footbridge.

11 Looking back towards Guildford at Farncombe boathouse (Boat Hire here). Carry straight on over the bridge towards Godalming.

12 Follow the path to the car park, then turn left over the bridge. Just after the bridge go straight ahead and up this street. Turn right at the top for the main high street and shops and refreshments. Follow signs to station, which is right, at the far end of the high street.

13 Alternatively just after the bridge, turn right along Bury Road for 200 yards. Take the path right off the road, on the left of St Peter and Paul Church, for the train station.

interesting building in the old centre is the former town hall, affectionately known as **The Pepperpot**, which was built at the western end of the High Street in 1814. This unusual arcaded building once contained an interesting museum of local history, but **The Museum** is now opposite the Pepperpot at the fascinating Wealden House, parts of which date from the 15th and 16th centuries but which also has Victorian and Georgian additions. The museum has displays on geology and archaeology as well as local history, including a display detailing Godalming's claim to fame as the first town to have a public electricity supply. Two of Godalming's most renowned former residents – Gertrude Jekyll, the gardener and Sir

Edward Lutyens, the architect – are celebrated in a gallery exhibition and there is a Jekyll-style garden. The timber-framed house once belonging to Gertrude Jekyll can be found in dense woodland on the opposite side of town. **Munstead Wood** was designed for her by Edwin Lutyens in characteristic rural vernacular style and partially constructed of Bargate stone, a locally quarried hard brown sandstone that was much loved by the Victorians. Lutyens also designed the tomb in which Gertrude Jekyll is buried in the churchyard at **Busbridge**, just south of Godalming.

Godalming's part-Norman parish church of St Peter and St Paul is also built of Bargate stone, as is

GODALMING ART SHOP

45 Bridge Street, Godalming, Surrey GU7 1HL
Tel/Fax: 01483 423432

In the ground floor of a redbrick building in a row of shops, **Godalming Art Shop** stocks an amazing range of materials for artists and craftspeople. At the helm are Alan Watson, formerly a professional illustrator, and his wife Charlotte, a talented artist and printmaker. All the leading makers of paints, brushes and associated supplies are stocked, and the shop also sells original paintings and prints, greetings cards, art-oriented gifts and books on art techniques. And as Alan says: "If we don't have what you want in stock we'll order it for you."

JEWELLED LTD

89 High Street, Godalming, Surrey GU7 1AW
Tel/Fax: 01483 869838
website: www.jewelled.info

Opened in September 2001, **Jewelled** offers a refreshing and energetic modern approach to jewellery design and manufacture. New and innovative designs in platinum, gold, silver and diamonds are handmade in the workshop by Jane Graham and Jamie Railton. They create jewellery that could be contemporary or classic, trendy or traditional, but is always individual and exciting. They

also specialise in making jewellery to individual customer specification, creating engagement and wedding rings, wedding bands and other pieces that follow customers' ideas right through from concept to the finished article.

Another service offered at Jewelled is the redesign and remodelling of existing pieces of jewellery. They also undertake valuations of customers' pieces, and the expertise, the quality and the all-important personal touch that accompany all their services have established Jewelled as a leader in its field. And the praise extends even to the building in which Jewelled is located: the interior of the Georgian premises was designed and refurbished by Jane's husband David – for which he earned a commendation in the Godalming Trust Civic Design Awards for 2002.

GODALMING PACKET BOAT COMPANY

57 Furze Lane, Farncombe, nr Godalming, Surrey GU7 3NP
Tel: 01483 414938
website: www.horseboat.org.uk

There can be few gentler, more relaxed ways of spending a summer afternoon than a horse-drawn boat trip with the **Godalming Packet Boat Company**. Jenny Roberts, who runs the company with her daughter Lynne, bought the narrow boat Iona in 1986 and started the trips, thus keeping alive the tradition of horse-drawn boating. The two-hour round trip (usually starting at 2pm) begins and ends at Godalming Wharf on the National Trust-owned River Wey Navigation, passing through a lock on the way. Iona, a full-length narrow boat, was built in 1935 by Harland & Wolfe for service with the Grand Union Canal Carrying Company. She did duty in several places and appeared on TV and in films before

taking up her current job. She retains her traditional colourful painting and has seats for up to 48 passengers and a tea bar.

Iona is drawn by one of two splendid heavy horses – the piebald mare Rosie, who used to appear in coloured horse classes at shows, or the blue roan gelding Ben, who started his working life pulling a trap in Brentwood. Iona can be chartered for a birthday outing, a corporate event or any other special occasion, and buffet meals or cream teas are available by arrangement.

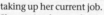

Charterhouse, the famous public school, which moved from London to a hillside site on the northern side of Godalming in 1872. Among its most striking features are the 150-foot Founder's Tower and the chapel designed by Giles Gilbert Scott as a memorial to those killed in the First World War.

Three miles along the B2130 to the southeast of Godalming lies the renowned **Winkworth**

Godalming in Snow

Arboretum, a 95-acre area of wooded hillside which was presented to the National Trust in 1952. The grounds contain two lakes and a magnificent collection of rare trees and shrubs, many of them native to other continents. Hascombe, one mile further on, is another characteristic Surrey village with great charm.

LOSELEY PARK

3 miles N of Godalming off the B3000

Loseley Park, a handsome Elizabethan country estate, was built in 1562 of

Bargate stone, some of which was taken from the ruins of Waverley Abbey. **Loseley House** is the former home of the Elizabethan statesman, Sir William More. Both Elizabeth I and James I are known to have stayed here, and the interior is decorated with a series of outstanding period features, including hand-painted panelling, woodcarving, delicate plasterwork ceilings, and a unique chimney-piece carved from a massive piece of chalk. The walled garden is a beautiful place to take a stroll, the surrounding gardens contain a terrace and a moat walk, and the nearby fields are home to Loseley's famous herd of pedigree Jersey cattle. Visitors can take a trailer ride to the traditional working dairy farm, where they can see the Jersey herd being milked every afternoon and discover the history of the estate.

COMPTON

4 miles N of Godalming off the B3000

The historic community of Compton was once an important stopping place on the old Pilgrims' Way. The village

Winkworth Arboretum

KD Fine Art Ltd

The Old Pottery Building, Down Lane, Compton, Surrey GU3 1DQ
Tel: 01483 811344   Fax: 01483 810616
e-mail: studio@kdfineartltd.co.uk
website: www.kdfineart.co.uk

Hidden away in the heart of the Surrey countryside, yet close to Guildford and the A3, **KD Fine Art Ltd** is an art gallery, gift shop and picture framing centre. In a lovely old pottery building on the site of the famous Watts Gallery, Keith and Denise Davenport first opened a small gallery in 1992. Since then the business has expanded rapidly, and now offers one of the largest selections of framed prints and original paintings in Surrey.

Two spacious galleries exhibit paintings by local and internationally known artists in a variety of styles and mediums, and the thousands of

prints in stock range from hand-coloured engravings and limited edition prints to modern lithographic reproductions. Complementing these is a large selection of picture frames, photo frames and mirrors. The Davenports' son Guy is a highly skilled, award-winning picture framer, and the large, well-equipped workshop on the premises offers a bespoke picture framing service that combines top quality with competitive prices. The gift shop stocks a superb selection of design-led giftware that includes Polish glass, Italian ceramics, pottery, candles, greetings cards and much more. KD Fine Arts is open every day from 10.30am to 5.30pm.

possesses an exceptional part-Saxon church, St Nicholas, with some remarkable internal features, including a series of 12th century murals, which were only rediscovered in 1966, an ancient hermit's, or anchorite's, cell, and a unique two-storey Romanesque sanctuary which is thought to have once contained an early Christian relic.

Compton is also renowned for being the home of the 19th century artist G F Watts, a largely self-taught painter and sculptor whose most famous work, *Physical Energy*, stands in London's Kensington Gardens. At the age of 47, Watts married the actress Ellen Terry, but the couple separated a year later. Then at the age of 69, he remarried, this time to Mary Fraser-Tytler, a painter and potter 33 years his junior who went on to design Watts' Memorial Gallery, which today contains over 200 pieces of the artist's work, along with the Watts

Mortuary Chapel, an extraordinary building which was completed in 1904 and is decorated in exuberant Art Nouveau style. The Watts Gallery is a fascinating place to visit, housing a unique collection of his paintings, drawings and sculptures. The nearby memorial chapel is also worth visiting.

EASHING
1 mile W of Godalming off the A3100

The tiny hamlet of Eashing is noted for the lovely medieval Eashing Bridge, which has segmented arches and uses cutwaters - pointed upstream and rounded downstream to stem the flow of the river. It is one of several surviving Wey Valley bridges of that period, the others being at Elstead and Tilford. Just to the east of the bridge is **The Meads**, an ancient house of two distinct parts. Half of it is 16th century, with timber framing and an original Tudor doorcase.

The other is 18th century and brick and stone, with small dark chips of stone set in the mortar.

WITLEY

4 miles S of Godalming on the A283

The historic village of Witley comprises an attractive collection of fine tile-hung and half-timbered buildings loosely arranged around the part-Saxon church of All Saints, a much-altered structure which contains some rare 12th century frescoes and a delicately carved 13th century font, and incorporates a 17th century tower. The present village inn, the White Hart, was constructed in Elizabethan times to replace an even earlier hostelry. It is believed to be one of the oldest inns in the country and at one time stood adjacent to a market place which hosted a busy Friday market.

Witley's Old Manor was visited by a number of English monarchs, including Edward I and Richard II, and the village centre contains some delightful 15th and 16th century timber-framed houses, many of which are hung with characteristic fishtail tiles. These include the Old Cottage, Red Rose Cottage (so-called because the lease granted on Christmas Day 1580 called for an annual rent of one red rose), and Step Cottage, a former rectory that was once the home of the Reverend Lawrence Stoughton; this worthy gentleman died aged 88 after serving the parish for 53 years and outliving five wives.

At one time, Witley was a summer haven for artists and writers, the best known of which is perhaps George Eliot who wrote her last novel, *Daniel Deronda*, here between 1874 and 1876. Her home, the Heights, was designed by Sir Henry Cole, the architect of the Royal Albert Hall, and was visited by a series of eminent guests, including the novelist Henry James. Today, the building has been converted into a nursing home and is now known as Roslyn Court.

A large proportion of the common to the north of Thursley is a designated nature reserve which is known for its unusually large and varied population of dragonflies. The **Witley Common Information Centre** lies a few minutes' drive from Thursley Common on the eastern side of the A3. This purpose-built nature centre is managed by the National Trust and is set in woodlands at the edge of a substantial area of Trust-owned heathland. Inside, there is an audio-visual display and an exhibition outlining the history, geology and natural history of the area.

Tigburne Court, which is regarded by many as Lutyens's finest work, is just over a mile south of Witley, standing right on the main Milford to Petworth road. It was built between 1899 and 1901 for Sir Edgar Horne. Lutyens was 30 years old when he designed Tigburne Court, and the house shows him at the height of his powers yet still full of youthful exuberance. He playfully mixed Tudor styles with 18th century classicism and used horizontal bands of tiles with the Bargate stone to create a powerful geometric effect. The gardens, like those of so many of the best Lutyens houses, are by his collaborator Gertrude Jekyll.

HAMBLEDON

5 miles S of Godalming on the A283

This scattered settlement contains a number of interesting buildings, including the tile-hung **Court Farm**, which stands near the part-14th century church, the Old Granary, School Cottage, and Malthouse Farm and Cottage. The National Trust owns a small timber-framed dwelling in Hambledon known as Oakhurst Cottage which has been restored as an old artisan's home and is open in the summer by appointment only.

A memorial to one of the Trust's founders, the social reformer Octavia Hill, stands at the top of nearby **Hydon's Ball**, an unusual conical hill which at 593 feet above sea level offers some fine views over the surrounding landscape.

HASLEMERE
9 miles S of Godalming on the A286

The genteel town of Haslemere lies in the southwestern corner of the county. Now a quiet and comfortable home for well-to-do commuters, it has central streets filled with handsome Georgian and Victorian buildings, most of which were constructed following the arrival of the railway in 1859. The building styles, including stucco, redbrick and tile-hung, combine to form an attractive and harmonious architectural mix. Some of Haslemere's finest pre-Victorian structures include the Town Hall, rebuilt in 1814, the **Tolle House Almshouses** in Petworth Road, Church Hill House, the Town House, and two noteworthy hotels, the Georgian and the White Horse.

Towards the end of the last century, Haslemere became something of a centre for the arts. Alfred Lord Tennyson settled nearby, and a group known as the Haslemere Society of Artists was formed whose number included Birket Foster and the landscape painter Helen Allingham. At the end of the World War I, the French-born musician and enthusiastic exponent of early music, Arnold Dolmetsch, founded what has become a world-famous musical instrument workshop here. Dolmetsch's family went on to establish the Haslemere Festival of Early Music in 1925; it is still held each year in July.

Another of Haslemere's attractions is the **Educational Museum** in the High Street, an establishment which was founded in 1888 by local surgeon and Quaker, Sir James Hutchinson, and which now contains an imaginative series of displays on local birds, botany, zoology, geology and history.

CHIDDINGFOLD
6 miles S of Godalming on the A283

With its three-sided green, waterlily-filled pond, part-13th century church, medieval pub and handsome collection of Georgian cottages, this attractive settlement contains all the features of a quintessential English village. During the 13th and 14th centuries, it was an important centre of the glass-making industry, a once flourishing trade which used local sand as its main ingredient and employed skilled craftspeople from across northern Europe. Some fragments of medieval Chiddingfold glass can be seen in the small lancet window in **St Mary's Church**, below which a brass plaque is inscribed with the names of several early glass-makers. The church itself was much altered during the 1860s. However, its west tower is 17th century and contains a peal of eight bells, one of which is believed to be around 500 years old. The churchyard is entered through an exceptionally fine lych-gate, a covered gateway with a wide timber slab which was used to shelter coffins awaiting burial.

Of the many handsome buildings standing around Chiddingfold's village green, the Crown Inn is perhaps the most impressive. This is another hostelry which claims to be the oldest in England, its existence having first been recorded in 1383. The structure is half-timbered and incorporates a medieval great hall; Edward VI is reported to have stayed here in the 15th century. Other buildings in the village worthy of note are Chantry House, Manor House, and Glebe House, the last two of which have elegant Georgian facades.

DUNSFOLD

6 miles S of Godalming on the B2130

From Chiddingfold, a pleasant journey eastwards through the country lanes leads to another settlement with fold (a Saxon term meaning 'forest clearing') in its name. Dunsfold is a narrow ribbon of a village, which lies on either side of a long unmanicured green. It contains a number of fine old brick and tile-hung cottages and houses, several of which date from the late 17th century, and an excellent pub, the Sun Inn which stands beside a towering oak tree which is said to have a girth of over 20 feet.

Dunsfold's finest feature, however, is situated half a mile from the village on top of a raised mound which may once have been the site of a pre-Christian place of worship. The **Church of St Mary and All Saints** dates from around 1280 and apart from the addition of a 15th century belfry, has remained virtually unchanged since. The structure was much admired by William Morris, the Victorian founder of the Arts and Crafts Movement, who particularly approved of the simple, rough-hewn pews, which were made around 1300 by the inhabitants of the surrounding farms. A leafy glade at the foot of the mound is the location of a holy well, whose water is reputed to be a cure for eye complaints and blindness. The site of the holy well is marked by a timber shelter erected in the 1930s.

ALFOLD

9 miles S of Godalming on the B2133

A former clearing in the Wealden forest, Alfold is an exceptionally attractive village that was once an important glass-making centre. It reputedly supplied material for the windows of Westminster Abbey. Evidence of the medieval glassworks can still be made out in the woods on the edge of the village. The area around the church contains a number of interesting features, including an ancient yew tree in the churchyard, a charming Tudor cottage, and an old village whipping post and set of stocks. Just at the edge of the village is the **Countryways Experience**, a series of interactive exhibits that covers the history and natural history of this area, giving visitors some perspective on how living conditions adapted to new styles of farming over the centuries. Visitors can feed a range of animals, including lambs, goats, piglets, calves and chickens, with food from the farm shop.

ELLEN'S GREEN

9 miles SE of Godalming on the B2128

This tiny hamlet on the Sussex border is one of the best preserved Surrey villages. It is set in unspoilt Weald country, with thick woodlands giving way to small fields. Cottages line the green but in a way that has no suggestion of excessive self-consciousness. Although singularly lacking in dramatic sights, Ellen's Green offers the visitor the chance to see an example of the small villages that were once typical of the area but are now much rarer.

CRANLEIGH

7 miles SE of Godalming on the B2128

The parish church, St Nicholas, in the quiet residential town of Cranleigh contains a carving of a grinning feline which allegedly provided the

ONE FORTY

140 High Street, Cranleigh, Surrey GU6 8RF
Tel: 01483 272627
e-mail: info@oneforty.co.uk website: www.oneforty.co.uk

Richard and Elaine Graham, with years of experience in fashion retailing and marketing, have recently opened **One Forty** on the main street of Cranleigh. Replacing their previous shop in the same Victorian building, One Forty sells an impressive selection of clothes and accessories for both men and women and aimed mainly at the 30 to 60 age group.

The shop is equally well stocked with major brands and smaller independent manufacturers, and

apart from the clothes and accessories there is a wide range of homeware and gifts suitable for any occasion. The owners have totally refurbished the shop, and behind the broad frontage and enticing window displays the decor includes seagrass and wooden floors, pendant lighting and strong colours distinguishing one department from another.

One Forty is a great place for browsing, and shoppers can take a break with a drink and a snack in the bright, spacious café on the first floor.

TIFFINS TEA ROOMS

6 Bank Buildings, 159 High Street, Cranleigh, Surrey GU6 8BB
Tel: 01483 272320

Part of a late-Victorian parade of shops in the centre of Cranleigh, **Tiffins** offers a selection of freshly prepared food served in delightful traditional surroundings. A hearty English breakfast is available from 9am until noon, when light lunches take over until 3pm: these include ham, egg and chips, chilli con carne, cod and chips, suet puddings with a choice of tasty savoury fillings, and delicious hot puddings. Sandwiches, jacket potatoes, hot snacks, cakes and pastries are on the menu all day, and the special cream tea with scones, strawberry jam and Devon clotted cream is a treat not to be missed. Closed Wednesday and Sunday.

inspiration for Lewis Carroll's Cheshire Cat. The town also contains the country's first cottage hospital, opened in the 1850s, and a public school founded by local farmers in 1865, which still incorporates a working farm.

EWHURST

8 miles SE of Godalming on the B2127

Ewhurst is a long village containing a sandstone church, **St Peter and St Paul**, whose nave and south door are considered to be among the finest examples of Norman church architecture in the county. The rest of the structure would have been of a similar age had it not been for an unfortunate attempt to underpin the tower in the 1830s, which resulted in the collapse not only of the tower but of the chancel and north transept as well. The structure was eventually rebuilt in Norman style with an unusual shingled broach spire. Inside, there is a carved 14th century font and a Jacobean pulpit, and outside, the churchyard contains a number of mature trees native to North America.

The remainder of the village, part of which is set around a small square, contains some fine 18th and 19th century residential buildings, including the Woolpit, built for the Doulton family in the 1880s. The 843-foot Pitch Hill is situated a mile to the north and can be easily reached along a pleasant footpath from the village.

DORKING

Dorking is a long-established settlement, which stands at the intersection of Stane Street, the Roman road which once connected London with Chichester, and the ancient **Pilgrims' Way**, the east-west ridge way route, which is roughly followed by the course of the modern **North Downs Way**. Despite evidence of Saxon and Viking occupation, present-day Dorking is a congested commuter town, which owes most of its character to the Victorians.

There are a small number of older buildings, most notably the part-15th century former coaching inn, the White Horse, and the shops and houses in North Street, West Street, and at the western end of the High Street. However, the town's two most distinctive architectural features are characteristically 19th century: the unexpectedly grand **Church of St Martin** with its soaring spire, and the Rose Hill housing development, an assortment of Victorian villas arranged around a green and entered from South Street through an unusual neo-Gothic arch. **St Paul's Church** in Dorking is a

fine piece of architecture, designed by Benjamin Ferray and constructed in 1857.

Perhaps Dorking's most attractive feature is its close proximity to unspoilt countryside, a testimony to the success of the southeast's Green Belt policy. As well as the open spaces in the downs to the north, **Holmwood Common**, two miles along the A24 to the south, is another tract of National Trust-owned land which offers some pleasant way-marked walks through mature oak and birch woodlands and disabled access to the pleasant picnic area around **Fourwents Pond**.

Box Hill
2 miles N of Dorking off the A25

The 563-foot Box Hill lies a couple of miles from Polesden Lacey on the eastern side of the River Mole. This popular local landmark rises sharply from the valley floor to an impressive tree-covered summit high above. The hill takes its name from the mature box trees which once grew here in profusion but which were seriously depleted in the 18th century to supply the needs of London wood-engravers. By then, the site had already been known for over a century as a beauty spot and had been visited and recorded by, among others, the diarist John Evelyn.

Today, the National Trust owns over 800 acres of land around Box Hill which has now been designated a country park. The area around the summit incorporates an exhibition centre, a late-19th century fort and a café, and can be reached either by footpath or by a narrow winding road leading up from Burford Bridge. The hillside is traversed by a series of nature walks, and there are also several picnic sites, which enjoy breathtaking views across the Weald to the South Downs.

FIRE AND IRON GALLERY

Rowhurst Forge, Oxshott Road, Leatherhead,
Surrey KT22 0EN
Tel: 01372 386453
e-mail: lucy@fireandiron.co.uk
website: www.fireandiron.co.uk

Described by Miranda Innes in *Country Living* Magazine as 'a mecca for metal maniacs', Lucy Quinnell's **Fire and Iron Gallery** is a lively, eccentric and eclectic collection of metalwork and jewellery produced by some leading local, national and international craftspeople. Delightfully situated in a 15th century Surrey farmhouse in several acres of pleasant countryside, the Gallery hosts one of the finest displays of the art of the metalworker to be found anywhere. A working forge produces metal works for private commissions and huge public installations, and throughout the year a series of special exhibitions by individual artists complements a slowly changing permanent display of work from the world's leading artist-blacksmiths.

The spacious interior of the Gallery has five separate rooms displaying work - often combining metal with other media - by more than 300 British and international makers. There is always a wide variety of designs on display, ranging from unusual wedding rings to bowls, fire accessories, furniture, garden sculptures and amazing life-size steel animals, and a small sculpture trail running through the garden showcases the work of some of the current artists in residence. One of them is Carlos Dare, who produces breathtakingly beautiful sculptures in aluminium. Lucy is happy to arrange for a specially commissioned piece from any of the artists, which might be anything from a simple ring to a weather vane. Making the gates of the Globe Theatre in London was one of the Gallery's largest and most ambitious public projects, taking 10 years to organise and involving the participation of no fewer than 120 blacksmiths from all over the world.

Other works include a number of trophies presented by the actor Sir Michael Caine at a drama festival, and the list of prestigious clients includes the Eden Project in Cornwall. Lucy has appeared on several TV and radio shows promoting the craft of blacksmithing, including Fuji TV in Japan, the Craft Show, Woman's Hour and Blue Peter (the Gallery made the weather vane for the Blue Peter garden). Visitors who would like to try their hand at producing artwork like that seen in the Gallery can sign up for one of the popular weekend blacksmithing courses.

The Burford Bridge Hotel stands on the banks of the River Mole at the foot of Box Hill and is connected to it by stepping stones across the river. In the early 19th century, the establishment was known as the Hare and Hounds and it was here in 1805 that Admiral Nelson said his farewells to Lady Hamilton prior to the Battle of Trafalgar. Keats is also believed to have completed his second volume of poems *Endymion* here in 1818. **Chapel Farm** at nearby West Humble is an open farm, where visitors can see at close quarters how a livestock farm works.

MICKLEHAM

3 miles N of Dorking on the A24

Mickleham is a highly picturesque village with a good pub, the Running Horses, and a restored Norman church, **St Michael's**, containing a rare Flemish stained-glass window. It is worth examining the churchyard because this is one of the few parish churches to preserve the Surrey tradition of grave-boards. These are wooden tombstone planks carried between two posts. Most of the grave-boards in St Michael's are 19th century and have been carefully preserved and renovated where necessary.

LEATHERHEAD

5 miles N of Dorking on the A24

Leatherhead is a pretty Mole Valley town that manages to retain some measure of tranquillity despite being crossed by a number of major trunk routes.

Several buildings in the narrow streets of the old town are worthy of note, including the 16th century Running Horse Inn and the attractive part-12th century parish church of St Mary and St Nicholas. The grave of

VECCHIA TRATTORIA

24 High Street, Leatherhead, Surrey KT22 8AM
Tel: 01372 383290

Chris, Susan, Richard and Anne bring a wealth of varied skills and experience to **Vecchia Trattoria**, their excellent High Street restaurant specialising in traditional Italian dishes. The room is bright and modern, with a warm Mediterranean feel assisted by a feature ragwashed wall with green shutters on trompe l'œil doors, and the atmosphere is always happy and relaxed. Risotto marinara is a great favourite, and other

tempting dishes include scallops cooked with wine and lemon, veal with porcini sauce and a classic osso buco. The great food is complemented by a well-chosen list of Italian wines.

Anthony Hope (real name Sir Anthony Hawkins), the author of *The Prisoner Of Zenda*, can be found in the churchyard, and a short distance away in Church Street, the informative **Leatherhead Museum of Local History** is housed in a charming 17th century timber-framed cottage with its own small garden.

GREAT BOOKHAM

4 miles N of Dorking on the A246

Although heavily built up since the Second World War, the residential area to the west of Leatherhead manages to retain something of its historic past. The earliest mention of a settlement in the area dates back to the 7th century, when a manor at Bocheham is recorded as belonging to Chertsey Abbey.

Present day Great Bookham contains an exceptional parish church, **St Nicholas**, which has an unusual flint tower with a shingled spire dating back to the Norman era in the 12th century. A substantial part of the building, including the chancel, is known to have been rebuilt in the 1340s by the Abbot of Chertsey, and the church was again remodelled by the Victorians. Inside, there are some fine 15th century stained glass windows and a number of noteworthy monumental brasses and memorials to the local lords of the manor. An early 18th century owner of

the Bookham estate, Dr Hugh Shortrudge, left an endowment in his will to four local churches on condition that an annual sermon be preached on the subject of the martyrdom of Charles I. St Nicholas continues to uphold the tradition of the 'Shortrudge Sermon' which is preached each year on the final Sunday in January.

Nearby **Little Bookham** has a small single-roomed church with a wooden belfry that is believed to date from the 12th century. The adjacent 18th century manor house now operates as a school. Bookham Common and Banks Common to the northwest of Little Bookham provide some welcome relief from the commuter estates and offer some pleasant walking through relatively unspoilt open heathland. The commons are recorded in the Domesday Book as providing pannage, the right to graze pigs on acorns, for Chertsey Abbey. Now in the ownership of the National Trust, they are particularly known for their rich and varied birdlife.

Another National Trust-owned property, **Polesden Lacey**, stands on high ground two miles to the south of Great Bookham. The estate was once owned by the writer R B Sheridan, who purchased it in 1797 with the intention of restoring its decaying 17th century manor house. However, a lack of funds prevented him from realising his

Polesden Lacey

Margaret's personal collection of photographs provides a fascinating record of British high society at play during the early part of the century. The surrounding grounds amount to over 1,000 acres and incorporate a walled rose garden, open lawns, a YHA youth hostel and a large area of natural woodland. An annual festival in late June and early July is held in the charming open-air theatre. This has expanded over the years and now presents a variety of theatre and entertainment including Gilbert and Sullivan, light operetta, grand opera, ballet, classical concerts, jazz, big bands, music hall, folk dancing and spectacular fireworks. The programme always includes a Shakespearean production.

The Polesden Lacey estate is bordered to the south by Ranmore Common, another area of National Trust-owned upland, which is criss-crossed by scenic footpaths and bridleways.

ambitions, and following his death in 1816 the building was demolished and the estate sold. During the 1820s, the architect Thomas Cubitt built a substantial Regency villa in its place which was subsequently remodelled and enlarged by successive owners throughout the 19th century.

In 1906, the estate was acquired by Captain Ronald Greville and his wife Margaret, the daughter of a Scottish brewing magnate and a celebrated high society hostess. Over the following three decades, they invited a succession of rich and influential guests to Polesden Lacey whose number included Edward VII, and George VI and Queen Elizabeth (later the Queen Mother), who spent part of their honeymoon here in 1923. The Grevilles carried out a number of alterations of their own during this period and the extravagant 'Edwardian-Louis XVI' internal decoration remains as a testimony to Margaret Greville's taste - or lack of it.

Whatever the perspective, the house contains an undeniably fine collection of furniture, paintings, tapestries, porcelain and silver, which the Grevilles accumulated over 40 years, and

RANMORE COMMON

1 mile NW of Dorking off the A2003

Ranmore Common's location on the top of the Downs provides excellent views, especially to the south. This unspoilt setting, which can feel remote in bad weather despite its proximity to Dorking, is a testament to enlightened Green Belt policy. The common is in reality a long green, with only a few houses dotted around it, thereby preserving its exposed nature. Owned in part by the Forestry Commission, it is a Site of Special Scientific Interest and provides an excellent habitat for many birds and small mammals.

EFFINGHAM

5 miles NW of Dorking on the A246

Effingham is an old village that was famous as the home of the Howards of Effingham, one of whom was the Commander-in-Chief of the English fleet, which defeated the Spanish Armada in 1588. His home was **Effingham Court Palace**, which survives only as remnants at Lower Place Farm. There were two other important manors in Effingham. One is the moated grange in Great Lee Wood, once the manor of Effingham la Leigh. The other was the medieval property of the Earls of Gloucester, East Court, which is now incorporated in a boarding school, St Theresa's Convent.

EAST HORSLEY

6 miles NW of Dorking on the A246

Suburban building has caught up with East Horsley, leaving the town centre bereft of the sort of charm associated with Ranmore Common or some of the other villages that are nearer Dorking. It does, however, possess one of the more dramatic country houses in Surrey, at least as it is viewed from the road. **East Horsley Towers**, built in the 1820s, seems to capture the spirit of the 19th century imagination as it moved from Romantic to the nostalgic re-creations so loved by the Victorians. A long entrance leads to the house, which presents itself with a huge round tower by the entrance. Another tower, to the west, is built in the Gothic style. The house itself displays Tudor influences but has multi-coloured vaulting ribs throughout for support. Another tower, this time Germanic looking with a pointed roof, dominates the east wing of the house. It now operates as a luxurious management training centre.

F CONISBEE & SON

Park Corner, Ockham Road South, East Horsley, Surrey KT24 6RZ
Tel: 01483 282073 Fax: 01483 248859
website: www.f.conisbee.co.uk

In a distinctive three-storey pebble-fronted building on a corner site in East Horsley, **F Conisbee & Son** are high-class butchers, poulterers, graziers and caterers who have been masters of their trade since 1760. The current Conisbee is Neil, who runs the business with his sons Stephen and James. They use the very best sources, including local Surrey farmers and the weekly local fatstock market, and on their farm in Fetcham they rear beef cattle and prize-winning turkeys. All their meat is hung as carcasses and quarters, allowing the meat to mature naturally, ensuring tenderness and improved flavour without the tainting or discoloration often found in vacuum-packed meat.

The business now has a resident chef, Robert, who makes an excellent range of award-winning meat pies. He also provides meat platters, salads and specialities such as Beef Wellington - part of the full catering service offered by this outstanding firm. Another of the Conisbee specialities is a range of superb sausages in over 20 varieties (one is gluten-free), and they are also widely known for their barbecues and spit roasts, providing whole or part pigs served on a spit over a bed of hot coals, with all the trimmings, all the equipment and all the staff to ensure a great occasion for up to 1,000 people.

Oскнам

10 miles NW of Dorking on the B2039

Ockham once possessed a fine Jacobean mansion, **Ockham Park**. A serious fire in 1948 destroyed everything except for the orangery, stables, kitchen wing, and a solitary Italianate tower. The village church of All Saints still stands within the grounds of the estate; this largely 13th century building was constructed on the site of a pre-Norman structure and is known for its remarkable east window, a surprising combination of seven tall pointed lancets finished in marble with distinctive carved capitals. The window dates from around 1260 and is thought to have been brought here from nearby Newark Abbey following its dissolution in the 16th century. The church incorporates a brick chapel, which contains a robed marble effigy of the first Lord King, a former owner of Ockham Park who died in 1734. The name of Ockham is chiefly associated with the expression Ockham's Razor. William of Ockham was a 13th century Franciscan intellectual whose maxim was that every hypothesis should be sliced to its essentials and all unnecessary facts in the subject being analysed should be eliminated. William is commemorated by a small stained-glass window in the church.

On **Chatley Heath**, a mile to the north of Ockham, there is a unique **Semaphore Tower** which was once part of the Royal Navy's signalling system for relaying messages between Portsmouth and the Admiralty in London. Although the semaphore mechanism soon fell into disuse, the structure has remained in good order and is open to the public at weekends. As well as offering outstanding views over the surrounding landscape, the Chatley Heath Semaphore Tower houses an interesting exhibition and model collection. It can be reached along a pleasant woodland pathway and is open throughout the summer at weekends and Bank Holidays.

East Clandon

7 miles W of Dorking on the A246

This attractive small village straddles the A246 Leatherhead to Guildford route. The road zig-zags between brick and half-timber cottages, several of which are clustered around the Norman church of St Thomas. This small church was extensively restored at the end of the 19th century but the architects ensured that one of is most distinctive features - the bulky shingled bell tower - retained its original appearance.

The village also contains an interesting old forge and a lovely old manor farmhouse dating from the late 17th century. A striking National Trust property is located one mile to the northeast: **Hatchlands Park** is a distinctive brick-built house designed in the mid 18th century for Admiral Boscawen after his famous victory in the Battle of Louisburg. Inside, there are some splendid examples of the early work of Robert Adams, some fine period furniture and paintings, and a wonderful assortment of historic keyboard instruments, the Cobbe collection, which was moved here in 1988. Among the pianos are those owned or played by Beethoven, Mahler, Mozart, Chopin, Marie Antoinette and the Medici family. Elgar's piano is the very one on which he composed the *Enigma Variations*. The grounds, originally laid out by Humphry Repton, were remodelled by Gertrude Jekyll. In recent years, parts of the garden have been restored to the original designs and planting plans of Jekyll and Repton.

KINGFISHER FARM SHOP

Abinger Hammer, Dorking, Surrey RH5 6QX
Tel: 01306 730703 Fax: 01306 731654
e-mail: kingfisher@watercress.fsnet.co.uk

Run by Barrie Arminson, his wife Margaret and their daughter Marion, **Kingfisher Farm Shop** is continuing a long family tradition of providing high-quality food for the discerning consumer. Barrie's great grandfather started growing watercress in 1850 and Barrie still produces watercress for a few small retail outlets. It is grown in natural spring water, which provides all the necessary nutrients without the aid of fertilisers or insecticides.

The Farm Shop has been an increasingly important part of the business since the family started selling fruit and vegetables in 1971, and the watercress packing shed at Abinger Hammer became the present shop in 1999. As well as their own fresh watercress, the family sell as much regional and local

food as they can. Outside are seasonal displays of pumpkins, squashes, plants and herbs, while in the brightly lit interior an abundance of fresh fruit and vegetables greets the visitor. Nearby shelves are groaning with bread, cakes, pies and biscuits alongside locally produced jams and chutneys; in chill cabinets and freezers there are fresh and frozen meats, while dairy products include milk, cream, ice cream and a great selection of cheeses. Vegetarian and wholefood products are also available.

The off licence section stocks English wines, beers from Surrey and Sussex and cider from Herefordshire.

As members of Taste of Sussex, the Kingfisher Farm Shop is committed to providing high-quality local and homemade food of a kind not to be found on the shelves of supermarkets. The latest addition to the offerings at this outstanding farm shop is the adjacent Flower Shop, opened in October 2003. Here the family sell fresh-cut seasonal flowers, exotic stems, house plants and hand-tied bouquets and sprays (made to order), growing aids and ceramic and terracotta pots. The Farm Shop is open every day, the Flower Shop every day except Sunday and Monday.

A sight not to be missed on a visit to Abinger Hammer is the famous 'Jack the Smith' hammer clock that overhangs the main road. It stands on the site of an old iron forge, and the figure of a blacksmith strikes a bell with his hammer every hour.

WESTCOTT

2 miles W of Dorking on the A25

Westcott is a tidy village that lies on the
main road linking Dorking with Shere.
Although most of the houses are from
the same Victorian period, they display a
variety of building styles. This diversity
stems from the fact that Westcott lies
almost exactly at the junction of the
chalk North Downs and the sandstone
Surrey Hills. Both of these stone types
figure in the design of the cottages, and
sometimes both are used in the same
house. **Churtgate House**, built in the
16th century, pre-dates nearly all the
other buildings in Westcott; it is located
on the main road at the corner of
Balchin's Lane.

ABINGER

4 miles SW of Dorking off the A25

The parish of Abinger contains two
villages, Abinger itself (or **Abinger
Common**) which lies one mile west of
Friday Street at the southern end of the
parish, and Abinger Hammer which lies
on the A25 Dorking to Guildford road to
the north. Abinger claims to be one of
the oldest settlements in the country,
having been settled by Middle Stone Age
people around 5000 BC. The remains of
a Mesolithic pit-dwelling were discovered
in a field near Abinger's old Manor
House, which, when excavated in 1950,
revealed over 1,000 tools and artefacts
which are now on display in an
interesting little museum.

Abinger's parish **Church of St James** is
an unlucky building. This part-12th
century structure was largely destroyed
by an enemy flying bomb during World
War II. It was rebuilt, with great
sensitivity, but was severely damaged in
1964 after being struck by lightning. In
the churchyard is a war memorial
designed by Lutyens, and in the corner

THE STEPHAN LANGTON INN

Friday Street, Abinger Common, nr Dorking,
Surrey RH5 6JR
Tel: 01306 730775

Since taking over the **Stephan Langton Inn** at the end of
2000, Jonathan and Cynthia Coomb have made it one of
the best-regarded and most popular eating places in the
region. They brought with them experience in several top
London restaurants, and their expertise and the delightful
woodland setting have won many new friends. Adnams and
Sussex Best Bitter are among the ales on tap in the cosy wooden-floored bar, but the true heart of the
inn is the black-beamed, non-smoking dining room, where customers come to feast on Jonathan's
superb modern British cooking based on the finest ingredients.

Typical dishes on his daily changing menu run from potato pancake with smoked salmon and
pickled cucumber or country terrine of chicken livers, pigeon
and bacon with pumpkin chutney for starters to main courses
of roast cod with white beans, chorizo and salsa verde, or slow
roast pork with bubble & squeak, morcilla (Spanish black
pudding) and piccalilli. The pleasure level stays sky-high with
desserts such as blood orange and campari sorbet or raspberry
and almond tart with mascarpone ice cream. Wine is also taken
very seriously at this outstanding establishment, with both
Old and New Worlds well represented and many wines
available by the glass. Meals are served Tuesday to Saturday
evenings and Sunday lunchtime.

of the three-side village green a set of old wooden stocks and a whipping post.

Abinger Common is a delightful hamlet that lies one and a half miles north of Leith Hill, the birthplace of the first Archbishop of Canterbury whose name lives on in the title of a delightful pub, The Stephen Langton Inn.

Abinger Hammer, just over a mile to the northwest, lies in the valley of the River Tillingbourne, a fast-flowing stream which in the 15th and 16th centuries was used to power the mechanical metal-working hammers from which the settlement takes its name. At one time, the village was known for the manufacture of cannon balls and a busy blacksmith's workshop can still be found here. Abinger Hammer's industrial past is reflected in the famous 'Jack the Smith' hammer clock, which was erected in 1909. This unique clock overhangs the road on the site of an old iron forge and is characterised by the figure of a blacksmith who strikes a bell with his hammer every half hour.

HOLMBURY ST MARY

6 miles SW of Dorking on the B2126

Until 1879 the village was called Felday and was a hideaway for smugglers, and many of the oldest stone cottages have unusually large cellars dug into the hillside - perfect for hiding goods in transit! Holmbury St Mary was the invention of well-to-do Victorians, one of whom, the eminent George Edmund Street, designed and paid for the church in 1879, giving it to the parish in memory of his second wife. The village is ideally situated for access to the 857-foot Holmbury Hill, an upland with an altogether wilder feel than Leith Hill, its taller neighbour across the valley.

BULMER FARM

Holmbury St Mary, nr Dorking, Surrey RH5 6LG
Tel: 01306 730210

David and Gill Hill offer a choice of self-catering and Bed & Breakfast accommodation at **Bulmer Farm**, a working beef farm set in the delightful village of Holmbury St Mary in the heart of picturesque rural Surrey. Bed and Breakfast is available in five en suite bedrooms (three doubles and two twins) in a stylishly converted barn, and other old farm buildings now provide two quiet, relaxing self-catering units.

Badgerholt, for two people, was designed with disabled guests in mind and is suitable for wheelchairs; it comprises a twin-bedded room, shower room with WC, sitting room and kitchenette. Foxholme, for four people, comprises one twin and one double-bedded room, bathroom with WC, sitting room and kitchenette, ideal for a family break.

All the accommodation at Bulmer Farm is provided with bed linen and towels, and the two kitchenettes are fully equipped with cooker, refrigerator, crockery and cutlery. There is also a communal laundry room, and the large garden is available for guests' use. The area round the farm is excellent for walking, riding and birdwatching, and the village itself has plenty to interest the visitor, including a church designed by the renowned Victorian architect G E Street, who lived locally.

century BC. The fort is oval in plan, covering more than 11 acres, and is defended by triple banks with double ditches to the north and northeast.

LEITH HILL

5 miles SW of Dorking on the B2126

The 965-foot National Trust-owned Leith Hill is the highest point in the southeast of England. In 1766, a 64-foot tower was built on the tree-covered summit by Richard Hull, a local squire who lived at nearby Leith Hill Place. He now lies buried beneath his splendid creation. Present-day visitors climbing to the top on a clear day are rewarded with a panorama that takes in several counties and stretches as far as the English Channel.

The part-17th, part-18th century **Leith Hill Place** stands within beautiful rhododendron-filled grounds that are open to the public throughout the year. In its time, the house has been owned by the Wedgwood and Vaughan Williams families, and contains a fine collection of Wedgwood pottery and paintings by such eminent artists as Reynolds and Stubbs. An Edwardian country house designed by Sir Edwin Lutyens can be found on the northern slopes of Leith Hill. Goddards on Abinger Common, now the centre of activities of the Lutyens Trust, stands within attractive grounds laid out by Gertrude Jekyll.

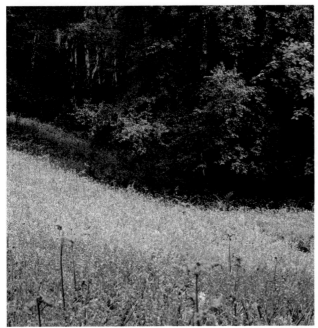

Bluebell Woods, Leith Hill

A pleasant walk leads to the remains of an eight acre Iron Age hill fort whose fading earthwork fortifications lie hidden amidst the undergrowth on the hillside

COLDHARBOUR

5 miles SW of Dorking off the A29

A remote hamlet set 700 feet up in the Surrey Hills, Coldharbour has an atmosphere that is light-years away from most people's preconception of surrey as a county of cosy suburbs and smiling farmland. Sturdy, stone-built houses cling to the hilltop, from which there are magnificent views sweeping south over the Weald.

Just to the north of Coldharbour is **Anstiebury Camp**, an Iron Age fort probably dating from the 1st or 2nd

THE HANNAH PESCHAR SCULPTURE GARDEN

Black and White Cottage, Standon Lane, Ockley, Surrey RH5 5QR
Tel: 01306 627269 fax: 01306 627662
e-mail: hpeschar@easynet.co.uk
website: www.hannahpescharsculpture.com

Situated in a wooded valley with natural running water this sculpture garden has been developed over the last 18 years by **Hanna Peschar** and her husband Anthony Paul. The water was previously channelled into millponds and an earlier 20th century garden had added paths and exotic plantings. Now the remains of the old water garden have been combined with an ever-changing display of sculpture and ceramics in a specially designed and unique setting.

Anthony Paul is a freelance landscape designer, whose work on the landscape of this lively, unorthodox, garden has been so subtle as to be easily mistaken for nature itself. Streams, ponds, waterfalls and bridges provide the artwork with a setting that is dramatic and theatrical and at the same time sensuous and tactile.

Existing trees have been trimmed to improve their form and new plants chosen for both form and colour to provide dense planting and contrasting open areas. Tall grasses and massive leafed plants frame and enhance the art collection.

It's a place where surprises abound. *Fragment* a stoneware and lead face by Graham Clayton lies on the ground beside a tree and may evoke memories of Shelley's poem *Ozymandius of Egypt*. Neil Wilkin's *Umbrella Tree* is a study in crystal and stainless steel, which appears to be in a perfectly natural setting on the banks of a stream, surrounded by wild flowers and grasses while the bronze mesh forms of David Beggbie's *Three Truncs* create an almost ghostly, ethereal atmosphere as they hang suspended between two tree trunks against a backdrop of lush vegetation.

Hannah Peschar has built up an international reputation for promoting young and exciting talent. All the art works in the garden have been chosen by her and most are by British artists. The range is wide with styles covering everything from the figurative to the abstract. Materials can be metals, glass, wire, ceramic, marble, wood and even plastic or fibreglass. It is not a static exhibition and the installations are changed regularly. Most of the sculptures are for sale and with a possibility of paying in instalments. Sculptures can also be shipped and placed worldwide, and individual commissions arranged with any of the artists exhibiting.

The garden is easy to find. Exit the M25 at Junction 9 and take the A24 south towards Dorking. Bypass that town and at the Beare Green roundabout take the A29, signposted Bognor Regis, to the village of Ockley. Look out for the Old School House pub on the right and just after it, turn right into Cat Hill Lane. Turn left at the T junction into Standon Lane and the garden entrance will be on the right some 500 yards past the left turning to Oakwood Church.

OCKLEY

8 miles S of Dorking on the A29

At Ockley there is a village green which, at over 500 feet in diameter, is one of the largest in Surrey. In summer, village cricket is played in this classic English setting which is enhanced by a number of handsome period houses and cottages. Ockley has had a long and eventful history: the village once stood on Stane Street, the old Roman road between Chichester and London which is now partially followed by the route of the A29, and in the mid 9th century, a momentous battle between the forces of King Ethelwulf of the West Saxons and the marauding Vikings reputedly took place near here. Following the Norman invasion, the surrounding woodlands were designated a royal hunting forest and in the 12th century, the Normans built a fortification half a mile to the north of the present village green which has long since disappeared. However, the nearby part-14th century church of St Margaret remains, although this was extensively remodelled by the Victorians during the 1870s.

Among the many other noteworthy buildings in Ockley are the 18th century **Ockley Court**, which stands opposite the church, and the groups of cottages surrounding the green, built in a variety of styles and materials, including brick, tiling and weather-boarding. An interesting private sculpture and ceramics gallery, the **Hannah Peschar Gallery-Garden**, which incorporates a delightful water garden can be found in Standon Lane (see panel opposite).

A short distance to the southwest of Ockley, a chapel was built in the 13th century to serve the population of this once-isolated part of the Weald. Known as the Okewood Chapel, it was later endowed by a local nobleman after his son narrowly avoided being savaged by a wild boar when a mystery arrow struck and killed the charging animal.

NEWDIGATE

5 miles S of Dorking off the A24

A turning east off the A24 at Beare Green leads to the village of Newdigate. This historic settlement contains an interesting parish church, St Peter's, which is believed to have been founded in the 12th century by the Earl de Warenne as a 'hunters' chapel', a place of worship built to be used by Norman hunting parties during their expeditions in the Wealden forest. The tower, with its shingled spire, was constructed around a massive cross-braced timber frame in the 15th century, a time when Newdigate was relatively prosperous thanks to its flourishing iron-founding industry. The oak shingles on the spire had to be replaced in the late 1970s after their Victorian predecessors had warped in the hot summer of 1976.

Present-day Newdigate contains a number of exceptional old timber-framed buildings, several of which date back to the 16th century and earlier.

CHARLWOOD

8 miles SE of Dorking off the A24

A charming period village on the Sussex border, Charlwood is all the more admirable in that it is so near Crawley and Gatwick Airport and yet preserves so much of its own rural identity. Although it lacks the sense of remoteness which it must once have possessed, Charlwood still has many 18th century cottages and a sprinkling of earlier, slightly larger yeomen's houses such as the 15th century Charlwood House to the southeast of the village centre.

The parish Church of St Nicholas was built in the 11th century and underwent a series of alterations, extensions and renovations beginning in the 13th century. The impression, surprisingly, is one of an organic building that has evolved with the centuries. One of its prized possessions is the late medieval screen, one of the most intricately carved pieces of ecclesiastical woodwork in Surrey.

BROCKHAM

1 mile E of Dorking on the A25

Brockham is a picture-postcard village set around a quintessential three-sided village green on which cricket is played in summer, a Guy Fawkes bonfire is lit in November, and Christmas carols are sung in winter. The legendary cricketer W G Grace is even said to have played here. This delightful tree-lined setting is enhanced by a splendid view of Box Hill, some fine old cottages, and an elegantly proportioned parish church with a tall spire which was built in the 1840s in uncomplicated Early English style. Other noteworthy buildings in the village include the late-18th century **Brockham Court**, which can be seen on the eastern edge of the green, and the part-17th century Feltons Farm, which lies a short distance away to the southwest. The remains of some 19th century industrial kilns can be seen on the Downs above the village in the disused Brockham Quarries.

SOUTHEAST SURREY

The southeast corner of Surrey abuts both Kent to the east and Sussex to the south. Not surprisingly there are elements of both counties in some of the Surrey border villages, noticeable in particular in the way that Kent weather-boarding features in the villages and hamlets near Lingfield.

The M25 marks the northern extremity of the area covered in this chapter. As with so many other parts of the county, the towns and villages lying just south of the motorway have fought - and largely won - a battle to preserve their sense of identity. Perhaps it is simply because they have had many centuries to grow accustomed to east-west traffic. The valleys and ridges here comprised the route followed by religious devotees on their way from London and further afield to Canterbury. Indeed many stretches of the original Pilgrims' Way, which is now a well-marked trail along much of its route, look down on its modern, secular, counterpart, the M25.

The countryside in this southeastern corner is far less wooded than south-central or southwestern Surrey. Instead it is a land of open fields and church spires spotted on the horizon. Only at the southern edge, where it nears the Weald of Kent, does the landscape begin to become defined by its dense woodlands.

REIGATE

Reigate is a prosperous residential town whose expansion at the hands of postwar developers has done much to conceal its long and distinguished history. The settlement was once an important outpost of the de Warenne family, the assertive Norman rulers whose sphere of influence stretched from the Channel coast to the North Downs. As at Lewes, they built a castle on a rise above the village streets of which nothing remains today except for an arch, which was reconstructed in the 1770s from material recovered from the original castle walls. Today, this striking neo-Gothic reproduction stands at the heart of a pleasant public park.

A steep path leads down from the castle mound to the attractive mixture of Victorian, Georgian and older

La Lanterna

73 Bell Street, Reigate, Surrey RH2 7AN
Tel: 01737 245113
e-mail: tony@lalanterna.co.uk
website: www.lalanterna.co.uk

La Lanterna is a traditional family-run ristorante Italiano where diners go to have a good meal in friendly, relaxed surroundings. Everything about the place is warm and inviting, from the cheerful red blinds and the restaurant sign sporting the Italian national colours to the smiling welcome from owner Tony Marcazzo and his staff. In the lovely old-world dining room, with whitewashed walls,

black beams and copper ornaments, the menu offers a splendid range of classic Italian dishes, from a wide choice of antipasti to spaghetti and penne pasta, and fish, chicken, veal and steak prepared in a variety of ways and generously served.

House specialities include filetto alla lanterna (fillet steak filled with parma ham and mozzarella, cooked in a mushroom, wine and cream sauce) and flambés prepared with panache at the table. Good house wines head an extensive list, and the desserts and coffee round off a meal in style. La Lanterna is a great place for a party, and the lovely trellised garden, complete with pergola, is the perfect spot for a summer wedding reception. The restaurant is closed Saturday lunchtime, all Sunday and Monday lunchtime.

buildings, which line Reigate's High Street. The **Old Town Hall**, a handsome redbrick building constructed in 1729, stands at its eastern end, and a short distance away to the north, the entrance to a disused road tunnel can be seen. This was built beneath the castle mound in 1824 to ease the through-flow of traffic on the busy London to Brighton coaching route.

Other noteworthy buildings in this part of town include the timber-framed and tile-fronted La Trobes in the High Street, and the 400-year-old **Old Sweep's House** in the charmingly named Slipshoe Street.

As well as being effective administrators, the de Warennes were known for their devout religious beliefs,

and, as at Lewes, they founded a priory in the town some distance from the centre. After the Dissolution, this became the home of Lord Howard of Effingham, the commander-in-chief of the English navy at the time of the Spanish Armada. **Reigate Priory**, now a Grade 1 listed building set in 65 acres of parkland, has been remodelled on a number of occasions, in particular during the Georgian era. It now operates as a school and museum. The interior contains some fine period features including a Holbein fireplace and a fine 17th century oak staircase. Also set away from the town centre, and probably standing on the site of pre-Norman Reigate, is the pale stone-built church of St Mary Magdalene. This contains a number of striking memorials, including one carved by Joseph Rose the Elder.

AROUND REIGATE

BETCHWORTH
3 miles W of Reigate off the A25

Betchworth was once a much more important settlement than it is today. In the 14th century, it had its own fortress, Betchworth Castle, which stood beside the River Mole on a site now occupied by the local golf course. This has now virtually disappeared and the only reminder of Betchworth's past glory is the parish **Church of St Michael**, a surprisingly imposing structure which incorporates some ancient Saxon masonry, a Norman arch and a succession of more recent architectural modifications. Inside, there is a fascinating map of the local manor dated 1634 showing the vestiges of the feudal field system and a wooden chest which is reputed to have been made before the Norman invasion from a single piece of timber taken from a 1,000-year-old oak tree. There is also an unusual font dating from the 1950s. The church is situated at the end of a wide cul-de-sac, which also contains an early 18th century vicarage, an old long barn, and a collection of attractive 17th and 18th century cottages.

A number of interesting buildings can be seen in other parts of Betchworth, including the 16th century Old Mill Cottage, the slender **Queen Anne Old House**, and **Betchworth House**, an impressive part-Georgian manor house which is surrounded by pretty parkland.

BUCKLAND
3 miles W of Reigate on the A25

Buckland is a pretty settlement which suffers from being sited on the busy main

road. The road divides Buckland's tidy rectangular green from the parish church of St Mary, a part-13th century structure whose interior is worth a look for its 15th century stained-glass east window and 17th century pews and oak panelling. The A25 to the east of Buckland passes along the northern edge of Reigate Heath. This narrow area of open heathland is the home of the unique **Windmill Church**, surely the only church in the world to be situated in a windmill.

LEIGH
4 miles SW of Reigate of the A217

Leigh (pronounced Lye) is a well-kept village, which, like at least a dozen others in Britain, takes its name from the Saxon term for forest clearing. Like Newdigate and Charlwood to the south, Leigh was an important centre of the Wealden iron-founding industry which prospered from the 14th century until it was superseded by Northern-based coal-fired smelting in the 18th century. Indeed, this now-tranquil area was once known as Thunderfield-in-the-Forest because of the number of iron furnaces it contained.

HORLEY
5 miles S of Reigate on the A23

The pleasant town of Horley lies on the Sussex border and not far from Gatwick Airport to the south. The proximity to the airport, surprisingly, has done little to alter the character of Horley although the town did undergo a transformation in the Victorian era after the arrival of the main railway line. The present arrangement of streets, set mostly in a gridiron pattern, branched out from the railway line to provide housing for railway workers and shops to cater to their needs. This neighbourhood, which constitutes most of the core of Horley, is trim and neat, and the overall effect is pleasant. Dotted among the 19th century buildings are a few survivors of earlier eras, including a lovely tile-hung cottage by the church.

Outwood
5 miles SE of Reigate off the M23

Although Outwood is accessible from the M23, a more pleasant approach leads southwards from Bletchingley along a country road across the Weald. **Outwood Common**, the area of high ground to the east of village, is best known for being the location of one of the most interesting windmills in the country.

The Post Mill is acknowledged as the oldest working windmill in England. It was built in 1665 and it is said that from the top of the mill, some 39 feet up, the Great Fire of London was visible 27 miles away. Unlike other ancient buildings in England, the Post Mill's early history is not shrouded in mystery and conjecture. It was built by Thomas Budgen, a miller of Nutfield, and the original deeds are still in existence.

The term 'post mill' describes the structure and mechanism of this remarkable building. The whole body of the mill, including its sails and machinery, balances on a huge central post. This post is made from oak, which, it is said, was carried seven miles by oxcart from Crabbet Park, near Crawley, where it was felled. It is supported by four diagonal quarter bars and two crosstrees. These in turn rest on four brick piers. The purpose of this post system is to allow the mill to be turned to face the breeze, and it is so finely balanced that a single person can turn the sails into the wind. Another special design feature incorporated around 100 years later allows the angle of the sails to be adjusted to suit different wind

conditions using a system of elliptical springs.

For over a century, a second smock windmill stood nearby, and the pair were known locally as the Cat and Fiddle; sadly, the Fiddle blew down in a storm in the early 1960s.

Burstow
8 miles SE of Reigate off the B2037

The lanes to the south of Outwood lead through Smallfield to Burstow, a well-kept village whose church, St Bartholomew's, has a surprisingly well preserved late medieval timber-framed tower. This hefty 15th century structure supports a peal of six bells, the largest of which weighs over half a ton. The church itself is an attractive mixture of Norman, Perpendicular, and Victorian influences; the chancel contains the remains of John Flamsteed, a former rector and the first Astronomer Royal, who is best remembered for his maps of the night skies which were compiled in the late 17th century as an aid to marine navigation. Flamsteed was presented with the living of Burstow by Lord North in 1684.

About one mile north of Burstow is **Smallfield Place**, regarded by many as the best example of a stone-built country home in Surrey. Its almost forbidding appearance is at odds with the mellow brick or aged timber exteriors of so many Surrey manor houses. The house was built at the beginning of the 17th century and presents a long, largely unadorned two-storey Wealden stone face to the curious public.

Lingfield
12 miles SE of Reigate off the A22

Lingfield is a large village, which is set within delightful wooded countryside in the southeastern corner of the county.

THE WILLOW TREES NURSERY

Newchapel Road, Lingfield, Surrey RH7 6BL
Tel: 01342 834961 Fax: 01342 832237

Richard and Jennifer Day bought the **Willow Trees Nursery** in 2002, having previously owned a treework and garden maintenance company. Fuchsias are their speciality, and the 300 plus varieties on the list include irresistible names like Ballet Girl, Circus Spangles, Pink Marshmallow, Voo-Doo and Tennessee Waltz. All the fuchsias are propagated at the Nursery, with Richard taking the cuttings and Jennifer doing the potting.

They also grow and sell a wide range of shrubs, alpines, hardy perennials and summer bedding plants, and they have built up a fine reputation for their hanging baskets. They sell fully planted baskets or will supply plants for baskets, and customers can bring back their baskets for replanting.

This neat, well-run and very attractive nursery is open from 10am to 5pm every day except Tuesday. It is closed From November to January.

Almost large enough to be called a town, 'leafy Lingfield' is perhaps best known to the world at large for its racecourse. However, the settlement has long been an important agricultural centre, whose largely Perpendicular **Church of St Peter and St Paul** has been enlarged over the centuries to create what has become known as the Westminster Abbey of Surrey. As well as having a rare double nave and an exceptional collection of monumental brasses, the church also contains a number of memorials to members of the Cobham family, the medieval lords of the manor who lived at the now demolished **Starborough Castle**, a mile and a half to the east. Each of the first four barons has a sizeable tomb showing an effigy of its

occupant. These date from between 1361 and 1471 and are particularly fascinating to those with an interest in the development of late-medieval armour.

The broad thoroughfare leading down from the church is lined with characteristic weatherboarded and tile-fronted buildings, including Pollard Cottage, with its unusual 15th century shop front, the 16th century Old Town Stores, and the Star Inn Cottages, built around 1700. The country library on the opposite side of the church is a former farmhouse built in the 17th century on the site of a Carthusian college founded in the 1400s by Sir Reginald Cobham. Elsewhere in Lingfield, a couple of interesting features can be found near the pond in Plaistow Street: the 15th century village cross and the old lock-up, a small local jail built in 1772 and in use until 1882.

Greathed Manor, to the southeast of Lingfield, is a substantial Victorian manor house built in 1868 for the Spender Clay family.

CROWHURST
11 miles SE of Reigate off the A22

Crowhurst contains a yew tree estimated to be around 4,000 years old and thought to be one of the oldest in the country. Its branches are said to enclose an area over 30 feet in diameter. During the 1820s, a covered café was formed by removing some of the central branches and installing tables and chairs.

Crowhurst Place, to the southwest, was rebuilt after the First World War on the site of a 15th century moated manor house.

DORMANSLAND
12 miles SE of Reigate off the B2029

Dormansland presents itself as evidence for a bit of social history detective work. The cottages in this hamlet near the Sussex and Kent borders date from the Victorian era, with some 17th and 18th century examples mixed in. However, they share a common limitation - their size. Other Surrey hamlets have workmen's cottages but there is usually much more diversity in scale. Several social historians have proposed that these tiny cottages were built by people who were squatting in common land.

Just outside the village is an altogether grander structure, **Old Surrey Hall**, built in 1450 on the remote border with Sussex. Much of the 15th century section, with its close timbering exterior, survives, but the

overall moated quadrangle of today's house dates from 1922 and represents a renovation work of near genius by the architect George Crawley.

REDHILL
2 miles E of Reigate on the A23

Redhill developed around the railway station after the London to Brighton line opened in the 1840s. The new rail line ran parallel to the corresponding road (now the A23) and cut through previously open landscape. Most of Redhill's buildings consequently date from that period or the decades shortly afterwards. The parish church of St John has an exceptionally tall and elegant spire, and the Harlequin Theatre in the Warwick Quadrant shopping precinct offers a full programme of drama, film and musical entertainment in addition to having a pleasant bar, restaurant and coffee shop.

BLETCHINGLEY
4 miles E of Reigate on the A25

Bletchingley is a highly picturesque village and former "rotten borough" which once had its own castle and street market. Traces of the Norman fortification thought to have been built by Richard de Tonbridge in the 12th century can be seen in the grounds of **Castle Hill**, a private house lying to the south of the A25. Closer to the centre, the old market in Middle Row is an exceptionally handsome thoroughfare, which, like the nearby High Street, contains some wonderful old timber-framed and tile-hung houses and cottages.

Some fine early buildings can also be found in **Church Walk**, the lane leading to Bletchingley's Perpendicular Church of St Mary. The oldest part of this sizeable sandstone structure, the Norman

Bletchingley

Distance:	5.5 miles (8.8 kilometres)
Typical time:	180 mins
Height gain:	90 metres
Map:	Explorer 146
Walk:	www.walkingworld.com ID:537
Contributor:	Nina Thornhill

Access Information:

Buses run to Bletchingley from Redhill and Oxted. Cars can be parked in the High Street on the A25. The walk starts from Castle Square opposite St Lychens Lane at the Red Lion pub end of the High Street, reached by heading uphill from the High Street.

Additional Information:

Some of the walk is on bridleways, which are likely to be muddy after heavy rain, so boots are advisable. Bird lovers may find it useful to bring their binoculars, as Bay Pond Nature Reserve provides plenty of opportunities to see a wide variety of birds all year round. Just to the west of waymark one at the start of the walk, the remains of Bletchingley castle can be seen. Nothing of the castle itself remains, just a series of mounds and ditches. Refreshments and supplies are available at Bletchingley, which has four pubs and Godstone which has two pubs and a sandwich bar. These are the only places where you are likely to find toilets.

Description:

This walk shows that there is more to the Surrey Hills than just the more widely known North Downs. The Greensand Hills lie to the south of the North Downs, forming a ridge from Haslemere in Surrey to Hamstreet in Kent. This walk follows the Greensand Way for approximately 2½miles from Castle Hill, Bletchingley, along Tilbustow Hill to Brakey Hill. Here we depart from the Greensand Way and head north to Godstone. En route a series of ponds are passed before entering Church Town, the older part of Godstone. It has quite a selection of period cottages and houses, some dating from the 16th century, as well as the church of St. Nicholas. Right on Godstones' doorstep sits Bay Pond, a nature reserve managed by the Surrey Wildlife Trust. Godstone Green is an ideal place to stop and have lunch. There are two pubs here, one on either side of the green, both serve meals. On summer Sundays the green makes a good picnic spot where you can enjoy your lunch and watch a game of cricket. After Godstone, we head westwards over open farmland. It is here that we travel between the North Downs and the Greensand Hills. At Brewer Street, a half-timbered farmhouse can be seen, dating from the 15th century. The walk ends at the village of Bletchingley, which has several buildings of historic interest. formed by the streams which gather into the Coombe Haven. The latter part of the walk takes you through the quiet residential streets of Bexhill. It ends at a car park beside a park in which are a museum and the ruins of a manor.

Features:

Hills or Fells, Lake/Loch, Pub, Church, Wildlife, Birds, Great Views

Walk Directions:

1 From Bletchingley High Street, turn left into Castle Square. Keep ahead until a two-way fingerpost is reached. You are not going to take either of these paths, instead turn around and face the way you came. You should see a single fingerpost on your right marked Greensand Way, this is the path to take. When you reach a road, turn right and walk along the road until you come to a fork.

2 Turn left at this fork onto a bridleway. Keep to the path, ignoring a stile on the left (after a pond) and also ignore a path further on, to the right, until you arrive at a junction, by a tree stump.

3 Bear right here, ignoring the path on the left. Keep ahead on the main path, ignoring any going off to the left until another fork is reached. Turn right here. When you reach a junction, turn left. After approx 50 yards, look out for a downhill path on your right. Go down this right hand path and at the junction turn left. When you get to the road, turn left. Look out for a bridleway on the right after passing the white house.

4 Follow the bridleway here. Be careful to keep to bridleway when you are going around the fields.

5 Keep to the bridleway as it bears left and goes slightly uphill around the field. Do not take any paths which go through gaps in the hedgerow. When the road is reached, turn left. Look out for the bridleway on your right in approx 250 yards. Follow the GSW arrows (Greensand Way) on the bridleway, keeping straight ahead. When you come to Tilburstow Hill Road go over to the bridleway (marked GSW). Keep ahead on this bridleway, ignoring a path that comes up on the right, until you arrive at a junction.

6 Bear right at this junction. After a few yards look out for a stile and path on the right. Turn right onto this path, which goes through a field heading towards the B2236. When the road is reached, turn left and walk along it until you get to a fork opposite a building suppliers.

7 You need to turn right at the fork signposted Tandridge. At the millrace, look out for a stile on the left. Leave the Greensand Way and turn left onto this path by the millrace. Passing between two ponds at Leigh Place, ignore the path going off to the right. When a three-way fingerpost is reached, turn left to join the bridleway. Look out for another three-way fingerpost.

8 Come off the bridleway and turn right onto the footpath here. Keep to the path until you reach a post. Once in the field turn left to see a marked post. At this post, turn left into the wood and follow the path downhill and on past Glebe Water. Continue ahead through the graveyard, to pass through the lychgate. The path continues almost ahead on the other side of the road. This path passes Bay Pond Nature Reserve, then passes some buildings before coming out by the road at Godstone green. Cross the green, making for the A25 on the other side. Cross over and turn left along this road until you come to a garden centre.

9 Look out for this footpath on the right opposite the garden centre. This passes some sandworkings. When the road is reached turn left. In a few paces you should see 1 North Park Cottage on the right.

10 Turn right onto this track by North Park Cottage. In a few yards turn left through a metal gate and keep to the sandy path until you reach the road. Do not turn right onto a cycle route track, instead turn right and walk along Place Farm Road. You need to stay on this road, ignoring any paths going off. At the road junction turn left into Brewer Street. Keep ahead until the road forks off to the right.

11 At this fork you leave the road and continue ahead on the track. Keep ahead on the path ignoring other paths going off. The path comes out by a road next to Dormers Farm.

12 When this road is reached, be sure to take the path on the left that follows the road. In approx 200 yards a small workshop unit is reached on the left.

13 You need to turn left onto this path by the workshop unit. When you reach a church bear right around the front of the church. This path comes out behind Bletchingley High Street.

west tower, dates from the end of the 11th century; it had a spire until a bolt of lightning destroyed it in 1606. Inside are a 13th century hermit's cell, a wonderful assortment of medieval gargoyles, a 16th century monumental brass of a local tanner and his wife, and an extravagant sculpted monument to Sir Robert Clayton, a City money lender and former Lord Mayor of London who died in 1707. The church also contains the sizeable tomb of Sir Thomas Cawarden, the former owner of Bletchingley Place, who acquired the manor house from Anne of Cleves after she had won it from Henry VIII as part of her divorce settlement.

A couple of interesting settlements lie within easy reach of Bletchingley. **Pendell**, a two-minute drive to the northwest, contains the striking Jacobean-style Pendell Court, which was built in 1624, and the neo-classical Pendell House, which was built 12 years later on an adjacent site. Brewer Street, one mile to the north, contains the remains of Anne of Cleves's manor house, remodelled in the 18th century and known as Place Farm.

GODSTONE

6 miles E of Reigate off the A22

Although Godstone is now thankfully bypassed by the A22, the A25 east-west route still passes through its heart, making a sharp change in direction as it does so. Fortunately, the village's Tudor and Elizabethan character has survived relatively intact. Godstone's most distinguished building, the White Hart Inn in the High Street, claims to have been visited by Richard II, Elizabeth I, Queen Victoria, and even the Tsar of Russia, who broke his journey here in 1815. A series of attractive lanes and alleyways connects the High Street to the

village green, a broad open space with a cricket pitch, which is surrounded by a wonderful collection of 16th and 17th century buildings, including the Tudor-built Hare and Hounds Inn.

Godstone's parish church of St Nicholas is situated half a mile east of the centre and can be reached from the White Hart along an old thoroughfare known as Bay Path. Although Norman in origin, the building was virtually rebuilt in the 1870s by Sir George Gilbert Scott, a local resident at the time. Inside, there is a marble memorial to a cousin of John Evelyn, the 17th century diarist. The area around the church contains some fine old buildings, including a row of 19th century almshouses and the 16th century timber-framed Old Pack House, which lies a short distance away to the south. Bay Path also leads to a former hammer pond, **Bay Pond**, which is now a designated nature reserve. At one time, its water would have been used to power the mechanical hammers in a nearby iron foundry, an indication of Godstone's lost industrial past, which also included the manufacture of gunpowder and leatherware. **Godstone Farm**, in Tilburstow Hill Road to the south of the village, is an open farm where children can experience life on the farm at first hand.

OXTED

8 miles E of Reigate off the A25

Oxted is an old town that prospered because of its position just below the Downs and consequently a good trading link with the rest of Surrey. Today, however, Oxted constitutes two distinct parts. New Oxted lies between the original town and Limpsfield. It grew up around the railway station, which was built in the 19th century.

PUSH THE BOAT OUT

15 Station Road East, Oxted, Surrey RH8 0BD
Tel: 01883 722665

Cards for every occasion are the speciality of **Push the Boat Out**, and owner Diana Millard offers what is probably the largest selection in the region. Her splendid little shop also stocks stationery for normal and specialised use, wrapping paper and ribbons, T-shirts, Beanies and cuddly toys, picture frames, fashion bags and purses, jewellery, board games and puzzles, wooden plaques and keepsake boxes, wind chimes, fragrances and toiletries – and since the stock is constantly changing, every visit to this delightful place will reveal something different, either practical or decorative, to keep as a treat or give as a special present.

Old Oxted is also largely Victorian to the eye, but occasionally the visitor notices some survivors of earlier centuries such as the Forge House and Beam Cottages, with their medieval core and 17th century exteriors. Streeters Cottage, built in the 17th century, presents a large timber-framed gable to the road.

CALICO

35 Station Road East, Oxted,
Surrey RH8 0AX
Tel: 01883 714904
website: www.calico-oxted.co.uk

Since opening in 1997, **Calico** has built up an enviable reputation as a retail outlet offering an impressive and ever-growing choice of desirable lifestyle items for the home as well as imaginative ideas for gifts. Owner Deborah White and her staff pride themselves on their wide experience in the retail sector, and their product knowledge inspires confidence and trust: customers visit

and re-visit knowing that they will be given every assistance in finding exactly the right purchase to fit any occasion.

The items in the window tempt passers-by inside, where bright, colourful displays cover the product ranges of manufacturers both familiar - Portmeirion, Dartington, Woods of Windsor, Orrefors, Spode, Crabtree & Evelyn - and less well known. There are vases and pots, figurines, cushions and fabrics, stylish lighting, beautiful crystal and an eye-catching range of jewellery to appeal to all ages.

LIMPSFIELD

9 miles E of Reigate on the B269

The churchyard at Limpsfield contains the grave of the composer, Frederick Delius, who died in France in 1934 but had expressed a wish to be buried in an English country graveyard. Sir Thomas Beecham, a great admirer of Delius, read the funeral oration and conducted an orchestra playing works by Delius. Sir Thomas died in 1961 and was originally buried at Brookwood cemetery near Woking. In 1991 his body was transferred to Limpsfield, where he was buried close to Delius. Also lying here are the conductor Norman del Mar and the pianist Eileen Joyce.

Detillens, a rare 15th century 'hall' house, is also located in Limpsfield.

This striking building has an unusual 'king-post' roof, and despite having been given a new façade in the 18th century, is a good example of a house belonging to a Surrey yeoman, a member of the class of small freeholders who cultivated their own land. Inside, there is an interesting collection of period furniture, china and militaria.

Limpsfield Chart, or simply The Chart, constitutes a hilltop common with some lovely views eastwards across Kent. Next to the common is a 17th century Mill House. The windmill itself was removed in 1925. Elsewhere in The Chart there are handsome groupings of stone-built houses, cottages, and farm buildings, best exemplified by the ensemble at Moorhouse Farm.

SAUVARIN WITHERS

High Street, Limpsfield, Surrey RH8 0DT
Tel: 01883 715060

In an attractive 18th century building that used to be the village bakery, **Sauvarin Withers** is a jewellery and engraving business owned and run by Dudley Withers. With a period at art school, a silversmithing course and a diploma in engraving under his belt, he started his professional career in 1974 in a friend's workshop; he started up in his first shop in 1980 and moved across the road to his current premises in 1986. He is a Freeman

of the Goldsmiths Company and a member of the Institute of Professional Goldsmiths.

Items are displayed in the shop on antique furniture in simple, elegant style, and besides his own work the stock includes silver and jewellery by contemporary designers, 18th and 19th century silver, old Sheffield plate, glass and decorative objects and wine-related antiques. Sauvarin Withers also offers a full repair and restoration service for silver and glass and a complete engraving service.

TOURIST INFORMATION CENTRES

KENT

ASHFORD

18 The Churchyard
Ashford
Kent TN23 1QG
Tel: 01233 629165
Fax: 01233 639166
e-mail: tourism@ashford.gov.uk

BROADSTAIRS

68 High Street
Broadstairs
Kent CT10 1LH
Tel: 01843 865650
Fax: 01843 868373

CANTERBURY

34 St Margret's Street
Canterbury
Kent CT1 2TG
Tel: 01227 766567
Fax: 01227 459840
e-mail: canterburyinformation@
canterbury.gov.uk

CRANBROOK - SUMMER ONLY

Vestry Hall
Stone Street
Cranbrook
Kent TN17 3HA
Tel: 01580 712538
Fax: 01580 712538

DEAL

Town Hall
High Street
Deal
Kent CT14 6ER
Tel: 01304 369576
Fax: 01304 380641

DOVER

Townwall Street
Dover
Kent CT16 1JR

Tel: 01304 205108
Fax: 01304 245409
e-mail: tic@doveruk.com

EDENBRIDGE

Stangrove Park
Edenbridge
Kent TN8 5LU
Tel: 01732 868110
Fax: 01732 868114
e-mail: edenbridge.tic@sevenoaks.gov.uk

FAVERSHAM

Fleur de Lis Heritage Centre
13 Preston Street
Faversham
Kent ME13 8NS
Tel: 01795 534542
Fax: 01795 533261
e-mail: faversham@btinternet.com

FOLKESTONE

Harbour Street
Folkestone
Kent CT20 1QN
Tel: 01303 258594
Fax: 01303 259754
e-mail: tourism@folkestone.org.uk

GRAVESEND

Town Centric
18a St George's Square
Gravesend
Kent
Tel: 01474 337600
Fax: 01474 337601
e-mail: towncentre.initiative@
gravesham.gov.uk

HERNE BAY

12 William Street
Herne Bay
Kent CT6 5EJ
Tel: 01227 361911
Fax: 01227 361911
e-mail: hernebayinformation@
canterbury.gov.uk

HYTHE

En Route Building
Red Lion Square
Hythe
Kent CT21 5AU
Tel: 01303 267799
Fax: 01303 261161

LONDON BEXLEY

Hall Place
Bourne Road
Bexley
Kent DA5 1PQ
Tel: 01322 558676
Fax: 01322 522921

LONDON SWANLEY

London Road
Swanley
Kent BR8 7AE
Tel: 01322 614660
Fax: 01322 666154
e-mail: ticstaff@swanley74.fsnet.org.uk

MAIDSTONE

Town Hall
Middle Row
High Street
Maidstone
Kent ME14 1TF
Public enquiries: 01622 602169
Tel: 01622 602048
Fax: 01622 602519
e-mail: tourism@maidstone.gov.uk

MARGATE

12-13 The Parade
Margate
Kent CT9 1EY
Tel: 01843 583334
Fax: 01843 292019
e-mail: margatevic@yahoo.com

NEW ROMNEY

Magpies
Church Approach
New Romney
Kent TN28 8AS
Tel: 01797 364044
Fax: 01797 364194

RAMSGATE

17 Albert Court
York Street
Ramsgate
Kent CT11 9DN
Tel: 01843 583333
Fax: 01843 585353
e-mail: ramsgatevic@yahoo.co.uk

ROCHESTER

95 High Street
Rochester
Kent ME1 1LX
Tel: 01634 843666
Fax: 01634 847891
e-mail: visitor.centre@medway.gov.uk

SANDWICH

The Guild Hall
Cattle Market
Sandwich
Kent CT13 9AH
Tel: 01304 613565
Fax: 01304 613565

SEVENOAKS

Buckhurst Lane
Sevenoaks
Kent TN13 1LQ
Tel: 01732 450305
Fax: 01732 461959
e-mail: tic@sevenoakstown.gov.uk

TENTERDEN - SUMMER ONLY

Town Hall
High Street
Tenterden Kent
TN30 6AN
Tel: 01580 763572
Fax: 01580 766863

TONBRIDGE

Tonbridge Castle
Castle Street
Tonbridge
Kent TN9 1BG
Tel: 01732 770929
Fax: 01732 770449
e-mail: tonbridgecastle@tmbc.gov.uk

TUNBRIDGE WELLS

The Old Fish Market
The Pantiles
Tunbridge Wells
Kent TN2 5TN
Tel: 01892 515675
Fax: 01892 534660
e-mail: touristinformationcentre@
tunbridgewells.gov.uk

WHITSTABLE

7 Oxford Street
Whitstable
Kent CT5 1DB
Tel: 01227 275482
Fax: 01227 275482
e-mail: whitstableinformation@
canterbury.gov.uk

EAST SUSSEX

SUSSEX COUNTRY NORTH

Ashdown Forest Llama Park
Wych Cross
Forest Row
East Sussex RH18 5JN
Tel: 01825 713862
Fax: 01825 713812
e-mail: ticnorth@wealden.gov.uk

SUSSEX COUNTRY SOUTH

Boship Roundabout A22
Lower Dicker
Hailsham
East Sussex BN27 4DT
Tel: 01323 442667
Fax: 01323 449584
e-mail: sussexcountry.tic@wealden.gov.uk

BATTLE

88 High Street
Battle
East Sussex TN33 0AQ
Tel: 01424 773721
Fax: 01424 773436
e-mail: battletic@rother.gov.uk

BEXHILL-ON-SEA

51 Marina
Bexhill-on-Sea
East Sussex TN40 1BQ
Tel: 01424 732208
Fax: 01424 212500
e-mail: bexhilltic@rother.gov.uk

BRIGHTON

10 Bartholomew Square
Brighton
East Sussex BN1 1JS
Fax: 01273 292594
e-mail: brighton-tourism@
brighton-hove.gov.uk

EASTBOURNE

Cornfield Road
Eastbourne
East Sussex BN21 4QL
Tel: 01323 411400
Fax: 01323 649574
e-mail: eastbournetic@btclick.com

HASTINGS

Queens Square
Priory Meadow
Hastings
East Sussex TN34 1TL
Tel: 01424 781111
Tel: 01424 781186
e-mail: hic_info@hastings.gov.uk

HASTINGS

The Stade
Old Town
Hastings
East Sussex TN34 1EZ
Tel: 01424 781111
Fax: 01424 781186
e-mail: hic_info@hastings.gov.uk

HOVE

Church Road
Hove
East Sussex BN3 3BQ
Tel: 01273 292589

LEWES

187 High Street
Lewes
East Sussex BN7 2DE
Tel: 01273 483448
Fax: 01273 484003
e-mail: lewestic@lewes.gov.uk

RYE

The Heritage Centre,
Strand Quay
Rye
East Sussex TN31 7AY
Tel: 01797 226696
Fax: 01797 223460
e-mail: ryetic@rother.gov.uk
website: www.visitrye.co.uk

SEAFORD

25 Clinton Place
Seaford
East Sussex BN25 1NP
Tel: 01323 897426
e-mail: seafordtic@lewes.gov.uk

WEST SUSSEX

ARUNDEL

61 High Street
Arundel
West Sussex BN18 9AJ
Tel: 01903 882268
Fax: 01903 882419
e-mail: tourism@arun.gov.uk
website: www.sussexbythesea.com

BOGNOR REGIS

Belmont Street
Bognor Regis
West Sussex PO21 1BJ
Tel: 01243 823140
Fax: 01243 820435
e-mail: tourism@arun.gov.uk
website: www.sussexbythesea.com

BURGESS HILL

96 Church Walk
Burgess Hill
West Sussex RH15 9AS
Tel: 01444 247726
Fax: 01444 233707
e-mail: touristinformation@
burgesshill.gov.uk

CHICHESTER

29a South Street
Chichester
West Sussex PO19 1AH
Tel: 01243 775888
Fax: 01243 539449
e-mail: Chitic@chichester.gov.uk

HORSHAM

9 The Causeway
Horsham
West Sussex RH12 1HE
Tel: 01403 211661
Fax: 01403 217581
e-mail: touristinformation@horsham.gov.uk

LITTLEHAMPTON

Visitor Information Centre
Look and Sea Centre
63-65 Littlehampton
West Sussex BN175AW
Tel: 01903 721866
e-mail: tourism@arun.gov.uk
website: www.sussexbythesea.com/

MIDHURST

North Street
Midhurst
West Sussex GU29 9DW
Tel: 01730 817322
Fax: 01730 817120

PETWORTH

Market Square
Petworth
West Sussex GU28 0AF
Tel: 01798 343523
Fax: 01798 343942

WORTHING

Chapel Road
Worthing
West Sussex BN11 1HL
Tel: 01903 210022
Fax: 01903 236277
e-mail: wbctourism@pavilion.co.uk

SURREY

CROYDON

Croydon Clocktower
Katharine Street
Croydon
Surrey CR9 1ET
Tel: 020 8253 1009
Fax: 020 8253 1008
e-mail: tic@croydononline.org

FARNHAM

Council Offices
South Street
Farnham
Surrey GU9 7RN
Tel: 01252 715109
Fax: 01252 725083
e-mail: itourist@waverley.gov.uk

GUILDFORD

14 Tunsgate
Guildford
Surrey GU1 3QT
Tel: 01483 444333
Fax: 01483 302046
e-mail: tic@guildford.gov.uk

RICHMOND

Old Town Hall
Whittaker Avenue
Richmond
Surrey TW9 1TP
Tel: 020 8940 9125
Fax: 020 8940 6899
e-mail: information.services@
              richmond.gov.uk

INDEX OF ADVERTISERS

ARTS AND CRAFTS

FASHIONS

GIFTWARE

HOME AND GARDEN

INDEX OF WALKS

Looking for more walks?

The walks in this book have been gleaned from Britain's largest online walking guide, to be found at *www.walkingworld.com*.

The site contains 300 walks across eastern England, so there is plenty more choice in this region alone. If you are heading further afield there are walks of every length and type across England, Scotland and Wales – ideal if you are taking a short break as you can plan your walks in advance.

Want more detail for the walks in this book? Next to every walk in this book you will see a Walk ID. You can enter this ID number on Walkingworld's 'Find a Walk' page and you will be taken straight to the details of that walk.

- Over **1850** walks across Britain

- Print routes out as you need them

- No bulky guidebook to carry

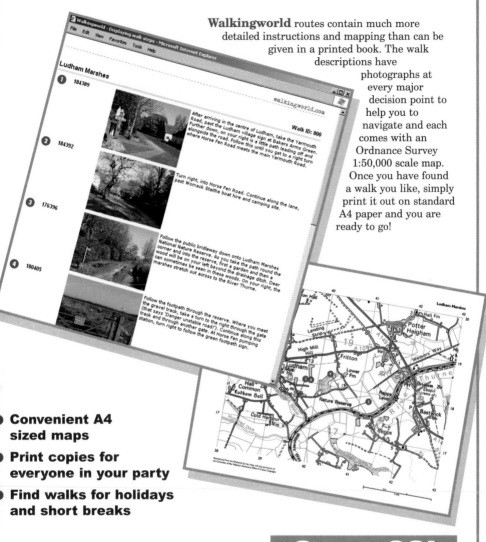

Walkingworld routes contain much more detailed instructions and mapping than can be given in a printed book. The walk descriptions have photographs at every major decision point to help you to navigate and each comes with an Ordnance Survey 1:50,000 scale map. Once you have found a walk you like, simply print it out on standard A4 paper and you are ready to go!

- **Convenient A4 sized maps**
- **Print copies for everyone in your party**
- **Find walks for holidays and short breaks**

A modest annual subscription gives you access to over 1850 walks, all in Walkingworld's easy to follow format. The database of walks is growing all the time and as a subscriber you gain access to new routes as soon as they are published.

Visit the Walkingworld website at *www.walkingworld.com*

Travel Publishing

The Hidden Places

Regional and National guides to the less well-known places of interest and places to eat, stay and drink

Hidden Inns

Regional guides to traditional pubs and inns throughout the United Kingdom

Golfers Guides

Regional and National guides to 18 hole golf courses and local places to stay, eat and drink

COUNTRY LIVING
MAGAZINE
RURAL GUIDES

Regional and National guides to the traditional countryside of Britain and Ireland with easy to read facts on places to visit, stay, eat, drink and shop

For more information:

Phone: 0118 981 7777
e-mail: info@travelpublishing.co.uk

Fax: 0118 982 0077
website: www.travelpublishing.co.uk

Easy-to-use, Informative
Travel Guides on the British Isles

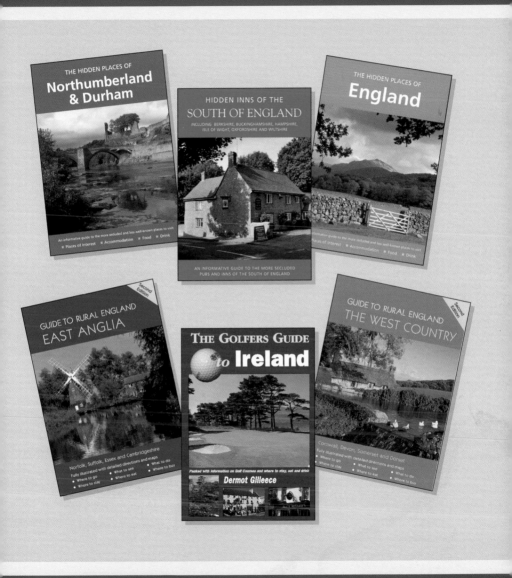

THE HIDDEN PLACES OF
Northumberland & Durham
An informative guide to the more secluded and less well-known places to visit
■ Places of Interest ■ Accommodation ■ Food ■ Drink

HIDDEN INNS OF THE
SOUTH OF ENGLAND
INCLUDING BERKSHIRE, BUCKINGHAMSHIRE, HAMPSHIRE, ISLE OF WIGHT, OXFORDSHIRE AND WILTSHIRE
AN INFORMATIVE GUIDE TO THE MORE SECLUDED PUBS AND INNS OF THE SOUTH OF ENGLAND

THE HIDDEN PLACES OF
England
Informative guide to the more secluded and less known places to visit
■ Places of Interest ■ Accommodation ■ Food ■ Drink

GUIDE TO RURAL ENGLAND
EAST ANGLIA
Second Edition
Norfolk, Suffolk, Essex and Cambridgeshire
Fully illustrated with detailed directions and maps
● Where to go   ● What to see   ● What to do
● Where to stay   ● Where to eat   ● Where to buy

THE GOLFERS GUIDE to Ireland
Packed with information on Golf Courses and where to stay, eat and drink
Dermot Gilleece

GUIDE TO RURAL ENGLAND
THE WEST COUNTRY
Second Edition
Cornwall, Devon, Somerset and Dorset
Fully illustrated with detailed directions and maps
● Where to go   ● What to see   ● What to do
● Where to stay   ● Where to eat   ● Where to Buy

Travel Publishing Limited
7a Apollo House • Calleva Park • Aldermaston • Berkshire RG7 8TN

ORDER FORM

To order any of our publications just fill in the payment details below and complete the order form. For orders of less than 4 copies please add £1 per book for postage and packing. Orders over 4 copies are P & P free.

Please Complete Either:

I enclose a cheque for £ [ ] made payable to Travel Publishing Ltd

Or:

Card No: [ ]   Expiry Date: [ ]

Signature: [ ]

NAME: [ ]

ADDRESS: [ ]

TEL NO: [ ]

Please either send, telephone, fax or e-mail your order to:
Travel Publishing Ltd, 7a Apollo House, Calleva Park, Aldermaston, Berkshire RG7 8TN
Tel: 0118 981 7777   Fax: 0118 982 0077   e-mail: info@travelpublishing.co.uk

	PRICE	QUANTITY		PRICE	QUANTITY
HIDDEN PLACES REGIONAL TITLES			**HIDDEN INNS TITLES**		
Cambs & Lincolnshire	£8.99	....	East Anglia	£7.99	....
Chilterns	£8.99	....	Heart of England	£7.99	....
Cornwall	£8.99	....	Lancashire & Cheshire	£7.99	....
Derbyshire	£8.99	....	North of England	£7.99	....
Devon	£8.99	....	South	£7.99	....
Dorset, Hants & Isle of Wight	£8.99	....	South East	£7.99	....
East Anglia	£8.99	....	South and Central Scotland	£7.99	....
Gloucs, Wiltshire & Somerset	£8.99	....	Wales	£7.99	....
Heart of England	£8.99	....	Welsh Borders	£7.99	....
Hereford, Worcs & Shropshire	£8.99	....	West Country	£7.99	....
Kent	£8.99	....	**COUNTRY LIVING RURAL GUIDES**		
Lake District & Cumbria	£8.99	....			
Lancashire & Cheshire	£8.99	....	East Anglia	£10.99	....
Lincolnshire & Nottinghamshire	£8.99	....	Heart of England	£10.99	....
Northumberland & Durham	£8.99	....	Ireland	£11.99	....
Sussex	£8.99	....	North East of England	£10.99	....
Yorkshire	£8.99	....	North West of England	£10.99	....
HIDDEN PLACES NATIONAL TITLES			Scotland	£11.99	....
			South of England	£10.99	....
England	£11.99	....	South East of England	£10.99	....
Ireland	£11.99	....	Wales	£11.99	....
Scotland	£11.99	....	West Country	£10.99	....
Wales	£11.99	....			

Total Quantity [ ]

Total Value [ ]

READER REACTION FORM

The *Travel Publishing* research team would like to receive readers' comments on any visitor attractions or places reviewed in the book and also recommendations for suitable entries to be included in the next edition. This will help ensure that the *Country Living series of Rural Guides* continues to provide its readers with useful information on the more interesting, unusual or unique features of each attraction or place ensuring that their visit to the local area is an enjoyable and stimulating experience. To provide your comments or recommendations would you please complete the forms below and overleaf as indicated and send to:

The Research Department, Travel Publishing Ltd,

7a Apollo House, Calleva Park, Aldermaston, Reading, RG7 8TN.

Your Name:

Your Address:

Your Telephone Number:

Please tick as appropriate: Comments ☐ Recommendation ☐

Name of Establishment:

Address:

Telephone Number:

Name of Contact:

READER REACTION FORM

Comment or Reason for Recommendation:

....

....

....

....

....

....

....

....

....

....

INDEX TO TOWNS & PLACES OF INTEREST

C